PEOPLE
I HAVE LOVED,
KNOWN OR
ADMIRED

Leo Rosten

PEOPLE
I HAVE LOVED,
KNOWN OR
ADMIRED

McGRAW-HILL BOOK COMPANY

New York   St. Louis   San Francisco   London
Toronto   Sydney   Düsseldorf   Mexico   Panama

Library of Congress Catalog Card Number: 79-132099
First Edition
07–053976–6

The author is grateful to Harper & Row for permission to adapt and expand one story from *The Return of Hyman Kaplan*, three from *Captain Newman, M.D.*, and three from *The Many Worlds of Leo Rosten;* and to Cowles Communications, Inc., for permission to use portions of several articles printed in *Look* and protected by individual copyrights.

To Helen and George

CONTENTS

. . . and all he did was tell tales, and multitudes came to hear him; and some left honey and myrrh for the pleasure he had given them. But whether the things he recounted had truly transpired, or were spun from the golden strands of his fancy, or were the sorcerer's own sweet blend of both, no man could say save the sagaman himself. And once when asked where truth did end, and fable begin, he looked puzzled, then sighed, "But much is true that doth not happen, and much that happens gaineth not in verity because of blind occurrence."

—*Der Goldener Mozzik,*
author unknown; Vaysichvaus
Press (Chicago), 1911

To the Reader

LET me admit it: I have enormously enjoyed writing
these stories about people I have loved, or have known and
not loved, or have admired but never knew.

Most of the characters, drawn from what is mushily
called "real life," have greatly enriched the unreal life of my
imagination. Most have given me immeasurable delight; for
to me, at least, they are very funny. Others are off-beat, or
sad, or bafflers I simply cannot shake out of memory.

I have tried to make them all seem human, which is to
say childish, mature, vain, humble, flabbergasting, charming,
gifted, giftless, shallow, brilliant, cheerful, somber, lyrical,
flat, sublime, outrageous, ordinary, and astonishing.

Sometimes I think that the longer you know someone,
and the harder you strain to understand him (and certainly
her), the more you begin to wonder whether we are not all
possessed, driven by needs we cannot articulate, trapped
within mazes we cannot unriddle. Even those I know best
seem, from time to time, to be inhabited by elves or demons
of the contrary.

I have always envied artists the freedom we give them
to paint the same subject, again and again, without criticiz-
ing them. Renoir painted Gabrielle, whom he hired as a
servant, three hundred times—because "her skin does not

reject the light." No one censured him for painting the same skin so often. (It was, of course, never the same, which is why Renoir returned to it.) Hokusai, who called himself "mad with drawing," drew hundreds upon hundreds of views of Mount Fuji, seen from different places, at different times and seasons. Claude Monet became so enthralled by the changing play of light that he painted the same cathedral many times, trying to capture the variant tints and hues of color that splashed down the spires and stones; and he became so obsessed with the water lilies in his pond that he filled no fewer than fifty canvases, each 7 feet high and 15 feet long, with nothing but his matchless, magical *Nymphéas*. No one frowned at the replication of so *many* water lilies. . . .

I mention this because in some chapters I have written afresh about an experience, a character, or a story I once sketched in another context, but in much shorter space, from a different point of vision, with wholly different highlights and shadings and emphases. The profiles of Freud or Groucho Marx; the stories about Potch, the master criminal of my boyhood, or Wilbur, my *nudnick* friend; my ruminations on Leonardo da Vinci or Broadway's dime-a-dance girls; the chapters on the tantalizing baroness in Vienna or the altogether surprising Mr. Washington—all are vastly different, quintuple the length and fathoms deeper, I think, than my earlier efforts to find their essences. Many chapters, of course, are printed here for the first time.

So no story in this book has been seen by you before, not in these words, or in this mood, or at such length. I can best explain what I mean by quoting words written by Francis Bacon long ago:

> The human understanding is like an irregular mirror, which distorts and discolors the nature of things by mingling its own nature with it. . . . For everyone has a cave of his own, which refracts and discolors the light of nature. . . . Numberless are the ways in which the affections color and infect the understanding.

I have worked in my cave happily, using my imperfect mirror to refract afresh, with new colors and affection, the people who infect my understanding.

—Leo Rosten

East Quogue
New York

PEOPLE
I HAVE LOVED,
KNOWN OR
ADMIRED

A Few to Admire

~~~~~~

O UR times are so dangerous, our crises so multiplex, our problems so intricate, our choices so painful, the Middle East so terrifying, the Far East so fortuneless, our cities so savage, our air so noxious, our streets so disgusting, our traffic so monstrous, our students so bellicose, their teachers so buffaloed, and the price of everything from parking to popovers so distorted by unfamiliar affluence and political lunacy (pause, inhale) that it pleases me to relieve the surrounding darkness by telling you about a few rare members of our foolish race who may brighten your mood, as they have mine.

1. *The unknown genius* who ran this one-line ad in the Los Angeles *Times:*
>   LAST DAY TO SEND IN YOUR DOLLAR.
>   —Box 153
Thousands of idiots sent in their dollars.

2. *Joseph Pellegrino,* who makes square spaghetti. This unorthodox—nay, revolutionary!—pasta offers many advantages over conventional spaghetti: It does not slip off the fork so often; it does not slide on the plate so readily; it is also firmer, less gooey and holds on to the tomato sauce

better than run-of-the-mill pasta. I think square spaghetti also inspires confidence in its character, because of its sturdy, self-reliant appearance.

Signor Pellegrino did not just sit down at his drawing board and spin farinaceous magic out of a superhuman imagination; nor did the great idea attack him in the bathtub so that he could cry *"Ecco!"*, which is the Italian equivalent of *"Eureka!"* Oh, no. Signor Pellegrino, a spaghetti buff of long standing, was served the square surprise while lunching in a modest little *ristorante*. As stunned as a saint receiving a revelation, Pellegrino rushed into the kitchen, where he saw the Mamma of the establishment rolling a slab of dough across a wooden frame on which was stretched a multitude of—guitar strings!

Today, Signor Pellegrino turns out quadrilateral spaghetti on wire, instead of catgut strings, and it is a boon to Romans and tourists alike.

So far as I can see, this splendid pasta *may* have one trivial fault, a defect implied, though not foreseen, by Christopher Morley, who once said: "No man is lonely while eating spaghetti; it takes so much *attention*."

3. *The beardless American youth*, returning from Paris, who was asked by a U.S. Customs inspector, "Do you have any pornographic literature?" and wailed, "Gee *whiz*, I don't even have a pornograph!"

4. *Charles Babbage*, a crank, a crackpot, a neurotic, a nut —and a mathematician who dreamed up the miraculous machines we call computers.

Babbage, a Cambridge (England) professor who never delivered a lecture, was a bundle of crotchets and kookeries: The moment he heard an organ-grinder or street-singer he would run out of his house and give chase, with homicidal intent. He just went wild if anyone disturbed his inner, furious peace. When the children of Cambridge learned of Babbage's acousticophobia, which is how psychiatrists with time to kill describe a fear/hate of noise, the little darlings began to blow their bugles right under his windows. He never married.

Back in the 1820s, Babbage noticed how many mistakes there were in the tables used by seamen and astronomers, and began to play with the idea of a computer that would perform mathematical computations. He was not entering virgin forests: Napier had produced logarithms, Pascal had built an adding machine, and Leibniz had invented a contrivance that could multiply and divide. But all these ingenuities had one crucial drawback: they had to be reset for each step of an arithmetical process. What enfevered Babbage was the idea of a mathematical machine that would work automatically throughout. It is this that makes him the grandfather, if not the father, of UNIVAC.

Babbage's vision, as unrealistic as only a visionary's can be, shot much too far beyond the existing technology (electronics did not appear for a century). The genie of his imagination was cluttered with springs, cogs, weights, pawls, cams, and doo-hickeys galore—literally thousands of heavy moving parts. He spent over twenty years bulling his way through the mazes of his fantasy and once cried in despair: "This is the most entangled and perplexed thing which ever occupied a human mind!" I do not doubt it.

Babbage never completed his task. He quarreled with his sponsors and frittered away grants from Parliament with excited and balmy digressions. . . . He died in 1871.

A tantalizing footnote to all this is that Babbage desperately needed someone to work out ways of feeding equations into his imagined "Analytical Engine." By a stroke of uncommon luck, he found a remarkable girl, a gifted mathematician and a great beauty, who, apart from her cerebral dexterity, wrote up Babbage's work in such a clear way that laymen could understand what he was up to. Her name was Ada, and she was the daughter of a poet named Byron.

The airport manager of a smallish Western field who put up this memorable sign in the Pilot's Room:

WARNING

ABSOLUTELY NO FLYING ALLOWED OVER THE NUDIST COL-
ONY THAT IS 10.5 MILES SSW ON TRUE COURSE OF 180.

6. *Henrietta Blueye*, a twenty-one-year-old Seneca Indian from Basom, New York, who, while on a summer tour in Europe with fellow students from Radcliffe, tried to smuggle an East German student out of Hungary into West Germany. She was caught and sentenced to six months at hard labor.

Miss Blueye confessed that she had helped smuggle another East German out of Czechoslovakia. And when the Hungarians asked her why she had committed this crime on their sovereign soil, she said: "I felt it was my duty."

I wish there were some medal (and a lavish reward) for people like Henrietta Blueye. She performed an act of great courage and unembroidered human decency.

7. *Charles Dillon ("Casey") Stengel*, who has ornamented baseball with his spellbinding soliloquies (a Joycean orgy of *non sequiturs* inside verbal fogs even he gets lost in), who once declared: "They say you can't do it, but sometimes that doesn't always work."

More recently, Mr. Stengel explained the meteoric world championship of the New York Mets in these jeweled words: "This is a team that came up slow, but fast." He also used karate on the commonplace: "A lot of people my age are dead at the present time."

I have long dreamed of attending a bull session between Casey Stengel and Yogi Berra. To make it perfect, you might throw in Dizzy Dean.

8. *Lyndon B. Johnson*, whom it is considered *infra dig* and even grotesque to admire these days, who, during a long and exhausting meeting on some crisis, heard a member of his Cabinet sigh, "If we only knew what the American people want us to do!" and replied in these poignant and, I think, supremely honorable words: "And suppose we did know what the people want us to do; can you be sure we ought to do it?"

My Father

WE buried my father not long ago, and wayward memories of him—a laugh, a sigh, a smile—keep washing over my mind in unexpected wavelets.

He was a simple man, without a shred of affectation. His tastes were innocent, his desires easily satisfied. He was unfailingly agreeable. He made no demands on anyone. He disapproved of gossip and simply did not know the meaning of rancor or envy. He was entirely without self-righteousness. He never pried or probed or stuck his nose into anyone else's affairs. I rarely, rarely heard him complain, and though he was far from prudish I never heard him use profanity. And not once, in over fifty years, can I remember his uttering a mean or malicious or spiteful thought.

He loved nothing more than spending his hours with my mother, my younger sister, and me, and he spent a good deal of that time just beaming. His contentment was contagious—literally, I mean, infecting others. He was always pleasant to be with. I suppose that's the word people would be most likely to use in characterizing him: "pleasant," or "nice," because he never made a fuss about things.

He adored my mother, to whom he always deferred, considering himself unbelievably lucky to have won someone so beautiful, so intelligent, so dignified and proud. In his

later years, he would get up before she did and make coffee
(he made splendid coffee) and sip it as he read the morning
paper and waited for her to join him in his happiness.

I never knew a man who so loved newspapers. He read
them with the utmost care, savoring every item. He could
derive pleasure from every story—whether world-shaking
or picayune. He even devoured the space fillers. He would
pore through his bifocals over the speech of a President or
the yarn of a two-headed calf, marveling and clucking and
tchk-tchking: "Imagine!" "How do you like that?" "Who
could expect such a thing?"

He particularly enjoyed interviews; he read any interview
with anyone—a scientist, an actress, a lifeguard, a thief.
To him, the morning paper renewed the newness of life
each day, without fail: a glorious bazaar, a circus of wonders and follies, a forum, a sideshow, a school, a stage.

He loved to make people laugh. He could not wait to tell
you the latest joke or story he had heard; and no one
enjoyed hearing a story more. He was surprisingly fresh
and original in his humor. When I was a little boy, he used
to divert me with silly stories and pantomimes. He was a
natural storyteller and mimic. Puffing up his cheeks or crossing his eyes or imitating a walk, a frown, a comic glare,
he could create a character before your eyes.

Once, when I was five, he told me a story about three old
sisters who lived together, and each night, before retiring,
had to pool their resources in order to blow out the candle
which gave them their only light. You see, the first sister
could only blow upward; the second, downward; the third,
out of the corner of her mouth. I watched with unbounded
enchantment as he acted out each sister's part, mimicking
how each one tried to blow out that recalcitrant candle, and
failed, and how all three had to blow in unison to drown the
light, as it were, in their frantic exhalations.

He had an instinct for the amusing aspect of any event,
even the most commonplace, and he often tricked us into
laughter with delicious nonsense. He would exclaim with
excitement,

"*Guess* who I met this morning?"

"Who?"

"The mailman."

Or he would slap his knee as if he had just thought of something frightfully important: "How could I forget to tell you? *Guess* what I found, right on the street?"

"What?"

"A handkerchief."

Do these stories sound absurd? You have no idea what delight they gave me, for it flattered me to see my father trying to please me; and it impressed me to think a man could find such an amplitude of pleasure in pleasing a child.

And when I had children, my father would tell them silly stories they were young enough to marvel over, and old enough to find the "catch" in. He would sigh, "Ah, when I was your age, I could raise my hand all the way up to here" (raising his hand above his head) "but now, I can only raise it up to here" (holding his arm out shoulder-high).

The child would frown and wrinkle his or her brow, and wonder what was—what *had* to be—wrong.

"Oh, yes," my father would say, giving the child time to penetrate the deception, "it's very sad. Imagine not being able to raise your hand higher than this—when I used to be able to raise it way up to here—"

And then a shrill voice would cry, "But, Grampa, look, you just *did!*"

"Did what?"

"Raised your hand up there! !"

"Sure. That's how high I *used* to——"

"No, no, Gramps, you did it *now!*"

"Oh, I can't raise it this high now——"

"But *zayde,* look, you *are*. You're doing it!"

And he would pretend that he saw their point, or would slap his forehead to complain that he had been taken in by his own gullibility, or he would marvel how he had never before realized the absurd self-contradiction of his gesturings, or he would thank the furiously cerebrating child for such a lesson in reasoning; or he would simply laugh, and when the child looked sheepish over having been gulled, my father would deliver the swift reward of a proud hug or kiss, or a lift high in the air, or a magnified admiring or mock-rueful remark like, "My! You're too smart to be fooled."

He was often funny unintentionally. He went to a night school for foreigners, soon after arriving in Chicago, and after the teacher explained the principal parts of speech, she called upon him:

"Can you give me a noun?"

"Door," said my father.

"Very good. Now, another noun?"

"Another door," said my father. (I used this in a book about Hyman Kaplan.)

Once, ending a long-distance telephone call from California, he said: "Good-bye—and give my regards to anybody."

But mostly, his humor was intentional and improvised on the moment. If my sister or I got up for some milk or water, he would say, "As long as you're up, get yourself a glass, too."

Once he raised his index finger slightly and asked, "Do you know why Woodrow Wilson couldn't write with this finger?"

"No," I said. "Why?"

"Because it's mine."

My mother and father were immensely proud, and he somewhat in awe, of my scholastic efforts. I learned as a boy that I could usually get out of a chore—taking out the garbage, sifting the ashes in the cellar for unburned coal, pasting labels on the sweater boxes in the store (our living room)—by picking up a book. And when my father saw me reading, he would pat me on the head, saying, "That's good, that's good; you're laying in stock—" tapping his temple—"up here!" He never ceased to marvel over the miracles that came from men's minds.

No one ever loved this country more deeply. He thought America a truly golden land, a *Gan Eden*, a haven, a heaven of endless promise. "Why, here you can talk, you can argue, you can disagree, you can call a mayor a crook—you can even complain to a *police*man! !"

My father had been a stocking-maker in Poland, and became a sweater-maker in America. He came to Ellis Island in his early twenties, alone, and later brought over my mother and me, and in Chicago he spent sixty hours a week at work pulling the heavy carriage of a knitting machine back and forth across the inverted-V bed of needles.

He would get up before dawn, during the ferocious Chicago winters, and take a streetcar for an hour or more to be at work by eight. When he returned from his long workday, he would eat his dinner (we called it "supper" in those days) and then start working on a secondhand knitting machine in our front room—to make sweaters on his own. My mother was determined to start "a business of our own," so they would never be at the mercy of a "boss." She had gone to work as a girl in a textile plant in Lodz and had been so swift and skillful that they made her a foreman at fifteen.

My father was always full of talk about great wealth, which I do not think he ever really believed he would acquire. But the thought and talk of being rich warmed his hopes. My mother never denied us anything really important, but the memory of great hardships left my father forever uneasy, even frightened, about spending money. Even when he would concede that he was "well-off," he would add "—but not *that* well-off." For instance, he considered airmail stamps an unneeded luxury, and he would enter a taxi, even one he knew I would never let him pay for, only after obligatory protestations. "Who *needs* it? We can take a bus."

He never tired of admiring millionaires (of anyone whom rumor rated as slightly richer than "comfortable," my father would say, "I'll bet he's a regular millionaire!"), but only if they made their fortune by their own brain and effort. He scoffed at—nay, resented—those who inherited wealth. His own dreams of affluence led him to undertake a strike-it-rich scheme that turned into a fiasco which became a legend.

While working at the knitting mills by day, and on his own machine at night, he decided to spend his spare time (!) making stove polish. Since everyone had a kitchen stove in those days, "a good, inexpensive stove polish," my father announced, "is sure to make a fortune!"

So he went out and bought the ingredients, consulting heaven only knows what expert on stove polishes, and we plugged up our bathtub and mixed great batches of arcane, smelly liquids in it, stirring with a paddle, and he dipped a pitcher into the Stygian brew and poured the polish through a little funnel into a vast field of six-ounce glass bottles arrayed on the kitchen table, sink, and sideboards. I proudly helped him paste the labels ("Statue of Liberty Stove Polish," I think) on the bottles.

He put two dozen bottles in a cardboard carton, I remember, then went around to the neighborhood grocers, carrying four cartons at a time. When he found the storekeepers understandably reluctant to buy a totally unknown product, my father hit upon the idea of letting them take the bottles for nothing, no deposit, no commitment, entirely "on consignment" (a dazzling invention): The shopkeepers would pay, at the end of the week, only for the number of bottles they had actually sold! How could anyone lose from so honest, ingenious, and riskless a course? My father began to plan ways of expanding his possible production of stove polish, dreaming of hiring others to deliver them far and wide throughout the nights ahead, while he would concentrate on production, labeling, packaging, and bookkeeping.

I remember how excited we were as we waited for him to return from his call upon the storekeepers to whom he had delivered his first batch of bottles, after a week of imagined riches had passed. As he came through the door, my mother and uncle and I showered him with questions: "How many bottles did they sell?" "How many reordered?" "How much did you get?"

"Get?" My father looked ashen. "I'm lucky I wasn't murdered!"

My mother turned dead white. "What happened?"

"What *happened?*" he echoed. "I'll tell you what happened. They chased me out of the store! They hollered and *kvitched* and came at me with brooms! They told me never to come back or they'd break every bone in my body!"

"But *why?*" my mother cried. "Why?"

"Why?" my father sighed. "Because all the bottles *exploded*, that's why. Exploded right on the shelves! Knocked all the corks out! Sprayed black stove polish all over the groceries and pickle barrels and vegetables and merchandise! . . . Did you ever hear of such a thing?"

My mother sank into a chair and my uncle nodded in irony, blaming the fates or the capitalistic system, and said, "But Sam, how did it happen?"

"I *suppose* I mixed something wrong," sighed my father. "I wonder what it was. . . . I tell you, Idy, if we can make a good stove polish, it will sell like hotcakes, and we'll make a fortune!"

In my imagination, I still see all the corks popping out of all those little bottles on the astonished grocers' shelves, and the goo spurting out in inky geysers over all the food and soaps and flour, and blackening the Statue of Liberty, to boot.

My father loved to sing, and he often sang with the "company" who came to our home. We had a victrola and many records, of Caruso and Chaliapin and Galli-Curci. My father sang quite well. He was the only man I ever heard of, though, who sang in his sleep. He usually hummed while asleep, rather politely, but sometimes was so carried away by his dreams that he would trill out an aria from *Tosca* or *Aida*. His favorite was the lament from *The Pearl Fishers*. He was also the most powerful, rattling, unregenerate snorer I ever heard. Between the snores and the arias, and the fact that my sister occasionally walked in her sleep, the night hours in our house were often unsedative.

He met disappointments, accidents, emergencies, with a sigh. To no one was a display of drama more alien. He treated his own anxieties, when he could not evade them, with a certain mild regret. In fact, he embraced soft regret where others roared rage or hatred or rebellion. He was unbelievably patient. He simply took it for granted that greed, stupidity, hypocrisy, lunacy were rife in a world he never made. He also took it for granted, I think, that life was not very kind or reasonable or just. But he did not *blame* anyone for these things, except maybe God, with whom he had little in common. He had stopped talking to God long before I was born.

He was a man of great hopes, but not great ambition. My mother was the restless, driving, doctrinaire one. Her conviction that he must emancipate himself from the ranks of labor, whom everyone knew to be heartlessly exploited, spurred him on. They worked together as a team: my mother designing and cutting sweaters (pullovers, turtlenecks, cardigans), then stocking caps, skating scarves, toques, stoles. She was remarkably deft, swift, and ingenious in her craft. My father bought the yarn and equipment and manually operated the machine.

In time, he hired his first employee, in the "shop" that was our commandeered front room. We lived, like so many other immigrant families, "behind the store," but not in or behind a real store, on the ground floor, which my mother considered horrifying and outrageously *déclassé*. In time, my parents opened a *real* store, that is, a store away from where we lived, and my father was the proprietor and manufacturer, and my mother waited on customers behind a real counter in premises on the street level.

My parents were ardent trade unionists, loyal members of the Workmen's Circle, and the transformation from the status of workers to "bosses" never ceased to plague them with unease. I shall never forget my father trying to persuade four of his own employees to organize a union—and strike for higher wages! His employees could not see it that way, because they *liked* to work for my parents and thought they were being paid quite adequately. Besides, they said, "If you think we ought to get higher wages, why don't you just give us a raise? Why should we form a union and go on strike?"

"Ah," said my father, "don't you see, if I am the only sweater-maker to raise wages, I won't be able to compete against the other manufacturers who *won't*. But if all the textile workers in Chicago get together, and make a union, and send a delegation to *all* the sweater-makers—then we would all have to raise wages!" He did not win them over. . . .

In economics courses at college, years later, I would remember that paradoxical scene—the boss urging his workers to organize and strike, and the exploited workers, content with their lot, puzzled by the unorthodox capitalist in their midst.

My father made my uncle the foreman of the shop. My uncle was a passionate union man and organizer. (He had been badly beaten up once, by company thugs, as an "agitator.") Encouraged by my parents, my uncle used every lunch hour to propagandize their workers on the desirability, the wisdom, the economic *necessity* of organizing Chicago's first sweater-makers' union! That didn't work either.

My father had many friends, but no very close friends, because he was so emphatically a family man, a husband and father. He responded to those qualities in others that he possessed himself: simplicity, good cheer, unneurotic pastimes. He venerated in others those blessings he thought he did not possess: education, analytic power, creativeness. He paid his highest respect to plain character. His greatest praise was to say of someone, "There is a prince . . . a man, a *prince!*" I think he meant "a prince of a fellow," but he only said "a prince."

He had seen banks fail and more prosperous men than he go broke, but it was not hard for my mother to get her way with expenses whenever "education," that holy word, was concerned. So my sister was given piano lessons and elocution lessons and singing lessons; and I, who *hated* to practice anything, was forced to take violin lessons for eighteen grueling months. Freed at last, I made the mistake of strumming on an imaginary guitar (a broomstick), and drooling romantic songs, just as I had seen my idol, Ramon Novarro, do in a movie. For my next birthday, I was given a mandolin. I never had the heart to tell my father or mother that a mandolin is as much like a guitar as a penny whistle is like a flute.

My father taught me to play chess when I was eleven. He loved that game. And when I first beat him, six or seven months later, he was as proud as you can imagine, chuckling and clucking and boasting to "friends of the family."

My father had supreme respect for the privacy of others. When my older daughter visited my sister and brother-in-law in Deerfield (my parents were spending the summer with them), my father, the first to get up each morning, always prepared breakfast. And each morning, when my daughter came down, the dialogue between them ran like this:

"Good morning, Grandpa."

"*Well,* Maddy."

That was all. Having said this, he gave her half the morning paper, served her, sat down, sipped his coffee, reading his half of the paper, and did not bother her with conversation again.

On political issues he was alternately idealistic, skeptical, naive, cynical. He had begun as a staunch believer in socialism and the brotherhood of man, but in time came to distrust all politicians, and many union leaders, too; but he loved Norman Thomas, worshiped Franklin D. Roosevelt, and admired Adlai E. Stevenson beyond description.

He loved movies, but even more lectures, "so long as the speaker has something new to say." He was impatient with those who repeated themselves from year to year, or rehashed old ideas, or used platitudes their audiences already subscribed to. He had an instinctive dubiety about demagogues, which often made his judgment unsure because he loved oratory. His years at a machine and in business for himself had diminished his susceptibility to the spellbinder, the visionary, the unrealistic. "But a man has to have ideals."

He *detested* Communists, whom he saw at work in the labor and philanthropic organizations to which he contributed. What offended him most about the Communists was not that they were leftist but that they were liars: "A man who lies can't be trusted," he would say. "I don't care how fancy they talk or how much they promise." He had contempt for the doglike fidelity of about-facers whenever the party reversed itself. He could never excuse the purges in Russia, the fake trials, the forced labor camps, the outlandish "confessions," the to-him clear brutality of bureaucrats become omnipotent. "Some Marxists!" he once told me. "Plain murderers."

He loved the water and spent a thousand happy hours on its shores, in Michigan and California and Florida. He could not swim a stroke, so he would never go into the water above his knees. As he got older, he would sit at the edge of the sea and let the water lap up to him. He took to wearing a hat in the sun, and it was a sight to see him sitting at the water's edge, with his hat on, like a child playing in a bathtub, reading a newspaper.

Danny Thomas once told me how his father—a very strong, proud Lebanese—died. The old man sat up in his bed for the last time, breathing hard, glared toward heaven and shook his fist at it and cried, "God damn death!"

My father did not die that way. He slept away his life, in an oxygen tent, numbed of consciousness by the drugs they'd given him, and worn out, literally worn out, by a year of heart troubles and coughing and emphysema. He was more sad than angry over the thought of dying; he was—disgusted by his long ailing.

Once, as I sat by him in an ambulance, he removed the oxygen mask from his mouth and put his hands out, palms up, as if to say, "What's the use?" The oxygen tank was empty.

And once, in the hospital in South Haven, to which my mother had brought him, he complained that his face felt itchy. So I brought over my electric razor and shaved him. As the razor whirred away, he asked, "Why did you bother coming—all the way to Michigan—from New York?"

"I didn't," I lied. "I happened to be in Detroit for a convention. I was lucky."

"Some lucky," he sighed; then, smiling: "You're the most expensive barber I ever had."

In a moment, I said, "Go like this," pulling my mouth to one side to tighten the skin on the cheek.

He did that, and chuckled: "That joke: 'Go like this.' Remember? . . . That was a good one."

He was always rating jokes, saying, "That's a good one" for the funny, and making a moue or saying "mnyeh" for those he deemed mediocre.

When he came out of the hospital, he was unrecognizably frail. He had to use a cane when he walked. And when we took a stroll now, I had to hold his arm, and help him down the curb and up again, and I could not help thinking of the Yiddish saying: "When a father helps a son, both laugh; when a son helps a father, both cry."

But we never cried, for I kept talking away about work, my wife, my children, my plans—things he never tired of hearing. I always stored up new stories I'd heard, or old anecdotes he might not remember—anything to distract him from his final, fading imprisonment within the shell of his body. He would smile as I talked, rarely laughing now, as if it took too much strength to laugh; but he always pretended that his ailment would pass in time and there would be a thousand hours yet to talk and a thousand tales to tell and hear.

I say he was "pretending." I mean he was pretending to the rest of us; I do not think he retained much hope himself. He simply saw no purpose in inflicting upon us his pains or symptoms or apprehensions. I think he was terribly afraid of dying, but he never once so much as hinted at that.

At the end, he weighed no more than ninety pounds.

He looked desiccated, a shrunken, waxen figure, the skin stretched tight across the bones of his face, his ribs sticking out of him like prongs of a hayfork.

The last time I saw him, he was in the hospital again, in Chicago, under the canopy of an oxygen tent, propped up, dozing.

My wife and I said good-bye to him, but he could not hear us. I blew him a kiss. I did not think he saw it. But he had. He nodded and made a wry, wrinkled-up grimace—the face he always made when he said, "Don't worry about me," or "Don't wait," or "Go home now." Then he managed to raise two fingers to his lips and blew me a kiss in return.

He was a dear, kind, gentle man, and I loved him.

After he died I swam a lot, every day. You can weep in the water, and when you come out red-eyed, people attribute it to the swimming. The sea my father loved is a fine place for crying, and so is the indoor pool in which I swim in the winter.

And now, as I write this, adding to what I wrote before, it is over four years since my father died, and I still ache when I think of him. I never knew how much you can miss someone. I miss him more than anyone I have ever known. It pleased him so to be with me; and it was so simple and happy for me to be with him.

How very much of him lives on in my mind—so vividly; and portions of him rush into unexpected recollection at the oddest moments. And then I hear myself crying, "Oh, Papa, Papa, you were a prince."

Wilbur

～～～～～～～～～～

I'VE known Wilbur since he was knee high to a *Romalea microptera*—and the fact that I write "*Romalea microptera*" instead of "grasshopper" shows you the peculiar influence he (Wilbur, not the grasshopper) has had on my life.

I first began to wonder whether Wilbur was some kind of nut when we were in high school in Chi-ca-go. We were walking along Douglas Boulevard one afternoon, Wilbur munching on a cube of yeast, to improve his complexion, when, without warning, he announced:

"Schatzski's Ring is a constriction of the lower esophagus."

I stopped. "Is anything wrong with your esophagus?"

"No," said Wilbur.

"Then why did you tell me that?"

"What?"

"About Schatzski's Ring."

"I don't know," he said. "I thought it would interest you."

"Interest me? I am panting for more. But what made you think of it?"

"I don't know," frowned Wilbur; then his face lighted up. "B-because I swallowed!"

That is the way Wilbur's mind worked.

Or take the time we were all hanging around the corner, discussing you-know-what, and Wilbur, who seemed de-

34

void of normal adolescent hankerings, suddenly declared, in his warm adenoidal voice, "A conger eel can lay fifteen million eggs a season!"

The incredulity that froze our band was cracked by Zack Pichnik's deadly, "What'd you say, Four Eyes?"

Wilbur pushed his cheaters up across the fallen bridge of his nose and repeated, quite bravely, I thought: "I said a conger eel can lay fifteen m-million eggs a season."

"Willy," said Zack, "you are the type who one-a these days they are gonna throw a net over his head so's you will spend the rest of your life playing 'Chopsticks' for doctors in white coats. . . . Eels," he echoed in disgust. "'F' cryin' out loud, why *eels?*"

Wilbur flushed. "I—thought it would interest you. . . . I mean, you were all talking about sex. I mean, that many *eggs*, Zack! I mean, f-fifteen *million!*"

Or take the sweltering, sizzling August afternoon Wilbur and I were pitching pennies, to improve our vision, and he went into a fit, shouting: "Yes, sir! Yes, siree! Carpathian peasants trim their bunions only under a new moon! How about *that*, Zoltan? Huh? *Wow!*"

After I sobered him down, I asked, "Is that true, Wil?"

"What?"

"That Carpathian peasants trim their bunions only under a new moon?"

"Sure it's true! It's five-hundred and fifty per*cent* true!" shouted Wilbur. "I will give you book, author, and page. I *never* make things up. I only deal in facts!"

I have never forgotten that. First of all, my name never was Zoltan. Second, I checked the source Wilbur gave me, and he was absolutely right: certain Carpathian mountain peasants would rather be boiled in yoghurt than trim their bunions at any time except a lunar-crescent night. Third, here is a striking, solid piece of information that will never be dislodged from the neural reservoir of my mind. Only Wilbur could have put it there. Just as he did with, say, Kuru, which is not the name of a Hindu god, or even the way Japanese pronounce "coolie"; Kuru is a laughing disease that is *100 percent fatal!* Fortunately, it afflicts only the Fore tribe in eastern New Guinea.

I often wondered what quirk in Wilbur's nature made him store up such motley odds-and-ends. And after closer observation and deeper analysis I came to the conclusion that Wilbur must have discovered, early in his life, that ideas confused him—so he began to collect information. There's nothing wrong in that, mind you: some boys collect stamps or coins or match-book covers; well, Wilbur collected trivia. In that way, he was able to substitute facts for conversation. This was shrewd of him, I think, because the truth is that Wilbur's brain was neither deep, swift, wide, nor sharp; but it *was* retentive. It was a stroke of inspiration, therefore, for him to become a dataphile. He is the only person I know who made so unusual an asset out of so common a deficiency.

Whenever any of us asked Wilbur what in hell impelled him to announce out of the blue that Trinidad produces asphalt of surprisingly high quality, or that Descartes said monkeys could talk if they wanted to—they just act nonverbal so they won't be put to work, Wilbur would reply, "I—just thought it would *interest* you."

Notice, he did not say "I thought it was interesting," which was true, but "I thought it would interest you," which was debatable. Yet there, in his very way of saying it, lay the key to Wilbur's character. He desperately wanted to be liked, and he gave you the only treasures he possessed. He was so eager to make friends, and so klutzy in the ways he went about it, that he reminded me of the old Chinese proverb: "He is like a fellow in a barrel of rice with his lips sewed up." Come to think of it, I heard that one from Wilbur.

II

As Wilbur grew older, which he did, he became plumper and perspired a great deal, but since his adenoids shrank (he told me) he stammered less. This was a good thing, because in all other respects Wilbur retained, and even expanded, his core of clumsiness. I think God had chosen Wilbur to be one of his shlemiels—well-meaning, generous, and hopelessly inept.

When you took a walk with Wilbur, for instance, you found yourself bumping into him, even though you were both in the normal, side-by-side arrangement for walking, which should make a collision impossible. Or when you introduced Wilbur to someone, he would pump the other person's hand as if there was a water shortage.

I always felt sorry for Wilbur. No one seemed to *like* him, except me, and I—well, I just tried to befriend him. I won't deny that maybe I did that because I am a masochist, or because I need to fortify my sense of virtue by being kind to someone whom everyone else treats as if he were a carrier of lockjaw *(clostridium tetani)*.

After high school, Wilbur enrolled in the Henrietta Knippel Business College, where he studied ledger entries, categories for filing, changing typewriter ribbons, and so on. He racked up such good grades at Knippel that immediately upon receiving his certificate, eighteen months later, he went to work for Wieboldt's Department Store, in basement curtain rods. I never really saw Wilbur as the curtain-rod kind, but inside of two months Wilbur's zeal, honesty, and erudition gave Mr. Gensen, the basement manager, a complete nervous breakdown. The department *supervisor*, Mr. Bosey, who turned out to be a Knippel man himself, now asked Wilbur to replace Mr. Gensen "temporarily." And within nine days, I think it was, Wilbur made such a powerful impression on Mr. Bosey that he was fired.

Now, Wilbur started door-to-door selling. He swiftly progressed from ironing-board covers to cemetery plots. He neither shone nor starved in his new profession, since he took plenty of time "breaking the ice," he told me, employing smiles, chuckles and friendly small talk—about things like the origin of the word "bloomer," or the mischievous tributaries of the Wabash River.

I left Chicago for Washington, then Hollywood, and after

some years in the citric paradise moved to New York. I had
not heard a word from or about Wilbur for eight years.
One morning, my phone rang and I heard that unmistak-
able, warm, adenoidal voice. My heart either leaped or sank.
"I now live in Queens!" the voice shouted. "My uncle has a
Tastee-Freeze franchise and put me in charge of one station!
I can't wait to see you. Have you changed?"

We lunched at a dairy restaurant Wilbur recommended.
All of its waiters looked pessimistic. As for Wilbur, he had
not changed. "Say, it will be great, living just across the
river," he burbled. "We can catch up on a million things.
Did you know I had geographic tongue?"

"What?"

"Geographic tongue," said Wilbur. "That's when your
tongue has entire areas or blotches that differ in color, like
a map."

"How did you get it?" I asked.

"What?" asked Wilbur.

"Geographic tongue."

"I don't know," said Wilbur. He plopped sour cream into
his borscht until it looked like a strawberry cake with white
icing. "That's one of the most interesting things about it. *No
one knows what causes it or what makes it disappear!* Look."
He stuck his tongue out. I had never realized what a long
tongue Wilbur had, but it looked perfectly normal: pink,
moist and in no way like a map.

"Your tongue looks perfectly normal," I said, "pink, moist,
and in no way like a map."

"That's because it disappeared," said Wilbur.

"What was the treatment?" I asked.

"What treatment?" asked Wilbur.

"The treatment for geographic tongue," I said.

"Oh. . . . None. It just went away. That's because it was a
benign, migratory *glossitis!*"

I ate my blintzes thoughtfully.

"Thank God it wasn't the *rhomboid* type!" Wilbur blurted.
"How about you?"

"I'm glad it wasn't, too," I said.

"No, no, I mean have *you* had any unusual ailments since we last met?"

I felt a genuine twinge of regret. "I'm afraid not, Wil."

A week later Wilbur telephoned again. "My uncle—well, more my aunt is the reader—is a *great* fan of yours, and when she heard you are my best friend said she is dying to meet you. So I can pick you up in their car and drive you to Kew Gardens, where we'll have supper with them, and I'll——"

"I'm going to San Diego!" I cried.

"So? A few days won't matter."

"—then Hong Kong——"

"Hong Kong!" echoed Wilbur, in rapture. "My uncle and aunt were just there. They can give you some wonderful tips——"

"But Wil, I'm swamped——"

"You'll love them, I know."

"—I can't promise——"

"I bet you even get an idea for a story out of it!"

"—God knows when I'll have a free evening."

"So make it a Sunday brunch! That would be even better! Sunday brunch or even supper is a weekly feature, my aunt being such a versatile cook."

"Maybe after Christmas..." A child was using my lips.

"Anytime you're free. They're very flexible people. I'll keep calling——"

"No, no, Wil. Let me call you."

His euphoria caressed my ears. "It will mean a lot to me. Career-wise. I told them how you are my best and oldest friend."

I was in Kew Gardens on Sunday.

III

There were ten for "supper" and Wilbur's aunt's cooking made a lasting impression on me. I think she had attended the *Cordon Noir*. After an *apéritif* of rum and coconut milk, and *hors-d'oeuvres* such as pistachio nuts, sunflower seeds and tiny "pigs in a blanket" with a sweet sauce, we sat down at the festive board for "the informal Sunday night supper." It was not entirely informal, despite the splendid garlic pickles, because the chopped liver was served in flaky pastry shells and the salad was called Green Goddess. To wash down our viands (pastrami, ham, tongue, and hot meatballs) we had a choice of Pabst '68, Tab '69, or Dr. Brown's Celery Tonic, which is an entirely new taste thrill when you drink it from a champagne glass.

Apart from the cuisine, that was an evening that will long live in my memory, because every time Wilbur said something, the guests reached for their potions and took very slow, long swigs. During these moments, Wilbur's uncle and aunt kept exchanging a look (it was really two looks, each having one, but since they were identical I say "a" look) that I find hard to describe. I can understand it; I just can't describe it.

Wilbur's uncle had barely finished describing the fascinating thermostats and valves that control the temperature on his Tastee-Freeze machines, when Wilbur leaned forward and exclaimed,

"In Blowing Rock, North Carolina, *snow falls upside down!*"

Now, when a sophisticated group of people at a dinner table hear someone announce that in Blowing Rock, North Carolina, snow falls upside down, you can be *pretty* sure someone will pick up the ball and respond, "Why?"

A Mrs. Alvin Nussbaum, I believe, did.

I felt uneasy. I expected Wilbur to stammer out his usual anticlimactic "I don't know," which was not the kind of answer I would advise anyone to give a woman with eyes as fierce as Mrs. Nussbaum's; but to my relief and surprise Wilbur responded, in a manly, knowledgeable way: "The snow falls upside down in Blowing Rock, North Carolina, because a wind sweeps up through the rocky flume below, in the immense cliff that overhangs a gorge in the Blue Ridge mountains! Thus," Wilbur rushed on, "if you stand on the edge of the cliff and throw down an empty bag, piece of tissue paper, bus ticket, or something like that, *it is returned to you by the powerful updraft!*"

It was the first time I ever heard Wilbur explain one of his inapposite references—so I could understand why he looked disappointed by the ensuing silence. I think he had kind of dreamed of having the men leap up to hoist him on their shoulders and circle the table singing "Boola, boola," or songs from *The Student Prince.*

Mrs. Nussbaum narrowed her eyes to maximize her attitude, and spaced her words to stress her skepticism: "Did *you* throw an empty bag, bus ticket, or piece of tissue over the cliff only to have it returned to you by that powerful updraft?"

"N-no," said Wilbur, with a hurt expression.

"I thought so!" she snapped. *"Then how can you be sure the goddam updraft is that powerful?!"*

"I r-read it," sputtered Wilbur, "in a——"

"So do you believe every stupid thing you read? Ha! It could just of been propaganda! Put out by the Chamber of Commerce! A come-on, to get suckers like you to go all the way down there just to see a Kleenex drift around—on account of that type tissue is so light it will float right here in Kew Gardens, or rise on a windy day. 'Snow falls upside down' my foot, and I am being polite. You should go see a psychiatrist, that's what you should do, young man, to cure your naive way of accepting things!"

Mrs. Nussbaum was not a nice lady, even though (Wilbur later told me) her husband had deserted her for a beautician from Rego Park.

I spent the summer—the loveliest of summers—in Europe and returned to New York on a September 18 with a fine tan, a brisk gait, and notes for a book. On September 19, Wilbur appeared in my office. A Band-Aid called attention to the left corner of his upper lip. "I need to c-confide in someone," he said.

"What's the matter?" I exclaimed. "You look green."

It seemed that Wilbur's uncle had given him quite a heart-to-heart talk, which Wilbur, with his uncanny talent for data retrieval, repeated word for word.

"Willy," his uncle had said, "you are an unusual type young man who I see a great future for, but I have to tell you I do not see you in Tastee-Freezes or similar enterprises that involve direct relations with the public. You should go in for something more on the inhuman side—like warehouses, or stock inventory, or a thing like that which lets you use your brain to the full of its powers but does not require you should make conversation with the customers."

"What brought *that* on?" I asked. "I thought things were going well . . ."

"My uncle said he had been thinking over my whole personality—with all its pluses and minuses—for some time," moaned Wilbur. "What finally made up his mind to suggest I move upward, but somewhere else, was that crazy episode that transpired Thursday night."

What had happened the preceding Thursday night, stripped to its essentials, was that a yellow convertible had pulled up to Wilbur's station, quite late, and three couples had gotten out and ordered double Tastee-Freezes. As Wilbur was making change for the host of the party, a burly fellow in a crew-neck sweater with a big chenille "G" on the chest, one of the girls, a recent blonde who seemed a little hopped up, began to stroke the buttons on Wilbur's white uniform suggestively, one by one, murmuring, "Hey, cool cat, I bet your hands are not always as cold as they get handling these crummy Freezies all night!"

Wilbur answered, "Oh, you are absolutely right. My hands are usually quite warm."

"You'd have a *ball* in Alaska," purred the blonde.

"Do you think so?" asked Wilbur eagerly. "You know, an Eskimo will lend you his wife, if you stay overnight——"

"What the hell kind of talk is that?" cried the athlete.

"I just try to keep abreast of things," said Wilbur.

The first blow cut his lip pretty badly, but luckily a police car pulled up just as Mr. G. and the other man, whose initial I do not know, had dragged Wilbur through the window and were proceeding to pummel him severely.

One policeman stopped the mutilation with the classic "Break it up, break it up!" while his partner, who was somewhat older, demanded, "Hey, what's going on around here?"

"I'll tell you what's going on around here!" yelled Mr. G., poking and jabbing at Wilbur over the restraining officer's shoulder. "That son-of-a-bitch offered to put his cold hands on my wife's boobies! He said I should make like an Eskimo and lend her to him overnight!"

The blonde provocateuse and her sister-rinse managed to pull Mr. G. sidewards, and when the police asked if anyone wanted to file charges, Wilbur said, "N-no!" and Mr. G. drove his posse away, leaving a sonic trail of colorful language. They had not even paid for the Tastee-Freezes.

So no charges were filled, but the police car dutifully reported the fracas over the radio, and a feisty desk sergeant phoned Wilbur's uncle and told him he'd better take a *pret*-ty good look at the smarty-pants employee who had created an incident through blatant sexual advances. "Why, he made a pass at a lady right in front of her husband!" Such a type might have rapist leanings, said the sergeant, or could even be a recidivist. Wilbur's uncle did not know what "recidivist" meant, but the mere sound drove an ice pick into his heart.

"My uncle drove right over," Wilbur lamented, "and closed the stand for the night and took me home—and that's where he gave me that long heart-to-heart talk I told you . . . I think he also fired me."

I did not know what to say. Wilbur was sighing and pushing down the Band-Aid, which had upcurled. With false aplomb, I ventured, "That's too bad, Wil—but that was just a bad break. Don't let it get you down. Why, in no time at all you'll find a much better job——"

"I have!" Wilbur sang out, his face lighting up. "At Weisshaupt Orthopedic Shoe Stores. I answered an ad. They need someone to handle delivery receipts, and check stock so that models in all sizes of the most popular numbers and colors are available at all times. I think it will be very *int*eresting.

... Orthopedic shoes are not only used by orthopedists, you know!" He removed his glasses and wiped them with the lint-free glass-wiping cloth he always carried in its own lint-free cover. "The *largest* shoe store in the world is Lilley and Skinner, in London. Mr. Weisshaupt told me they have a quarter of a million pairs for sale at all times!"

A load seemed to rise from my back as I heard these words.

IV

Wilbur did very well in orthopedic shoes. I know, because I did not hear from him for quite a while. He had no doubt made new friends. He also no doubt soon lost them, because he began to drop me postcards suggesting, with his unique brand of gaiety, that "we break bread together" or "take a weekend stroll, for the sake of our cardiac welfare."

To each postcard I dashed off a plausible excuse: I would be attending a funeral next Sunday; I was giving a lecture in Sag Harbor; I had a maladjusted kneecap. But I could not forever increase the death rate, the lecture circuit, or the neuroses of my knee, hip, and instep. And, I suppose, I just could not bring myself to turn down Wilbur for good.

So I decided to cushion the *effect* of Wilbur's company —by inviting someone else to join us. And to launch this stratagem properly I went through my address book and chose, out of all my acquaintances, the one who would be most likely to find Wilbur the most interesting—or, at least, the least peculiar: Hans Ecklish. Hans is a computer programmer. He is completely uninterested in food, girls, boys, politics or the underdeveloped countries. What he *is* interested in is French madrigals, Portuguese *fados,* and the influence of Speusippus. Hans has been that way since his *gymnasium* days in Schleswig-Holstein. He is an especial fan of Speusippus, who was Plato's nephew, I believe.

Well, Wilbur and I met in front of the polar bears, and I soon saw Hans coming toward us with his Harry Truman stride and green hat with a pheasant's feather in the band.

I felt the self-congratulatory glow of a man who has made an uncannily astute decision.

But no sooner did I introduce Wilbur to Hans (who always frowned upon being introduced) and Hans to Wilbur, than Wilbur, in his most ingenuous manner, said, "This is my *dies faustus.*"

"I beg your pardon?" asked Hans.

"My *dies faustus*," repeated Wilbur. "That is how the ancient Romans said 'my unlucky day.'"

"Wilbur doesn't mean that in a personal sense," I hastened to explain.

"Then why did he say it?" asked Hans.

"Why did you say that, Wil?" I asked.

"What?" asked Wilbur.

"That this is your unlucky day."

"I don't know. I—was thinking about Julius Caesar."

"Did you think I was about to assassinate you?" inquired Hans, in a dangerous murmur.

"Oh, no," Wilbur flushed. "Oh, *no!*"

"Are you Italian?" asked Hans.

"No," said Wilbur.

"Are you an historian?"

"Oh, no. I'm in orthopedic——"

"Aha!" cried Hans. "Then it is not your everyday habit to walk around thinking about Julius Caesar and quoting *Latin,* which you insult me by translating. Did you take me for a barbarian? Did you——"

Wilbur was sputtering and hopping up and down and pushing his glasses halfway up his forehead, explaining that he had just realized that he thought of Caesar because he had passed an Italian parade on the way to the park, but the Gothic wrath of Hans Ecklish was not to be stilled by feats of association and recall. He was still shouting *ad libidum.*

"*Did you think I have no education?* No breeding? No culture?" Hans bellowed. "I will match my knowledge of Greek against yours any day!"

"But *I* don't know Greek—" blubbered Wilbur.

"Then don't quote me your goddam Latin!" thundered Hans. *"Dies faustus! . . .* Bah! Bah!"

I think you can see why it turned out to be an afternoon full of awkward hiatuses; they were not helped, I fear, by Wilbur's periodic, frantic stabs at propitiation: that there are only 4,000 telephones in all of Haiti; that the most expensive cheese in the world comes from goats; that you can heat a living room if twelve people just keep walking around it, since each walker throws off 800 BTU's an hour, and even on the coldest day in New York a five-room *house* requires only 5,000.

I did not see Wilbur for months after that.

One day, I was lunching at Schrafft's with Cy Harnish, and Wilbur materialized before us. He said he had finished his buttermilk at the counter and just came by to wish us *"Bon appétit!"*

I introduced him to Cy before he could explain that *"bon appétit"* was actually French and meant "Eat hearty."

Wilbur sat down, sighing. "Did you know that hair grows one seventy-second of an inch a day?"

Cy coughed up some refractory object in his food.

"The interesting thing is that the club- or bulb-shaped end of a dislodged hair is *not the root,* as most people think! Oh, no. A hair becomes club- or bulb-shaped *after* it comes out; and new hair does grow out of the vacated follicle!!"

Cy rose. "My wife Hilda is having a hysterectomy in twenty minutes," he said. "I think I'll scrub up, in case the surgeon loses his way," and strode out.

"For God's *sake,* Wilbur," I exploded, *"why* did you have to say that?"

"What?"

"How the bulbous end of hair is not really the root——"

"I thought he would find it *in*teresting," blinked Wilbur.

"Sure he would! He is as bald as an eggshell! Didn't you notice? He has been hairless since he was twenty-eight and

I do not think you made his day joyful and carefree by saying that hair will grow out of vacated follicles!"

Wilbur began to stammer badly. "I-I was kind of excited, I guess, b-because I just learned those facts——"

"Why would anyone get excited about the rate at which hair grows? !" I fumed.

"I *have* to know that," protested Wilbur. "Where would I get at Marco's if I didn't know a basic thing like that?"

"What," I asked, "is Marco's?"

"Where I work," said Wilbur.

"Since when does hair grow on orthopedic shoes?" I asked.

"I left orthopedic shoes in April," explained Wilbur, surprised that I had not heard it on television, "for a f-fantastic opportunity with a new 'growth' firm, as they are called. Mr. Palestrina, whose first name is Marco, says there's a gold mine in his X-14—shampoo or ointment!"

"What," I heard myself respond, "do you do for Mr. Palestrina?"

"P-public relations. Mostly, I answer letters of complaint. But that's only to break me in."

V

Blissful time passed during which I did not hear from my poor, dear old schoolmate. Just as I was beginning to understand why I was enjoying so many good books again, I received a letter: Wilbur hoped I would come to a "little housewarming party" at his new "digs," on Saturday, and "meet a charming young lady. We have had six dates! ! R.S.V.P. New phone: 756-7334."

I could understand the exclamation points after "six dates." Wilbur had always had this problem with girls: the day after any girl went out with him, she became engaged to someone overseas, she told him, or contracted tularemia and was quarantined, with a fierce guard from the Department of Health at her door. I could not help being curious about Wilbur's latest grope toward normalcy.

I phoned him. "What time is your housewarming?"

"Two-thirty!" flashed Wilbur. "Tickled you can come, old man!" I wondered what was getting into Wilbur now; first, "digs" and now—he had never called me or anyone "old man." "Do jot down my new address," Wilbur was saying. "It's 1420 Second Avenue, a new building that is faced in white tile and has three very swift self-service elevators. Its name is Ilium Towers."

"What?"

"What do you mean 'what'?"

"Skip it."

"I'm on the second floor. Apartment 'L.'"

Ilium Towers *was* faced entirely in bathroom tile, and the self-service elevator was so swift that rocketing up to the mere second floor left it insufficient time for smooth deceleration, so the abrupt murder of motion reactivated an old war wound in my elbow when I banged it against the elevator rail and realized with new keenness how momentum becomes inertia according to Newton's $F=ma$, where "F" is force, "m" mass, and "a" stands for acceleration.

Apartment 2-L was the last cell on the floor, by far the most convenient to the incinerator.

I lifted the tormented Trojan on the knocker and rapped his little helmet against the brass shield. The door flew open. "Hello, hello, hel*lo* there. Come in, old boy!" beamed Wilbur.

He was wearing a maroon velour smoking jacket, slippers to match with an embroidered crest, and an unlighted pipe. (He was not actually wearing the pipe; he had it clenched between his bared teeth.) Since Wilbur never used nicotinic substances, I suddenly realized where the "old man" and "old boy" were coming from: the pipe. Whenever Wilbur put that London pipe between his choppers, phrases from Piccadilly came out. Maybe they had been packed in with the pipe; or maybe it was osmosis, or some symbiotic process.

"Enter, enter!" Wilbur was chuckling. "Or, as a Spaniard would say: 'Sir, consider yourself in your own *casa!*'"

" '*Casa*,' I assume, is the Spanish word for 'house'?" I ventured.

"Quite," said Wilbur.

The apartment overlooked the ramp to the garage in the basement of Ilium Towers, but Wilbur closed the draperies, turned on some lamps, and snapped on his hi-fi to an FM program of Chinese widows wailing quarter-tones in some burial rite. Now, the only way you would even suspect you were overlooking the ramp to a garage was from an occasional irate automobile horn, or a shout of "Stop blocking the *ramp*, you stupid bastard!"

"She'll be here any minute," Wilbur burbled. "Sit down; do unwind. I know you'll like her!"

"What's her name?" I asked.

"Naomi."

"How many people did you invite to this housewarming?"

Before he could explain his suave, mysterious smile, the Trojan fell twice and Wilbur leaped for the door as if there was a fire and he had to escape before the gas tanks in the garage below exploded. His speed caused him to fling the door open so fast that he opened it too wide, which knocked a bowl of flowers off the nearby end table.

"Well, well, well, well," crowed Wilbur, stooping to pick up the glass shards and homeless daisies. "Come *in*, Nao, here, I'll take your coat." He was so excited that he hopped up and down as he introduced us. "—and this is N-Naomi Spredforth."

I would like to say I had no difficulty acknowledging the introduction. "How do you do, Miss Spredforth."

She was a thin, pleasant waif of a girl, slightly bucktoothed, with a retroussé nose and fine, tortoise-shell glasses. Her eyes were navy blue.

"Sit here, sit here!" cried Wilbur. To me, he said, "Something to drink, old boy? Four Roses? Manischewitz wine? Some other alcoholic c-concoction?"

"At 2:30?" I frowned. "No, thank you."

"Perhaps coffee," Naomi Spredforth whispered to him.

"Perhaps you prefer coffee?" shouted Wilbur.

"Not yet," I said, regretting my rejection of stronger stuff. "What about you, Miss Spredforth?"

"I never drink coffee," she said. She took her seat on the Castro convertible ("That's the Monte Carlo model," explained Wilbur proudly) and placed a tote bag, carpet-patterned, beside her.

In the silent, precommunication communion, Wilbur glanced from me to Miss Spredforth and from Miss Spredforth to me, beaming and clucking to encourage us to get to know each other. A damp suspicion grew inside me that the total number of people in Wilbur's party would be three. I cleared my throat.

"Do you live in New York?" I asked.

Miss Spredforth nodded sweetly. "Since a quarter to five, March fourth, nineteen hundred and sixty-six."

"Oh, did you hear that?" moaned Wilbur.

"I remember the exact time," she sighed, "because that was when I closed the door to my own flat, on Tenth Street, saying to myself, 'This is now your home, Naomi, your own flat on Tenth Street in New York City, on the island of Manhattan, and thank God, thank *God* you are no longer in that dreadful School of Library Administration——'"

"Naomi comes from Comfort, Texas!" boomed Wilbur, who had never been good at keeping a secret.

"Really?" I said. "You don't have a Texan accent."

"That," said Miss Spredforth, "is because I was only born in Comfort; financial reverses compelled my father to take us to Waco, where I spent the first year of my life—scarcely the crucial period, formatively speaking, insofar as inflection and accent in speech are concerned."

"True!" cried Wilbur.

"Where *were* you brought up?" I asked.

"Cos Cob, which is a tiny community five miles west of Stamford," she said. "Do you mind if I tat?"

"What?"

She opened her tote and removed a tiny hand shuttle with a needle stuck in some embryonic lace.

"Oh," I said. "Please do. I have always wanted to see some-one tatting."

"Since I neither smoke nor drink," smiled Miss Spredforth, "tatting serves to canalize my nervous energies."

"Not that she's nervous now!" Wilbur sang out. "You're not nervous now, are you, Nao?"

"No, no. But would you mind reducing the decibel volume on that loudspeaker? I have a slightly impaired tympanum, from an obscure infection of the ear that did not respond to antibiotics when I was eleven."

When Wilbur terminated the Chinese funeral we could hear the growling engines and oaths much more clearly, but Miss Spredforth did not seem to mind. Neither did Wilbur, who moved to the very edge of his chair, leaning forward, his heels rising out of his slippers, pushing his glasses up his nose, taking the pipe out of his mouth, totally prepared in mind and posture for Miss Spredforth to lift her head from her tatting so that he could look her right in the lens. When she did, he did, blurting: "Did you know that in Burma girls born on a Sunday are supposed to marry only boys who were born on a Tuesday?!"

Naomi's mouth stayed open wider than is customary. "Gracious! Why is that?"

"I don't know," said Wilbur, but promptly recovered with a blasé, "I suppose it's some ancient superstition!"

A knowing, Delphic expression crept into Naomi Spredforth's eyes. "The Greeks," she lilted, "think Tuesday, not Friday, the unlucky day of the week."

"*Really?*" gasped Wilbur. "The Burmese drive bamboo stakes into the ground so that their numerous governing spirits will have a place to sit! That's how considerate the Burmese are!"

Naomi laughed, clapping her girlish hands once—not to applaud, but in a reflex of admiration. "That reminds me of something my brother Hasdrubal, who is in the Foreign Service, told me. In Cambodia, an American virtually takes his life in his hands if he pats a native child on the head!

The Cambodians think it is sacrilegious to pat a child on the head."

Wilbur almost whined in his rapture. "Did *you* know that in Japan they place a very high value on having a son, and a very low value on having a daughter?"

"Yes," murmured Naomi, "I know."

"Then why do Japanese couples *actually pray for their firstborn to be a girl?!!*" Wilbur paused dramatically, his eyes shining.

Naomi gave the low, confident laugh of a master and, one eyebrow arched to underline her accomplishment, smiled, "Because if the Nipponese firstborn is a girl, then, when the all-important little *boy* comes along, there is an older sister waiting to raise, pamper and slave for him! !"

They were married three weeks later.

I hear they are very happy. They moved from Ilium Towers right after their honeymoon in the Museum of Natural History, because Naomi understandably disapproved of overlooking a garage ramp. Now they have a three-room floor-through in the west seventies, from the front room of which they have a fine view of a charming brownstone stoop across the street where nothing but marijuana is sold —no heroin, "speed," or ugly stuff like that.

Last Christmas, Naomi gave Wilbur a set of *World Almanacs* (in remarkably good condition) for the years 1927–47. Wilbur gave Naomi *The Proteptics of Iamblichus*.

I don't know how two squirrels can be happier than that.

And I don't have to see Wilbur anymore.

Dear Miss O'Neill

O N the hellish hot days (and the only city more hellish
than Chicago, where this happened, is Bombay), Miss
O'Neill would lift her wig and scratch her pate. She did it
absently, without interrupting whatever she was saying or
doing.

I always watched this with fascination. Miss O'Neill was
our seventh-grade teacher, and it was the consensus of my
cynical classmates that Miss O'Neill had, until very recently,
been—a *nun*. That was the only way they could explain the
phenomenal fact of her wig. Miss O'Neill, they whispered,
had been nudged out of her holy order for dire, mysterious,
heart-rending reasons, and the punishment her stern superiors had decreed was that she teach the emphatically
non-Catholic heathens in the George Howland Elementary
School on Sixteenth Street.

None of us ever knew Miss O'Neill's first name (actually,
teachers never *had* a first name), and when my mother
once asked me how old she was, I answered, "Oh, she's *old.*"
"Old" meant at least thirty, even forty—which, to an eleven-
year-old, is as decrepit and remote and meaningless as, say,
sixty or seventy, though not one hundred.

Miss O'Neill was dumpy, moonfaced, sallow, colorless,
and we hated her. We hated her as only a pack of West Side

barbarians could hate a teacher of arithmetic. She did not teach arithmetic—but that is how much we hated her. She taught English. She was a thirty-third-degree perfectionist who drilled us—constantly, endlessly, mercilessly—in spelling and grammar and diction and syntax. She had a hawk's eye for error, for a dangling participle or an upright *non sequitur*, a "not *quite* right" word or a fruity solecism. (Did you know that "solecism" comes from the contempt of Greek patricians for the dialect that thrived in Soloi?)

Whenever one of our runny-nosed congregation made a mistake, in composition *or* recitation, Miss O'Neill would send the malefactor to the blackboard to "diagram" the sentence. Going to the blackboard for the public self-exposure of a grammatical tort, which in Miss O'Neill's eyes partook of at least venial sin, was the classroom torture we most resented.

Miss O'Neill's diagramming made us lay bare the solid, irreducible anatomy of a sentence. We had to separate subject from predicate, the accusative from the dative. We had to explain how each part of a sentence works, and how the parts fit together, and how they mesh and move to wheel out meaning. We had to uncover our mistakes ourselves, "naked to our enemies," then offer a correction and explain the reason for *that*—all as Miss O'Neill impassively waited. She waited as if she could sit there until Gabriel blew his kazoo, as our devastating humor had it.

And if an offered correction was itself wrong, Miss O'Neill compounded the heartlessness of her discipline by making the culprit parse *that* on the board, and see where and why *that* was in error, and how *that* must now be remedied. It was inhuman.

Some kids broke into the sweats as they floundered around at the blackboard, guessing at (and failing to pinpoint) their mistake, praying that Miss O'Neill would end the fearful ordeal either by identifying the awful error herself or, at least, by hinting, eyebrowing, murmuring a sound (positive or negative) that might guide them to the one true redeeming answer. But that Miss O'Neill would never do; instead, she shifted her inquisition from the criminal at the blackboard to the helots in the chairs. "Well, class? Who sees the mistake? . . . Jacob? No? . . . Sylvia? . . . My, my . . . Harold? . . . Annie . . . Joseph? . . . Come, come, class; you must concentrate. There is an error— an error in grammar —on that blackboard. . . ." So pitiless and unyielding was her method.

Each afternoon, as we poured out of George Howland, like Cheyennes en route to a massacre, we would pause for a time in the schoolyard to pool our misery and voice our indignation over the fate that had condemned us to such an abecedarian. Had we known Shakespeare, we would have added one word to Hamlet's command to Ophelia, making it, with feeling, "Get thee *back* to a nunnery."

What added frustration to our grievance was the fact that Miss O'Neill never lost her patience, never grew angry, never even raised her voice. Worse, she was impervious to the sly infractions, the simulated incomprehensions, with which our most talented saboteurs baited and riled other teachers. Nothing disturbed Miss O'Neill's tight, shipshape classroom. She was unrufflable. She simply ignored, or outflanked, the ruses and traps and malingerings of our minor Machiavellis. Nothing impeded the steady pace and purpose of her tutelage.

I say that my comrades and I hated Miss O'Neill—but that is not entirely true. I only pretended to hate her. In our sidewalk conclaves, on weekends, when we chortled over the latest *tour de force* of Douglas Fairbanks, who could hold off fifty of Richelieu's swordsmen with his single blade, or outwit a platoon of Pancho Villa's ruffians with no more than his acrobatics and celestial smile; or when we mourned the unaccountable defeat of our noble Cubs by the disgusting White Sox; or when we matched extravagances about what we would do if we happened to find *ten million dollars* at that very moment; or when we licked our Eskimo Pies and, for the umpteenth time, shared fantasies about the hot-breathed surrender of one or another seventh-grade nymph to our lascivious fumblings—sooner or later Miss O'Neill would be damned by some indignant freeman, and I would at once join in the howlings about her cold-blooded despotism, cursing her as fervently as any of my companions: So strong is the desire of a boy to "belong," to be no different from the grubbiest of his fellows.

But secretly, my respect for Miss O'Neill—nay, even my affection—mounted, week by week. I was exhilarated by what I can only call the incorruptibility of her instruction. I found stirring within myself a sense of excitement, of discovery, a curious quickening of the spirit that attends initiation into a new world.

Though I could not have explained it in these words, I sensed that frumpy Miss O'Neill was leading me, not through the musty labyrinth of English Composition, but into a sunlit realm of order and meaning. Her iron rules, her inflexible demands, her meticulous corrections, were not, to me, the torment or irritation they were to my companions. They were sudden flashes of light, giddying glimpses of the magic that hides within the arrangement of words, intoxicating visions of that universe that awaits understanding. It was as if a cloak of wonder had been wrapped around the barren bones of grammar.

For it was not just grammar or diction or syntax to which Miss O'Neill, whether she knew it or not, was introducing me. She was revealing language as the vehicle for thinking, grammar as the servant of logic, diction as a chariot for the imagination, the prosaic sentence as the beautiful, beating life of the mind at work. She was teaching what an earlier generation called "right reason."

The most astonishing thing about Miss O'Neill was that she proceeded on the assumption that she *could* teach a pack of potential poolroom jockeys how to write clear, clean, correct sentences, organized into clear, clean, correct paragraphs—in their native tongue.

I do not think Miss O'Neill had the slightest awareness of her influence on me, or anyone else. She was not especially interested in me. She never betrayed an iota of preference for any of her captive and embittered flock.

Nor was Miss O'Neill much interested in the high, grand reaches of the language whose terrain she so briskly charted. She was a technician, pure and simple—efficient, conscientious, immune to excuses or flattery or subterfuge. Nothing derailed her from her professionalism.

And that is the point. Miss O'Neill did not try to please us. She did not try to like us. She certainly made no effort to make us like her. She valued results more than affection, and, I suspect, respect more than popularity.

She was not endowed with either loving or lovable attributes, and she did not bother regretting it or denying it or trying to compensate for it. She went about her task with a forthright "I want" or "You go" instead of the sanctimonious "Shall we?" She concentrated solely on the transmission of her knowledge and the transferring of her skill.

I think Miss O'Neill understood what foolish evangelists of education are bound to rediscover: that drill and discipline are not detestable; that whether they know it or not, children prefer competence to "personality" in a teacher; that communication is more significant than camaraderie; that what is hard to master gives students special rewards (pride, self-respect, the unique gratification of having succeeded) precisely because difficulties have been conquered, ramparts scaled, battles won; that there may be no easy road at all to learning some things, and no "fascinating" or "fun" way of learning some things really well.

Popular teachers often leave residues of uncertainty in their pupils, I think, suspicions of things untested, therefore unresolved. Children's unease with ambiguity, especially when it is the product and the price of lenience, surely leads to discontent. But "hard" teachers earn gratitude—perhaps not immediately, perhaps not articulated, no doubt grudging —for respecting the *subject* no less than the student, for teaching that refuses to diminish the subject's size or debase its importance.

I do not know whether Miss O'Neill infected any other

varmint in the seventh grade with a passion for, or even an abiding interest in, English. To me, she was a force of enlightenment.

Miss O'Neill must long ago have retired from her mission to elementary-school aborigines. Perhaps she has been called from this unkind world to don wings—and, I hope, golden locks, to replace the wig under whose gauzy base she scratched her relief from itching on those broiling days in Chicago. If she is still alive, she must be in her dotage: I hope she somehow gets word of these thanks, so long belated, for a task so well performed.

I have never forgotten what she taught me.

To this day, whether I am wrestling a slipshod sentence or stand glazed before a recalcitrant phrase; when I must drive myself to tame a rebellious paragraph, or burn out the fog of careless prose; whether I begin to puff over an involuted passage in Proust or get knocked cold by an unsaintly clause in Talcott Parsons, I promptly find myself thinking of dear Miss (What-oh-what?) O'Neill—and, sighing, reach for a sheet of paper and proceed to diagram the English until I know—and know *why*—it is right or wrong, and how it can be swept clean of that muddleheadedness that doth plague us all.

Groucho

HE is seventy-five and frail (at least he *looks* frail) and the sardonic rasp of the crow in his throat is softer. But he is no less scornful of the inanity of most conversation, the mendacity of most mortals, the heartless slings of fortune, the deadly arrows of *l'amour*. He moves slowly, loves to have the soles of his feet scratched, and observes the idiot parade of human events with mournful skepticism. He exudes the ambience of a larcenous undertaker. And he is part of our national treasure.

I have written about Groucho before, but there are things I have never published about him; and now *he* has published his letters to friends and fans. In these Epistles to the Galitzianers, my hero sounds off with supreme indifference to All That Americans Hold Dear. His correspondence is a hall of mirrors, full of vertiginous wisecracks, unexpected backswipes, pop-up coolers, lunacies, triple entendres and blasé variations on the theme of Indignant Insult which is his hallmark. I do believe he is vaudeville's Voltaire.

The Library of Congress (no less) preserves Groucho's memorabilia of six decades in show biz, on Broadway, in Hollywood, on radio and TV. This treasure trove contains some choice *aperçus:*

"You don't have to have relatives in Kansas City to be miserable."

"Home is where you hang your head."

"Azusa is a town where a drugstore sells straw hats for horses."

"Writing to you is like corresponding with an aching void."

"*Ciao* is an Italian salutation. It is also a breed of dog who will bite off your ass for no reason."

"My plans are still in embryo, a small town on the edge of wishful thinking."

I became Groucho's slave at the State and Lake Theater in Chicago, on a day I played high-school hooky from Crane Tech, a robust seminary for steamfitters, where I was learning to draw blueprints, forge horseshoes, splice, solder, mortise, and injure odd parts of my body. The year was, roughly, 1863, and I played hooky thereafter whenever the Four Marx Brothers brought a new vaudeville act to the Loop.

I have seen every movie the blessed brothers made, and every play they endowed with glory. I rejoiced in their inspired insolence, howled over their non sequiturs, grew drunk on their madcap repartée, and lost control of my senses altogether (as they so joyously did of theirs) as I watched their triumphant defiance of convention, manners, logic, and propriety.

As for the lugubrious Groucho, the cork-moustachioed roué with the half-crouch lope and the visage of a sardonic owl, he was clearly doing to Reason what Einstein did to Time and Space. I just wish I had the time and space to tell you what Groucho did to reason. He still is the iconoclast *par excellence*, a master of contempt, the freshest, sanest lunatic on earth.

And who dares challenge my conviction that the love scenes between reprobate Groucho and Margaret Dumont (that glorious travesty of a *grande dame* with her Newport diction and Uffizi bosom) are a high point in western civilization?

After college and a stretch in graduate school, I came to

Hollywood to do research for a study of the movie colony. Eager to plunge neck-deep into the native culture, I attended a charity baseball game between teams representing the Actors and the Comedians. Groucho, captain of the comics, told his lead-off man, Jack Benny, "Benny, get up there and hit a home run."

Benny got up there and struck out.

Marx promptly stalked out of the dugout with Homeric indignation and resigned: "I can't manage a team that won't follow instructions!"

I was his guest once in his box during a Hollywood Angels' night game. It was the most disorienting two hours I ever endured in a ball park. My host uttered antiseptic advice and dissent throughout the nine innings:

When one batter poked feebly at an outside curve, Marx shouted, "You haven't enough strength to beat your wife!"

When the Hollywood pitcher was yanked and began his long, sad trek to the showers, Marx rose, put his beret over his heart, and bowed his head in silent tribute.

When the Angels' second baseman (who had struck out, popped out, and struck out) finally managed to draw a base on balls, and advanced to second base on another walk, Marx observed bitterly: "That's the first time I've seen that guy on second without his glove."

After my Hollywood tome appeared, I returned to more conventional fiction and, as a free lance, wrote a story for (I hoped) a movie. I cast Groucho, in my dreams, as "Emil Keck," a flatfooted waiter and shlemiel who all his life had yearned to be a swindler. Emil so passionately admired crooks, con men, card sharps, sap suckers, pigeon pluckers, title tappers, grifters, and gully-miners that he had for twenty years lovingly collected and filed every scrap of data about swindlers he could lay his hands on. He thus became a walking *Who's Who* on the masters of the special arts of malfeasance. From a reverent memory he could respond, as I do now, recalling my script: "Green Gloves Cantrell? One of the finest scratch scribes who ever came out of the old South! Flim-flammed the yokels in St. Looey for fifty thousand bucks in 1948. Boodled a *banker* from Memphis for ten thou' in '50. He was double-crossed by a gimpy fink named Chowder-head Brown and did four years for the Feds in the clink. And his very first week out, son, in ole San Antone, he pulled as pretty a bunco caper as you ever saw, made it clean with twenty-five grand—and headed for the Mexican border! . . . Ah, Green Gloves . . . What a man! They don't make clip slicks like *that* anymore."

Groucho did play the part of Emil, to my everlasting satisfaction, and with a perfection even that prince of scoundrels, W. C. Fields, would have applauded. Groucho wedded hypocritical benevolence to subliminal derision with a nonchalance few con men could hope to match.

The movie, incidentally, costarred a young hopeful named Frank Sinatra and an ex-dentist's–secretary named Jane Russell; it was called *It's Only Money* until Mr. Howard Hughes, who owned RKO before he owned the Humboldt Current, changed the title to *Double Dynamite*. It takes no mental labor, if you remember Miss Russell's figure, to figure out what Mr. Hughes considered his main attraction's main attractions.

Groucho loved the part of Emil Keck, as did I; but Mr. Hughes decided either to sell RKO or buy Q.E.D., during which transaction, greatly complicated by Mr. Hughes' propensity for vanishing into thick air, the lovely tale of Emil Keck got lost in a publicity vacuum. It has rested there forever after.

II

Mr. Marx has a mind of considerable originality and supersonic speed. He is a satirist who uses the flattest, most bored of monotones to puncture the time-honored platitudes of social discourse. What knight of civil rights ever put his case as succinctly as Marx did when he (a Jew, married to a woman who wasn't) expressed interest in joining a posh beach club in Santa Monica?

"Groucho," a friend said uneasily, "don't apply for membership in that club."

"Why not?"

"Well, frankly—they're anti-Semitic."

"Mmh," sighed Groucho. "Do you think they'd let my son go into the water up to his knees?"

Contrast this with the immortal *coup de grâce* he administered to a club that invited him to join their hallowed ranks: "I do not wish to belong to the kind of club that accepts people like me as members."

I leave it to logical positivists to figure out what kind of club a man of such refined sensibilities *can* join. I also recommend the problem to students of Zeno's paradoxes.

It pleases Groucho more than he lets on that he was (and is) the pet comic of highbrows around the world, from Oxford to Bombay to Jerusalem: T. S. Eliot, James Thurber, Thornton Wilder, James Joyce (who neologized "Groucho" into a verb in *Finnegans Wake*). And he will tell you that when a Foreign Office emissary came to 10 Downing Street, during a fearful night of the War, with some documents that needed the Prime Minister's signature, Winston Churchill growled crossly, "You must wait until I have seen tonight's film. It's the *Marx* Brothers!"

My favorite Marxism, of the hundreds I cherish, involves the time Groucho was driving back from Mexico; his car stopped at the U.S. immigration post on the California border and the government officer asked him the usual questions:

"Are you an American citizen?"

"Sure," replied Marx.

"Where were you born?"

"New York."

"What's your occupation?"

Groucho's eyes narrowed: "Smuggler."

Among his unique attributes this cream of jesters possesses the uncanny faculty of *hearing* with originality. One night, as he was driving me to a rally, I suddenly remembered that it was my father's birthday.

"Would you mind stopping at a Western Union office?" I asked. "I want to wire my father."

"What's the matter?" leered the Master. "Can't he stand by himself?"

I should confess, in all fairness, that I do not carry on a correspondence with Mr. Marx, because: (1) I am a poor correspondent; (2) I am nowhere as close to him as three-dozen old friends I can mention; and (3) his answers give me the feeling that I have fallen into a centrifuge. He once wrote me this confounding and cockamamy reply to a note: "Excuse me for not answering your letter sooner, junior, but I've been so busy not answering letters that I couldn't get around to not answering yours in time."

He makes no effort to inhibit whatever outlandish notion may float into that serene, anarchic mind. In the middle of a heated political discussion, Groucho may rise, intone, "Gentlemen, they have fired on Fort Sumter!" and leave the room.

And in 1942, our hero, scheduled to entertain the troops at an Army post, was waiting in the general's office when the telephone rang. Since the general was out, Groucho picked up the instrument, crooning, quite accurately: "World War Two-oo-oo."

He derives special pleasure from pulverizing the phony. At one time, many of his friends in Hollywood kept recounting the supernatural powers of a spiritualist under whose spell they had fallen and who was cashing in on séances for movie luminaries. This sorcerer might still be plying his occult wiles had not some of skeptical Groucho's friends challenged him to attend a séance and appraise the psychic's wizardry for himself. Marx went.

He sat silent and baleful through a demonstration in which the turbaned spiritualist stared into a crystal ball and, uttering arcane mumbo-jumbo, broke the barrier between those who are here and those who are hereafter, answering the most difficult questions with aplomb, revealing awesome secrets from beyond the grave, and generally advising, warning, instructing, and uplifting. After two hours of such exhausting omniscience, the seer intoned in eerie timbre, "Now my spirit-medium grows weary.... Our journey into the other world must draw to a close. . . . There is time for—one more question."

Marx asked it: "What's the capital of South Dakota?"

Groucho abhors the innocent clichés of social discourse. I was lunching with him at the Brown Derby once when a dowager barged over and gushed, "Oh, *do* pardon me—but aren't you Groucho Marx?"

"No," said Marx, "are you?"

When a tipsy delegate to some convention of cretins slapped Marx on the back with that hallowed American anthem, "You old son-of-a-gun, you probably don't remember me!" Marx impaled the oaf on his misanthropic glare and replied, "I never forget a face, but in your case I'll be glad to make an exception."

In his study, once, he asked me to look at a framed photograph of a boy—nine or ten years old—who was facing the camera stiffly. The boy was wearing high-button shoes, stockings, knickers, a mackintosh, a stocking hat and mittens. "He looks familiar. It's not you?" I ventured.

"No. That's Harpo. . . . Count the gloves."

I stepped closer to the picture. Harpo was holding a leather glove in one of his mittened hands.

"How many gloves do you see?" asked Groucho.

"Three," I said.

"Right. Do you know why?"

"No."

"Well," said Groucho, "Harpo heard early in life that a gentleman never appears in public without holding a glove."

III

He was born Julius (a name he loathes) Marx, in New York. His uncle was Al Shean, of the memorable Gallagher and Shean vaudeville act. Marx's mother, a woman of prodigious enterprise and confidence in her brood, put all five of her sons into show business at a tender age, with an aunt, in an act called "Six Musical Mascots."

The five shrank to the Four Marx Brothers, using names

of faultless acuity: Groucho, because he never laughed and dripped lugubrious pessimism; Chico, the "Ravelli" of the team, a scruffy gambler, thimblerigger and pianist; Harpo, a faun in heat, who never spoke a line, plucked the harp like an angel, and excelled in stealing silverware; and Zeppo, who had the profile of Apollo and a talent hard to detect—he played the straight man and romantic lead. They remain the most original, brazen, delicious bounders in the history of what is known as "stage or screen."

This is the barest of biographical outlines, of course. When Groucho is asked about his career, his answers tend to resemble those of a defrocked preacher:

> I was born during a volcanic eruption in one of the banana countries of Central America, where a stranger apprenticed me to a basket weaver in Guatemala. I soon learned to weave with such dexterity that, by the time my second teeth arrived, I was known throughout the village as the basket child of Guatemala.
>
> I met two fellows named, I believe, Harpo and Chico. They are brothers but strangers to me. As for Sam Marx of MGM, he is their joint child by a former marriage.

During the years that the Four Marx Brothers cast their luster on the stage (*Coconuts, Animal Crackers, I'll Say She Is*), Groucho's siblings often tried to throw him off balance with outlandish ad libs. Once, while Groucho was in the middle of one of those unforgettable parodies of courtship with Margaret Dumont, brother Chico suddenly appeared onstage, announcing, "The garbage man is here."

"Tell him we don't want any," said Groucho.

In another play, in which Groucho played Napoleon with a caddish panache that taught me more about the mighty than Carlyle's *Heroes and Hero-Worship*, brother Zeppo, in the wings, bribed a bugler to blow the opening chords of the "Marseillaise." Zeppo cried, "Our national anthem—the Mayonnaise!"

Onstage, Groucho rose, saying, "The army must be dressing."

It was on a New York stage that Marx, feeling an actor's

pulse, scaled Parnassus with the line: "Either this man is dead or my watch has stopped."

And what red-blooded American can forget the time Zeppo burst into Groucho's office exclaiming, "Sir, Mr. Jennings has been waiting to see you for an hour and is waxing wroth!"

To which Groucho responded, "Well, let Roth wax Jennings for a while."

A passing *caveat:* Envious souls may charge that some of the japeries strung throughout this eulogy are not original with Groucho, but were taken from plays or movies written by such celebrated wits as S. J. Perelman, George S. Kaufman, Morris Ryskind, Irving Brecher, *et alia.* There is a grain of truth in this. But a grain is not a wheatfield. Groucho has not been in a play or movie for years; and no ghost writes his letters, and no wit whispers *ad libs* into his ears. The influence of Perelman on Marx's kind of humor is obvious, so I sing to Sid: *Gaudeamus Non Sequitur;* but when I asked the late George S. Kaufman about the demented dialogue in the Marx Brothers plays, his jaw sagged lower than usual as he scowled, "I used to go back stage, after the boys were settled into a play, and listen. And every so often I'd say, 'Ah, *that* line is mine.'"

Groucho's dispatch in turning a banality into a laugh is startling. "I came into my hotel room one night and found a strange blonde in my bed. I would stand for none of that nonsense," he said. "I gave her exactly twenty-four hours to get out."

He can toy with a sentence the way a mathematician plays with a slide rule. He once asked a friend, "How did you like my show last night?"

"I only caught the first ten minutes," the friend apologized. "I had to catch a plane——"

"A fine friend you are!" Marx glowered. "*I* heard the whole program from start to finish: that's the kind of friend *I* am."

He can push puns to the edge of dementia. In the middle of a letter about football, Marx remarked, "I have been studying the Notre Dame lineup. Did you know there is only one Irishman on the team? And his mother is a Pole—a ten-foot pole, in fact. They are the best kind for football, because when they die they die by inches, so it takes them that much longer to kick off."

Marx is repelled by back-scratching, in or out of business. He once wrote Arthur Murray, the ballroom pedagogue:

> Dear Mr. Murray:
>   When an actor mentions a product on a program, it has become customary for the manufacturer to show his appreciation by sending a gift-in-kind. If I were to mention Old Taylor on my show, for example, they would send me a case of bourbon.
>   Well, I am going to mention the Arthur Murray dancers on next week's program. Will you therefore please send me a medium-sized dancing girl, about 5'2", with the customary measurements. I am not particular as to what kind of hair she has, as long as she has hair.
>
> Yours,
> Groucho Marx

He also detests the fraudulent friendliness of business practice. When a bank wrote him: "If we can ever be of assistance, please let us know," Marx replied with a directness unequaled in English letters:

> Frankly, the best assistance you can give me is to steal some money from the account of one of your richer clients and credit it to mine.

And when *Variety,* the Bible of Show Biz, editorialized that the Marx Brothers could earn $20,000 a week if they would only work together again, Marx educated the editor:

> Dear Sir:
>   Apparently you are under the impression that the only thing that matters in this world is money. That is quite true.
>
> Groucho Marx

He once asked a professional wrestler if, as is alleged,

television's grunt-and-groan matches are fixed. The gladiator replied, "That's just a dirty rumor!"

"Well, how many dirty rumors have you wrestled lately?" asked Marx.

IV

I suppose that what most deeply gratifies us in his wit is its sheer audacity. Groucho says things we are too timid or inhibited or conventional to think of, much less say. But how does repartée so abrasive avoid giving offense? I think it is because it outflanks resentment by diverting umbrage to pleasure. Marx is so cheeky *and* funny that you laugh at what he says and forget it is at your expense. People who have been needled, chivvied, baited, and harpooned by Groucho, far from getting angry, can't wait to tell everyone about it. It is this, I think, that lets him get away with such outrageous brusqueries as these, which I cull from a priceless collection:

When someone told him, "I am my own worst enemy!" Groucho said, "Not as long as I'm alive."

He left one party with this farewell to his hostess: "Don't think this hasn't been a long, dull evening, because it has."

Of a movie producer not noted for literacy, Marx suggested, "He thinks Somerset Maugham is next to Epsom Downs."

Earl Wilson's wife once remarked, "We ate home last night. I made a stew."

"Anyone I know?" asked Groucho.

Groucho's dry, deflating mockery owes much to the mental and semantic agility of the Ashkenazim. In *The Joys of Yiddish*, I wrote:

> Yiddish lends itself to an extraordinary range of observational nuances and psychological subtleties. Steeped in sentiment, it is sluiced with sarcasm. It loves the ruminative, because it rests on a rueful past; favors paradox, because it knows that only paradox can do justice to the injustices of life; adores irony, because the only way the Jews could

retain their sanity was to view a dreadful world with sardonic, astringent eyes. In its innermost heart, Yiddish swings between *shmaltz* and derision. . . .

A very large part of Jewish humor is cerebral. It is, like Sholom Aleichem's, reason made mischievous, or, like Groucho Marx's, reason gone mad. Jewish jokes drape their laughter on logic—in despair.*

Groucho's comedy of complaint would indeed have delighted Sholom Aleichem—or Charles Dickens. During a low spot in his career, he told a friend: "I am up to my ears— in activities that don't bring in a dime. Last week, I did a show for the Army—free. Then I auditioned for radio—no money. Then I wrote a guest column—gratis. Today, I'm recording a speech for the Heart Fund in Chicago. The only thing I can get out of *that* is that someday I may be lucky enough to have a heart attack in the Loop."

Not working always depressed Groucho, as it does most comedians. He wrote the following lamentation to Sam Zolotow:

For the past nine weeks, I've been leading a life that parallels Swain's Rat and Cat Act. This offering, in case you are too young to remember, consisted of six rats dressed as jockeys, perched on six cats dressed as horses, galloping furiously around a miniature race track. It was an extraordinary act. Alan Dale wrote in the New York *Journal:*

"Last night, Swain's Rats and Cats gave a performance that for beauty and sincerity hasn't been equaled since Beerbohm Tree played King Lear at the Old Garrick."

Of course, I get more salary than Swain paid his actors. They didn't get any salary; Swain paid them in cheese. Each rat got two pounds a week. This may not seem like much, but it was all net.

The rats didn't have an agent—they knew their own kind and booked themselves independently. They didn't even have to shop for their cheese; they just sat in their dressing room and waited for Swain to throw their salary over the transom.

* Printed by permission of the author.

Frankly, I don't see where I am as well off as they were. Oh, of course, I get paid in money—but most of it goes for fuel, shelter, and taxes. With the pittance that remains, I, too, buy cheese. But I have no manager to throw it over the transom. I have to take a bus to the grocery store and shop for mine.

If my next picture turns out disastrously (and there is no reason why it shouldn't), I am going to look up Swain and ask him if he would be interested in reviving his act. I could play one of the jockeys.

Groucho

V

On his memorable radio and television shows, *You Bet Your Life*, Groucho was unlike any comedian in the republic. He simply chatted with his contestants, and about the most mundane matters: "Are you married?" "Have you any children?" "How many banks have you robbed lately?" and so on. The questions led to complications of an unearthly character.

GROUCHO:

Where are you from?

GIRL:

Australia. I flew here by plane.

GROUCHO:

A girl would be a fool to try it any other way.

On one program, a schoolteacher confessed she was "approaching forty."

"From which direction?" asked Groucho.

To a Chinese contestant who said he was twenty-four, Groucho asked, "In years or yen?"

The Chinese lad said, "You don't count age in yen."

Groucho replied, "No? I have a yen to be twenty-one again."

On another program:

GROUCHO:

Well, sir, what do you do for a living?

CONGRESSMAN:

I'm in Congress.

GROUCHO:

How long have you been incongruous?

The wildest night in his TV asylum, I think, erupted with an innocent enough opening:

GROUCHO:

Are you married?

MAN:

Well . . . yes and no.

GROUCHO:

Good for you! That's the way to be.

MAN:

I mean I'm going to marry the same woman I was once married to.

GROUCHO:

Didn't it *take* the first time?

MAN:

I guess not.

GROUCHO:

No guessing, please; not on this quiz show. How did you meet your wife?

MAN:

We were kids together.

GROUCHO:

Kids together? That's possible—but still, how did you meet her?

MAN:

Well, I drive a truck——

GROUCHO:

You ran over her?

MAN:

No, she was in the barn——

GROUCHO:

You drove the truck into a *barn*?

MAN:

No, no. She was a farmer's daughter, and they had been missing their chickens——

GROUCHO:

They were lonely for chickens?

MAN:

No, they had been *missing* them, so they turned a light on in the barnyard, and one night I drove up to get some turkeys, and her father said the turkeys were in the barn——

GROUCHO:

You married a *turkey*?

MAN:

No, no. As I went to the barn, a skunk started for the chickenhouse—and she yelled, "Get that skunk!"—and I jumped on the skunk, and she fell on the skunk, too, and we started going out together because no one else would go out with either of us!

GROUCHO:

That's the most romantic story I ever heard.

Groucho has an encyclopedic knowledge of the golden age of vaudeville, and boundless affection for its wizards; it saddens him to see them, and their legendary acts, die. Once, in a restaurant, after studying the menu thoughtfully, he asked the waitress, "Do you have frog's legs?"

"I don't think so," she said.

"That's the wrong answer," mourned Groucho. "You should have said, 'No, it's my rheumatism makes me walk this way.'"

He still enjoys spontaneous flights of candor. At a party honoring a celebrated actress, Groucho rose to say: "I toast your beauty, your talent, your charm, your wit—which gives you a rough idea of how hard up a man can be for a drink."

When a beautiful tennis starlet said she was practicing hard "to improve my form and speed," Groucho assayed her frontal hills and said, "If you improve your form any further, you'll need every bit of speed you can turn on."

When a young actress asked his advice on how to win fame and fortune in the theater, Marx, appalled by the invitation to play Polonius, replied, "My advice to you and to all struggling actresses, is this: Keep struggling. If you keep struggling, you won't get into trouble; and if you don't get into trouble, you'll never be much of an actress."

And in 1948, when the pollsters predicted that Governor Thomas Dewey would walk all over President Truman at the polls, and the American voters proved the reverse, Groucho issued his own postmortem: "The only way a Republican is going to get into the White House is by marrying Margaret." (The only other comment on that election I think worth recording was Bob Hope's telegram to Governor Dewey: "Unpack.")

VI

Like most great comic talents, Mr. Marx seems discontented with the role in which fate cast and so amply rewarded him. He wanted to be a doctor. Despite his immense success and fame, I think he still considers a lifetime spent in making millions laugh not especially praiseworthy.

Groucho's wit is a masterly flirtation with schizophrenia. He puts reason through dizzying rides on his mental roller coaster. He can dress lunacy in paralogic until he achieves that state of dementia best illustrated by the philosopher Lichtenberg who puzzled over "a knife without a blade that has no handle."

Groucho is devilishly adept in setting up contexts within which you cannot be sure whether he is serious or satiric: as a result you are bewildered. Sometimes he seems unable to moderate his badinage, like a computer which has been set for scorn and cannot stop. He will turn any line, any phrase, any name, into a pun or a barrage of buffoonery. It is dazzling and demonic, and too much. Whenever I have found him in one of these compulsive moods, I felt like the bird that got caught in a badminton game.

In his Beverly Hills house once, taking leave at the door, I said, "I'd like to say good-bye to your wife."

"Who wouldn't?" he murmured. (They have since been divorced.)

At seventy-five Groucho shows a wistfulness that is aging's sadness. He has gone through dry and tragic seasons, and his letters reflect the long days of a wealthy man who does not like to socialize, does not play much golf, and has lost, through death, brothers Harpo and Chico and many a friend he loved: e.g., Fred Allen.

He sees small justification for optimism—in the domestic, international, or geriatric universes. He lives a quiet life, venerates Gilbert and Sullivan and can sing their lyrics by the hour. He also reads more than you do.

I hear he recently remarked to a beautiful model, "You must have all sorts of exciting experiences in your work."

The model said, "Oh, no, it's just routine."

"What," graveled Groucho, "are you modeling: clay?"

It is a privilege to salute such a man.

The Sorcerer of Vision

THE first painting by Klee I ever saw puzzled me. The second fascinated me. The third hooked me. Since then, I have never seen a Klee that did not intrigue or enchant or send me spinning into a realm of fantasy that differs from all other fantasies, I think, in that it is lyrical, crowded, playful, and crystal sharp.

Klee is not a "big," grand, overpowering painter. He is a minor master, quite special, off-beat, clearly not part of the mainstream of art. He seems to have had no ancestors; but his heirs are without number. It is impossible to spend an afternoon in any town in the world without seeing some delight of pattern, some juxtaposition of color, some whimsy of design—in a poster, a gallery, an advertisement, a window display—inspired by, or derived from, this altogether fresh genius. The kiosks of Paris and Kyoto and Rome, the billboards of Dubuque or Dakar, the trolleys of Rio, the cafés of Capri—each, in some symbol or arrangement, is indebted to the precise and intricate intuition of Paul Klee. And so, in a different way, was Pollock or Miro, Avery or Shahn or Kline.

Klee said he wanted art to "sound like a fairy tale, a holiday ... a transfer to another world ..." And in his search for that other world, he began to paint not only what the unimaginative could not see, and not those fragmented impressions with which the French liberated art: Klee painted meditations, feelings, fantasies, ideas. He once said, "I try to push myself away from the earth."

To stand before a wall covered with his work—at the Basle Museum, or the indifferent nook assigned the Klees in the great Barnes Collection—is to fall victim to a feat of sensory deception: the pictures seem to ruminate, sometimes in amusement; this is visual music, from a sorcerer of whom one can never tire.

Everyone has a favorite Klee. The best phrase to characterize his artistry is his own: painting is "a trip into the land of deeper insight."

Klee was a small, pale, gentle man who worked on a dozen pictures at a time. He would sit before the different easels for hours, enveloped in blue clouds of smoke from his pipe, totally lost in what he liked to call "inner watching," trying to weave his reveries into new harmonies of design, color, hieroglyphs.

His pictures are small, all strange, all lovely or disturbing. He used every conceivable material: paper, canvas, silk, glass, linen, burlap, cardboard, tin. Fascinated by shapes and textures, he studied the most commonplace and the most exotic things: shells, mosaics, African masks; stained glass, coral, feathery moss; butterflies' wings and Chinese pottery, Coptic embroideries and Eskimo drawings and the pictographs of ancient Aztecs. You will find them all, in symbols or echoes, laced through his work.

"Art does not render what is visible," he said. "Art *makes* visible." He said his work owed more to Bach and Mozart than to any of the masters of painting. In Italy, as a student, greatly impressed by Leonardo and the frescoes of Pompeii, he nevertheless wrote: "Imitate nothing." When he visited Paris and beheld the work of Cézanne and Renoir, he wrote: "I have nothing to learn from the French."

He had so odd, so *personal* a vision that when he saw a child asleep, he said, "I saw the circulation of his blood, the regular breathing of his lungs . . . and in his head a world of dreams in contact with the powers of fate."

Once he noticed a man strolling down the deck of a ship,

and suddenly saw the man's movement and the motion of the ship and the rotation of the earth and the orbit of all the stars whirling and wheeling in the heavens—until his mind embraced the immense system of the cosmos, "centered on that man on the steamer."

"I don't want to represent a man as he is," he once declared, "but only as he might be." It was at the heart of this man's distinctive imagination that he could say that he saw in the moon "a dream of the sun."

Klee was born near Berne in Switzerland, in 1879, the son of a German music teacher and his Swiss wife. Young Klee became so good a violinist that he could not decide whether to devote his life to music or painting.

He once dawdled in the aquarium in Naples, fascinated by the dreamlike world under water in which fish and flora moved like phantoms through dark, lyrical light. Here was a realm "where things fall upward," where a flower looked like a fish, a turtle like a rock. Again and again, his paintings echoed the enchantment he had experienced there.

He married a pianist when he was twenty-seven, and kept house, literally, while she gave piano lessons; after four years he complained that the housework took too much time from his art—asking a half day, each day, for each.

He was deeply affected by Cubism—but much more by his visits to North Africa: to Tunis in 1914, to Egypt fourteen years later. Called to service in World War I, he wrote, after Franz Marc and August Macke, his closest friends, were killed: "The more horrifying this world becomes, the more art becomes abstract."

He began to teach at the famed Bauhaus in Weimar, where Kandinsky also taught, and became a professor at the new Bauhaus in Dessau and the Dusseldorf Academy of Fine Arts. When Hitler denounced the "culture Bolshevists," Klee fled to Berne. Over a hundred of his paintings and drawings were confiscated by the Nazis, who displayed some of them in the Exhibition of Degenerate Art. . . . But Picasso and Braque came to Berne, to do Klee homage.

His work, at first sight so naive, rests on immense discipline, masterful drawing, and most acute and original perceptions. His capacity to attain luminous effects through the juxtaposition of marginal colors is breathtaking. He uses color and design as if he were the first to discover them. "My hand is merely a tool, guided by something higher, more distant, somewhere." He taught himself to paint with either hand, sensing the variance in muscular control and point of vision.

Klee was as prolific as he was poetic: he created 8,926 (!) pictures and drawings, no one of which does more than hint at his boundless range and inventiveness. He was, in turn, charming, satirical, brooding, idyllic, mischievous, and morbid. Sometimes his images are startling: flashes of that dread he saw in the faces of those he called "consecrated to suffering." Some portraits, with their eccentric lines and unexpected planes of color, their skewed mouths and fanciful foreshortenings, capture the essence of the insane.

His tight, incandescent patterns are small carnivals of delight: mazes, fields of flowers, two-dimensional villages, or simply dabbed and exquisitely muted hues. Popping up like secret messengers come curious things: letters of the alphabet, a fossil form, an arrow, a balloon, antique artifacts, a sign or glyph—all embedded in a frieze that might have been inspired by the Pharaohs or the Aztecs, or in nonrepresentational streams and stripes of enchanting color. It sometimes seems to me that Klee uses encoded symbols from a kingdom no one else has ever seen.

"Our instinct drives us downward, deep down to the primal source," he reflected. "Whatever emerges from this activity, call it what you will—dream, idea, fantasy—should be taken quite seriously [and] given form. Then curiosities become realities, which add something more to life than it usually possesses. For then we no longer have things seen and reproduced... [but] visionary experiences made visible."

And so he went through life in a kind of dreamy pleasure, mesmerized by the world of wonder on every side. He fell under the spell of Bedouins and the desert, Persian tiles and

Ottoman minarets. "I am possessed by color," Klee wrote. "I do not need to pursue it. I and color are one. . . . I am a painter."

He drew phantom cities, for which he invented mysterious names: Beride, City of Water, Prhun, Uol, Air-Tsu-Dni. He could render illusion in a few crafty shapes, as in his *Arab Song*, where a large veil, two hard-to-see eyes, sandy texture, a quaint palm, bring Araby to life.

"The artists with real vocations," he said, "are those who travel to . . . that secret cavern where the central organ of all temporal and spatial movement—call it the brain or the heart of creation—makes everything happen. What artist would not wish to dwell there, in the bosom of nature . . . where the secret key to everything is kept?"

He never ceased observing and imagining and "seeing *in*," which is what insight means. "I have tried pure drawing; I have tried chiaroscuro painting; and I have tried all sorts of experiments with color . . . in meditations on the color wheel." His meditations led him to use colors as magic.

I began by saying that the first Klee I ever saw puzzled me. It puzzled me, as Klee first puzzles many others, because I was unprepared for such "childish" drawing in a portentous museum. Years later, I was struck by his own explanation: "The myth about the childishness of my drawing must have started with those linear structures in which I attempted to combine the *idea* of an object—a man, say— with representation of the pure linear elements. If I wanted to render a man 'just as he is,' I would need such a bewildering complex of lines that pure representation . . . would be impossible; they would be blurred to the point of being unrecognizable." Only Klee would see infinity in a face, a square, a dome, an insect's grace.

"No other painter of the last half-century," the *Dictionary of Modern Painting* tells us, "has exercised such a widespread influence. Even more than the variations of Picasso, whose genius recapitulates the history of form, Klee's art opens on the future."

This unconventional, wholly independent painter said,

"Sometimes I dream of a work of vast expanse which would encompass the whole realm of elements, objects, contents, and styles." Leonardo would have smiled; Blake would have understood; Freud would have been pleased. And we may wonder how that vast, dreamed universe of objects and moods and symbols and visions could have been imprisoned within the miniature scale on which Klee worked.

He died in 1940. On his tombstone is carved this disturbing revelation:

> I cannot be understood in purely earthly terms. For I can live as happily with the dead as with the unborn ...

Winston

N the visitors gallery of the House of Commons, one un-
eventful day decades ago, my host pointed out the luminaries
in that small but stately hall. "And that, of course," he whispered, "is Winston."

I saw a plump, beaming, pink-cheeked, roly-poly, slope-
shouldered oval of a man, his hair reddish in cast. He was
wearing a faultlessly tailored suit, a polka-dot bow tie, and
an expression so sunny, so impish, so pleased with the state
of the universe, that I could not help smiling myself. But
when a speaker from the opposite benches tossed some gibes
at His Majesty's Government, the cherubic countenance
changed before my eyes: the jaw jutted out to granite, the
mouth lowered, and that whole soft round countenance
turned into a glowering, defiant bulldog. If ever I saw John
Bull, it was then.

Later, I asked my friend, whose name was John Strachey
(his *The Coming Struggle for Power* had made a great impression in Europe and the United States), "Do you know
Churchill?"

"Only just."

"You call him Winston."

"Oh, *everyone* calls him Winston," he smiled. "He's a national nuisance, but one can't help being fond of him. He's

a romantic, reactionary, a blood-and-thunder jingoist. Crossed the floor *twice,* you know. . . . One can't ever be sure what he'll do or say. Frightfully good orator and writer. Smells of Gibbon, but awfully bright. . . . He's had his day, of course. *No* one, not even the wildest Tories, would dream of trusting power to Winston."

Then I used to hear about "Winston" a good deal in Hollywood, before the war, from John Balderston, to whom I was devoted. John had been London correspondent for several American papers, was a ravenous reader, and a conversationalist whose gamut ran from Cleopatra and Pericles to Parnell and Babe Ruth. John, to my awe and envy, received an air-mail edition of *The New York Times,* a dozen English papers and journals, and a stream of confidential letters from Washington, London, and Paris. It impressed me no end whenever a cable arrived at the house on Angelo Drive, or the one on Rodeo Drive, and John read it briskly, humphing or grinning or looking grave, then tossed it to me, and I was made privy to some message signed "Brendan" (Bracken), or "Nye" (Aneurin Bevan) or "Jennie" (Lee)—and "Winston."

And when the war broke out and the world went dark, as Germany smashed Poland and paralyzed France, John thundered: "Winston's the only one who can save them now! Why don't the bloody fools *see* that? . . ."

Six long, long years later, just after the war in Europe was won, I flew into London from Paris with my general, Paul Thompson, and hastened to the places I had lived in. They were gone, demolished, burned out, rubble.

For days I wandered about London with an awful weight on my heart. Near Bloomsbury, whole blocks were leveled, carpeted with hummocks of ash and brick and burned timbers; off Piccadilly, the crippled chimneys stood askew against the sky, dead sentinels gazing down on layers of collapsed floors; Chelsea was serried with dangling sconces and tilted pictures and broken mantelpieces clinging to the gaunt, surviving walls. There were no iron gates in Berkeley Square, no railing around Soho, no gilted fence-tips fronting

Mayfair's lovely mansions: every precious piece of iron had been melted into shells and cannon.

On countless sidewalks, wooden planks bridged gaping craters in which the water mains, fire hose, gas lines, conduits, dolls, shoes, wiring, oil tanks, pianos, hats, kettles, beds, canes, parasols, clocks, stoves, basement beams and attic rafters lay heaped in serpentine entanglements, cindered and stiff in their obliteration.

I made my way to the East End, and my throat dried up as I beheld the lifeless sea of shards and ruins in the mourning shades of St. Paul's. And I remembered the mockery of those moonlit nights when Nazi bombardiers could negate London's blackout simply by following the shining ribbon of the Thames from Gravesend to the city's heart. In my mind London was in flames once more, the citadel made hell, and numbly I remembered how, each night in Washington, we had pressed close to the radio, hoping to hear the treasured "This . . . is London" in that compassionate pause Edward Murrow invested with an emotion professional reporters are not supposed to betray.

And then . . . and then I heard the voice of England's lion, her leader, her savior, her talisman, Churchill, uttering that indomitable growl, that defiant scorn, that triumphant contempt for the Monster. In that abyss of desolation, echoed the unexpected upbeat to end a sentence, the teasing intervals, the occasional lisped sibilants; and, singing above all, the rolling pride and glory of those majestic passages that lifted the free world's heart. The shining phrases had indeed "armed the English language and sent it into battle. . . ."

But what I am trying to say was said better by the historian A. L. Rowse:

> Even now with the dust lying upon so much ardor along the way, one can hardly see for the tears in transcribing those words that bring back that glorious, unforgettable summer, the long hot days full of catastrophe and suspense, the country's sudden and complete uncovering, the mortal danger we stood in.

When I had my reunion with John Strachey, who was slated to become Under Secretary for Air, I asked about Churchill. He answered, "I don't think we could have made it without Winston. He was the decisive factor, magnificent, the incalculable weapon. . . . A great man. A *very* great man. . . . When he walks into the House, it is as if History itself materializes before our eyes, and is holding us accountable."

Since those distant days, I have read almost every book Churchill wrote, a hundred of his speeches, every biography or reminiscence I could lay my hands on. But I doubt that I can do justice to that miracle of a man.

•

He looked like a Toby jug, a character out of Dickens, but he was born to command, to fight, to inspire, to prevail. He lived with unquenchable gusto, sipping massive quantities of champagne, brandy, whiskey, wine; fondling long cigars all day long; working in bed until noon, lunching at three, taking a siesta—one hour, two hours, unclothed, in bed—then working again, and again after dinner until three or four or dawn. He loved dashing hats and splashy uniforms, the trappings of heraldry, the posture of chivalry, the panoply of kings.

He was a complete anachronism—a royalist, an imperialist, an Elizabethan thrust upon the stage of the twentieth century, to be charged with nothing less than the deliverance of Western civilization from the most hideous threat in history. The undefeated Wehrmacht smashed across Russia; Norway was seized; German submarines wreaked a horrible havoc on British ships and seamen and supplies; France collapsed, with and behind her vaunted Maginot Line; the evacuation at Dunkirk seemed one small, bitter *coup* in an unbelievable catastrophe; Nazi planes made London a holocaust; Hitler's boasts brought daily apprehensions of invasion; old men drilled in villages with pikes and pitchforks; road signs in Sussex, Kent, Dorset, Hampshire, were removed or reversed to confuse landing armies; Japanese airplanes sent the precious *Repulse* and *Prince of Wales* to the bottom of an eastern sea; Singapore, the very hinge of power in the Pacific, was stormed from the *land*, after "a sinister twilight," and to the world's astonishment surrendered; aid to Russia suffered shattering losses as U-boats wiped out merchant convoys on the dread run to Murmansk; Rommel rampaged across the North African desert with a speed and craft that shook the gates of Alexandria; the Mediterranean, swept by German and Italian fighter planes, was no longer England's lake; and one day a new scourge, flying missiles, unseen, silent, untrackable, soared high over the Channel and plunged into London's very breast....

And throughout this entire infernal visitation, as pundits predicted England would have to sue for peace, leave the Continent to Germany and lick her dreadful wounds, through all of this, the incredible Mr. Churchill talked of Honor, Duty, Valor—as if they were real; invoked Defiance, Fortitude, Glory—as if words mattered; sent his moral passion and glowing sentences from the very brink of chaos to lift the heart and galvanize the will of the proud "island race" whose Galahad he had become.

He was a cartoonist's dream, a doughty cherub by Lewis Carroll, with that round belly, puckish smile, pouting lips, bowler hat, chubby-fingered "V," that infantile "siren suit" for sleep—or flight—during air raids....But he truly became, as the London *Times* said, "the largest human being of his time."

It was typical of Churchill that while the Luftwaffe was making London a charnelhouse he could quip that "at the present rate" it would take "the Naaazis" about ten years to burn down one-half of London's buildings: "After that, of course, progress would be much slower."

•

He was in every way a genius, as paradoxical as he was gifted: an aristocrat who loved nothing so much as the House of Commons; a warlord who wept over human suffering; a cavalry officer who could quote 1200 lines of Macaulay from memory (or all the odes of Keats, or endless passages from Shakespeare) without hesitation or flaw; a romantic who loved to play polo, laid bricks for pleasure, and joined the Bricklayers Union; a Victorian who was ambushed at the Khyber Pass and lived beyond Hiroshima; a political "reactionary" revolted by any form of bigotry, cruelty, or injustice; a Lord of the Admiralty who was an excellent painter and won the Nobel Prize for Literature; a swashbuckler who fought in five wars, brushed death with exhilaration, and called war "once cruel and magnificent [now] cruel and squalid"; a Tory fiercely devoted to democracy and human rights; a monarchist who fashioned Britain's first social-welfare legislation; an apostle of ancient tradition who declined a dukedom or any noble rank he cared to choose, to remain a commoner; a military victor beyond compare who was a splendid biographer with a rare sense of history—which he wrote like a master (biased, but brilliant), casting himself in the starring role.

As a young man, he once had mused, "We are all worms ... but I do believe that I am a glowworm." He was at home with lightning.

He was often juvenile, petulant, exasperating; pugnacious and flamboyant, entirely egoistic, always unique. He monopolized conversation, nagged his colleagues, chivvied his staff, and employed every conceivable ploy to get his way, from tantrums to charm, sweet cajolery to Olympian wrath, anything and everything "to soften the heart, move the emotions—and intimidate," Dean Acheson has told us. And when Winston was forced to hear out others, said "Nye" Bevan, his gadfly, the curmudgeon would hunch up in pique and glower "like a ferocious clam."

Yet even those who opposed him, or suffered his obstinacy, or were stung by his acerb wit found it impossible not to like him. He was incapable of rancor. He could neither harbor nor nourish a grudge. After any quarrel, he was swift to make amends, always friendly, amiable, unbelievably considerate—to, say, Neville Chamberlain, whom he had derided, fought tooth-and-nail, and supplanted as Prime Minister. He could say even of the Germans: "My hate . . . died with their surrender." Labor's Clement Attlee called him "the most magnanimous man of his generation."

No man ever loved his country more: its heritage, its people, the abiding values of "our island race." And he so treasured the English language that he acted as if he had been appointed to police its purity. He snapped at any who misused the tongue or made it shabby with cant. To an official who tortured a sentence to avoid ending with a preposition, Churchill tartly wrote: "This is English up with which I will not put." He once illustrated the perverse versatility of prepositions in this delicious japery: "Why did you bring the book I don't want to be read to out of up for?"

His wit was famous. At one grand dinner, when he was a callow subaltern, a dowager exclaimed, "Lieutenant, I care for neither your politics nor your moustache!"—to which Winston replied, "Madame, you are unlikely to come into contact with either." When someone commented on a colleague's humility, he said, "He has a great deal to be humble about." As the austere Stafford Cripps walked by, Churchill sighed, "There, but for the grace of God, goes God." Of a Conservative in an easy by-election who switched to the Liberal ticket, Churchill remarked, "That's the only case on record of a rat swimming *towards* a sinking ship." In a parliamentary debate, obeying the rule that under no circumstance may the word "lie" ever be used, Winston charged an opponent with "terminological inexactitude." Bernard Shaw once sent him two tickets to an opening, with a note: "Please come to my play and bring a friend, if you have one"; Winston replied that he could not make the opening, "but I'll come to the second night, if there is one." And when a lady proudly remarked that her baby looked exactly like him, Churchill said, "Madame, *all* babies look like me."

But the banter stopped under stress, or whenever England was in peril; then Churchill loomed up like a massive and unshatterable rock. He could be all moral wrath and outrage, searing the enemy with contempt. In a worldwide broadcast he called Mussolini "this whipped jackal . . . this absurd impostor." He raked Hitler: "this bloodthirsty guttersnipe . . . a monster of wickedness, insatiable in his lust for blood and plunder . . . a monstrous abortion of hatred."

No Prime Minister was ever so *fondly* regarded by his people, so trusted and so loved. The sight of "good old Winnie" climbing over some smoking ruination inflicted by the Blitz warmed the hearts of England's workers, tradesmen, clerks, air-raid wardens. His mere presence seemed to assure them that this one staunch, indomitable figure would somehow, in some undiscernible way, surely, inevitably, however long it took, save them from annihilation. In one devastated London slum, the crowd swarmed upon him, to touch his sleeve, his coat, his arm. He was the messiah of their manumission. "One would have thought I had brought them some fine substantial benefit which would improve their lot. I was completely undermined and wept." An old woman in the crowd said, "You see, he really cares. He's crying."

The dauntless warrior was an unabashed sentimentalist. Throughout his life, he kept a picture of his Nanny in his bedroom. In the corridors of Commons, he discussed Hitler's savagery to the Jews, with tears rolling down his cheeks. During the Battle of Britain, returned from a town where he had seen the shambles of a small house and shop, all the walls blown off by a Nazi bomb, he cried to his Cabinet, "We must do something about that, *now!*" (This led to the novel and notable War Damages Commission.) It was typical of Churchill that he could not bear the unfairness of letting workers or tradesmen suffer losses as individuals in a war in which the nation's survival was at stake. And again, his car passed a long queue of shopgirls shivering in London's winter twilight, with the sirens howling and frantic searchlights stabbing at the ominous skies, and he asked what on earth the girls were buying, lined up at a time like this. An aide said, "Birdseed." Winston wept.

•

Winston Leonard Spencer Churchill was born beneath the dazzlement of chimney stacks of Blenheim, one of the grandest palaces in the world, a resplendent castle of 320 rooms and almost 3,000 acres of gardens and parks as fine as can be found anywhere in Europe. This estate was a gift from grateful Queen Anne to England's military genius, John Churchill, first Duke of Marlborough, to celebrate his brilliant victories on the Continent. Winston was born in a hastily transformed servants' room at Blenheim: his mother, visiting her husband's boyhood abode, was attending a ball, against her doctor's stern admonition.

The parents were fit for fiction. Jennie (Lady Randolph Churchill) was an American, beautiful, intelligent, vivacious, a fine pianist, painter, equestrienne—and flirt. She was, perhaps, one-sixteenth Iroquois, daughter of the notorious Leonard Jerome, a New York nabob, stock speculator and yachtsman, part owner of *The New York Times,* who lent his name to Jerome Avenue in the Bronx. A flagrant womanizer, Jerome named his daughter after Jennie Lind, his theninamorata.

Jennie met Lord Randolph Churchill during the posh Cowes regatta. They were married within the year, in the British Embassy in Paris. Neither the Duke nor the Duchess of Marlborough, the groom's parents, attended the wedding. ... Winston was born seven months later. England's Society lifted its eyebrows over the premature event. The year was 1874.

Lord and Lady Randolph deposited their chubby, red-haired infant with a wet-nurse and took off on one of their interminable social rounds. The Prince of Wales (later Edward VII) became extremely fond of Jennie, who visited him and the Princess often, and him sometimes alone, while Randolph pursued his own passions: a fascinating, moody man, a dandy and a rake, with neither a profession nor a goal, who lived on the Duke's patrimony and finally went into Parliament to represent the family fiefdom.

Winston adored his parents. He called his mother his "Evening Star," describing her beauty and finery when she came to kiss him good night. He absolutely worshiped his father, who "embodied that force, caprice, and charm

which so often spring from genius." But the morose Lord
Randolph treated his child with heartless indifference and
unconcealed distaste. The one who gave the boy affection
and trust for twenty years was his nurse, Mrs. Everest: "If
there be any ... who rejoice that I live, to that dear and
excellent woman, their gratitude is due."

He was a brash, bumptious, inordinately stubborn boy.
The Duchess besought Consuelo Vanderbilt to present her
oldest son with a son so that "that insufferable brat Winston" would not inherit the title, and Blenheim's domain.

At seven, the moon-faced, lisping redhead was sent off
to a boarding school, in Ascot, which was famous, fash-
ionable, grim in accommodations, wretched in food, savage
in discipline. The boys were caned or beaten until they bled.
So severe was the regimen that young Churchill's health
collapsed. He was transferred to Harrow, where he became
the poorest scholar in the bottom form.

The letters he sent home were pathetic. He begged "Dear
Papa" to write, to answer his letters, perhaps even to bestow
the priceless beneficence of visiting him, as other fathers
did. He asked his glamorous mother why it was that other
mothers seemed to want their sons home for weekends or
holidays, but his did not.

Yet he seems never to have lost confidence in himself, nor
in his conviction that he would one day "walk with destiny."
Once, when he was not nine years old, he was caned by an
upper classman, and said in a quaver, "I shall be a greater
man than you." When a headmaster summoned him to his
study to announce, "Churchill, I have grave reason to be
displeased with you," young Winston replied, "And I, sir,
have grave reason to be displeased with you."

He never succumbed to self-pity and, after a shame-laden
episode during which he hid behind a tree to escape the
stones thrown at him by jeering boys, resolved never again
to be the puppet of fear. He sought excitement and welcomed peril. Trapped on a bridge, in a game, he jumped
down, twenty-nine feet, in a ravine: he was unconscious
for three days. He won one Public School championship—

in fencing. And because he was so poor a student, he was placed in a special class, spared Latin and Greek, and assigned to a master who taught "the stupidest boys the most disregarded thing—to write mere English." He was lucky enough, he said, to spend three terms learning the structure of "that noble thing," the English sentence.

Young Winston spent endless hours playing with toy soldiers; he massed almost 1500 of them on a vast platform, executing intricate maneuvers, popping pebbles to simulate shells, ordering charges and retreats, learning self-administered lessons in strategy, in the tactics of surprise, the turning of flanks, the power of the phalanx, the deployment of reserves. It was, indeed, after watching this martial precocity for twenty minutes one day that Lord Randolph, who thought the boy too stupid for either the bar or the ministry, glumly asked if he would like a career in the army. "The toy soldiers turned the current of my life."

Twice, Winston failed to pass the entrance examinations to Sandhurst. During a fortuitous illness, a tutor was brought in daily to drum facts into his head, especially mathematics. He took a third examination, and passed. . . .

He never ceased to idolize his father, whom he never knew. Lord Randolph was, in fact, half-mad. Queen Victoria herself deplored the erratic moods of this gifted blue-blood, his party's leader in Commons, a speaker who held the House spellbound, the advocate of a liberal and invigorated "Tory democracy," who in private indulged in startling outbursts of insolence, anger, or spite. He became Chancellor of the Exchequer when only thirty-six, and rashly resigned over a secondary issue, confident that the Party would call him back, that he would soon be Prime Minister, as everyone had predicted. He waited in vain; for ten years he was a political pariah. . . .

Winston dreamed of redeeming his father's reputation. He also worried about his own handicap, a speech defect, an inability to pronounce "s," a slurring of words. So he went to a specialist: "Cure my impediment, please. I shall be in Parliament one day and I can't be haunted by the

knowledge that I must avoid every word that begins with
's.' "

Lord Randolph died in 1895, only forty-six years old, in
delirium—probably of syphilis.

•

Winston was commissioned a second lieutenant in the
Fourth Queen's Own Hussars. His salary barely paid his
expenses as a cavalry officer, and most of his personal allowance went to maintain his polo ponies; for his mother
was spending his inheritance as well as her own, cavorting
with the rich and the highborn, courted by a succession of
French and Russian noblemen. (She married twice more;
her last husband was younger than Winston.)

The ambitious and impatient subaltern "searched the
world for some scene of adventure," and talked his way into
an assignment as a correspondent for a London paper, at-
tached to the Spanish Army (!) in Cuba, to cover the guer-
rilla uprising—at £ 5 per dispatch. On his twenty-first birthday he first heard the sound of shots fired to kill. And in
Cuba he discovered the salubrious effects of daily siestas
and fine cigars.

He now sped to India's Northwest frontier, joined the
Malakand Field Force, fought in the hills of the Khyber Pass
—and sent vivid dispatches to London about the rebellion
of the Pathan tribes under "the Mad Mullah." (Military regulations did not prohibit a soldier-correspondent role in those
curious times.)

It was from India, as a member of the 31st Punjab In-
fantry, that Winston asked "Dearest Mummy"—to send him
books. He yearned to fill the considerable gaps in a thoroughly insufficient education. ("I never went to a university.") And Jennie chose wisely: she mailed him the
Greek and Roman historians, Macaulay and Burke and
Gibbon. And now the young cavalry officer began, at last, to
read.

All through the torrid afternoons, while the horses cooled
off in their stables and his comrades snored in the Indian
heat, "until the evening shadows proclaimed the hour of

Polo," Lieutenant Churchill read. He read Gibbon from cover
to cover, and more than once, and scribbled excited notes,
questions, comments, reminders in the margins of the
pages. He also read, in that remote and exotic outpost,
Plato, Aristotle, Schopenhauer; Burke, Darwin, Malthus;
Samuel Johnson and Macaulay. And he asked his mother to
send him the debates in Parliament, which he studied and
annotated.

One can only marvel over the image of this descendant
of Marlborough, at Bangalore, drilling and playing polo and
educating himself down the months of steaming afternoons,
immersed in the glories of Greece, the fortunes of Rome, the
history of England—of Henry V and Queen Elizabeth, Drake
and Chatham and Disraeli. He developed a special fondness
for Bartlett's *Quotations*, which he winnowed again and
again.

One episode in his *My Early Life* has always stuck in my
mind. Reading W. E. H. Lecky's *The Rise and Influence of
Rationalism*, Winston waxed indignant over the "deceptions"
of the Christian pastors of his youth. He entered upon a
"violent anti-religious phase"; but then he noticed that he
always asked for divine protection before braving enemy
fire, and "even asked for lesser things than not to be killed
too soon." He escaped death in a dozen hair-breadth moments, and concluded that prayer served him just as well
as reasoning, "which contradicted it sharply." Besides, the
prayer "was comforting, and the reasoning led nowhere."
So he decided he might as well warm himself with faith
without subjecting it to reason. He followed that soothing
and patrician principle for the rest of his life.

His newspaper dispatches began to win notice, and he
received compliments from far-off England. Winston was
beside himself with delight: "I had never been praised before." (!)

He next volunteered for service in Egypt, with General
Kitchener, who was preparing to invade the Sudan and
suppress the rebellious forces of the Mahdi, one Muhammad
Ahmed, a messianic Muslim with a hundred thousand fa-

natical followers. And in his classic gasconade, *The River War*, Churchill described the Battle of Omdurman, in which he led a cavalry charge of the 21st Lancers in a battle that raged for five hours and might have happened five hundred years ago. The Dervishes suddenly appeared from concealment in a gully: "The whole side of the hill seemed to move...Above them waved hundreds of banners, and the sun, glinting on so many hostile spearpoints, spread a sparkling cloud."

The zealot hordes slashed at the infidels' horses with curved swords, aiming for hamstrings or bellies, or hurled spears into the frantic beasts and riders, then massacred the Englishmen who were downed: disemboweling, decapitating, slicing men in two, the whole frightful mêlée cloaked in swirls of red choking dust, the carnage made bedlam by the howlings of the natives, the screams of the horses, the cries of pain and terror from the gored and the dying. Six times Churchill shot his pistol at close quarters, and each time struck a Dervish: one poised to fling a spear at him, another about to hack his horse from under him, a third straining to dismember him with a saber. He fought his way through the butchery, and with Kitchener entered Khartoum.

That night he contemplated "the dirty, shoddy business of war, which only a fool would undertake," dismissing the illusions of war's glory, but knowing "some things must be done, no matter what the cost." He wrote this about the enemy:

> When the soldier of a civilized Power is killed . . . his body is borne by friendly arms reverently to the grave. . . . But there was nothing *dulce et decorum* about the Dervish dead; nothing of the dignity of unconquerable manhood; all was filthy corruption. Yet these were as brave men as ever walked the earth . . . destroyed, not conquered, by machinery.

•

Young Winston returned to England, ran for Parliament (his mother campaigning alongside him), lost—and went off to South Africa, to cover the Boer War.

He was soon captured by the Boers, who announced it to the world, proud to have an English lord's son in their hold. They marched him sixty miles to a prison camp at Pretoria.

He so hated captivity that the hours "crawled by like paralytic centipedes." After three weeks he escaped, alone, three hundred miles from a sanctuary. He had no map, no compass, not the faintest knowledge of either Dutch or Kaffir.... He found his nocturnal way to the only man within twenty miles who would not have turned him over to the Boers. Never again did Churchill question his luck, or his conviction that fate was saving him for some illustrious pinnacle.

The manager of a Transvaal colliery hid him in the bottom of a mine, where, by candlelight, with white mice as companions, Winston read *Kidnapped*. He hid in a loaded freight car to cross Boer country into Portuguese territory.

When he landed in South Africa, he was hailed by hysterical crowds. The news, flashed around the Empire, was cheered in London's streets.

He was twenty-six, and famous.

•

But I must stop myself. I did not intend to undertake a capsule Life of Churchill, or to follow the incredible chronology of crises and triumphs in that altogether incredible life. I started to sketch a portrait, not write a biography.

The young hero was resoundingly elected to Parliament, as the twentieth century was born. "Ten minutes after he had been sworn," the Daily *Mail* marveled, "he was leaning back on the bench, silk hat well down over his forehead, figure crouched in the doubled-up attitude assumed by the ministers, both hands deep in his pocket, eyeing the place and its inmates critically as if they were all parliamentary novices." He clearly was not.

He announced that were he a Boer, he, too, would be fighting for his country, against England; and soon he was baiting the government with the follies of a plan to reorganize the Army:

...if we went to war with any great Power, three army corps would scarcely serve as a vanguard. If we are hated, they will not make us loved. If we are in danger, they will not make us safe. They are enough to irritate; they are not enough to overawe. Yet while they cannot make us invulnerable, they may very likely make us venturesome.

Churchill's speeches (he published a volume of them before he was thirty) were forcefully organized, beautifully embroidered, written out in advance, and—for all their appearance of oral spontaneity—had been committed to memory. He also distributed the orations to the press in advance, to ensure proper publicity, blandly inserting parenthetical anticipations: "Cheers," "Prolonged cheering," "Ovation."

The House of Commons was his perfect element. He served there for half a century—supporting himself, in considerable luxury, as a journalist, author, historian, biographer, and public lecturer. (In his first American appearance, he was introduced by Mark Twain; in a tour during Prohibition, his contract called for a bottle of French champagne before each speech.) He served under six different monarchs and he held six different Cabinet posts.

But he never built a powerful personal following. For he flabbergasted lesser men: by his monumental confidence, his penchant for romantic action, his need to stir things up, his blazing drive for distinction, his incessant quest for power. He was like a prodigal child in the range of his appetites and his interests, the dazzling play of his intelligence and imagination.

The most innocent and loyal of friends, he could never understand why he was distrusted. He was indeed "the Peter Pan of politics," quick to critize, improvise, give advice as if from on high. He always ran with the bit between his teeth. Five Prime Ministers complained that whenever he was in the Cabinet, "Winston acted as if he were already prime minister." Admiral Beatty called him "an impossible nuisance" and "a succubus."

Yet his good humor, his singular awareness of his foibles, were irresistible. He confessed to having "overcome my repugnance to the taste of whiskey." He solemnly told the House, "All the years I have been [here] I have said to myself: 'Do not interrupt,' and I have never been able to keep that resolution." When one eloquent adversary in Commons, annoyed by Winston's constant grunts and derogatory grimaces, complained, "My right honorable friend keeps shaking his head—but I am only expressing my views!" the cherubic Churchill replied, "And I am only shaking my head."

He was so absorbed in politics that he paid small attention to the eligible maidens whom illustrious mothers paraded before him. He did not marry until he was thirty-three, when he instantly fell in love with Clementine Hozier, a handsome young lady with a classic profile, a quick mind, and strong feminist opinions. Churchill ends one of his books: "In 1908 . . . I married and lived happily ever after."

His marriage was, for all of its fifty-three years, a rare and idyllic one; but Churchill did not really live happily ever after, even though he wrote:

> I have been happier every year since I became a man. . . . All the days were good and each day better than the others. Ups and downs, risks and journeys, but always the sense of motion, and the illusion of hope.

It was not so. We have learned from the diaries of Lord Moran, his doctor, that throughout his adult life Churchill suffered severe and recurrent depressions. He called these seizures of melancholia "the Black Dog." Outsiders never suspected his conflicts and his despair. The periodic ravages of anxiety make his bounce, his gallantry, his unyielding courage all the more remarkable. He did not weep only for others.

•

He strode upon the main stage of politics as First Lord of the Admiralty (1911–15). Boldly and with immense foresight, he strengthened Britain's sea power: replacing cruisers with battleships, accelerating the production of submarines, and converting the Navy from coal to oil in a move of historic importance. When Germany declared war on Russia in

1914, Churchill held the Navy at Portland, where war games had been going on; then, on his own initiative, he ordered the Fleet to strategic battle stations. He sent an unauthorized, secret alert to his bases and squadrons around the globe. He guaranteed England control of the seas.

He had himself learned how to fly, and founded the Royal Air Force—in the Navy. And when he grasped the stalemate of trench warfare, and brooded over the appalling human costs of "going over the top" directly into machine-gun massacres, he ordered technicians to design an armored vehicle that would ride across the trenches. This absurdity, the tank, was dubbed "Winston's Folly." It was opposed and obstructed by the military; and tanks were first built for Winston's Navy.

His audacious scheme to force the Dardanelles ended in the catastrophe of Gallipoli, and his total political disgrace. It took him a quarter of a century to live it down. How close the Gallipoli expedition came to succeeding we now know from the archives of Turkey and Germany: the German staff was fleeing Constantinople; defeat seemed a matter of hours. What accounted for the crushing failure was not Churchill's plan: the Navy compromised and delayed; the Army blew hot and cold, sabotaged coordination with the Navy, moved in support too late, too cautiously, with inadequate men and materiel.

But Churchill's vision had been stupendous, for had Gallipoli been a success, Turkey would have surrendered, the opened Dardanelles would have freed a Russian fleet bottled up in the Black Sea, the war would have ended much sooner, and the Bolsheviks could not have seized the power they seized only in a reeling, beaten, hungry and embittered Russia. To experts on warfare, the Dardanelles expedition remains the most original military idea of the War.

Churchill left the Admiralty in ignominy—for France, determined to command troops in battle. Sir John French offered him a brigadiership, but the Prime Minister cried: "For God's sake, don't give him a brigade! He might try to march straight into Berlin!" So Winston was made a colonel in the Fusiliers. He visited his front lines three times a day, often after midnight, when he would climb up the trench ladders to reassure the young, unblooded sentries, kindly explaining how little chance there really was of their being wounded.

Lloyd George made him Minister of Munitions. Within six months, he had increased the number of English planes by 40 percent, the tank corps by almost 30. When over 400 tanks attacked at Cambria, leading a battle in which six miles of German trenches were overrun, "one of the most astonishing ba*tles in all history had been won."

•

Peace never favored his talents. He was wrong on Irish independence, but effected a treaty with the rebellion's leaders. As Chancellor of the Exchequer, he most unwisely pushed England back on the gold standard. (Keynes pilloried him for his economic policies.) He acted foolhardy in the General Strike of 1926. He courted certain political disaster in the crisis over Edward VIII and Mrs. "Wally" Simpson, the American divorcée the king was determined to marry. Churchill's friends were aghast when he told them what he intended to say in Commons; they pleaded with him not to oppose Baldwin and the Archbishop of Canterbury, powerful lords and Catholics; they told him it was a lost and hopeless cause. But Churchill would not compromise his loyalty. He made his speech. The entire House booed and hissed, an unthinkable breach of parliamentary decorum, in a way Earl Winterton said he had not heard in over forty-seven years in Commons.

Churchill was, in truth, a poor politician. He thrived on the dramas of public life, but was bored by the requirements of party politics. In the 1922 elections he even lost his seat to a Prohibitionist (!) named Edwin Scrymgeour. (I know of no other distinction to grace that improbable name.)

Nor was Churchill skillful in handling Parliament, except (but what a mighty "except" that is) in wartime. Twice he switched party allegiance, from Tory to Liberal and back— than which there is no more heinous sin in English politics.

He shifted not to abandon a course, but to persist in it from the benches opposite—but without even a week's decorous silence, at least, to provide a veneer of reluctance.

He was despised by Labor, disowned by the Liberals, loathed by most Tories. The press lampooned him as a *poseur*, the public wrote him off as an opportunist, his adversaries castigated him as reckless, unstable, a dangerous adventurer. Even Anthony Eden, desperate for support against the appeasement of Nazi Germany, held Winston at arms' length. He was a political albatross.

The man baffled his admirers no less than his antagonists. Labeled a warmonger, he supported collective security: "There is not much collective security in a flock of sheep on the way to the butcher." Hated as a militarist, he exhorted England and France to build up their military strength—to guarantee the peace.

From 1933 to 1939, in a succession of magnificent and prophetic speeches, many to a half-empty House, most pooh-poohed by Britain's press and all "sensible" statesmen, Churchill hammered away at the growth of German power, the dangers that must attend a resurgent Luftwaffe, new U-boats, "pocket battleships," the inevitable confrontation that Hitler's arms and maniacal ambitions would force upon an England so sanguine, so pacific, so unwilling to contemplate the unthinkable.

Winston seemed better informed than the Foreign Office, or the Ministers of War and Navy and Air—as, indeed, he often was. For in addition to his sources within the government, he was carrying on an energetic correspondence with friends in embassies all over Europe; with military experts in a dozen countries; with foreign correspondents in Paris, Berlin, Warsaw, Moscow, Rome; with a network of friends around the world—including my friend John Balderston, in far-off Beverly Hills.

Churchill warned, argued, exhorted, denounced. He coined phrases that could not be shaken out of mind: "the deadly, drilled, docile, brutish masses of the Hun"; "Hitler has liberated Austria from the horrors of self-government"; "The flying peril is not a peril from which one can fly. We cannot move London"; "It is better to be frightened now than killed hereafter."

His scorn was withering. He called Ramsay MacDonald "the Boneless Wonder." He blistered "the baboonery of Communism." He had described his foes in Parliament as "good, honest men who are ready to die for their opinions, if only they knew what their opinions are." Of Baldwin's government, he said: "So they go on in strange paradox, decided only to be undecided, resolved to be irresolute, adamant for drift... all-powerful to be impotent."

His speeches and writings and arguments sparkled with epigrams: "A fanatic is a man who can't change his mind and won't change the subject." "Anecdotes are the gleaming toys of history." "We cannot say 'the past is past' without surrendering the future." "I cannot remain impartial as between the Fire Brigade and the fire."

But he was ignored or ridiculed from every political quarter for his allegedly dramatic obsessions with an exaggerated German threat. And when England embraced its short, shortsighted euphoria over Chamberlain's deal with Hitler at Munich, Churchill rose in the House to say:

> All is over. Silent, mournful, abandoned, broken, Czechoslovakia recedes into the darkness. . . . It is a fraud and a farce to invoke the name [self-determination].

> We have sustained a defeat without a war. . . . We have passed an awful milestone in our history. . . . The whole equilibrium of Europe has been deranged. . . . Terrible words have been pronounced against the Western democracies: "Thou art weighed in the balance and found wanting."

> And do not suppose that this is the end. . . . This is only the first sip, the first foretaste of a bitter cup which will be proffered to us year by year. . . .

It was Churchill's very refusal to be "expedient" or utopian that made him the one man to whom England, on the brink of disaster, had to turn. The Germans invaded

Poland; Belgium and Holland were about to be smothered; France was demoralized; Hitler's planes, tanks, and Storm Battalions were smashing out victory after victory in apocalyptic *Blitzkrieg.* An exhausted, sick, shamed Chamberlain resigned. Winston became Prime Minister. And who but he could have slept happily that night, feeling "a profound sense of relief"?

> At last I had the authority to give directions over the whole scene. I felt as if . . . all my past life had been but a preparation for this hour and for this trial. . . . I was sure I should not fail. Therefore, although impatient for the morning, I slept soundly and had no need for cheering dreams. Facts are better than dreams.

One can only marvel at the "facts" he could find comforting.
•

He began on May 13, 1940, telling a gloomy, apprehensive House:

> I have nothing to offer but blood, toil, tears, and sweat. . . . You ask what is our policy? . . . It is to wage war, war by sea, land, and air, with all our might and with all our strength that God can give us: to wage war against a monstrous tyranny, never surpassed in the dark, lamentable catalogue of human crime. That is our policy.
>
> You ask, What is our aim? I can answer in one word: Victory—victory at all costs, victory in spite of terror, victory, however long and hard the road may be; for without victory, there is no survival . . . no survival for the British Empire . . . no survival for the urge and impulse of the ages, that mankind will move forward. . . .

He had once said, "Nothing in war ever goes right except by accident. . . . There is only one thing certain about war, that it is full of disappointments and mistakes. . . . There are no safe battles." But he also knew that the British "are the only people who like to be told the worst."

What can one say of Churchill's speeches to the Commons, the people of Great Britain, the breathless world? Henry Grunwald recalls:

It is necessary to have sat in a dim room listening to that incomparable voice at moments when a Nazi victory seemed entirely possible, to understand that Churchill's speeches were not ornamental but, literally, an essential contribution to the war. Nothing else and no one else could so surely buoy up flagging hopes or restore confidence—in Britain and in oneself.

He never prettified disasters: After the awful defeat and miraculous deliverance at Dunkirk, he dryly reminded the Commons: "Wars are not won by evacuations," and went soaring into a passage that surpasses Cicero:

> We shall not flag or fail. We shall go on to the end. We shall fight in France, we shall fight on the seas and oceans, we shall fight . . . in the air. We shall defend our island, whatever the cost may be. We shall fight on the beaches, we shall fight on the landing grounds, we shall fight in the fields and in the streets, we shall fight in the hills; we shall never surrender. And even if, which I do not for a moment believe, this island . . . were subjugated and starving, then our Empire beyond the seas, armed and guarded by the British Fleet, would carry on the struggle, until, in God's good time, the new world, with all its power and might, steps forth to the rescue and the liberation of the old.

After France fell, "the Battle of Britain" about to begin, the invincible lion said:

> The whole fury and might of the enemy must very soon be turned on us. . . . Let us therefore brace ourselves to our duties, and so bear ourselves that, if the British Empire and its Commonwealth last for a thousand years, men will still say, "This was their finest hour."

Aneurin Bevan said:

> Some of the speeches he delivered are beyond description. Nobody could have listened and not been moved. There has never been anybody who could speak for history as Churchill could. . . . When the people . . . might have been depressed by the brute facts about Dunkirk, Churchill was persuading them to think about Queen Elizabeth and the defeat of the Armada. . . . He could fling a Union Jack over

five tanks and get people to behave as though they had become fifteen.

Phrases from those orations will always echo in my mind:

Never in the field of human conflict was so much owed by so many to so few.

Russia is a riddle wrapped in a mystery inside an enigma; but perhaps there is a key ... Russian national interest.

If Hitler invaded Hell, I would make at least a favorable reference to the Devil in the House of Commons.

This is not the end. It is not even the beginning of the end. But it is, perhaps, the end of the beginning.

His words were worth battalions to the men and women and children who slept in London's subways night after night; to soldiers cursing the broiling Sahara; to sailors hunting U-boats and dreading torpedoes. To all of them, and especially to the weary, blooded, battered people of London, "Winnie" typified far more than English spunk.

He *understood* war; and he instructed his countrymen in war's awful requirements. He gave them a grammar of courage. He showed them how to be heroic: how to manage fear; how to invest despair with grandeur, and anger with purpose; how to wrap pain and suffering and death in the habiliments of nobility.

He made every man feel a part of history, touched by glory, fortunate to be alive in so sublime an ordeal. He spoke for the future with a confidence that was hard to believe, but men believed him. He was the best of Britain, incarnate.

"In the hour when all but courage failed," said the London *Times,* "[he] made courage conscious of itself, plumed it with defiance, and rendered it invincible."

•

For more than five long, harrowing years, Churchill wielded supreme power. He ran the war with a torrent of written memoranda. He never issued verbal instructions. He hated secondhand information. He would not let his staff summarize anything. He insisted on reading all cables from the theaters of operation. He never asked anyone to draft orders; he dictated them himself, striding back and forth as ministers and counselors waited; then the prose would roll out in impeccable, resounding sentences.

His curiosity was boundless, tireless and, as Harold Macmillan sighed, "exhausting." He reveled in details, mixing deliberations on grand strategy and global war with observations on the plumbing in Yalta or the fleshpots of Marrakesh. He had written a score of books—on history and war, thick biographies of Marlborough and Lord Randolph, brilliant pen portraits of contemporaries from Lloyd George to "Chinese" Gordon; and now he deluged his captains with prickly "minutes" that discombobulated them, but kept them on their toes: "What are we doing about the tents for signalers on Salisbury Plain?" Why was the time of clerks, encoders, telegraphers, decoders, being wasted in three words, "Admiral von Tirpitz, when surely Tirpitz is enough for the beast"?

His working habits, his conferences at two and three in the morning, his crossing of departmental lines drove his colleagues to distraction, but his own energy and exuberance flourished. "Nothing could turn him aside," said Sir Ian Jacob. "The narrower the field of study, the hotter burned his scrutiny and the deeper went his drive. His power seemed to be turned on all the time." Sometimes, late at night, he would turn on the phonograph, always the record of a band playing military marches, and he would strut back and forth to its beat like a schoolboy, composing those luminous phrases of resolution and hope.

In War Cabinet meetings, he held forth endlessly, sparking ideas (some brilliant, some impossible), shooting unnerving questions at colleagues, always making clear who would make the decisions—and take responsibility for them. He invented stratagems that were nothing short of inspired: e.g., the "Mulberry" breakwaters and landing docks that were towed across the English Channel in the invasion of Normandy. He made calamitous mistakes, reckless moves born of his unalterable faith in audacity and attack: the *ad hoc* expedition to Norway; the perilous gamble of running the *Repulse* and the *Prince of Wales* without air cover through waters controlled by Japan; the quixotic drop into Crete; the firing on French warships in the Mediterranean, after France surrendered, while his admirals were negotiating their transfer.

But—he kept England in the war. He exemplified her resourcefulness. He kept her fighting after defeats, impervious to anything but persistence. It never occurred to him to seek a truce, or consider the compromise Hitler was ready to accept. He refused to countenance the idea that England would *allow* herself to be beaten. . . . It was quixotic; it was heroic; but it was not empty bravado, for Churchill's knowledge of history fortified his confidence: he knew that no encircling alliance in Europe for three hundred years had failed to win out in the end.

And he knew, with that prescience that led him to the psychological heart of a crisis, with that unerring sense of the ingredients of morale, that he could summon infinite fortitude from Englishmen's pride in their history. "He was leading a nation," writes J. H. Plumb, "more committed to its sense of the past than any the world has known since imperial China."

He had a much clearer, harder, longer view of the future than Roosevelt ever did—about the Russians, the Balkans, "the soft underbelly of the dragon," the inevitable postwar conflicts of power. He inspired the patriots of Poland and France and Czechoslovakia. He supported the intractable de Gaulle, confessing "my cross is the cross of Lorraine." He backed Tito in Yugoslavia. In Moscow, Yalta, Casablanca, he stood up to the obdurate Stalin, fighting for a settlement that would not put Eastern Europe under Russia's heel. That he failed was a function of power and geography, not a failure of foresight or principles.

He was that rarest of statesmen: the man who masters events; and, I think, the rarest of geniuses: a triumph of character.

And he won.

•

"Whenever we got on the subject of planning for postwar Britain, Winston was ill at ease," wrote Attlee.

The great war leader was unattuned to social or economic problems. Once the war ended, Churchill looked like a redoubtable relic. He was a genius of the Renaissance, in the modern age, and he could not contend with technology. He could not counter Labor's plans for the reemployment of England's labor force, for fiscal reforms, for tax and welfare programs. His oratory now sounded Victorian, his eloquence archaic, his imperial vision Kiplingesque. He was hopelessly stubborn and insular about the independence of India. He called Gandhi "a malignant and subversive fanatic . . . a seditious Middle-Temple lawyer now posing as a fakir." He rashly condemned Nehru.

He seemed bewildered by the profound discontents England's class structure generated. The problems of an industrial society baffled and eluded him. "The pageantry of a coronation superimposed on the steelworks of Sheffield . . . never struck him as odd." His unease in the postwar clamor was summarized in a bright but halting sentence: "We want a lot of engineers in the modern world, but we do not want a world of engineers."

In one swift, unbelievable turn of the tide of public favor, Churchill was voted out of office, in 1945—a fall so unexpected that even the new Labor ministers, to say nothing of foreign observers, were dumbfounded. No one dreamed the English people would be so "ungrateful. . . ."

The old man never understood it. When the King offered him the prized Order of the Garter, he declined: "How can I accept the Garter when the people have just given me the Boot?" He became Leader of the Opposition. He was not effective. And though he was voted back to 10 Downing Street in 1951, he was out again in four years (and he did accept the Garter).

He turned away from politics, as he had done earlier after defeat. He finished his monumental six-volume history of the Second World War, and his four-volume *History of the English-Speaking Peoples.* Both were huge successes. He fed his goldfish (the only "exercise" he had taken for decades) and painted and was made the first and only Honorary Citizen of the United States. He traveled to Fulton, Missouri, to electrify the world with his prefiguration of Russia's plans behind "an iron curtain." He coined the phrase "talks at the summit." He was awarded the Nobel Prize.

When an admiring photographer said he hoped to photograph him on his hundredth birthday, the eighty-year-old sprite gibed, "I don't see why not, young man. You look reasonably fit."

He had ruminated with relish: "I am ready to meet my Maker. Whether my Maker is prepared for the great ordeal of meeting me is another matter."

•

He died on January 24, 1965, in the ninety-first year of a career unparalleled in history. "We are a free people," *The Spectator* declared, "because a man named Winston Churchill lived."

He died like King David, "in a good old age, full of days, riches, and honor."

For three days and nights, the long, long line of mourners, young and old and from places with unpronounceable names, over 320,000 of them, passed the body that lay in state in the beautiful, vaulted emptiness of old Westminster Hall.

Then the valiant giant was borne through the silent frieze of the streets, in a bitter wind, to the monotone beat of one drum among all the kettles wrapped in black crepe, the world's renowned behind, in cloaks and plumes and equipage —scarlet, purple, gold—kings and queens, great generals and ministers and princes of the East, all the way to St. Paul's Cathedral, which had never seen such a rite.

Then the coffin was borne to a funeral barge on the Thames, where the iron spires of the cranes and derricks that line the river bent half-down in awkward homage.

It was almost as if Winston had planned it so.

My Night
at the Opera

O NLY once in any man's lifetime can he hope to be rewarded by such a Donnybrook as exploded that night in Constitution Hall. I certainly am a different creature since that glorious eve: my doctor tells me there is a firmer beat to my stride, a brighter bleam in my eye. I know that a stronger sense of comedy burns in my breast, and a more fervent conviction of man's matchless capacity for creating chaos.

It all began quite prosaically. The National Opera Association (Edouard Albion, President, Director, Impresario, and Bass) was scheduled to present *Lakmé*, with Bidú Sayao, "the Brazilian nightingale," in the leading role. It was the first opera performance in our nation's capital in over four years.

There were 1600 in the audience, and a more bedecked and bespangled congregation you never saw. White ties and tails, lorgnettes and ermine wraps made the main floor resemble a Metro-Goldwyn-Mayer set of La Scala the night Caterina Cacciatore, famed prima donna, is devoiced by laryngitis, and her understudy, Mary Lou Saunders, a nice, clean American girl from Keosauqua, Iowa, sings the leading role on ten minutes' notice to set the music world on its ear with her high "D."

The auditorium bulged with celebrities: The Ambassador from Brazil, in a box, the envoy from G————y, in another. You could not move your head three inches in either direction without seeing senators, diplomats, members of the DAR, the Supreme Court, or the RFC.

Constitution Hall can be emptied in two minutes, according to a prophetic note in my program. It is built like an amphitheater: the occupants of boxes, balcony or "gallery" (a figure of speech, since the gallery is only the last rows of the balcony) get an unimpeded view of their peers on the main floor. This is more than worth the price of admission. I was in the *infra-dig* balcony, but I couldn't have chosen a more strategic position from which to view the embranglements of that memorable night.

It was 8:15, announced as curtain time. The *crème de la crème* of Washington (D.C.) Society was still drifting in. Soon it was 8:30. No peep came forth from the touted forty-piece orchestra, which was not in the pit. 8:40. The large India print which served as the curtain this gala night hung inert and noncommittal.

Then it was 8:45, and the audience began to clear their throats and tap their toes. A few bumpkins in the gallery started to clap-clap their impatience. Then, time being what it is, it was 8:50. The *noblesse oblige* of the main floor was seeping away. Restlessness, like a soft wind, passed across the starched chests and bared bosoms. Scions of unimpeachable lineage began ironical applause. This emboldened the balcony folk, who began to groan and mutter, which in turn encouraged the peons in the gallery to break through the thin veneer of their grade-school education and stamp their feet. One vulgarian emitted raucous noises of the genre known as the Bronx Cheer. These expressions of public opinion continued, according to my calculations, for ten minutes.

At 9:01, hitherto staunch patrons of opera began to rise in the boxes and put on their capes and stoles. At 9:05 the first distinct hoot punctured the air. Now, all over that testy audience, people began to clap and stamp and boo and whistle.

Then (could it be?!) the curtain parted. A hush fell upon us as a formidable matron strode onto the proscenium, waving a little piece of paper in a frantic way. Her gown was gorgeous, but her eyes bore infant tears.

"Oh, mi*god!*" gasped a girl in the row below me. "That is Mrs. Edouard Albion!"

"Ladies and gentlemen!" Mrs. Albion cried. "'Let me explain. The orchestra *refuses to accept this check* for $1500! This check is signed by one of the leading singers in the country, yet the musicians refuse to accept it! They will not play!! They—want—*cash!!*"

A roar welled up in Constitution Hall. People howled, hissed, booed. Someone cried "Shame! Shame!" Any number of people looked as if they were muttering "Disgusting!" under their breaths.

"Will some prominent Washingtonian in the audience please come forward—and endorse this check?" asked Mrs. Albion.

A second hush gripped us. But where our first hush had proceeded from a thirst for information, this one came from paralyzing ambivalence.

"Won't someone—*any*one—please underwrite this check?" wailed Mrs. Albion.

There was no doubt about it now; no one would underwrite that check.

Some hothead yelled, "Down with the union!"—an editorial opinion swiftly reinforced by cries of "Boo!" "Sssss!" and an unmistakable "Pthrrrr!"

A new woman appeared on stage and approached Mrs. Albion.

"Oh, mi*god,*" the girl below me gasped. "That is Mrs. Gertrude Lyons!"

Her escort whispered, "A singer?"

"Migod, *no!* She is President of the Washington Federation of Music Clubs!"

"Ladies and gentlemen," Mrs. Gertrude Lyons announced in a rather shrill, accusatory voice. "I want to tell you that every human effort has been made to persuade the musicians to play! We have even called Albert C. Hayden, president of Musicians' Protective Union, Local 161—in person. He said it is *against union rules to accept checks!*"

A hurricane of hisses and sisses and sizzling catcalls shook the hallowed walls of Constitution Hall, which was built in 1929.

Mrs. Lyons raised her hand to still the furor. "They *will* play—if someone puts up a U.S. Government Bond as guarantee . . ."

I am sorry to say that an icy silence followed this suggestion.

"The opera can also go on if ten—people—give—$100— *each!*" offered Mrs. Lyons.

Alas, there were not ten people in the hall that night to whom *Lakmé* was worth $100 (each).

Some hothead in the audience shouted: "Wait until those musicians play in the symphony! We'll show them what we think of this!"

A cannonade of applause ratified this warning, and opinions rang out *ad libitum:*

"Shame!"

"Boooooo!"

"Ssssss!"

"Pthrrr!" (Bronx cheer.)

Now, her voice treading grapes of wrath, Mrs. Edouard Albion proclaimed, "THIS OPERA IS MAKING HISTORY! . . . I am going backstage to plead with the orchestra once more!"

This brave maneuver won the salvo it deserved and Mrs. Albion disappeared behind the India print.

Operaphiles were departing the hall in droves now. And the audience suddenly turned into an extemporaneous forum, where defenders of Unionism leaped up to mount an attack on the forces of Anti-Unionism. Argument, debate, insult, recrimination soared into a verbal free-for-all more vehement than any I ever heard around the soapboxes of Hyde Park.

Applause was heard from the front rows; a few musicians had come into the pit! They were greeted by cheers from the Left, and caterwauling from the rest. The musicians sat down—but played nary a note.

A goateed gentleman in the first row leaned over the rail, engaged the musicians in earnest dialogue, then turned to face the main floor. "*La*dies and *gen*tlemen!" he brayed. "All we need is a money collection! *Let's take up a collection!*"

"Collection! Collection!" came from every side.

Legal tender—ones, twos, fives, tens—now shot up in hands waving above the boiled shirts and curled coiffures.

"How much is needed?" a go-getter bawled.

Out flew Mrs. Albion from behind that India print. "Fifteen hundred dollars!"

The cries of "Collection!" stopped cold. The green oblongs fluttered, swayed like limp grass, and disappeared. Mammon had triumped over *Lakmé.*

At this, an oaf in the gallery jumped up, threw his coat to the floor, shook his fist over his head, and hollered: "I have been a union man all my life and I want to say——"

No one ever heard what he wanted to say. On the main floor, otherwise sedate men and women leaped to *their* feet —howling and hooting and hissing the union man.

Mrs. Albion was waving her hands at one and all, calling tearfully: "Come on down here, everybody! Come *closer!*" She indicated the seats vacated by those of little faith.

The invitation brought people forward from rows H to Z, and down from the balcony.

An elderly musicomane near me began to laugh idiotically: "This is better than *Lakmé!* This is a three-ring circus! This is wonderful to behold."

What I beheld was certainly wonderful: a beautifully groomed damsel running up and down the main-floor aisle, bleating, *"What will the nation's music lovers think of all this? I Down with the union!"*

The Democrat in the gallery who had thrown his coat to the floor bellowed, "Wait, wait! Be fair! Let's hear the *union's* side of this! You fools!" He made a funnel of his hands and yelled down to the musicians in the pit. "Get up on the stage! Tell your side of it!"

This suggestion, proper enough to me, precipitated pandemonium in others.

"Go back to Russia!"

"Stooge!"

"Troublemaker!"

"Booooo!"

"Sssss!"

"Down with unions!"

"Pthrrr!"

One of the violinists in the pit stood up and announced: "These people still owe us $1600 for a previous performance!"

The clarinetist exclaimed: "Everyone *else* got paid in cash, so why not us?"

More howls, more catcalls, plus unabashed curses.

Now a musician appeared in front of the India print. I knew he was a musician because he was carrying an oboe, which he raised aloft and, amidst the diminution of decibels, announced in tremulous timbre: "I think you should know that Mr. Edouard Albion still owes us money from four years ago which he never paid!"

A veritable simoon of boos ascended, but it was hard to tell which were for the oboist and which for perfidious Albion. A dowager shook all her glittering diamonds as she pounded her cane on the floor and screamed, "Debate, debate! I came here to hear *Lakmé,* not a debate!"

Mrs. Albion dabbed at her nose with a handkerchief. "Ladies! . . . Gentlemen! . . . May I have your attention?" She raised both hands, palms forward. "Listen! Would you like to hear this opera with just *piano accompaniment?*"

I need hardly tell you that this suggestion, certainly unprecedented in the annals of operadom, struck Constitution Hall dumb. The sheer novelty, not to say audacity, of the solution caught everyone flatfooted—until some lady trilled, "Why not?"

The challenge enlisted recruits to a cause revived:

"O.K.!"

"Yes!"

"Let's *go!*"

Mrs. Albion, flushed with success, called, "If there is a piano we can wheel onstage..."

Some cynic guffawed, "Is there a piano in the house?"

"Another promise you can't deliver!" came a disenchanted voice.

"We just can't find a piano back*stage!*" wailed Mrs. Albion.

Up welled fresh discontents: groans, moans, the dental despair of gnashing teeth. Succor came from an unexpected quarter: a succulent female on the main floor: "Where's the little organ?" her voice sang out. "Let's get the little *organ!*"

"It's in the basement!" someone shouted.

The musicomane on my left laughed and choked and jactitated on the brink of hysteria. "This is *better* than a three-ring circus!" he gasped. "It is worth ten dollars right now! Twenty! Thirty!" (He was obviously a man of means.)

The next thing I knew, a small portable organ was being rolled out from the wings. "WE HAVE THE ORGAN!" proclaimed Mrs. Albion.

Furious applause. A chorus of cheers.

Mrs. Albion dabbed at her upper lip feverishly. "Now will someone—we have a score—volunteer to play the organ?"

Fresh umbrage rocked the auditorium. But I was now on the side of Mrs. Albion: it is foolhardy to expect players of portable organs to hang around every auditorium in the land on the off-chance that they will be asked to substitute for an orchestra that calls a strike without the slightest advance notice.

More and more ticket-holders were moving toward the exits. Our sky looked very dark at that moment, but a benevolent god intervened, in the person of a frail, white-haired woman in the ninth or tenth row who rose and declared: "I will play that organ."

The girl below me sucked in her breath as if inhaling the last noodle in a bowl of soup. "My music teacher! Oh, mi*god!* It is Madame Maria Zalipsky!" (That girl knew everyone.) I am sure she said "Maria Zalipsky," because her escort, looking both as bollixed and dubious as I felt, asked, *"Who?"*

The maiden responded with a steely segregation of syllables: "Ma-dame Ma-ri-a Za-lip-sky."

By now Mme. Zalipsky had walked down the aisle, to spattering applause, and up the side stairs to the stage, where, with no superfluous nonsense, she seated herself at the little organ and began to pump away on the foot-pedals. She had to pump, herself: That is the type of organ it was.

A resuscitated Mrs. Albion was all over the stage now, leading, planning, coaxing. She shook hands energetically with Mme. Zalipsky, placed a score of *Lakmé* on the rack before her savioress, darted backstage—and promptly darted out front again, pale as a sheet.

"The—conductor—refuses—to—direct—the—chorus!" choked Mrs. Albion. "He is a union man, too!"

I was mighty glad I wasn't the maestro at that moment. You never heard such a vocal massacre: boos, hoots, yowls, skirls, the ululations of ferocious patronesses of the opera.

"And the costume man wants his costumes back!" cried Mrs. Albion; another blow. "And the electricians have walked off!" Blow after blow. "And *the stagehands won't shift scenes!*" It was too much, too much.

The truncated audience was calling for blood.

Mrs. Albion cried: "But if volunteers from the audience come up here, THE OPERA WILL GO ON!"

Tremendous applause, cheers, chortles of triumph replacing rage.

Up rose a fine figure of a man in the fifth row. "I will lead the choruses!"

He was like Caesar leaving for Gaul.

"Fortunately some of the cast have their costumes on."
Mrs. Albion exulted, "and *will not take them off for anyone!*"

Ah, the torrent of homage, the avalanche of gratitude
that rewarded the heroes who would not remove their
costumes for anyone.

"*Start the opera!*" cried Mrs. Albion.

Mme. Maria Zalipsky raised her taut, thin arms and flung
her thin, taut fingers upon the organ keys. There was no
squeak of sound.

Mme. Zalipsky (only God can make a tree or a name
like that) now pumped harder and flayed at the keys with
fiercer resolve. The infernal machine creaked, sighed and
stammered forth the opening notes of *Lakmé*.

It was 10:22.

The stage lights did not go on, but *Lakmé* did.

The rest of that beautiful performance is lost in a blur
of memory. For three long hours the portable organ
wheezed, Mme. Zalipsky pumped, and the cast sang and
sang and milled around in the vespertine light. I should
inform you that the chorus, who had obviously been driven
to extremities by an uncooperative wardrobe department,
were clothed in a chow-chow of costumery: Persian, Tartar,
Ottoman and assorted Oriental dress, street garb, half-and-
half, and specimens of the *al fresco* or catch-as-catch-can
period. The stage looked like an animated clothing rack
from a Greenwich Village bazaar.

Nor did bizarre bazaar dress end the *tsimmes*. For reasons
I shall never know, Lakmé's principal characters sang their
roles in French, whereas the chorus used safer English.
During the grand solo-*cum*-chorus arias, I felt as if I had
stumbled into a Berlitz school of music.

At one point (this I remember as vividly as my recurrent
dream about popping up naked in the Bryn Mawr chapel
during Commencement) a platoon of stout singing men,
playing England's soldiers, marched across the stage—in
American business suits, but carrying rifles. I found this
novel, but the audience yawned. They were spoiled rotten

by now: I don't suppose anything short of flying octopi would have unjaded them.

I also remember that at one point the little organ went mute. Mme. Zalipsky was sitting there, stricken, neither pumping nor pounding but gesturing that her copy of the music was exhausted. The tenor who played the part of Gerald showed admirable presence of mind; he soloed himself toward the wings, snatched a score from the hands of the prompter, *a cappella*-ed his way back across the stage, picked the insufficient score off the organ's music rack and plunked the new one down before Mme. Zalipsky— all without missing a note.

At another unforgettable juncture, the Frédéric of the opera, a Mr. Daniel Harris, discontented with Mme. Zalipsky's tempo, conducted her into another, waving one hand as he sang his felicitous lay.

The title role, I should say, was given a really bang-up performance, everything considered, by Miss Bidú Sayao, the "Brazilian nightingale," who turned out to be a coloratura such as had not been heard since Galli-Curci. She hit a clear high E—third line above the treble clef, pardner —at the end of the immortal "Bell Song" in the second act, and I have been her most ardent fan, courtesy of Columbia Records, ever since. In case you have never bothered learning the words of the "Bell Song," I gift the cream of them to you:

> *Où va la jeune hindoue, fille des parias,*
> *Quand la lune se joue dans les grands mimosas?*

These pearls may be Anglicized as:

Where goeth the young Hindu girl, daughter of pariahs,
When the moon disports itself among immense mimosas?

As for Mr. Edouard Albion, the bass and founding father of the suddenly historic National Opera Association, he did the role of Nilakantha, the fanatical Brahman priest, up brown, even though something seemed to be troubling him. He was wearing a Hindu turban, as I recall, and some sort of mustache. I could not tell whether the mustache was his own or pasted on, but you must remember I was seated in the balcony.

By 1:00 A.M. the audience—down to a paltry 400 (sponsors and relatives of the cast, I figured)—sparsely dotted the drowsy desert of Constitution Hall. Chauffeurs kept peering into the hall through the open lobby doors, trying to believe their eyes. The ushers made no effort to conceal their cavernous yawnings; some were dozing against pillars, others were snoring in the boxes. Something told me none of us would ever see a night like this again.

It was not until 1:30 that morn that the most unusual performance of *Lakmé* on record came to its exhausted end. The audience sort of applauded, Edouard Albion wheedled and beadled some curtain calls out of us, and brave Mme. Zalipsky staggered off the stage gasping, "I am dead, I am dead. Water, water!", according to the afternoon papers, and everyone went home. There just was no place else to go after an experience like that.

Sometimes, on long, moonless nights, when the world is too much with me, when the apprehension of man's evil and malice and hatefulness drives me from despair to despond, I dip into the precious miracle of memory and pretend I am back in Constitution Hall once more, and that it is January 21, 1936, and that that shining night will never end.

Potch

WE called him Potch, and he was as unprepossessing
as his nickname: a sallow, humorless gnome of a boy who
plunged me, at ten, into the greatest moral crisis of my life.

Potch, who was given to sucking air and muttering odd
maledictions, was not popular. He was never part of our
"gang." He had no athletic skills, no dreams of glory on
gridiron or diamond, and seemed actually to dislike the
noble, shining hours we spent on softball, basketball, hand-
ball, "pinners." No one wanted Potch when we chose up
sides for Run, Sheep, Run or Prisoner's Base or *Skoosh*,
which was what, in Chicago, we called punchball, played
right out in the streets, with a manhole cover as home plate
—and without a bat: you hit the ball with your fist.

Potch was a loner, skinny, moody, without luster. He was
so nonpopular that he did not even compete in our daily
tournament of loyalty, each boy screaming out his own All-
Time All-Star Baseball Team at the top of his lungs. Nor
did Potch, upon seeing a man with a beard, spit into his
left palm and jam his right fist into it, pronouncing the
proper abracadabra that, we all knew, exorcised (or, at least,
slowed up) the faceless demons who lurk around any familiar
with a beard.

We never invited Potch to undergo the mysterious rites,

performed in a cellar, of initiation into our secret club, whose sole function was to perform mysterious rites of initiation in a cellar. And whenever our volcanoes of adoration erupted, and we extolled the relative splendors of the Rover Boys or Tom Swift, the intrepid Nick Carter or the peerless Frank Merriwell, Potch merely made muffled, gargling sounds and drifted away. He never read *anything,* so far as we knew; and we (well, two of us anyway) were absolutely fanatical, insatiable addicts of print.

The only noteworthy thing about Potch was that he always seemed to have spending money, and more of it than any of the rest of us. I once saw him take a whole two-dollar bill out of his pocket. To me, whose allowance was five cents a week, this bordered on the supernatural.

We used to talk about Potch in front of the corner delicatessen, marveling over his readiness to buy a ten-cent baloney sandwich or a root beer, a Hershey-bar or piece of halvah *whenever he felt like it.* And we came to the only conclusion possible to explain so staggering "a stash of mazuma" (that's the way men of the world talked on my block): Potch had not inherited a fortune, since his mother was still a laundress and his father had long since been buried by a fraternal order; clearly, Potch worked at some secret, lucrative part-time job, and was well along the road to becoming a millionaire.

But what sort of a job could a callow schoolboy hold? We swiftly deduced that a job never mentioned, never even hinted at, was probably shady, possibly unlawful, perhaps even sinful! We tried not to show our envy. We failed. Potch came to enjoy an unvoiced prestige among us.

Once, Potch bought chocolate phosphates for five of us (!) and "Stomach" Ginsberg, who on a penny bet would eat matches, gravel, pencils, paper, etc., laughed, "Hey, Potch, watchado—robba *bank* or sumpin? !"

Potch paused, blinked, and tossed non-committal *"Khoo!"*'s and *"Flggh!"*'s around his throat.

"Well, Jesse James, *did*ja?"

At that moment, Potch must have realized the aura he had acquired in the minds of his peers; a glow spread beneath his pastiness, like watercolors fanning out from a blot, and he grinned and brought out, "*Pfrr . . . khnug . . .* woonchoo liketa know!"

It was the first time I had seen him approximate a smile, and I saw that he was missing a tooth on each side of his mouth. He looked like a dog—not a good dog, a mutt. But still, there was all that money. . . .

Once, Potch and I were alone, spinning our tops one flaming afternoon in July, moving like sleepwalkers, hearing our sweat splat on the burning sidewalk, and I said, "Hey, Potch, no fooling—where *do* you get all your dough?"

He produced various facial twitches, made several rabbity squeaks, then gargled: "*Hanh* . . . Presents! Presents f'my birt'day!"

"Oh," I said. "When was your birthday?"

"*Khroo . . . Skng. . . .* Las' March. . . . But you gotta remember I got fordy-fifdy uncles 'n' aunts! An' some of 'em live way far t'hellangone an' back, so it takes time, you have to figure, for alla my presents t'get here."

I did not know what to think, so I donned the liberating wings of fantasy. I thought of my book-heroes, especially the great Jimmy Dale, a socialite by day, a Robin Hood at night, who outwitted the finest police brains of the time. Jimmy Dale was a one-man Corrector of Injustice, self-appointed Punisher of Greed and Chicanery, a noble, saintly Redresser of life's inequities, the law's blindness, the helplessness of innocents. Jimmy Dale wore an opera cape and mask as he made his midnight rounds, concealing his ropes and "burgalizing" equipment beneath the voluminous carapace. Ah, Jimmy Dale: his wit, his agility, his intrepid courage and blazing virtue—what more could you ask in an idol?

But *Potch*? Holy macaroni! . . . Jimmy Dale was as handsome as Apollo, and Potch was a dish of oatmeal. Jimmy Dale was as courageous as Ajax, and Potch was "ascared" of mice. Jimmy Dale was as nonchalant as the Scarlet Pimpernel; Potch was only pimpled. Jimmy Dale wore tuxedos and was a paragon of sophistication; Potch, to put it in a nutshell, was a *shmendrick* and a *klutz.*

Still, I comforted myself with the uplifting thought that Potch was just beginning his career; if Fate only gave him a fair shake of the dice, a long and glorious career of crime might stretch beyond the springtime of his delinquency. In my mind, I even converted Potch's deficiencies into boons: since he was so small and skinny, he could become a human fly. I could see him scaling walls, shinnying up pillars or down rainpipes, crawling across balconies, pulling himself up parapets, leaping with cat-footed sureness from rooftop to rooftop on moonless nights, forcing open skylights, windows, transoms, ventilators, jimmying open doors, prying back iron bars, outwitting locks, chains, bolts, burglar alarms —all without leaving so much as the scratch of a fingernail to betray him—to reach at last the baronial bedroom of Throckmorton Spondulix, where Potch would glide to the safe secreted behind a Raphael Madonna, the safe in which the fabled Star of Samarkand reposed, and, with a knowing smile, breathing softly, without a vestige of his youthful *Phtrr!s* and *Shlgg!s,* would proceed to apply his genius to the tumblers, seducing them into revealing their magic numbers by the superhuman sensitivity of his fingers on the dial. . . . And then Potch—*Potch?!* The whole luminescent edifice collapsed. It was crazy. It was ludicrous. It was impossible. You might as well cast cross-eyed Ben Turpin in the role of Don Juan, or ZaSu Pitts as Juliet.

One afternoon, as I was stretched out on my bed reading *The Red-Headed Outfield,* I heard a soft tap-tap-tapping at my window. I rolled over. Potch was crouched on the porch like the Hunchback of Notre Dame, his face screwed up.

"Hey, boychik," he whispered hoarsely, "be quiet no one should hear . . . *Krrr. Flmm.* I wanna ask a favor."

"C'min," I said.

"Tru da *window?*" he protested.

"Sure." I raised it.

"Na, na!" He shot nervous glances around. "How's about you c'mon out?" He signaled to me vigorously, and snaked his way down the back stairs.

I climbed out of the window and followed him and sat down on the bottom step. He was standing over me now, looking down, unaccustomed to being taller, sniffling, then began to dance around in crazy circles, straining his neck and jerking his arms about in a new repertoire of tics. "So I had a birt'day yestiday!" he cried. "So my uncle and aunts and, boy, maybe one hunnerd tousand other relations from all over hellangone give me presents, see? So many presents you can't even count 'em up! So they're piled up in boxes an' I can't hardly squeeze in the goddam bedroom me and my brother use, it's so crowded. Yeh. *Phrr. Nyaa* . . . So I remember you got a bedroom. Alone. Right?" He kicked imaginary time bombs off the sidewalk. "So I figure—how about me bringin' over some boxes, and leave 'em in your closet, for maybe one-two weeks? Whaddaya say you hold somma dem boxes, huh?"

"Well," I said, "I guess so, but—what's in them?"

"Like I *told* you. Presents." He looked harassed and swallowed air and scratched at his neck. "Well, what's *in* all dem boxes is actually nuttin excep'—books."

I gulped. "*Books?*"

"Maybe two hunnerd. But I don't have no *place* for books an' I ain't gonna read 'em, for cryin' out loud, so we just pile 'em up in your closet, see, and . . . *phtrr* . . . *krsh* . . . you hold onto 'em, huh? Just till I take 'em away."

My heart was knocking a sizable hole in my ribs. The unbelievable vision of two hundred books resting in my closet made me delirious. "You'll *leave* them, Potch—I mean the books—in my closet?"

"Yeh. *Glawk. Chrr.* Why not?" He rubbed his fingers on his shirt like Jimmy Valentine. "Just till I take 'em away."

"Why'll you take 'em away?" I asked, already too greedy.

"To *sell* them. Jeeze! . . . *Chlog* . . . I take away maybe six-ten at a time . . . to peddle, thassall."

I tried to keep the hammering out of my voice. "While the books are in my closet—Potch, you wouldn't mind if I read them?"

"I have to *sell* dem books!" he cried, hopping up and down. "*Prsh! Shkr!* They have to be bran' *new!*"

I shouted, "I c'n wrap a towel or something around each book I read! No one'll know anyone even opened *up* a book!"

"Pipe *down,*" he moaned. "You wanna tell the whole goddam neighbahood?" He rolled his eyes and waggled his head in the throes of indecision. "Damn books have to be absolutely *clean,* I'm tellin' ya!"

"There won't even be a spot on 'em!" I exclaimed, with a fervor never exceeded on Kedzie Avenue. "Not one crease or *scratch* even. I promise! Ask any of the guys——"

"Don't you ask no guys! This is just between you and me only.... *Thrrp ... klup ... strr ...* So, O.K. I'll bring over da boxes. I'll come up the back, like just now, an' shove 'em t'rough ya window." He sniffed and snaffled and one eye twitched and teared up. "Hey, your old lady!... While I'm deliverin' the merchandise, you better see your old lady is busy in the kitchen or someplace, huh?... *Knrr ... Flggh* ... Old ladies stick their nose in everyt'ing!"

"I'll say," I warmly agreed. "Don't worry. She's in the front."

And so, in five separate trips, Potch carried cartons (not boxes) up the back stairs, soft of tread, but puffing and whirring away. He wiggled the cartons through the window onto my bed, then crawled in and placed each one in my closet. The cartoons were clean, brown—and sealed. "You open up a box real *careful,*" he whined. "You read a book don't even *touch* it, for luvvah Mike!"

"Holy smoke!" I feigned disgust at his unconfidence. "I *told* you I'd be triple careful!"

"*Hanh ... krr ...*" He disappeared down the steps, a ferret.

The moment Potch left, I dashed into the kitchen, opened a drawer stealthily, found a knife, and scurried back to my room. Silently I closed the door. I moved a chair under the knob with care and, my throat crowded with unfamiliar muscles and organs (my tongue seemed to have fallen into my larynx), I carefully cut along the divided top of the first carton. Slowly, I bent the covers back. Eldorado blazed before my eyes: there, in pristine, shiny, illustrated jackets, were books—a row, a line, a jeweled chain of them.

I washed my hands and took a pillowcase and reverently removed all the books from the first carton, using the pillowcase as a glove, spreading the books out on my bed, devouring the titles with my eyes. I repeated this ritual with the second carton, and the third, and the fourth—until over a hundred precious volumes shone their glory on my bed and dresser and desk. I resavored the titles, one by one, feasting on the names that glittered such promise and invitation. I must have done this for half an hour, like a gourmet prolonging the pleasure of caviar, then carefully placed all but one of the golden trove back in their unworthy containers.

Then I wrapped a fresh towel around my first choice and turned to page one. I was instantly transported beyond time, beyond space, beyond matter, beyond immediate sensation of the immediate, glossless world, far out into the kingdom of print, the only kingdom in which the humblest traveler can find his throne.

The first line (can I ever forget it?) was: "'Crack!' went the bat." These were scarcely surprising words, need I add; in those days, boys' fiction began with an instant hurdle over introductory nonsense to plunge you smack into the center of breathless crisis: "'Pow!' came the sound of Bob Sterling's boot against the pigskin." "'Look out!' shouted the frantic engineer." "'On your marks...set...Bang!' rang out the gunshot." Not even "Call me Ishmael" could have sent the blood racing through my veins so.

For three days, in the morning before breakfast, in the afternoon after school, from after supper until my eyes ached with fatigue, I read. I read and read and read.

On the third day, I heard an ominous tapping on my

bedroom window, and saw Potch's furrowed brow and vapid eyes above the sill. He was kneeling on the back porch, and he held up a large brown paper bag. "Gimme eight," he croaked.

My heart sank. I went to the closet, hating him: I had read only six books. Undiscovered worlds were slipping forever beyond my ken. I got the six books I had read and tried to select two more with the least enticing titles, but Potch was *krechtzing* and *"phtrr"*ing his impatient gibberish. . . . I handed the books through the window, two by two, suppressing my bitterness. He stuffed them into his bag and tiptoed off, trailing his rumblings and snufflings.

I was not caught short again. I now realized that I had to consume the books in the closet faster than Potch, an enterprising salesman, could retrieve them. And I did. I read earlier in the morning, and at the breakfast table, and after school (racing the four long blocks home each day), and after supper, and farther into the night. To explain my temporary resignation from the primal horde, my nonavailability for *Skoosh* or "pinners" (what New Yorkers call "stoopball," in which you threw a rubber ball at a flight of stairs, aiming for an edge so that you might catch the returned ball on a fly, for five points, instead of on a bounce, for one), or the hectic exchange of baseball stars' pictures, or the aimless, exquisite, interminable dawdlings at which the *genus* boy shows such genius—I explained my staggering renunciation of these ecstasies to my pals with a mish-mosh of excuses: I had to sweep out the cellar; a cousin was arriving from Moldavia; I had to stock up coal for the stove; my bike needed emergency readjustments on the "New Departure" brake that worked by reversing the thrust of the foot pedals. The coarse pleasures of sport and play were renounced; I entered the divine sanctuary of reading.

Behind my bedroom door, I soared away each day on great adventurings with the insidious Dr. Fu Manchu and fearless Henry Ware, brave Dave Porter, gentle Penrod, priceless roly-poly Mark Tidd. I lived in a haze of unutterable bliss, made drunk by deeds of valor at Chickamauga

and ninth-inning rallies (score 3–0, bases loaded, our hero
at bat) and last-minute touchdowns for God and Yale. I
chortled over the inspired pranks of the Prodigious Hickey
and the Tennessee Shad, matchless Doc Macnooder and
Hungry Smeed and Skippy Bedelle. I saw hand-to-hand combat against the shifty-eyed Boxers in Peking, and ran down
treacherous natives on the Amazon. I joined patrols against
the howling Berbers screaming "Allah!," and trapped skulking
guerrillas in the steaming Philippines. Down a most precious
and magical cascade of words—by Zane Grey and Sax
Rohmer, Booth Tarkington, Burt L. Standish, Joseph Altshe-
ler, and their immortal peers—I was borne from intrigue
in Singapore to vigils in Tangiers, from Apache massacres
to high crime in Mayfair or small-town deviltries or long,
cold nights on the Chisholm Trail. Was ever any boy more
blessed?

But——! A nasty, nagging unease gnawed at me in my
paradise of print. Those two hundred volumes...In our
neighborhood, a boy might receive a book for his birthday.
Maybe two books. *Possibly* three. But two hundred?!...
And if Potch's books were presents, I could not help wondering, why were they in sealed cartons? And why didn't Potch
keep them somewhere in his own house? I had to confront
the insistent, unremovable suspicion (how I tried not to)
that Potch wanted to conceal the books from his parents.
And why would anyone do that?...I twisted and turned
and dodged to keep from colliding with the awful, dreadful,
unevadable possibility that the books were (oh, dear God,
don't let it be!) stolen.

For a month, I pushed that horrendous thought away
with ever-new, ever-more-ingenious rationalizations. After
all, *I* was not the one who had stolen two hundred volumes.
And they had been purloined without the slightest knowledge, aid, comfort, or encouragement from me. And they
had come to me clearly represented by their possessor as
presents. And Potch surely had a right to lend, store, or sell
his own *presents*. ... But ... and still ...

I was too young to know what being accessory to a crime

(before *or* after) meant; but some basic moral sensor kept bleeping that it was wrong to reap the fruits of thievery; and wrong not to *ask* Potch, at least, if he had stolen the books; and wrong not to consult *someone*—my father, my mother, our gym teacher, a policeman. . . .

I did none of these. To ask Potch himself, however subtly, was to run the unbearable risk of learning that what I feared was true. And if it was true, I could not read on so happily, however skillful the rationalizations to soothe however gullible a conscience. . . . And if I asked Potch and it *was* true, Potch would bring no further loot to my bedroom! . . . And if it was not true, he might demand that I return his entire cache at once, in proper retaliation for being so unworthy a beneficiary.

There was no answer, no solution, no sop, no deliverance. What, then, did I do? I read faster.

I finished the last book not more than an hour before Potch came for the last volumes of his booty. He put them in a suitcase. The suitcase was new. So was Potch's cap. So were his mittens. So was his fob. So was the pearl-handled knife that fell out of his pocket. . .

An Infuriating Man

Y OU take my friend Fenwick. He is an exceedingly lovable little man. His disposition is so sunny, his character so open, that even the Most Hardened Cynics, of whom my wife is International Chairman, call Fenwick "utterly adorable." He is the very incarnation of the Boy Scout creed: "trustworthy, loyal, helpful, friendly, courteous, kind, obedient, cheerful, thrifty, brave, clean (great Scott! but he's *clean*), reverent."

Now you would think that with a personality like that, Fenwick would be just about the most popular man on our block. That is not so. Fenwick is just about the most unpopular man on our block. People can't *stand* him. I have seen Sunday-school teachers with unblemished complexions, and account executives with split-level ranch houses, throw conniption fits at the mere mention of Fenwick's name. Why? *Why?* I puzzled over this for years, using the finest puzzling equipment money can buy, before I discovered the answer: Fenwick is a man who goes around being logical. He even uses reason at cocktail parties.

Now, most people believe in reason the way they believe in cold showers: It's O.K. if you don't overdo it. Very few people are so insensitive as to go around applying logic to other people's beliefs. The consistent application of reason to human affairs is irrational. It is also dangerous, as you shall soon find out.

The basic trouble is that Fenwick, who is very intelligent, assumes that other people are very intelligent, too. And that, believe it or not, is the way he talks to them. This makes people uneasy, for nothing is more unsettling than to be treated as if you are extremely intelligent—especially by someone you hardly know. To avoid disillusioning such a man requires that you maintain a constant state of alert, and think before you speak, which imposes cruel demands on your brain. It even makes you examine the patly packaged platitudes you have always employed instead of thinking. Few activities tire one out so rapidly.

Fenwick has no understanding of such things. I think I should tell you that Fenwick *enjoys* reasoning. He uses his mind the way a sprinter uses his shoes: to get from one point to another with a maximum of speed and a minimum of nonsense. Such a discrepancy between the swift and the stupid ordinarily causes hubris in the former and dysphasia in the latter, hubris being the fancy name for cockiness and dysphasia a variety of depression. But these psychological reflexes do not click on where Fenwick is concerned, because the people he outruns (or, more correctly, outratiocinates) tend to save face by calling his speed a symptom and his skill a neurosis. Such people attain emotional serenity from believing that superior thinking is a sign of emotional disturbance. I am not sure they are wrong.

Of none of all this is my friend Fenwick remotely aware. For although he actually likes to think, even when no one is forcing him to, he also likes people. The exotic combination of cold cerebration and warm feelings throws people for a loop.

Even more enlooping, my friend Fenwick loves to *learn.* It does not matter what you do, like, think, or talk about: Fenwick is passionately interested in it. He listens intently to anything you have to say, which is both flattering and seductive; but if you mention something Fenwick does not know, his eyes become as wide as Frisbies and he asks

where you found that out, how you know it is true, and
how—assuming for the moment that you are right, which is
conceivable, though unlikely—you can account for any
one of fourteen cases which, if true, shoot your case as
full of holes as that of the couple with two children who
decided not to have a third because they had read that
every third child born these days is a Chinaman. And as you
bumble and blubber and flounder and flush, Fenwick sweetly soothes your ego by sighing, "Of course, you *may* be right
. . . but not for the reasons you presented."

Fenwick appears to own a brain that came equipped with
a sorting device that separates inference from information, allegation from argument, illustration from proof, and
preferences from conclusions. Despite this, he has more
friends than I do. His friends, it is true, tend to have strong
nerves and read statistics the way some men read pornography. But they *are* staunch, stout friends. Even the thin
ones are stout friends.

In ordinary conversation, Fenwick is a fellow-traveler. He
follows every chug in your train of thought—indeed, he
leaps right on the train with you. And you have barely begun to pick up steam before Fenwick excitedly demon-
strates that: (a) you have taken the wrong train; or (b) it
doesn't stop where you want to go; or (c) the tracks don't
lead from your premise to your expectations; or (d) you
had better jump off while the jumping's good or you'll land
in the swamp of mushy ideas you never suspected your
position rests upon.

Yes, my friends, Fenwick comes pret-ty close to being that
most odious and exasperating of human types: the persistent thinker. He may even (I hate to suggest this) be an
Intellectual. An Intellectual is a man who shamelessly uses
his brain most of the time. No one, of course, uses his brain
all of the time; such a man would be a monster—he would
not dig sandpiles by the sea, or fall in love, or observe
Mother's Day.

Oscar Wilde, who was diabolically clever (and just as
superficial), once quipped: "I can stand brute force, but

brute reason is quite unbearable. . . . It is hitting below the intellect." Fenwick, a beamish fellow, *never* hits below the intellect. He is always kind, fair, patient, moderate—which greatly increases his unpopularity. Do you follow me? Fenwick is so fair in discussions that people can't even accuse him of using unfair tactics, than which nothing is more aggravating when you are wrong.

I once heard Fenwick explain to a cocktail party full of decent, taxpaying liberals why it is that no socialist society, however well-intentioned, can give its masses anywhere near the standard of living of a competitive or capitalist society. After the dumbfounded humanitarians had finished stamping their feet, screaming "Reactionary!" and otherwise increasing their psychiatric bills, Fenwick kindly compared the postwar achievement of West Germany with East Germany, of Japan with Red China, of Italy with India, of France with Soviet Russia. He gave several of his listeners the veritable jim-jams by going so far as to compare the economy of Cuba before and after Castro, and the G.N.P. of liberated Africa before and after European imperialism.

If *that* episode doesn't tell you what kind of screwball Fenwick is, let me cite another. Fenwick and a friend of mine from Washington, a sociological *Meistersinger* named Rupert Shmidlapp, were talking about minimum wages, which Congress had just voted to raise from $1.25 an hour to $1.40—and ultimately to $1.60. Fenwick stunned Shmidlapp, whom I had forgotten to brief in advance, by mournfully remarking that the minimum-wage laws would of course create *un*employment, and that these particular laws would wreak havoc precisely among those unskilled workers (Negroes, teen-agers, Puerto Ricans) they were supposed to help.

"What?" gulped Shmidlapp.

"To begin with," said Fenwick, "the American wage-earner today gets twice $1.40 an hour, so the bill is not going to affect him——"

"The bill is designed to help the unskilled and the undereducated," retorted Shmidlapp.

"An *admirable* intention," beamed Fenwick, "because a tragic proportion of that group is unemployed. But if employers aren't hiring them at $1.25 an hour, is there any reason on earth why they will hire them at $1.40?"

I poured a stiff drink for Shmidlapp.

Fenwick continued: "Surely the unemployed will have less chance of finding a job under the new, higher minimum-wage laws than they had under the old."

"*What?*" cried Shmidlapp. "Can you prove that?"

"Yes," said Fenwick. "Every time minimum wages *have* been raised, the ratio of unemployed teen-agers has risen— and mostly among Negroes and Puerto Ricans, who are the teen-agers it seems absolutely insane, if you look at the crime rate, to force onto the streets with nothing to do! ... Don't you agree that every time you raise the minimum, you *must* push more unskilled or inexperienced or poorly educated or discriminated-against workers onto the unemployment and relief rolls?"

Instead of repairing his fences, Shmidlapp attacked on the flanks. "What about *the greedy employers*," he demanded, "who cruelly exploit their workers by not paying them enough to live on?!"

A twinge of pain crossed Fenwick's boyish features. "Oh, very, very few employers can hold on to their workmen if they pay them less than the workers can get elsewhere."

"It isn't what they can 'get,' it's what they're worth!" Shmidlapp thundered.

"Only God can decide how much a man is 'worth,'" sighed Fenwick. "Let us consider the best wage a man can *get*— for his labor, services or talent——"

"Some men just can't live on that! Or feed and clothe their children! Or pay their medical bills!" This was Shmidlapp at his best.

"We certainly ought to remedy *that*," said Fenwick. "No American who wants to work should go hungry because of the objective (and therefore efficient) forces of supply and demand. Let us by all means give and guarantee the poor a minimum *income;* that does far less economic and political damage than a minimum *wage.* A minimum income does not discriminate against the black, the illiterate, the inept——"

"Do you mean to stand there and tell me"—Shmidlapp was too agitated to notice that Fenwick was sitting, not standing—"that no workers are actually helped when Congress raises the minimum wage?!"

"Oh, *some* workers will have their wages raised from $1.25 to $1.40 an hour," said Fenwick, "but far more will not get a job they might have gotten at $1.25! And fewer teen-agers and Negroes will get on-the-job training, which they desperately need. It is just too costly to train them at $1.40, much less $1.60 an hour—especially for skills that take long training periods. This makes a raise in minimum wages absolutely *heartless,*" mourned Fenwick. "It prices decent, innocent, willing workingmen right out of the labor market!"

"Then why does Congress pass such laws?" shouted Shmidlapp.

Fenwick blinked. "Are you suggesting that Congress never passes foolish or short-sighted——"

"I am asking why, if minimum wages are so goddam stupid, far-sighted humanitarian leaders like Lyndon Johnson and Hubert Humphrey and Governor Rockefeller support them?!"

"Politics," chuckled Fenwick. "Or innocence. Or ignorance. Or all three. Politicians and labor leaders get a lot of public credit for raising wages, and considerable private satisfaction in imagining all the good they have done."

"I happen to know that many business leaders, Republicans and conservatives, favor minimum-wage legislation!" swooped Shmidlapp.

"Of *course* they do. They can be just as wrong, ignorant, or selfish as anyone else," said Fenwick. "Many of them are manufacturing products in the North——"

"What does geography have to do with it?" demanded Shmidlapp.

"Well, northern manufacturers are delighted to force up their competitors' costs in the South; in that way, businessmen in the North won't have to face the desirable effects of that free-enterprise system conservatives and Republicans love to extol."

"But opinion polls show that the *public*——"

"The public," sighed Fenwick, "is not well-informed about economics, and will pay for its innocence. Increased minimum wages lead to increased costs, which lead to higher prices. . . . Then many honest, low-wage earners in the South (where the cost of living is lower; which is one reason wages there stay lower) will become *dis*employed. And many more of the young and no-skilled, in Harlem no less than Dixie, will remain more hopelessly unemployed than they already are." Fenwick regarded Rupert Shmidlapp innocently. "Tell me, honestly: Would *you* rather work for $1.25 an hour or be unemployed at $1.40?"

While Shmidlapp was wrestling with many unkind thoughts, Fenwick gave his guileless smile: "I am strongly in favor of wages' *rising*—which is entirely different from raising wages. Let wages go up as far as they can and deserve to, for the right reasons, which means in response to demand and supply and freedom to choose. . . . Take domestic servants, Mr. Shmidlapp. Why maids, cooks, cleaning women, laundresses have enjoyed a *fantastic* increase in their earnings. And notice, please, that domestic servants are not organized; they don't have a union, or a congressional lobby. Or take bank clerks . . ."

But I can't bear to go on. I guess you can see why Fenwick is so unpopular. The man is *infuriating*.

P.S. Outraged letters should be addressed to P.O. Box 146, Tierra del Fuego, where I shall be spending the long, hard winter.

Coby

$\mathbf{C}$OBY Clay was an Alabama lad, exactly six feet five inches in height. He had baby-blue eyes, curly hair, and a cherubic spirit that spilled over from some inner reservoir of content. He walked around in a private cloud of delight, always grinning, chuckling, slapping his thigh in gratitude for his own inexhaustible good company. "Man, oh, man," he would chortle, to himself, "jest you listen to that. Man, oh, man, that's mighty fine stuff!"

He was at peace with the world and at home with himself: his body, his reveries, his Maker, his soul. His moods ran an exceptionally narrow gamut, being bounded at the lower end by pleasure and at the upper end by bliss. The only thing he was sensitive about was his height, which he reported, in rueful confession, as "five foot seventeen."

At Camp Colfax we always knew when Coby was about to materialize; we could hear, in advance, the whistling or humming or chuckling which accompanied his running colloquy with his beatific self. Hear it? No; overhear it. For his contact with any of us, with the unhappy universe beyond his own fantasies, was fragmentary—and oddly compassionate. I think he felt sorry for everyone who could not join him in the idyllic past with which he chose to replace the irksome now.

Coby was an exceedingly amiable soldier, but he was most oddly coordinated. His far-flung limbs seemed to live a life independent of his torso. When Coby drew those six feet five inches to attention, for instance, he did it in sequence—as if his brain was sending messages to the outlying provinces of its empire; naturally it took more time for a foot to respond than, say, a hand, since the one was so much farther from headquarters than the other.

Coby had a massive chest, immense biceps, and looked strong, very strong, which I'm sure he was; but he did not *feel* strong. And a man who does not *feel* strong simply is not able to lift heavy loads, or move burdensome objects, or heave, haul, toss, or carry things which weaker men manage to do because they want to be strong. This was an illusion Coby did not entertain. He did not care about physical strength; he sought harmony, not power.

At an early age, Coby had found himself in a world where men competed—for jobs, for money, for women, for promotions—and he had long since come to the conclusion that he did not care to compete for anything. He was content with himself, encouraged himself, enjoyed himself, and admired himself.

"His ego," Captain Newman wrote in the confidential report on Coby Clay which Colonel Pyser requested, "appears to be inaccessible to conventional appeals."

It certainly was.

Coby was the only private in the United States Army who never made his bed. May I repeat that? Coby was the only private in the United States Army who never made his bed. It was his desperate, frantic sergeant who made his bed for him, each and every morning. I think Coby was the only soldier in military history whom neither sergeants nor lieutenants nor captains nor majors nor colonels could prevail upon. They tried—all of them; Lord knows they tried. They tried command and cajolery, blandishment and bluster and threats of reprisal, but Coby just would not make his bed. He would hear out the orders, the coaxings, the reasoning, the threats; he would gravely consider the appeals to sense, to duty, to teamwork, to *esprit de corps,* to the glory of his uniform, to the Flag. Then all Coby would say, with the utmost kindliness, was: "But 'tain't fitten for a grown-up man to make his own bed."

All this broke upon our awareness the very first dawn after Coby was shipped to our unsuspecting installation, when his sergeant came into the barracks to find Coby stretched out on his cot, gazing out of the window happily, humming a roundelay. His bed was unmade.

Sergeant Pulaski, an uncomplicated Polish boy from Hammond, Indiana, called, "Clay!"

"Yes, Sarge," Coby beamed.

"On your feet, soldier!"

"Yes, suh!" Coby transferred his components from a horizontal to a vertical arrangement.

"Clay," said Sergeant Pulaski sternly, "you haven't made your bed."

"That's right, Sarge."

Sergeant Pulaski wrinkled his brow. "Why not?"

Coby said, "'Tain't fit for a grown-up man to make his own bed."

Sergeant Pulaski, who had a gift for unvarnished command, put his fists on his hips at once and barked, "What the *hell* kind of crap is that?"

"Back home," said Coby, "my maw always makes up my bed. Ever since I been born, my maw always made up that there bed."

"In the Army," said Sergeant Pulaski, in searing syllables, "there ain't no ma's to make up no beds. In the Army, soldier, everyone—*everyone* exceptin' officers—makes his own bed!"

Coby took thought and clucked his tongue in wonderment.

"Inspection is in ten minutes!" said Sergeant Pulaski.

"That's nice," said Coby.

"Now, boy, you make that bed!"

Coby sighed and shook his head with indubitable regret. "I ain't hankerin' to make no trouble for nobody, nohow, Sarge; but I jest cain't do it."

"And why 'cain't you just do it'?"

"Why, I jest couldn't look my maw in the eye agin if I made up my own bed."

Sergeant Pulaski stared at Coby in amazement, tightened his lips, declared, "A guy asks for trouble he's gonna get hisself an assful of trouble!" and stalked out.

Coby lay down on his cot and hummed himself a song from the gracious past.

In less than five minutes, Sergeant Pulaski returned with Lieutenant Bienstock, a second lieutenant with fuzz on his cheek but not on his chin. Bienstock was an enthusiastic exponent of that Come-on-fellows-let's-all-put-our-shoulders-to-the-wheel spirit which never failed to puzzle our allies, whose military observers expected an army to be divided simply into those who command and those who obey.

Lieutenant Bienstock now hastened into the barracks with shining eyes and palpitating disbelief. He was so excited he kept repeating himself. "Which one? Where, Sergeant? Which one is it? That one? Is he the one? He is, eh? Well, we'll just see about him. On your feet, soldier!"

As Coby solemnly undulated himself upward, part after part, until all of his five foot seventeen arrived more or less at attention, Lieutenant Bienstock paled—slightly, but in steady and visible degrees.

"Mornin,' suh," Coby smiled.

Lieutenant Bienstock glanced uneasily at Sergeant Pulaski and said, "Now listen, Clay. Just listen to me. Sergeant Pulaski has been very patient with you, I must say. *Very* patient. There are mighty few sergeants who would be one-half that patient! You don't want to get into any trouble, do you? And we certainly don't want to make *you* any trouble. Correct? Cor-*rect!* So—now, what's all this malarky about you refusing to make up your bed?"

Coby looked down at his superior from bland, unruffled heights. "Oh, I don't aim to make no trouble for nobody, nohow. I like it here, suh. But it jest ain't *right*, suh."

"What do you mean it ain't—I mean isn't, 'right'?!" demanded Bienstock.

"Well," allowed Coby, "I jest couldn't look my maw in the eye again if I made up my own bed."

Lieutenant Bienstock stared at the kind, forbearing face above him and in a strained voice asked, "Holy Je-*sus*, soldier, do you realize what you're saying? Do you know what this *means*? Why—you are deliberately refusing to obey an order from a superior officer!"

"Oh, no, suh," Coby drawled. "I ain't refusin' t' obey no one, nohow."

"Then you'll go ahead and make that bed!"

"Cain't," said Coby.

Lieutenant Bienstock glanced at Sergeant Pulaski uneasily, wetting his lips, not knowing what to do now, so he tapped his teeth with his forefinger (a nervous habit he had inherited from his uncle in Shamokin, we heard) and said with flimsy briskness, "Sergeant, you take this man over to Captain Howard's office!"

"Right!" Sergeant Pulaski saluted and nodded to Coby, who nodded toward Lieutenant Bienstock in the kindest possible way before ambling out.

Bienstock lighted a cigarette and inhaled deeply, organizing his thoughts. There were a great many of them. After due thought and confusion, he raced after his yeomen, heading for Captain Howard's office in Building Two. He found Coby Clay sitting on a long bench, one knee drawn up supporting his elbow, his hand dangling loosely, moving in lazy rhythm to his humming. Sergeant Pulaski was standing next to him in a correct military posture.

Lieutenant Bienstock regarded Coby sententiously, giving him one last chance to reconsider or recant. Coby started to mobilize his bodily ingredients for ascent, but Lieutenant Bienstock turned on his heel and strode into Captain Howard's office.

I disliked Captain Howard. He was a knuckle-cracker and a mint-sucker. He was efficient, crisp, hardworking, and mean. An automobile salesman from Wichita, Herbert Howard was a staunch believer in fair play, cold showers, and clean thoughts. His thoughts were so clean that he spent most of his evenings at the Officer's Club boring us with his plans for a five-minute car-washing service he was going to open up as soon as the war was over. He was the kind of incomplete personality known as "a man's man." He had few friends and many doubts. When he thought no one was watching, he bit his cuticles. I think that when he slept he looked puzzled.

Howard was tallying up some requisition forms when Lieutenant Bienstock entered. Bienstock saluted smartly, accepted Captain Howard's cursory "Proceed," and, while the latter continued to add and carry over, Bienstock recited the details of Private Coby Clay's defiance of the simplest and most universal requirement of military life. Bienstock's uneasy repetitions and occasional stuttering (the stuttering would never have happened if he had only been allowed to tap his teeth) gave his report added force and a curious verity.

Captain Howard lifted his head with an expression of incipient outrage. "He won't make his *bed*?"

Lieutenant Bienstock cleared his throat. "Yes, sir. That's what he won't do."

Captain Howard scrutinized Bienstock as if the man had just told him the sun had risen in the west that morning.

"He says—well, he says it's against his—principles, sir," Bienstock quickly added.

"His *principles*?" Captain Howard echoed. "What the hell is he, a Muhammadan?"

"No, sir. I'm almost sure he's not a Muhammadan. He's from the South."

"So what? Halfa this goddam installation comes from around the Mason and Dixie line!"

"He says his Maw always made his bed for him," poor Bienstock said, "and 'taint—it isn't *fit* for a grown-up man to —well, to make his own bed."

Captain Howard leaned forward, hunching his shoulders like a fullback plowing through the line, and cried, "His 'maw'? What the hell's the matter with you, Bienstock?"

"Nothing, sir," protested Lieutenant Bienstock with a pained expression. "I was just *quoting*."

"Well, stop quoting and talk sense, for Crissake! He calls his mother 'maw'?"

"Yes, sir."

"Is he a hillbilly or something?"

Bienstock hesitated. "I think he's from Alabama, sir."

"I don't care if he's a thirty-plus-three degree Shriner! Do you mean to stand there and tell me you let a dogface pull a gag like refusing to make his own bed on you, a lootenant in the U.S. Army——"

"Sir, I explained and insisted and *argued* with him. I even——"

Captain Howard's face assumed various variations of impatience as Lieutenant Bienstock proceeded. This made Lieutenant Bienstock more nervous, and he began to stammer. This made Captain Howard's lips thread themselves so that impatience was replaced by contempt. This made Lieutenant Bienstock blush. This made Captain Howard slap his desk with his open palm and snap, "You *argued* with him? Are you off your goddam rocker, Bienstock? You are an *of*ficer in the United States *Army!* This isn't a debating society. We're at *war!* Get the marbles out of your head and throw that no-good goldbrick in the little old guardhouse!"

"Sir?" gulped Bienstock.

"You heard me. Throw him in the jug!"

"I thought——"

"That's not smart of you, thinking. Thinking is obviously not your strong point. Give him to the MPs, Bienstock, to— the—MPs! Twenty-four hours in the little old cooler will cool off that smartass joker. It's as simple as that. 'Won't make his bed!' Oh, my aching back! 'It ain't fit for a grownup man.'" Captain Howard's expression was a masterpiece of condescension and disgust. "Holy Moses, Bienstock, even the *Com*munists make their own beds. Dismissed!"

Lieutenant Bienstock wiped his brow the minute he got outside the door, signaled to Sergeant Pulaski, and strode out.

Sergeant Pulaski snapped "Up!" to Coby and they marched after their officer.

When they were fifty feet from Captain Howard's office, Lieutenant Bienstock took Coby under a tree and made a last

earnest effort to save him from his fate. Bienstock spoke
softly but clearly and firmly and with impeccable logic.

Coby listened with the utmost consideration. Anyone
could see that he wouldn't want to hurt Lieutenant Bienstock's feelings for anything in the world. But what he said,
after Bienstock's moving appeal and summation, was, "But,
sir, 'tain't fit for a grown man to——"

"Sergeant," glared Bienstock petulantly, "take this man to
the guardhouse! That's all. By order of Captain Howard."

Coby spent that day behind bars singing, and all of that
night he slept like a particularly contented lamb.

When Coby returned to the barracks from the guardhouse
the next morning, Sergeant Pulaski was waiting at the
porch entrance with a knowing, superior smile.

Coby seemed delighted to see him. "Man, oh, man," he
chuckled, "I caught me up on plenty of snoozin'."

Pulaski said, "O.K., Clay. Let's you and me have no more
trouble for me from you, huh?"

Coby's eyes moved serenely around the barracks, coming
to rest on his own cot in the far corner. It looked as neat,
tight and oblong as a coffin.

"We got commended for neat quarters at inspection this
morning," said Sergeant Pulaski defensively. "O.K., O.K., so
I made up your bed. But no more trouble from you, huh,
Clay?"

"No, Sarge," said Coby. "I ain't aimin' to give nobody——"

"— no trouble nohow," Pulaski finished. "I heard you.
Now get the lead out of your tail and fall in with your
squad."

Coby spent the day training with his company, went to
sleep that night, responded to reveille nobly the next morning, helped his comrades mop the floor and sweep the porch,
lent a cheerful, helping hand to one and all—but he did
not make his bed.

Sergeant Pulaski looked both stunned and hurt as he ran
out to find Lieutenant Bienstock.

This time Bienstock did not shilly-shally. He told Sergeant
Pulaski to bring Private Clay to his office forthwith. And

when Coby appeared, Lieutenant Bienstock, staring directly ahead, gave Coby an icy ten-minute lecture on military discipline, and what would next happen, and what would occur if this open-and-shut act of mutiny went up "through channels." He stressed Captain Howard's cold heart, Major Forman's nasty temper, and the reputation of our Commandant, Colonel Pyser, an absolute Caligula *cum laude* in disciplinary matters.

Coby could not have been more interested in these novel insights into the military organization of which he was so small a part. But he would not sacrifice his principles; he would not sully his mother's image of him; he would not make his bed.

He returned to the guardhouse.

And, back in the barracks, Sergeant Pulaski made his bed again, while Coby sang for his colleagues in the can.

The next day Coby was back with his fellows. That night he slept in the bed which Sergeant Pulaski had made that morning. And the next morning he once more declined to make his bed, with genuine affection and regret, and was marched off to the guardhouse again.

This went on for a week, Coby spending alternate nights at the guardhouse, sleeping alternate nights in the bed which Sergeant Pulaski, hamstrung and half-crazy, made for him.

When it seemed clear that Coby was willing to spend the rest of his days in this idyllic double life, Sergeant Pulaski appealed to Lieutenant Bienstock with uncommon emotion. "Either he goes or I—go—nuts!" was they way Pulaski summarized the impasse.

"Let's not lose your head," said Lieutenant Bienstock, and proceeded to lose his, crying, "I'll get that Tobacco Road anarchist sent to Alcatraz in chains, if I have to!"

The outburst was cathartic, but of short duration, for when Lieutenant Bienstock reported to Captain Howard, an unmistakable frog had invaded his voice.

Captain Howard now cracked his knuckles, studied Lieutenant Bienstock with a disgust diluted only with disbelief, and, between his fine, well-brushed teeth, said, "OK., send that mother-lovin' bastard in to me." He had never laid eyes on Coby Clay, you must bear in mind.

When Coby presented himself, Captain Howard was tilted far back in his chair with his back to the door, barking into the telephone acidly at some noncom over at the PX. Captain Howard was feeling especially curt, concise and complete that day. He slammed the phone down, swiveled around, deliberately turning his cold eyes to some report on his desk, and waited for the familiar: "Private———report-ing, sir," from the soldier awaiting his dispensation. He did not get it, because Coby saw no reason to give it.

The seditious silence caused Captain Howard to put his pencil down slowly, exactly parallel to the blotter pad, as-sume an expression of fearful foreboding, then slowly lift his eyes up the height of the erect body before him. This maneuver of ascending appraisal had always before served Captain Howard's purposes; it effected a slow deflation of the other's ego; it smothered hope or illusion; it was a tactical gambit which made it crystal clear who was stand-ing and who was sitting, and who was going to continue standing at the sole pleasure of who was sitting.

But Lieutenant Bienstock had forgotten to tell Captain Howard that Coby Clay was six feet five in altitude. So by the time Captain Howard's gaze reached the unexpected eminence of Coby's chin, Herbert Howard, who was only five feet eight, had his head stuck far back in the socket of his neck and his eyes bugged in involuntary bulges.

Coby blushed, as he always did when people compre-hended his distance from the ground. "I come right over, suh, like that there other fellow told me."

"*Who?*" asked Captain Howard.

"That there other fellow. The one brought me here before."

Captain Howard could feel his neck getting hot. "That 'other fellow,'" he said frigidly, "just happens to be an officer, soldier! An officer named Lieutenant Bienstock. And you will *re*-fer to him hereafter by name!"

"He never told me his name," said Coby.

"Well, *I* am telling you his rank *and* name!" Captain Howard retorted, slamming his fist on the desk. "And even if you don't know his name, you could call him 'Lieutenant.' You understand that much, soldier, don't you?"

"Yes, suh!" beamed Coby, always grateful for increment to his store of knowledge.

Captain Howard turned sideward and poured himself a glass of water, noting with approval that his hands were steady. He sipped the water slowly, then lowered the glass, studied it, and placed the glass on the table. Then he leaned forward, put his palms together, and said in an even voice, "Soldier, I want you to listen very, very carefully to what I am about to tell you. I'll say it slowly, so there is not the slightest chance you'll misunderstand. This involves your making a decision that may affect your whole life! . . . Are you ready?"

Coby furrowed his brow, concentrating on every pearl of a word Captain Howard had uttered, and nodded.

"I asked, 'Are you ready?' " Captain Howard glared.

"Oh, yes, I heard."

"Then say you're ready!" shouted Captain Howard.

"Yes, suh, I am ready," sighed Coby.

Captain Howard took a long, deep breath and let it out, word by word: "*Either* you make your bed *ev*ery morning, without a single beef, or I will throw you in the guardhouse —for—ten—whole—days." He fixed Coby with his deadliest I-take-no-nonsense-from-anyone stare. "Is that clear?"

Coby nodded.

"You understand it?"

Coby nodded again.

"Any question you want to ask, boy?"

Coby shook his head.

"Fine. Now, soldier, which will it be?"

"How's that again, suh?" asked Coby.

Captain Howard closed his eyes. "Which—will—it—be? *Either* you make your bed in the morning, every morning— or go to the cold, cold jug for—ten—days!"

Coby blinked, regarding the man seated before and below

him with infinite compassion. "I don't aim to make no trouble for *no* one, nohow, suh, but still an' all, I cain't go along with the idea that it's fit for a grown-up man to ——"

The blood drained out of Captain Howard's simian features, and all sorts of evil thoughts welled up in him and had to be denied. He opened his desk drawer swiftly, harpooned a mint, placed the mint in his mouth and, sucking vehemently, pressed a button on his desk. "Good-bye, soldier!"

So Coby spent the next ten days in the guardhouse. It was, according to the reports we received (scuttlebutt raced through our post with the velocity of a brush fire), the happiest ten days of Coby's life.

That certainly was not true of the personnel to whom he was entrusted. The MPs and Captain Howard and Major Forman—to whom Captain Howard brought his problem, confessing defeat—simply could not believe it. They could understand it, but they could not believe it. Or perhaps it was the other way around.

The dominant philosophical point is that Coby Clay was behaving in such a way that the entire theory of punishment as a deterrent was endangered. Every day Coby spent happily in the guardhouse demonstrated that the punitive could be pleasant; this challenged the very foundations of military law enforcement, for the whole idea of a guardhouse, or any place of confinement, rests on the assumption that detention is hateful to man's free spirit and crippling to man's free soul.

But now the American Army was confronted by a man for whom detention held no terrors, confinement meant no deprivation, discipline represented no threat. The awful truth, which was beginning to confound our brass, was even worse: Private Coby Clay *liked* the guardhouse. There, he slept like a king and sang like an angel. In fact, he preferred the guardhouse to the barracks. There was something about that bounded, ordered microcosm that appealed to Coby no end; there, life was reduced to its simplest form—devoid of conflict, or the perplexities of choice.

The fact that Coby declined to make his bed in the guard-house, too—politely, but definitively—presented its own special problem to the MPs; after all, there is no other guard-house to which you can send a man in order to punish him for not making his bed in the guardhouse in which he is.

"What in hell can I *do*?" Major Inglehart, the commanding MP, often moaned to us.

No one knew what to tell him.

Nor was this the worst of it. The other prisoners, who regarded Coby with the awe that apprentices render a master, were beginning to be converted to Coby's unique philosophy, and an insidious idea began to germinate in their delinquent brains: perhaps they, too, need not make their beds. To nip this understandably alarming prospect in the bud, Major Inglehart transferred Coby to an end cell with one Lacy Bucks, a young enlistee from Louisiana who could not abide Yankees but felt kissing kin to practically anyone south of Chattanooga.

The major interviewed Private Bucks privately and, after a certain amount of beating around the bush, bribed Bucks ("double rations") to make up Coby's bed every morning. "And don't you tell anyone you're doing it," Inglehart warned him fiercely, "or I'll skin you alive!"

Lacy Bucks seemed contented to be silent for the Major, and the rations. And Coby Clay, of course, had no reason to tell anyone that Bucks was making his bed for him. He never felt the slightest need of initiating any discussion of the bed problem; it was no problem to him: at home his maw had made his bed; then Sergeant Pulaski had; now Lacy Bucks did. It was the most natural thing in the world to Coby.

I think you will agree that things could not be allowed to go on that way forever.

Besides, there was the dilemma of work details. Men who are suffering punishment in a guardhouse obviously cannot be permitted to spend their days in happy idleness, singing and goofing off, while all around them haggard and obedient comrades drill like furies, crawl through sand, contest barbed wire, run fiendish obstacle courses under a merciless sun, bivouac on a cold desert under a chilling moon. The Air Force of the Army of the United States of America could not be *that* naive.

So Major Inglehart, a canny captain, put Coby, Lacy Bucks, and a barrel-chested boy named Tony Caralucciano into a work detail to clean up the grounds. It seemed a sound enough assignment. But it soon looked as though that threesome would demoralize our entire installation. For American Army regulations require that every prisoner must have an armed guard whenever he (the prisoner) is allowed outside a guardhouse. This meant that as Coby, Bucks and Tony Caralucciano ambled happily across the grounds, in a memorable formation which I shall describe forthwith, three MPs, carrying rifles and wearing battle helmets, marched stiffly behind them. When the heat was very great, clawing at our senses with fiery fingers, the three prisoners in their loose and tieless fatigue garments were considerably more comfortable than their nominally freer custodians. The moral was not lost on any who witnessed this paradoxical transposition of values.

The formation of the detail added its own piquancy to the scene. Coby always took the middle spot, looming up above Lacy Bucks on his right and Tony Caralucciano on his left. Tony carried a long pole with a nail at the end; Lacy carried a burlap sack. And as the three good men moved lazily across the ground they had been assigned to make bereft of trash, Tony would spear a piece of paper—a chewing-gum wrapper, an envelope, a crumpled ball of unrequited love—on the end of the nail that was on the end of his pole, then brought the pole up horizontally across his chest toward Coby. Coby would thereupon remove the paper from the nail with the utmost delicacy, crooking his little finger, then bring his hand across from left to right, where Lacy Bucks was holding the sack open, and let the piece of paper drop daintily into the sack. He hummed or sang during the entire operation.

This did not help the morale of the guards.

To make things worse for Command, but delicious for everyone else, Tony Caralucciano had a fine barbershop bass and, in the tradition of his ancestors, loved grand opera. Lacy Bucks was strictly a hot-jazz type, the kind who tries to find in life the archaic excitations of the syncopated. And Coby, a man of broad and generous interests, liked to sing anything. So these three music lovers soon learned to float together on the sea of their common fantasies, singing or humming while they worked and as the spirit moved them. It was a thing beautiful to hear and, once heard, was not easily forgotten. It went like this:

Each morning when "The Prison Warblers," as someone dubbed them, moved into position ahead of their helmeted Cerberus, Coby Clay would open the day by humming a note —any note, whichever note best suited his mood. His mood was unfailingly happy. If Tony was feeling extremely operatic, he would take off, using Coby's theme note as a springboard, into anything from *Tosca* to *Madame Butterfly*. If it was Lacy Bucks who was in touch with his private muses, he would give out with *Johnny One-Note* or *Roll, Jordan, Roll*. And if Coby wanted to override his confrères, he would simply boom out his own immemorial hynms. There was no set pattern to it: whoever sang, the others accompanied; whatever one man finished, another would take up, on the last, long, expiring note, for his own. It was as close to true understanding as men can ever get.

As one of the MP guards was heard to mutter, struggling with his perplexity and dismay: "Them is the happiest goddam garbage collectors I ever did meet."

A second guard wondered whether the Army would one day put up some sort of monument to Coby Clay.

When Coby's term of incarceration ended, he appeared, refreshed and forgiving, in my office: Major Forman had told Captain Howard to tell Lieutenant Bienstock to tell Sergeant Pulaski to deliver Coby to "the head-shrinkers."

Major Forman had phoned me himself and said he wanted Coby Clay rigorously tested. "The works!" he said. "I want you to give him the toughest going-over you ever gave anyone. Then take him over to Captain Newman and let Newman start where you left off! Send all reports directly to me. I'm going to build up a case against this 8-ball that buttons down every angle, then I'm going to take it up directly with Colonel Pyser! If this soldier Clay is a fizzle-head we'll get him out of the army on a CDD; and if he's faking, we'll throw him out on a Section Eight. Either way, goddamit, this frigging farce has got to end!"

No one ever received as many tests as I administered to Coby Clay that long day. I gave him the whole battery from simple IQs to the Cornell Selectee Index. I gave him Self-Idealization scales and Sentence Completions ("I avoid people who . . . I feel nervous when . . . ") I gave him AGCTs and ACIOs. I tested him for mechanical aptitude, motor responses, minimum literacy, box counting, mental alertness, visual-motor skills. I gave him perception tests, emotional adjustment inventories, aptitude scales, visual classification series. I went through the entire lyrical manual published by the Personnel Procedures Section of the Adjutant General's Office to make triple sure there wasn't a semblance of a form, exam, quiz, catechism, probe or questionnaire I had missed.

It was exhaustive; it was inhuman; and although it left Coby with new reasons for self-enchantment (to him it was all a glass-bottom boat trip through his own subterranean wonderland), it left me spent. And then, relieved only by appropriate groanings and curses, it took me a good seventeen hours *after* my investigations to code, score, coordinate, and appraise my findings.

The results were indisputable: According to the accumulated diagnostic genius of all the psychological sciences of our civilization, Coby Clay was a perfectly healthy, sound, responsible, wholesome, brave, reasonable, well-adjusted, law-abiding, well-balanced specimen of American manhood. His schooling was not all that might be desired; his vocabulary was far from impressive; his spelling was atrocious—but then, so was the spelling of most of our GIs. Coby's IQ was 96—not high, to be sure, but you must remember that

50 percent of the men in our Army ranked between 95 and 105. It sort of dawned on me that, all in all, Coby Clay was probably more secure, sane, balanced and healthy than the psychologists who had devised the questionnaires.

I reported all this (my findings, not my suspicions) to the unorthodox Chief of our Neuro-Psychiatric Division, Captain Josiah J. Newman. At first he looked dubious, but soon he looked hornswoggled.

"How," Captain Newman finally frowned, "would you summarize all this? If you had to describe the patient—I mean prisoner—in one word, what would it be?"

I said, "Delightful."

Captain Newman put his head between his hands, moaning. "O.K., bring him around."

I instructed Sergeant Pulaski to escort Coby over to the hospital, to the NP ward. Sergeant Pulaski was beginning to look somewhat peaked, if not catatonic. I wondered if perhaps things would make more sense if the roles were reversed, and it was Coby Clay who was marching Ignatius Pulaski to the place the patients called "Psycho Beach."

Captain Newman interviewed Coby Clay for over an hour and returned him to the unhappy jurisdiction of Sergeant Pulaski.

The formal report which Captain Newman now wrote for Major Forman and, through him, Colonel Pyser, was precise, technical, thorough, and—to someone like West Point's Colonel Pyser—infuriating. I copied parts of Newman's summation, for the posterity I think it deserves:

> Coby Clay's physical reflexes are good, though not rapid. He shows excellent psychological equilibrium. He displays common sense, a sense of proportion, and a sense of humor.
>
> He sleeps well, eats well, and (aside from the singular problem for which he was referred to the undersigned) performs his soldierly duties in a responsible fashion.
>
> He may be classified as "Oral: Passive."
>
> He is somewhat euphoric but not neurotic, and in no way hypomanic.

He discusses his convictions about bedmaking (rather, about not-bedmaking) without anxiety, ambivalence, or hostility. This is impressive, clinically.

His attitude to his mother is one of respect and affection, not fear or libidinal fixation. No glib conclusions should be drawn about Oedipal complications. He seems to be equally affectionate to, and respectful of, his father.

Clay simply holds deeply encapsulated opinions about the masculine and feminine roles, placing some things firmly in the former category and others (such as bed-making) in the latter. . . .

I do not believe his opinions on this subject can be altered by therapy. I also do not believe they can be altered by punitive measures, or repeated threats thereof.

Clay may be described as having an unusual character structure. His aggressions are well in hand. His views about army life and military discipline are unique, but in no way subversive.

His ego appears to be inaccessible to conventional appeals.

In the considered, professional opinion of the undersigned, Private Coby Clay admirably illustrates the surpassing powers of a happy childhood.

(signed)

J. J. Newman,
Captain, MC

When Colonel Pyser called Captain Newman to his office, Major Forman and Captain Howard were already there, and a thick file on Coby Clay rested on Colonel Pyser's desk. The officers all looked terribly serious: Colonel Pyser kept fingering his mustache, Major Forman kept scratching one palm, and Captain Howard kept sucking his mints.

Colonel Pyser opened the conference bluntly: "Captain Newman, do you or do you not regard Private Clay as a mental defective?"

"I do not, sir."

"Do you regard him as a queer—I don't mean a fag, I mean *as* queer—in any shape, manner, or form?"

"No, sir."

Colonel Pyser cleared his throat significantly. "I take it, then, from your answers and your report, that you insist on considering Private Clay 'well adjusted?'"

"Yes, sir," said Captain Newman.

"You couldn't find *any* signs of neurosis, psychosis, or other incapacitating factors?" asked Pyser, almost plaintively.

"No, sir."

"Then how about moral turpitude?!" exclaimed Colonel Pyser. "Or antisocial behavior?"

Newman shook his head.

Colonel Pyser studied him hatefully. "So you probably would not recommend a Section Eight hearing for this feather-merchanting son-of-a-bitch?"

"No, sir."

Colonel Pyser put his hands on the arms of his chair in such a tense way that it looked as if he might spring at Captain Newman any moment. "Damn it to hell, Newman, you have recommended men for a Section Eight-ing out of the service who never gave us one-half the trouble this screwball has put the post through! And now, when we really need and can *use* an NP diagnosis, you go more conservative on me than Herbert H. Hoover!"

"But apart from not making his bed," Newman ventured, "Clay has created no difficulties——"

"'*Apart* from not making his bed!'" Colonel Pyser echoed, his cheeks turning flamingo. "'Apart from not making his *bed*'?! Man alive, what the hell more do you *want* from a nut than refusing to make his bed? And enjoying the guardhouse! I ask you again, Newman: Do you mean to sit there and tell me that you will not recommend we try this goldbrick or anarchist or whatever-the-hell-he-is on a Section Eight count?"

Newman met Colonel Pyser's glare steadily. "I *might* classify him as neurotic, a phobic type—say, a bedmaking phobia."

"Ah——"

"But Colonel, according to medical regulations that would only go with a recommendation for a CDD."

"A medical disability discharge?" shouted Colonel Pyser. "And give that galloping bastard a pension—on half pay—for the rest of his goddam life?! Over my dead body, Newman! O-ver—my—dead—body!" He leaped to his feet and paced back and forth furiously behind his high-backed chair, then wheeled on Newman. "The real, the final, the decisive question is this—*do you think this piss-cutter is fit for combat?*"

"Yes, sir," said Captain Newman.

"God!" Pyser groaned. "Look, Newman; if we send him overseas with his outfit, do you think he's going to change his opinion about making his bed on foreign soil?"

"No, sir."

"Right!" cried Pyser. "Then who the hell do you think will make his bed overseas?'"

"Someone else, sir," said Newman.

Colonel Pyser stared at Newman with a bitterness that is understandable. Newman later told me he could hear Major Forman's chair trembling from the palm-scratchings, and Captain Howard sucking on a mint as if it were an oxygen tube.

Colonel Pyser set his jaw and in his most cold, efficient, military fashion said, "One final question, Newman. *If* Clay finishes his training, and *if* I send him overseas with his outfit, then when the chips are down—when the bombs are falling and the flak is flakking and guys around him are being shot to pieces and blood is squirting high and low— what is your professional opinion? Is this joker going to fight, or is he going to wash out?!"

"This boy will never wash out," said Captain Newman.

"Oh, Christ," said Colonel Pyser.

And so when Coby Clay, that fine, delightful soldier, returned from his latest stretch in the guardhouse, rested and unruffled as of yore, and appeared before Sergeant Pulaski, smiling and considerate, the latter studied him in silence for a nervous moment before inquiring, "Coby, hey, pal, I hope you learned your lesson now? You don't want solitary and bread-and-water next. You gonna be a good Joe and make your bed?"

Before Coby could even finish the pleasant shaking of his head, Sergeant Pulaski threw his head back, crying, "Oh, hell! Oh, balls! O.K., O.K., I give up! You win! A couple million guys in this whole friggin' meathead Army, from North and South and East and West, and I have to draw you! So O.K., soldier. That's the way God wants it, that's the way He's gonna have it! I'll make your goddam bed from now on."

And he did. Every morning. Every single morning, an American sergeant made an American private's bed for him.

It was the talk of the post, of course, except at Head-quarters, where no one dared mention it.

Down the line, though, not a day passed but what Sergeant Pulaski got kidded and razzed and needled about this basic transmutation of the established order.

Then one day Private Clay loomed over Sergeant Pulaski and said, "Say, Sarge, can I ask you somethin'?"

"Come on, come on," said Pulaski crossly. "Talk fast."

Coby scratched his head. "Well, I been thinkin' out about this bedmakin'. 'Tain't fit for a grown-up man to make his own bed, like my maw says, but I been thinkin' an' scratchin' aroun' an' all, an' I don't see no right reason why a man cain't make up someone *else's* bed. Like you been doin' for me! I figger my maw or even my paw wouldn't hardly mind if I jest did that same little thing for you."

The kidding of Sergeant Pulaski stopped after that. For from then on, until that whole contingent of brave men was flown into action overseas, while Ignatius Pulaski made Coby Clay's bed each morning, Coby—humming of dark glades and promised lands—made Pulaski's.

A Handful of Heroes

EVERY man, I always say, is entitled to his own heroes. They come in all shapes and sizes: truly Great Men, triumphs of character and purpose, like Washington, Lincoln, Churchill; undiminishable titans, like Newton, Galileo, Einstein; important but detestable types, like Napoleon or Stalin; and geniuses of an order of human talent that simply surpasses explanation: Aristotle, Leonardo da Vinci, Willie Mays.

I preface *my* list of heroes by admitting that these are casual, even off-beat, idols, haphazardly collected down the years. But how I admire them! Here are seven mavericks for whose presence on Earth during my lifetime I am grateful.

1. *Konrad Lorenz,* the great Austrian naturalist; not only because he wrote *King Solomon's Ring,* as beguiling a book on animals as I ever read; and not because he discovered that a newly born gosling or duckling will accept as its mother (and obediently follow) the first moving object it perceives (!); but because he coined the truest, saddest epigram of the twentieth century:

"Man appears to be the missing link between anthropoid apes and human beings."

2. *Floyd Caves ("Babe") Herman,* outfielder for the much-mourned Brooklyn Dodgers, whose inspired confusions on the baseball diamond, in behalf of the Beloved Bums, forever enriched my memories.

Mr. Herman holds records to this day for achievement in categories no one had the foresight to dream up: Getting Entangled with Own Feet; Bumping into Teammates at Inopportune Moments; Running Bases in Wrong Direction; Trying to Catch Fly Balls with Head, Chin, Elbow or Shoulder.

Mr. Herman was surely the most *involved,* to say nothing of self-involved, outfielder our national game has yet produced. Malacologists tell me that he surpassed the octopus, which has eight arms and legs, in what he could do with only four. This is not meant as a compliment, mind you; it is a comment on Mr. Herman's habits as a fielder, in which capacity his mishaps verged on the spooky.

The moment Mr. Herman set forth in pursuit of a ball that had been hit into his neighborhood—whether to catch it, stop it, retrieve it, or just slow it down—either he or the ball went crazy. Sometimes both did. Baseball buffs with 20–20 vision have sworn by their mother's memory that line-drives headed right for Mr. Herman's station would pause, dodge, take abrupt detours, or even fight their way out of his leather grasp. Some students of the game claim that Mr. Herman was haunted and the baseballs knew it, hence placed maximum distance between themselves and him whenever they were batted within his ectoplasmic *gestalt.* I cannot say that I agree with this.

My theory is that there was something in Mr. Herman's molecular mass that physicists have only recently identified: antimatter. His nuclear singularity just screwed up Newton's Law of Universal Gravitation, because baseballs were *repelled,* not attracted, once they entered Mr. Herman's gravitational field. This astonishing reversal of the behavior of matter which varies inversely as the square of the distance between them, understandably confused Mr. Herman even more than the physicists in the box seats, and compelled him to improvise the most desperate stratagems to try to snag balls in anti-Newtonian orbits. What happened then?

Mr. Herman misjudged, dropped, bobbled, fumbled or lost balls with such frequency that he also upset experts on probability theory. Less scientific observers concluded that the man was a somnambulist, or was trying out for a part in a circus.

Whenever he committed a *faux pas*, rabid Dodger fans would wail that Mr. Herman's fingers were made of butter. Others cried that his brain was made of lard. Extremists charged that his feet were coated with glue.

Sometimes the inflamed fanatics would shift the zone to which they addressed their calumnies, accusing Mr. Herman of possessing an inordinately fat head, rubber tibia, or a cerebellum composed of mush. The unkindest of all, to my way of thinking, were the spectators who shouted questions about which team Mr. Herman was playing for.

What was even more humiliating to Mr. Herman than dropping, bobbling, fumbling, or altogether losing baseballs was the places the balls landed *after* Mr. Herman had done so: the spheroids showed a propensity for striking him on the knee, ear, elbow, or forehead. Whenever this occurred, the enraged sages in the bleachers would switch from aspersions on Mr. Herman's biochemistry to slander of his ancestry. One must have had a heart of stone not to sympathize with his plight; the emotions of an outfielder hit on the head by a fly ball are akin to those of a ballerina whose tutu drops to her knees in mid-jeté.

I should tell you that Mr. Herman always denied that baseballs actually struck various parts of his body after evading his glove. To hear him explain why his fielding went awry was to hear a master of creative alibi. But his efforts to correct his public image collapsed when one reporter inquired: "Well, how about your getting hit by a pop fly, today—right on your shoulder?"

Mr. Herman considered this thoughtfully before replying, "On the shoulders don't count."

Mr. Herman also complained about the report that he

carried lighted cigars in his pockets. I do not know how often Mr. Herman carried a lighted cigar in his pocket, but at least once, concluding a tête-à-tête with a sportswriter, he reached inside his coat pocket, removed a cigar, and proceeded to smoke it. Since he did not light the cigar, and since smoke was clearly seen to issue from it, I think we may conclude that Mr. Herman *had* placed a live or lighted stogy in his pocket.

Ring Lardner, the Rochefoucauld of baseball, once anathematized a baseball player thusly: "Although he isn't a very good fielder, he isn't a very good hitter, either." That, I am happy to tell you, could not be said about Babe Herman. He was a dandy hitter! In fact, it was only his hitting that kept him in there fielding—if that is what we may call his daily debate with ground balls.

But Mr. Herman's excellent hitting was often nullified by his heretical baserunning, in which he carried originality to extremes. Herman is the only man in history who twice invalidated home runs by the subsequent peculiarity of his movements. He accomplished this remarkable feat by suddenly reversing the direction in which he was running— reversing, that is, the conventional, or legal, course traversed by runners who desire to increase their team's score. Once, Babe was on base when a teammate walloped a home run over the wall; for reasons that have never been disclosed, Babe at once whirled around and ran *toward* the teammate, whom he then passed. Strategists of the game call this "Herman's Paradox." It has never been solved.

Babe also negated his own homer once. I know this sounds impossible, but it is true. He accomplished it by swatting the ball far out of sight and running around the bases, with laudable speed and determination, in the recognized, counterclockwise pattern. The only trouble this time was that he overtook and passed two teammates who happened to be on the bases ahead of him. This negated three runs and made men delirious for weeks.

Mr. Herman also once doubled into a double play. Of

course that sounds like a contradiction in terms, but it isn't. In fact, had there not been one man out for Brooklyn at the time, the Babe would have doubled into a *triple* play. The details of this historic achievement should be memorized by every schoolboy.

Mr. Herman came up to bat with the bases loaded and, as was his wont, dispatched a splendid high drive into deep right field. The Dodgers on first and second hesitated near their bases, naturally, before streaking ahead, in order to make sure that Herman's drive would not be caught; and it was while they were hesitating, in the manner approved by every authority on the game, that the Babe ran right past the man on first, full speed, head down, eyes glazed, intoxicated by team spirit and premonitions of glory. Herman's illegal passing so electrified his friend on first, and so paralyzed his colleague on second, that all three players reached *third* base at the same time.

This trail-blazing *contretemps* caused the beloved and long-suffering manager of the club, "Uncle" Wilbert Robinson, to announce: "That is the first time the men in this club have gotten together on anything."

3. *Harry S. Truman,* not only because of his spunk and dedication, as President, to doing what he believed to be "the right thing"; not only because of the clarity and vigor of his foreign policy; but because, at the age of eighty-one, looking back on his long, staunch, and tragically eroded efforts to establish a lasting peace, Mr. Truman concluded:

"Memories are short; appetites for power and glory are insatiable. Old tyrants depart. New ones take their place. It is all very baffling and trying."

4. *Richard Rodgers,* the Mozart of popular music, who has given me so many hours of delight—not just in listening, but in humming, singing, and whistling. I have heard Rodgers' songs played on every ocean liner I ever sailed, in every restaurant that accompanied food with music, in

every country—from Haiti to Turkey to Japan—I ever visited. And why not?

I will further brave the wrath of devotees of Poulenc by proclaiming that Mr. Rodgers is surely the most fluent, to say nothing of irresistible, musical talent of the last fifty years. Who above the age of ten does not know and love at least twenty of his captivating tunes? My favorites are: *Where or When?, With a Song in My Heart, Some Enchanted Evening, People Will Say We're in Love, Oh, What a Beautiful Mornin'!, When I Marry Mr. Snow, I Whistle a Happy Tune*—but I could go on until the corn in the sky reached an elephant's eye.

5. *Dr. Karl von Frisch*, who, after forty *years* of patient study, discovered how bees communicate with one another. Dr. von Frisch put glass sides on his honeycombs, marked his bees with different colors, placed saucers of sugar-water or honey at various distances from the hives—and watched. (He used red light, to which bees are blind.) He saw the scout bees fly out, locate the food, fill their stomachs and return to the hive—where they began to wiggle and waggle on the combs. Now, many an apiarist had seen bee scouts go through these excited dithers upon returning to their hive. What von Frisch dared to surmise was mind-boggling: Might it be that the agitated jitterbuggings of the scouts were a form of communication? And that is precisely what von Frisch's ingenious experiments proved them to be: precise signalings, in a geometrically oriented code, of where—in relation to the hive—food would be found!

Dr. von Frisch found that when food was ten yards or less away, the scout bee "danced" in a circle. As the distance of the food from the hive increased, this circular dance widened—in proportion—until, varying with distance, the dance-path assumed the shape of a sickle. And the sickle gradually changed shape, to show greater distances, into a figure-8—which meant: "over 100 yards from here"!

Nor was this all von Frisch learned. He proved that inside the hive the scout also communicates *direction*—i.e., the navigational angle along which the bees should fly—by using gravity itself as a language! The scout bee tells the swarm not only how far to go, but in which direction— *vis-à-vis the position of the sun!* How? Von Frisch, surely a genius, deduced (and then proved) that the angle at which the scout's promenade crosses an imaginary vertical line conveys the exact angle from the sun. Thus, if a scout moves straight *up* a honeycomb, that tells his hivesmen: "Fly straight toward the sun." If the scout's wagtail is 30 degrees, say, to the left of an imaginary vertical line, or 15 degrees to the right, that means respectively that food will be found 30 degrees to the left, or 15 degrees to the right, of the sun.

Nor is *that* all. The scout communicates the actual distance of food from home by the speed of his waggling: Twenty "runs" a minute signal one-half mile from the hive; twelve "runs" a minute, two miles. And if you are wondering what the scouts say, or the others learn, on cloudy days, when the sun is not visible—relax. The sun may not be visible to man, but it is to bees, who respond to ultraviolet rays with no difficulty.

Down the years of studying and experimenting with bees, von Frisch learned (I hope as much to his delight as to mine) that the language of bees changes with geography: Italian bees use dance patterns that differ from those of the Austrian bees he first studied! One of von Frisch's followers went to India, where he found added differences in the regional "dialects" of the bees' language. It seems that bees, no less than human beings, develop their own local patois.

I have no hesitation in nominating von Frisch for the Nobel Prize. In beology.

6. *Lord de l'Isle and Dudley,* about whom I know nothing except this (but what a "this" it is!): In England, after the war, he organized a legal defense fund for German Field Marshal Erich von Manstein, who was being tried as a war criminal.

You can imagine how many eyebrows were raised in London's clubs when this was announced; mutterings were heard the length and breadth of the Island, and invidious remarks raced through the Empire.

When reporters asked Lord de l'Isle and Dudley to explain why he had launched his puzzling philanthropy, he replied: "Had I met General von Manstein during the war, I would have shot him on sight." Pause. Muttered "Hear, hear!"s of approval from the press. "I am not concerned with whether von Manstein is guilty or not," milord continued. "I simply want sufficient money to insure that he will be properly represented in his trial, by a British barrister . . . I want Britain's reputation upheld."

He wanted England never to have anything to be ashamed of.

Dr. Freud

THEY came to his apartment on Vienna's *Berggasse*, in the 1880s, with diseases for which there was no physical cause, ailments unsolved by any branch of medicine: a "paralyzed" arm or suicidal depression, fits of mania or hysteria, outlandish compulsions and hallucinations as terrifying as they were inexplicable.

Herr Doktor Freud had treated the most bizarre neurasthenics, using hypnosis, under the celebrated neurologist, Jean Charcot, in Paris. Hypnosis had opened startling portals to an underworld of traumas a patient could not otherwise remember, and young Freud had achieved some dramatic cures. But he could not rid himself of the disconcerting knowledge that not everyone could be hypnotized, and —worse—that many symptoms vanished only to be replaced by others. . . .

So now Dr. Freud asked his patients to lie on a couch, behind which he sat, to minimize his presence, and utter everything that came into their minds—anything, everything, however weird or foolish or ugly it might be. He urged them to talk, that is, not in order to make sense, but with a resolute effort to disregard it. For he had the growing suspicion that, as he later wrote, any road leads to the center of that internal place where neuroses reign.

Freud listened. He noted the odd twists and turns of this new, aimless kind of talking: the rush of words abruptly stopped, with a blush or sweat or stammer; the unexpected coupling of totally incongruous ideas; the concatenation of facts and fears and fantasies that jumbled the now, the then, the never, in a turmoil where time does not exist. Could it be that "free association" simply could not remain meaningless? A patient's foolish pun would resurrect some childhood anguish; a slip of the tongue betrayed some secret shame or sin, real or but-imagined. Irrationality itself did not long remain pointless, for the unstructured ruminations of those patients on his couch again and again uncovered buried truths and unsuspected cravings. Patterns emerged —persistent, meaningful, and soon predictable—from even that carnival of masks we call dreams.

Freud listened. Occasionally, he would suggest to a patient that perhaps today's headache was a form of self-punishment for yesterday's hostile outburst; or he would remark on how a long-forgotten name had triggered some recollection of the denied. It began to seem to him that nothing in human behavior is undetermined, which meant that every symptom *served some purpose.* Behind a tic, a phobia, a formless anxiety or odd obsession, some inner conflict unfolded, conflict born of shame or lust or fear.

And then a stranger truth disclosed itself: this rambling, unguided talking, not supplemented by medicines of any sort, *cured.* . . . Could it be that symptoms were "substitute gratifications"? Could physical sickness represent a psychological need? A paralyzed limb, a tormenting eczema, tenacious insomnia or nonorganic illness—were these self-punishing expiations for unbearable (and uncommitted) transgression?

In 1896, Sigmund Freud described some of his cases and tentative findings to Vienna's Society of Psychiatry and Neurology. The furor that broke around him never abated. He was branded a charlatan, a near lunatic, a purveyor of "disgraceful bosh, rot, and nonsense." One learned professor charged that such vile material was fit for the police, not

the clinic. Freud was called a sex-ridden sensationalist, ped-
dling personal delusions that were nothing but "filth and
pornography."

No man less fitted so unsavory a role. Sigmund Freud was
a most moral, bourgeois, even prudish man. He was a considerate father and husband. He loved to walk in the mountains, and was a modest collector of antiquities from Egypt
and Greece. He disliked small talk, enjoyed a weekly game
of cards with his friends, and disapproved of off-color jokes.
Dignified, proud, slightly aloof, he was conservative in dress
and wore the proper physician's neatly trimmed beard. He
studied visitors or colleagues with a direct gaze many found
too penetrating for comfort. He adored his adoring mother,
who called him "my golden son," and he lunched with her
every Sunday as long as she lived. (She died at ninety-five.)
His only vice, to which he was truly addicted, was cigars:
he smoked twenty a day.

A brilliant student, Freud had entered medical school at
seventeen, ignoring the nasty anti-Semitism he encountered
in a Vienna where that seamy prejudice flourished. "I could
never grasp why I should be ashamed of my origin," he
wrote. "At an early date, I became aware of my destiny—
to belong to the critical minority . . . [and I developed] a
certain independence of judgment." It is revealing that he
could be so calm about discrimination, or analyze disagree-
able experiences so that he benefited from them.

His scientific record, after he was graduated from medical school, is impressive: first-rate laboratory research in
physiology, neurology, and the anatomy of the brain; disci-
plined attempts to explain the puzzling disorders found in
psychiatric wards or clinics. He used cocaine for a painful
condition and, noting its analgesic properties, recommended
it with such enthusiasm (he did not know its ominous ad-
dictive powers) that the error darkened his career.

He read six or seven languages and was a connoisseur
of the classics, immensely erudite about the Bible and the
mythology of ancient Egypt, Greece and Rome. He studied
for a year in London, where he formed a lifelong love of

Shakespeare and Milton, and translated a volume of John Stuart Mill into his native German.

Now, exploring the virgin domain he named "psychoanalysis," Freud accepted severe economic adversities, for he had to sacrifice much of an already meager medical practice. He felt guilty about the price his family paid for his choice of so aberrant a specialization. He offended all but a handful of men by presenting them with a picture of man that challenged the cherished moral bases of Christianity and Judaism. For forty years, his lectures, writings, clinical papers and books scandalized the world. Like Darwin, he especially horrified the religious.

Our behavior, said Freud, is only partly governed by morality or reason or will. In each of us, below consciousness, churns the "id," a cauldron of instinctual energy— primitive hungers and rages, savage greeds and hatreds and criminal desire. From this atavistic reservoir, ego and conscience are painfully formed. "Libido," the source of our sexuality, drives and dominates us all, even in our uninnocent infancy. The little boy is possessed by incestuous yearnings for his mother, the little girl for her father, and each child harbors murderous feelings for the parent who, possessing or possessed by the other, prevents the gratification of primeval concupiscence. In this fierce internal drama, which Freud named the "Oedipus complex," human character is formed. Siblings compete for parental love, and kill each other in their fantasies for the fantasy of incestuous fulfillment.

Freud saw love and hate as twins that torment us with lifelong "ambivalence." We are each born part male, part female, he observed, and toss throughout our lives between homosexual and heterosexual strivings. All of our prized individuality, our unique personality traits, are rooted in early "fixations" in eroticized zones: oral, anal, phallic. Eating, drinking, imagining; talking or writing or creating; questioning, searching, building, believing—everything from the satisfaction of our appetites to the marvels of art and science proceed from that fundamental organization of eroticized emotion. We "project" or "displace" our sexualized strivings into manifestations of reason or beauty or physical achievement. Music, mathematics, philosophy; ambition, cynicism, empathy—all draw upon our subterranean reservoir of libido.

The unconscious of man has no sense of time, and is blind to sense or proportion or restraint. It operates with its own system of logic, its own rewards, reprisals, and symbolic transactions. And in the controls we learn we must impose upon our desires, we come to punish ourselves for our wishes no less than for our deeds.

Guilt is the core, the center and the censor of civilization. It is the repression of our instinctual demands that makes human society possible. Guilt is our helmsman and our scourge. And when the unending, pitiless war between natural impulse and humanizing taboos becomes intolerable, some of us escape by a "flight into illness." For our defenses against our native destructiveness are sometimes too vulnerable to maintain our virtue, or too inflexible to preserve our sanity.

Freud saw men's basic experiences as universal. Genius or dolt, Oxonian or Senegalese, mystic or athlete or sage— we are each the product and the prisoner of our childhood. Everything we do or dream or wish is, in the ultimate analysis, determined.

We may forget (or think we forget what, in the deeper recesses of the psyche, we know) through fatigue, or evasion, or the erosions of time; but most of our forgetting is functional. We "repress," rather than forget. We push down, out of mind, the painful, the upsetting, the loathsome, the threatening. But what is repressed may one day break through the protecting dikes—in symptoms, in absurd or irrational conduct, and, most commonly, in our dreams.

Freud proposed the astounding doctrine that every dream, however grotesque, is packed with meaning. Dreams are a language, a secret language, a lexicon of symbols we can learn to decipher. Our dreams, like our legends and our myths, are in part "wish fulfillments" in which our forbidden impulses masquerade—for they must evade the stern suppressions of conscience (the "superego") and the vigilant controls of reason (the "ego"). So it is that, in the strange symbols of the night, balconies may stand for breasts or buttocks; the sea for birth; a snake or arch the organ each resembles. The dream, said Freud, in one of many brilliant metaphors, is "the royal road to the unconscious."

We break down emotionally not because we are immoral, said Freud, but because we so desperately try to be moral. The flaws in the architecture of feeling impair our capacity to adjust our needs to society's sovereign prohibitions. Parents cripple their children emotionally by punishing them for their natural exploration of their bodies, or their natural curiosity about where babies come from, or their inevitable interest in the "primal scene" of parental copulation.

Freud was as fertile in theorizing as he was uninhibited in observing. He made the most surprising correlations, linking paranoia to homosexuality, for instance, miserliness to the child's early fascination with its own excrement, philanthropy to penance for secret guilt, saintliness to an "overreaction" against sadistic temptations. The anger he provoked by such concepts was magnified by his refusal to prettify his vocabulary. He made no concessions to propriety, using words that shocked doctors no less than laymen: "Masturbation . . . penis envy . . . return to the womb . . . homosexuality . . . castration . . . anal eroticism."

In this chilling, furibund landscape, this harrowing world where "dark, unfeeling, unloving powers" shape our destiny, what hope can psychoanalysis, that long and painful process of self-dissection, offer the sick, the bewildered, the damaged, the neurotic? Psychoanalysis provides man with a new technique of thinking as well as healing; a new method of self-understanding: self-knowledge that enlists the irrational in the service of reason. Psychoanalysis is a way of exploring the buried continent of the unconscious—there to confront our hidden tyrants and rob them of their hidden power. It is a way to restore mercy to conscience gone vengeful and relentless. Psychoanalysis converts the random into

the purposeful; it reveals the unaccidental function of "accidents"; it makes the "trivial" significant; it endows the
"irrelevant" with unexpected consequence.

And the psychoanalyst himself? He is a neutral figure
who neither advises nor consoles nor condemns, no matter
how wicked or shame-laden the revelations which the self
wrests from its adamantine defenses. The patient "transfers"
his deepest affections and hostilities to the psychoanalyst,
as if to a father or mother or God, for the psychoanalyst
becomes a surrogate for anyone loved or hated, feared or
admired. The analyst helps the patient to dare to see what
swarms behind his "resistances," to confront his deepest
and most undesired impulsions—until he is strong enough
emotionally, freed from symbolic shackles, no longer to need
his neurotic defenses or the analyst's illuminations.

Psychoanalyzed, men are liberated from the despotism of
the unconscious. They are able to choose, no longer vassals
of the tyrants within them. They are strong enough to moderate the ferocity of their demands, upon themselves or
upon others. They are free, at last, to face the inescapable
frustrations and sufferings of living.

As if all this were not enough, Freud crossed psychology's
conventional frontiers, plunging beyond medical (albeit emotional) disorders and "psychosomatic" diseases to examine
men's shibboleths. In time, he modified some of the sardonic
opinions I now quote, but the world of ideas was profoundly
changed by his clinical, iconoclastic judgments:

Morality? It rests "on the inescapable exigencies of human cohabitation."

The meaning of life? "Nobody asks . . . the purpose of the
lives of animals."

God? A naive magnification of the kind, protecting, all-
forgiving father for whom all children long and, in their
imaginings, invent.

Religion? Once a bastion against the beasts within us,
religion has become a "mass obsessional neurosis . . . patently
infantile . . . incongruous with reality."

Love? "One is very crazy when in love."

Sexual morality? "As society defines it . . . [it is] contemptible."

Peace? Einstein wrote to ask Freud if and how the curse of war could be abolished. With care and melancholy, Freud replied that he had found no way to dispel the doubt that men will entirely subjugate their ferocious aggressions. Civilization is a barrier to human destructiveness, but it is a barrier periodically breached by the forces of instinctual insatiability.

History simply had no parallel for so harsh and corrosive a vision. Freud refused to appease men with emollient consolations. His frightening theories, his bluntness, his shriveling candor, seemed to drain virtue even out of childhood, altruism, idealism. He stripped motherhood itself of its encrusted sentimentalizations.

This cool, skeptical, ever-analyzing surgeon of the soul treated sin as sickness, not evil; he replaced innocence with insecurity; he brushed aside the precious "illusion" of our linkage to the divine. He made conscience the creation not of God but of parental punishments and displeasure. He paid not the slightest lip service to immortality. As for man's sacred soul: Where is it located; and of what elements is it composed; and how can its existence be confirmed—except in mystical assumptions that evade any semblance of evidence?

He was a stubborn, pragmatic philosopher who offered men no uplifting messages, only antiseptic clarifications. He saw maturity as the accommodation to unpleasant and undesired realities.

It is hardly surprising that the Vatican denounced psychoanalysis, that Moscow and her minion Marxists everywhere attacked Freud's "bourgeois, decadent deceptions," that preachers and teachers and parents and philosophers voiced outrage over a doctrine so "diseased . . . perverted . . . [or] obsessed with sex."

Yet, for all the condemnations, no twentieth-century figure so profoundly altered our thinking about ourselves. Freudian ideas invaded ordinary conversation, and were soon dinner-table clichés: "She's neurotic. . . . He isn't bad; he's *sick*. . . . Her cold is psychosomatic. . . . He was always in love with his mother. . . . She's a mess of ambivalences. . . . He never came to terms with his homosexual impulses. . . ."

What the pedants and moralizers shunned, artists seized upon with enormous excitement. Freud inspired poets, playwrights, painters to plumb the world below the surfaces men show the world; to break away from the constraining traditions of art and fiction and drama; to voyage into the cabalistic realm of symbols; to conjure new ways, new modes, new forms for self-expression; to ignore the authority of the conventional and the familiar; to experiment in nonrepresentational, nonrational creativity. Joyce, Picasso, Proust, T. S. Eliot, Eugene O'Neill, Arthur Schnitzler, Sherwood Anderson, Thomas Mann—they were all his beneficiaries.

Not that Freud approved of all the tumult he had inspired. A famous painter came to Vienna and spent an hour in enthusiastic praises of Freud's theories; when he left, Freud said, "That man is crazy." And of some painters' fragmentations of form, Dr. Freud, a classicist in taste, said, "That is not art; it is infantile."

He was a stubborn and opinionated man, difficult to know, easier to admire than love. He was ridden by inner conflict between systematic inquiry and what he called his "daemon of creative speculation." He was a naive judge of friends and colleagues, and often complained of having been betrayed. He was honest enough to write: "An intimate friend and a hated enemy have always been indispensable to my emotional life." He never forgave Jung and Alfred Adler for their "apostasy."

He could be unbelievably ingenuous. I cannot forget the episode, reported by Ernest Jones, concerning a letter Freud received from a woman in an English village, complaining that she had been seduced by her analyst. Freud demanded that the English Society of Psycho-analysis expose and expel the heinous culprit; and when an English analyst told him the woman must be hallucinating, since there was no psychoanalyst at all in the town mentioned, Freud tapped the letter indignantly and exclaimed: "I have the letter right here!"

Behind his self-control, Freud was a man of powerful emotions and recurrent melancholia. His love letters, during an extremely prolonged courtship, attest to the most intense jealousy and indecision. He guarded his privacy fiercely, even with his children; but he was indiscreet in discussing cases and colleagues, or in taking trips with his sister-in-law.

He held a gloomy view of mankind, once writing, "Most men are trash," or, again, expressing his "contempt of people and the detestable world." Yet when a critic asked him why he concentrated his attention and his work on man's immorality, Freud, surprised, replied, "But I take morality for granted!"

He was as unillusioned about himself as he was about others. "I have never done anything mean or malicious," he once wrote, "and I cannot trace any temptation to do so, so I am not in the least proud of it. . . . When I ask myself why I [behave] honorably, I have no answer. . . . Why I— and, incidentally, my six children—have to be thoroughly decent human beings is quite incomprehensible to me." It was a startling confession from the man who more than any other understood the massive power of the superego, the dominating force of childhood training, the lifelong hegemony of early indoctrination.

Freud held no high regard for his own talents. "I have always been dissatisfied with my gifts," he said; and he once complained that after thirty years of the most diligent research, he could not answer the simple question: "What does a woman *want*?" He expected women to be gentle, adoring, compliant helpmeets to men. His patient and devoted wife remained uninvolved in his work and was not at home with his theories.

He was very strong of will, capable of the most intense and prolonged concentration. He was also as self-critical as he was proud: "I am not really a man of science. I am by temperament . . . a conquistador," he said, and went on to list his governing qualities: "curiosity, boldness, and tenacity." When one of his disciples told him he was a great man, Freud dryly remarked "To discover great things is not to be great."

He withstood venomous calumny ("It rains abuse," he wrote a friend); and endured hostility for decades on end. During his self-chosen apprenticeship, in an area of knowledge no one had penetrated, he suffered "long years of . . . painful loneliness."

He was a brave man, and once charged into a crowd in Vienna that was chanting anti-Semitic slogans, brandishing his cane and inviting their attack. And when Nazi Storm Troopers came into his flat on the *Berggasse,* to confiscate his books and possessions, his savings and passport and personal treasures, he treated the invaders with contempt.

Freud carved out an immense new province for psychology; he gave sociology the long-missing bridge between individual and group behavior; he gave anthropology a new instrument of understanding: the developmental process, the study of how children are raised in different cultures and how that training affects character types and social values.

You have but to look around you to recognize the magnitude of his influence: How many nursery schools today accept love as the child's most precious anchor? In how many homes does "playing doctor" no longer incur stern reprisal? How many marriages separate passion from disgust? How many doctors now trace stuttering to inhibition, or impotence to fear, or asthma to anxiety, or ulcers to frustration?

But it is folly to stop there, to accept psychoanalysis as sacred revelation, or treat Freud as more infallible than, say, Newton. Freud erred, I think, in many ways. He made sweeping conclusions from meager or dubious evidence. (Unlike some of his disciples, he admitted it.) He elaborated theories that are self-fulfilling, which means that they are supportable only within a scheme that accepts his assumptions. He structured his findings in such a way that as they evolved they simply could not be *proved* to be right or wrong. He used categories that permit the same phenomenon to be either x or its opposite. (Among unsophisticated psychoanalysts, at least, if a patient accepts the analyst's interpretation of a dream, that is held to validate the analyst's hypothesis; if the patient does not, that is attributed to resistance, which also confirms the hypothesis. How and when can such analysts know when they are wrong?

Freud could not resist the striking metaphor, even in clinical reports whose effectiveness was diminished by their embellishment. He made interesting statements about, say, men's fantasies under perilous circumstances, but the statements did not jibe with the testimony of survivors, or the diaries of men who had died of cold, thirst, or hunger: Sexual dreams were not as omnipresent as he supposed.

He remained surprisingly uninterested in the processes of reasoning and learning, and he underestimated the leverage of both, I think, on character. He tried scrupulously to distinguish observation from speculation, but he was so much more creative than systematic that he poured out a wealth and a welter of untested intuitions, correlations, guesses, models. I think he underestimated the role of the psychoanalytic experience itself in persuading patients to accept the hardly sacrosanct premises on which the therapeutic enterprise rests. "The death instinct," as Freud originally presented it, appears to be dead and buried.

He was a marvelous writer, a gifted stylist with an unerring sense of the thrust of narrative. He wrote more like a novelist than a scientist, and won the Goethe Prize for German literature. He tried hard to guard against the power and impatience of his imagination, and he apologized to the world because his cases were so dramatic, devoid of "the serious stamp of science." But he never budged from the assertion that all of his theories, however singular or "grotesque," rested on "the most extensive and laborious observations."

His orthodox followers do him a disservice, it seems to me, in confusing intuition with data, in treating speculations as doctrines, in pushing attractive inferences to putative conclusions in circular parodies of thinking. The canonical keepers of the flame have made psychoanalysis a theology. They even excommunicate heretics who question unquestionable dogma. Many psychoanalytic theories have yet to be verified through research or experiment not precommitted to their validity.

The true believers forget that Freud had the courage to revise his theories many times. (It dawned on him, in early cases, that he had been too credulous with patients suffering from hysteria, who traced their symptoms back to "fictitious traumas," entirely imagined scenes of having been seduced. But he pressed on, to make the invaluable discovery that in man, and especially in the neurotic, "psychic reality" can operate as "actual reality.")

Please do not misunderstand me. All this criticism is overshadowed, for me, by the sheer brilliance, originality, depth, power and range of Freud's work. He was a genius—as an observer, an investigator, a theorist. He contended with surpassingly complicated phenomena that, like nuclear physics, circumvent consistency or play hob with the modalities of causation.

He had to invent techniques for his inquiry. He constructed a wholly new model of the human psyche. He discovered an interior universe, the unconscious, which thinkers from Plato to Blake to Nietzsche had dimly apprehended but never defined or examined or systematized. He explained the dynamic process and contests within that strange nether world.

He located the source of men's emotional disturbances not in medieval demons or imaginary vapors, mystical seizures or empty diagnoses made to sound important with Latin nomenclature; he focused his analysis on the ordinary, innocuous, observable family itself—to reveal forces as mighty and as tragic as any we find in Aeschylus or Shakespeare or

Dostoevski (from whom, incidentally, Freud said he learned more than from any psychologist).

He solved the ancient puzzles of dreams—and delusions, hallucinations, insanity. He swept aside the centuries-old division between mind and body, between normal and "abnormal," finding both, in varying mixtures, in "the psychopathology of everyday life." That electrifying phrase was the title of an early, simple book that opened new vistas to those who read it. (There were not many readers for his early writings.) Dealing with the most commonplace happenings—mislaying a letter, arriving too early or too late, losing a check or a purse or a wallet, being anxious about a child or parent or spouse—Freud's explanations made homely events reveal tensions that threatened the equilibrium of the self. And, of course, he demonstrated as no one before the far-reaching, many-faceted sovereignty of sexuality. He enriched the study of man more than anyone since Aristotle.

He was truly among those historic figures who, he sighed, "disturb the sleep of mankind."

Freud never set out to moralize, but he taught us new respect for the intricacy of man's burdens and men's fate. He surely enlarged our compassion. If his "cheerful pessimism," as he called it, holds any hope or promise, it is that we *can* learn to face the enemies within ourselves, whom our better selves can tame, if not destroy.

Freud bore the most excruciating pain for sixteen years. He underwent thirty operations (!) for cancer of the mouth, and was forced to wear a heavy, "barbarous" prosthetic device. He suffered unending torture, but rarely complained, and he refused to use the drugs his doctors urged upon him, saying, "I prefer to think in torment than not to think clearly."

He was eighty-two years old when Hitler drove him out of Vienna—or, better, permitted him to leave, after pressures from some of the most distinguished men in the world, discreet intervention from the American Embassy, tireless behind-the-scenes negotiations by Marie Bonaparte, herself a psychoanalyst, and the undisclosed greasing of Nazi palms in Austria and Berlin. William Bullitt supervised the abrupt departure to Paris and London.

Freud died in London in 1939, at eighty-three, wondering how "my many beginnings" would fare in the future, glumly characterizing his contributions as only "patchwork," hoping that "perhaps I have opened up a pathway for an important advance in our knowledge."

He had tried to alleviate human suffering, to understand things that had not yielded their secrets to healers and shamans and physicians down the centuries. But he was, in the last analysis, dedicated to analysis itself. He exemplified the scientist's respect for what *is*. He turned emotions into *materia medica*. He charted the dark ocean of the unconscious.

He would not camouflage the ugly, or sugar-coat the bestial, or soften the blasphemous. He could not view kings or saints or prophets except through diagnostic eyes. He would not court popularity, for his intelligence was an incorruptible as his sense of honor.

He was the Columbus of psychology, which still awaits its Euclid.

A Troubling Tale of
Good and Evil

𝓌𝓌𝓌𝓌𝓌𝓌𝓌𝓌𝓌𝓌𝓌𝓌𝓌𝓌𝓌𝓌𝓌𝓌𝓌𝓌𝓌𝓌𝓌𝓌𝓌𝓌

WE were in Rome again, making a pilgrimage to the loveliest open-air gallery in the world, the Museo Nazionale in the ancient, lofty ruins that were once the Baths of Caracalla. As we returned to the hotel one evening, the concierge handed me a cablegram. It was from New York:

> POPS SEVENTY-EIGHTH BIRTHDAY TUESDAY. KNOW
> HOW MUCH HE WOULD APPRECIATE A CARD, LETTER,
> OR CABLE FROM YOU. DON'T LET HIM DOWN. LOVE,
> KIDDO.
>
> ALBERTO

"Who's Alberto?" asked my wife.

"A friend," I said. "His name is Albert, but he likes to gussy it up—to suit the locale. He once sent me a cable to Madrid signed 'Don Juano,' and one from the Congo signed 'Albino.' "

"But are you close to his father?"

"N–no. It's just that each year Albert sends out these reminders of his father's birthday to friends around the globe. He wants the old man to be flooded by birthday greetings."

"What a sentimental son," she said.

"Albert?" I laughed. "He's the most cynical, skeptical, blistering misanthrope you ever laid eyes on."

Albert (I can't tell you his last name) has perpetually mocking eyes, his lips verge on a permanent sneer, and his most frequent gesture is a sarcastic lift of an unkiddable eyebrow. I have never heard Albert say "Hiya?" or "How's it going?" without an ironic tinge. He is as pessimistic as Diogenes, perhaps for the same reason. All this I told my wife.

"He sounds awful," she said.

"He isn't. He has the mushiest heart of anyone I know."

"Oh, no, he doesn't," said my lost rib. "You do; you are the world's champion sucker for pure, sheer *shmaltz.*"

II

I should tell you that I run into Albert only four or five times a year. He lives in Manhattan, a mere stone's throw from me, but has never thrown one. He loathes sentimentality, and has a horror of appearing to need company.

He practices no visible occupation except dissipation, and lives as though money should present a problem only to peasants. When people ask what he does for a living, as out-of-towners occasionally do, Albert answers gravely, "I advise embezzlers," or "I'm in economics: I spend money," or (to the curious and female), "I'm conducting advanced research for the Kinsey Institute; would you like to help advance the cause of science?"

Some Broadway night owls insist that Albert is on the payroll of a movie studio, as a scout for properties, literary and human, or illiterary. I happen to know that Albert had been a publicity wizard and made a fortune on A T & T in the days before the Internal Revenue Service went cannibal. I also know that for at least ten years Albert has been burning his candle at four ends (he cuts it in the middle).

No one has ever seen him erect before lunch, which he never eats, since he calls it breakfast; and it is hard to attend a Broadway opening or a ding-a-ling movie première, drop in at Sardi's or 21, without spying Albert and a beautiful date. Where he gets them, God certainly knows.

What makes all this so surprising, as I said at the beginning, is that Albert is the most old-fashioned, sentimental and devoted of sons. He adored, he revered, he worshiped his mother, and according to the Freudian savants at the Sixth Avenue Delicatessen, that's why Albert will never marry.

When his mother died, several years ago, Albert went into more than mourning: he vanished. He was not to be seen at any of the haunts—bistros, fooderies, theaters—he had, year after year, haunted. No one knew where on earth Albert could have gone. The Jamaica-to-Barbados circuit reported that he had clearly given up the sun. The *soigné* part of the Acapulco-Villefranches-Sardinia syndrome saw neither hide nor hair of him. As for, say, a de luxe Air Trip Around the World, the very thought was absurd: Albert detested tours almost as much as he despised tourists. Even a cruise to Buenos Aires, or the bright, bleached isles of Greece, was ruled out because Albert was in absolute terror of seasickness. He had once developed vertigo at pier 92, in a static stateroom on the *Queen Elizabeth*, where a champagne chorus of friends was seeing off Laurence Olivier or Ava Gardner or some other darling of the gods.

III

About three months after Albert's mother's funeral, I ran into him—literally—as he came lurching out of a dairy restaurant (alas, now departed) on Upper Broadway. He looked terrible: unshaved, no tie, a scarecrow in a trench coat that looked as though it had been used while tarring a chickenhouse.

"Albert!"

"Oh, Jesus," he groaned.

"How are you?"

"Just great," he glared. "Can't you see? I am sitting on top of the world——"

"You look terrible."

"Fancy that," he snorted.

"Where in the world have you been? No one——"

"Where have I *been*? I have been exactly four blocks from here, for Chrissake, *that's* where I have been! Where else would I be? With my old man! Since my mother, well, passed away"—(It was the only time I heard Albert use a euphemism)—"Pop is just *dying* of loneliness. Not pining or whining, chum: dying. . . . What the hell's the *matter* with everybody? Anyone I run into these days acts like I've been living it up in Vegas. People are too goddam stupid to know what life's all about! *Goom*-bye, Mary Sunshine."

"Wait a minute, you slob," I said. "Let's have coffee."

It was the "you slob" that got him. He turned back to me. "Sanka very much. Are you an Eagle Scout or a seeing-eye dog?"

"You'll pay," I said.

"Now I know you're for real."

Over coffee and blintzes, which I had minuscule difficulty in persuading him to test for taste and endurance, Albert blurted, "Honest to God, I'm worried sick. The old man has simply shut the world out of that apartment he shared for like fifty *years* with my mother: Pop just sits there, staring at—at what? At nothing. Oh, sure, he goes through old letters, and cries over old pictures, and I've steered him into pasting theater-ticket stubs and Philharmonic programs and flyers for rallies at the Garden—all the things he and my mother shared—into big scrapbooks. He must have fifteen of those goddam books bulging with mementos. And it's done him as much good as taking jasmine tea!"

Gloomily, Albert went on to describe the stratagems he had dreamed up in an effort to revive the old man's interest in living. He had phoned his father's cousin and old cronies, and asked his Masonic lodge fellows to drop in, and invited one and all up for lunch, coffee, drinks, a *nosh*. He had stocked Papa's apartment with liquor, soft drinks, beer, games: checkers, pinochle cards, Scrabble, backgammon. He had bought a color television set. Each day, magazines, candies, glazed fruits were delivered to the apartment. No Hollywood star Albert ever ballyhooed had received such attention, such affection, such prodigies of promotion as Albert lavished on his aging father.

And the old man pined, and was lonely, and only drew deeper into the shell of his sorrow.

"God!" Albert ended glumly. "I'll be a son-of-a-bitch if I know what to do now."

"Can I help?" I asked, not with confidence.

He studied me out of the colder corner of his eye. "Sure. Come up. See Pop. . . . I mean right now. Unless you're due at the White House."

"I'll come," I said.

His eyes widened. "Well, how do you like that?" he beamed. "Five gold stars for neatness."

The apartment was on Riverside Drive, a large, pleasant place, really, with what should have been a splendid view of the Palisades—had not all the shades been pulled down. Most of the furniture was covered with sheets; so were the mirrors.

Albert's father was sitting in a big, brown overstuffed chair. He was in his pajamas and a woolen robe.

"Hey, Pop!" Albert sang out before he even pulled the key out of the lock. "Look who's come to see you! *You* remember Leo. He wrote that story I read you last week——"

The old man stirred. "Oh, yes, yes." His eyes were watery.

"Aren't you going to shake hands, Pop?" Albert chided him.

"Oh, excuse me, yes," said the old man. Shakily, he raised a celery stalk of a hand. It was cold.

After some overly jolly banter and flat jokes, Albert chirped, "O.K., Pop, take a rest," and led me to the door. "See what I mean?" he whispered glumly. "But thanks for coming." He looked shattered, and I felt sorry for him.

IV

A week or so later, Albert telephoned. Would I meet him for lunch at Lindy's? "It's urgent, kiddo."

He was at his usual table. "Hiya! Still swindling your

readers? What'll you drink?...Me? Omigod, *you* ought to know I'm on the wagon! Booze nearly killed me. I go in strictly for simple, wholesome food....Waiter, I'll have a pastrami on pumpernickel, cole slaw on the side, and a bottle of root beer."

He ate almost absently, talking all the while. "Listen, Professor, I called you because I had a brainstorm. You must know people like sociologists, psychiatrists, experts in all that jazz. Well, why can't *they* come up with something good for Pop? Frankly, I'm at the end of my rope....I've even come to think is there maybe some old-folks home I can send him to? Never did I think the day would come I'd consider a thing like that! But I *have* to!...Pop has nothing to live for. He's just waiting to kick off!"

"I'm awfully sorry——"

"I'm awfully sorry, too, but what the hell good is that?" he cried. "I thought maybe you could ask some of those experts, the head-shrinkers, the group therapists..."

I had never before seen Albert uncertain, uncynical, or chastened.

"I'll do the best I can," I said.

"That's damn nice of you," sighed Albert. "I won't tell anyone you're a square."

I telephoned friends at N.Y.U. and colleagues at Columbia, a clinic in New Haven and a geriatorium on Long Island. I spoke to a bright young doctor at Montefiore who specialized in treating the old, and he referred me to a psychiatrist I've known since he was a nail-biter, and *he* passed me on to a Social Service Supervisor who was extremely informative but ended our dialogue asking if I knew of a job "in publishing or a bookstore or *anywhere* I can get away from these frustrated monsters I work with."

In several days, I called Albert, very cheerful, a raft of notes at my side. "Al, I've got some *ex*cellent leads!"

His tone was odd—mocking. "*Hel*-lo, sweetheart. Do tell."

I told him all I had found out, not skimping on the adjectives, describing several communities for "Senior Citizens" that——

"And what," he interrupted, "do they actually do all day?"

"Oh, they have a very rich program," I assured him. "Canasta tournaments, lectures, dances, handicrafts——"

"*Handi*crafts? You mean stringing beads and weaving trusses?"

"No, no, Al. They——"

"Forget it! Thanks for trying, but I couldn't wait for you long-hairs so I worked something out myself, and it's working!"

"And what," I asked coolly, "is that?"

"Friends," he said. "When you come right down to it, what's Pop's basic trouble? He's alone. That's all. He's lonely. . . . And what's the best cure for loneliness? People. Nice, friendly souls with time on their hands. So, I got a group of Good Samaritans and there's a regular schedule posted in Pop's apartment! A nice lady comes in to make him breakfast and reads him the papers. Another fixes his lunch and takes him for a little walk. Another cooks his dinner. Get it? *I just don't leave Pop time to be lonely* anymore! *Goom*-bye, genius!"

I was, of course, miffed. It was typical of Albert to act impulsively, without telling me to call off my research, and before I had even had a proper chance to tell him all that the experts had recommended. . . . And yet, the longer I thought of it, the more I was compelled to admire Albert's idea. His father was, after all, in a second childhood. And what is childhood's crowning solace? Who first comforted us in our sorrows, soothed our fears, dissolved our despair? Who first smiled over our errors, laughed at our humor, healed our bruises of defeat? Who, indeed, but the eternal Mother? And who could now better understand Pop, and minister to his grief?

Albert's instinct, I had to admit, was uncanny: to find a corps of maternal souls—not antiseptic nurses or neurotic social workers, but warm, middle-aged women—to cook for the old man, fuss over him, indulge his crotchets. It was really an inspired idea! Albert, I decided, was a genius.

V

I went to the beach for a long, working summer and it was a month after I returned, in October, before I heard that crooning, affectionate, maddening telephone greeting: "*Hel*-lo, pussy cat."

"Albert! How are you? How's your father?"

"How *is* he? He is a new human being, that's how he is." His voice dropped. "He can't hear me—he's taking a nap. Come up and see him for yourself. . . . Gu-reat! What do you mean 'when?' Right now! . . . But don't let on I called you, for Chrissake. Pretend it was your idea."

I took a taxi, a form of transportation usually driven, in New York, by recidivist Kamikazes; but the driver I drew in the deadly sidewalk lottery was a dyspeptic who stopped at every other green light to check his astigmatism. By the time I reached Riverside Drive and 84th Street, I had forgotten what day it was. And all *this* was forgotten the moment I entered Albert's father's abode, for the tableau that soothed my orbs was enough to last a man through a winter in Smackover, Arkansas. Pop was playing Parcheesi with an appetizing little redhead and a toothsome sweater girl whose salient attractions were not her teeth.

"Well, well, well!" called Albert. "Look who's here! What a surprise!"

Pop shook my hand firmly. "Say, this *is* a surprise." His eyes were dancing. "How nice of you to stop by, a busy man like you. . . . How do you like my boy Albert? *Such* a son! Who else would know so many charming librarians?"

I coughed, although there was nothing stuck in my throat.

"You know what a big reader Albert is," said Pop.

I was careful to glance toward Albert casually. He had made a little temple of his fingers and was gazing at the ceiling, a convert to Zen.

"Time for your treat, Pop!" I heard a dulcet voice sing out; a cherry-lipped Cyprian bounced out of the kitchen, carrying some Ovaltine. Her sheer mammary mass made me giddy.

Now the sister of mercy in the sweater exclaimed, "Got to run, Pop. See you tomorrow. Same time." She pecked him on the cheek and, dashing out, collided with the mother-figure who was checking in: an undulating Dionysian who flung her arms out, thrushed, "Oh, you great, big, beautiful *doll!*" and, sailing past Albert and me, planted a fat, wet smooch on the old man's cheek. "How's my fella?"

"Pretty good, Sandra," smiled Mr. Recent Depression. "How was the lecture?"

"The who?" asked Sandra.

"The U.S. Geodetic Program for the Seventies!" Albert blared at her.

"Oh, *that* lecture," said Sandra. "It was just wonderful, Pop. It was—well, like going to a church. I feel—well, *clean,* inside. . . . How about a game of checkers? Or should I read you Lenny Lyons' column?"

Things waxed (they never waned) that way around me for an hour. The front door kept opening and closing as therapeutic maidens drifted in and wafted out, "lookers" in every size, complexion and coiffure; one was carrying a Pekinese with an elaborate bow around its neck, who fortunately refused to lick my lobes in the way his mistress, if that is what she was, kept "tootsie-wootsie"-ing him to.

The telephone rang five or six times, during my dazed sojourn, and Albert answered the callers crisply, rather in the manner of a general issuing bulletins: "You're not scheduled until five, Marcia. . . . Tibby? Hel-*lo,* sweetie pie. Tomorrow, lunch. *Naturally* with Pop. I'll come in later. No. After my piccolo lesson, you little dreamboat."

I was muttering murky thoughts when I crept out, but no one seemed to notice.

VI

That night, bristling with virtue, icy in *Stimmung,* I spoke to the prodigal son.

"It was wonderful of you to come up," said Albert. "How do you think Pop looks?"

"He looks healthier, happier, and more longevitous than either you or me," I said. "But Al, who are all those—'librarians'?"

"What the hell difference does that make?" he exploded.

"They do not come from the U.S. Geodetic Service," I murmured.

"Very funny. O.K.! Who do you think has time to spend with an old man in the daytime? Men go to work. Women have children, mothers, shopping, bridge clubs. The only so-called human beings *I* know of who sit around with nothing to do all day are the ones who work at night. That means showgirls, dancers, hat-and-coat checkers, cigarette-tray cuties—*et–cet–er–a!*"

I paused. "Do you pay them? I mean, for their time."

"Wouldn't you like to know?" he cooed. "The important thing isn't whether I pay them. The important thing is that Pop thinks they really like his company. . . . You may not believe this, chum, but I recently detected a faint glimmer of a certain gleam in the old man's eye. . . ."

"That," I said sternly, "is why I decided to call you! Your father is approaching *eighty*, Albert. Do you realize what you may be doing? I mean—all that excitement. I mean, the—well—stimu*la*tion. Have you consulted a doctor?"

"I just *knew* you'd raise a goddam stupid question like that!" fumed Albert. "I don't give a flying hoot in hell *what* the doctors say! What good did all those knee-jerkers do for Pop all this time? They fed him tranquilizers for his nerves and roughage for his bowels. Period. Screw them! And all the Mayo Brothers, too. . . . I want my old man to have a few good years. I want it to be like each day he's on an excursion to Disneyland, with a chick on each arm——"

"It might *kill* him!" I could not help protesting.

I thought the telephone wire would snap from the vibrations of his laughter. "O.K., Billy Graham: Can you tell me a better way to go?"

VII

You are probably panting to ask, "Well, what happened?"
And I would be the last man on earth to blame you.

It offends my sense of rectitude to tell you that the regimen Albert had concocted for his dear old dad did not harm the old man one iota; *au contraire*, gang, Pop's color, spirits, gait, metabolism, muscle tone, kidneys, liver, lungs, blood pressure, garbage and water disposal became the talk of his neighborhood and the envy of his contemporaries, whose most noteworthy characteristics, when in public, were fits of wheezing.

The staunch comrades from Pop's Masonic lodge, who had initially displayed such stoicism anent his bereavement, were now falling all over each other in their concern for the old man's health and welfare. They visited him in daily delegations and weekend pilgrimages, bearing gifts: macadamia nuts, Tobler chocolates, Cadbury biscuits, glazed figs, Ottoman tangerines, flaky halvah, even a filigreed zither from the Holy Land. The Samaritans were equally attentive to, and appreciative of, their lodge-fellow's lady home companions. I think that the Masons hoped the fillies would be apportioned, in truly democratic fashion, in Pop's will.

As for the old man himself, he had by now revised his entire *Weltanschauung:* He told jokes, danced a brave (if shaky) cha-cha-cha, and held gentle court amidst his attending houris.

One of America's leading songwriters told me, with a lump in his throat: "That old goat is going to outlive us all!" I detected a note of envy, not to say resentment, in his prediction.

I next ran into Albert with a girl who must have been a Bunny, at a preview of some *avant garde* movie. (You could tell it was an *avant garde* movie because it was filmed partly in Marrakesh and partly in Omaha, shunned any conceivable resemblance to a story, and lingered lovingly on doorknobs, nostrils, and half-eaten tomatoes. In addition, the dialogue was pointless, there were pointed references to onanism, and to make absolutely sure the Lincoln Center crowd would recognize the higher aesthetic of *art nouveau,* all the crucial scenes were photographed through a wide-angle lens coated with shaving lather.) The New Crop of Emancipated Young Cinema Critics hailed this celluloid mishmosh: "A bold affirmation of alienation," "A searing revelation of the corroding *malaise* of capitalism," and "A hymn to hippie liberation." And the film chalked up $32,-000,000, after taxes, for two idealists of the New Left intent on exposing the materialistic values of Hollywood.

"How's your father?" I asked Albert.

He beamed: The old man was virtually bursting with beans and vinegar. He didn't put it quite that way, but that was the general idea.

I made no effort to hide my admiration. "You know, Al, I'd like to write up the story of you and your father——"

"Not as long as Pop's alive!" he scowled. "I don't want him ever to suspect I had anything to do with his popularity." He took me to one side. "Do you know what happened this afternoon? This will kill you. Pop, looking mighty embarrassed, apologized to me, because he thinks Sugar—a go-go chick from the Village—is taking a shine to him. He told me he didn't want to encourage her, because maybe I had a crush on her myself. Can you tie that, *bubele?*"

VIII

Well, I can tell the tale now *(loyauté m'oblige)* because Albert's father, dear soul, has left our mundane midst and entered the larger, lasting paradise. I hope it is the Muslim version.

He was eighty-one years old, and they say he died with a smile on his lips and a pretty young morsel patting his hand. Albert told a nosy reporter that the girl was his father's social secretary and had formerly worked in the Fine Arts division of the Boston Public Library. This caused considerable snickering around town when printed in the *Daily*

News' obituary, so Albert issued a corrected bulletin, saying
the reporter had misunderstood him: The girl had been with
the Art Fein Art Library in Pisgah, N.C. When it turned out
that there was no Art Fein Art Library in Pisgah, N.C., the
News, grievously wroth, would not even run Albert's perfectly straight letter to the Editor announcing that he was
donating 1,000 magnolia trees in his father's memory to
Menomonee Falls, Wisconsin, where the old man had been
born.

I think Maupassant or Damon Runyon would have understood this touching tale of father and son. But I'll bet
dollars to doughnuts, of which I am especially fond, that
neither Maupassant nor Runyon (nor Somerset Maugham
nor Noel Coward, for that matter) could have dreamed up
a more salubrious design for dying than my friend Albert
did for his dear old dad—in real life and glorious, living
Technicolor.

Father Divine

~~~~~~

I was grievously saddened the other night, talking to some college commandos, to discover that they had never heard of Father Divine. And I was more dismayed to find how little their parents remembered about that peerless evangelist. It is solely *pro bono publico,* therefore, that I write this memoir.

He was the most beguiling oracle ever to grace our land: a short, plump, bald, black pixie who always smiled and spouted a gospel so incomprehensible that it attracted a vast and enthusiastic clientele, black and white and lustrous hues in between. His adoring fold called him Father Divine. It is of the essence of his genius that he refused to recognize, much less discuss, questions about his divinity. "I don't have to say I'm God," he once declared, "and I don't have to say I'm not God. I have said there are millions of people who *call* me God. . . . I produce God and shake the earth."

Father Divine preached as overheated a theology as was ever heard on this unworthy planet. Consider this random sample: "God is not only personified and materialized, He is *re*personified and *re*materialized. He materalates and *re*materalates and is *re*materializatable!" Rarely has an insider given us so awesome a report on the Almighty.

Like many a holy man before him, Father always shied away from queries (or answers) concerning his mundane origins. His footwork with reporters was dazzling. But there is evidence that he was born George Baker, on Hutchinson's Island in the lovely Savannah River. He was an ordinary lad, apparently, who became a hedge-clipper and lawn-mower, through which humble arts he earned a living. Maturity made him cherubic, ever-pleasant of mien, and exemplary in habits.

He began sermonizing in a modest way in East Baltimore, around the turn of this century, and *circa* 1907 became "The Messenger" for one "Father Jehovia" (the difference between Jehovia and Jehovah is not entirely clear). But soon our hero transferred his allegiance to a celestial drummer named John Hickerson, who had launched a startling sect called "Live Ever, Die Never." With this sure-fire creed under his belt, the ever-ready hedge-clipper moved to Valdosta, Georgia, and in that sleepy, unsuspecting village set up his own theocratic practice.

Just as some men grow by degrees, George Baker grew by honorary degrees, which he gave himself. He became Major Devine, then Major Divine, then—but then this illustrious elf was tried for (it pains me to write it) lunacy. This insensitive action occurred in 1919, when the Major's black neighbors filed charges against him as a disturber of the peace and a sower of discord between husbands and wives —several of the latter having become so inspired by the Major's preachifying that they developed the habit of winging through town, screaming, "He is God! God has come! God is here!" These messianic tidings upset a good many religious folk, and whatever horses were on the street at the time.

So the dark patriarch was called to the jug and booked, by an admirably fair-minded constable, I think, as "John Doe, alias God." Although the legal proceedings, *State of Georgia vs. John Doe, alias God,* showed a profound respect for both the Constitution and the opinions of mankind, an unimaginative jury found Divine "unsound of mind." The judge offered him the choice of leaving Georgia with maximum haste or entering an asylum even faster. It did not take more than a moment, apparently without benefit of prayer, for "Alias God" to head for New York. This shows genuine foresight, I think, about growth stocks in the theosophy market.

In Manhattan, Father Divine struck out on his own, spreading his polysyllables with virtuous zest and hypnotic ambiguity. This swiftly won him reverent (and monetary) support from any number of pious folk, especially on Long Island, so the putative Father set up a house of worship in Saybrook. It became the scene for one of the most celebrated cases in history, a true milestone in the record of godly intervention. On November 16, 1931, Father Divine was haled into the local court by due process and protesting neighbors, who called him an inveterate encourager of deafening hymns and concerted prayings, and "a public nuisance" whose spiritual customers were driving them up the walls in their own homes.

Justice Lewis J. Smith fined Father $500 and sentenced him to six months in jail. And on November 20, four days after his blasphemous ruling, Judge Smith dropped dead. No warnings, no pains, no ailment, no occlusions, no clotting, no cardiac or vascular rhubarb. He just dropped dead.

I need not tell you what headlines and *tsimmes* this unloosed throughout the civilized world. What I do want to record is my admiration for how Father Divine explained the judge's departure to disoriented reporters: "I hated to do it."

Now, the great man's cause flourished, and so multitudinous were those who thirsted for his special salvation that he opened a branch in Harlem, where he set up Heaven—in fact, a whole string of Heavens, which is what he called the dormitories in which he lodged his growing, fervent synod. Several thousand converts, pink as well as black, became his "Angels." To win favor in the fold, they gave Father all their savings, assets, and current earnings—a procedure their gentle Vicar was prone to suggest, with a faraway glance that added spiritual uplift to the confrontation with Mammon.

Once they purged themselves of impure financial impediments to grace, the angels adopted new names, such as "Victory Love," "Faith Sweetness," "Peaceful Sam," and "Onward Universe." I shall always regret not having met "Onward Universe." The beatified then went about the sidewalks of New York joyously, laughing outright, shunning shopworn phrases of social discourse such as "Hello" or "Good-bye" to cry, instead, "Peace! It's wonderful!" This slogan unnerved many citizens who, though pacific themselves, were not accustomed to such vivid concurrence.

Father Divine bedizened his symbolic pulpit by naming his movement "The Peace Mission Cult." And in his Heavens the host of Angels ate, prayed, and slept in bliss. They did not copulate, because the earthly paradises were run according to the severe moral regimen Father imposed on his faithful: Lady angels and gentlemen angels were made to sleep in strictly separated dormitories. The geographical purity of these nocturnal arrangements won Father Divine a great deal of attention in the press—and a good many new supporters, I think, who needed external aid in their own wrestlings with the devil and the libido.

It is a testimonial to the extraordinary trust Father Divine was accorded by his flock that they reacted with rapture when he himself committed matrimony—with a twenty-one-year old Canadian lass, all white, named Edna Rose Ritchings. The puzzlement or grumblings from naive, literal-minded celibates were neatly outflanked by Father's masterly ratiocination: "We are married in name only," he announced, "because God is not married." I know of no way of faulting such sophisticated paralogy.

The increasingly publicized angels now made a slew of pilgrimages beyond New York's frontiers, enjoying the countryside, picnicking right and left, and conducting their evangelical crusades. They always traveled in beautiful

bright buses, on whose sides was painted "Father Divine,"
then "Father Divine (God)," then, without shilly-shallying,
"FATHER DIVINE IS GOD." The more impulsive apostles hailed
him as "Imperial Ruler of All the Universe!" This hubristic
claim was chastised by St. Clair McKelway in one of the
finest observations in English prose: "[Never] has Father
Divine ever hinted that he considers himself to be anything
more than God."

The earthly rewards of spiritual success were not spurned
by fortune's child. He (I use the capital only at the beginning of a sentence) was a sartorial sonata in his shiny silk
shirts and $500 suits, the latter as custom-tailored as the
most ingenious needlemen could drape on a five-foot-two,
short-necked, short-legged, barrel-chested, amply paunched
figure—a peculiar figure for one who figured as a father
figure to so many.

Among Father's unique traits was his practice of never
himself handling money, or opening bank accounts in his
name. Divinity spurned any possible *contretemps* with the
Internal Revenue Service, which is notoriously agnostic, but
adopted the ancient prerogative of not rendering unto Washington what Caesar might have been entitled to. Caesar, as
anyone knows, never held sway on the Potomac. But Father's
exquisite sense of monetary propriety did not forbid him
to accept nonfiscal expressions of love. He did not demur
when ardent parishioners insisted on giving him Rolls-
Royces, of which he utilized more than one; or when a white
tycoon donated a mansion in Gladwyne, Pennsylvania,
where Father swallowed his humility along with his victuals
off genuine 22-carat gold plates. Nor was the chocolate
santon austere in the way he ended all his letters: "This
leaves me well, healthy, joyful, peaceful, lively, loving, successful, prosperous and happy in spirit, body and mind and
in every organ, muscle, sinew, joint, limb, vein, and bone,
and in every atom, fiber, and cell of my bodily form." I doubt
whether even the late revered Everett Dirksen could have
topped that.

During the Great Recession, Father Divine won added international *réclame* because of the free meals he served every Sunday—to any and all comers. Whenever he was asked how such largess was financed, in such hard times, the prophet smiled serenely and murmured, "Father will provide." This formulation was flawless, for it could be interpreted literally or metaphorically—or both.

Actually, there was no mystery behind Father Divine's free dinners. Since the Angels who were employed outside of the various Heavens were giving him all their earnings, real money really presented no real problem. Besides, the cost of the Sunday feeds was drastically reduced by the sagacity Father Divine displayed in the first courses he unfailingly served and blessed: *mountains* of bread, spaghetti, macaroni and comparable appetite depressants.

Every so often Father Divine liked to announce: "No one ever dies in my house." This was not only electrifying, it was true: No one ever died in one of the Heavens. This was not because of immortality, instant resurrection, or mirific powers. No one ever died in Father Divine's Heavens because excessively balmy believers were hustled off to Bellevue Hospital, to be healed and/or forgotten; and seraphs who stopped breathing altogether on the premises were swiftly removed, during the understanding night, and deposited at some friendly address—from which the authorities were telephoned and notified to pick up a defunct mortal of insufficient faith.

The sunny, delightful founder of the Peace Mission Cult died (at least crass unbelievers *say* he died) at Woodmont, a thirty-two-room Tudor castle on a seventy-three-acre estate on Philadelphia's Main Line donated by a white disciple. No one was sure exactly how old Father was: He had replied with exalted imprecision whenever the question arose; once he gave his date of birth as "the time of Abraham." But the New York papers said his age was "estimated at about 100." I find it hard to believe he left us so young.

He departed this perplexing vale, which he had done so much to enrich and enliven, on September 10, 1965. He was an adorable mountebank; and I wish we had more like him—instead of the rancorous psychopaths who keep confusing politics with patricide, when they could be dedicating their paranoia, as Father Divine did, to a sweet and beneficent faith.

A Strange
and Special Beauty

ccccccccccccccccccccccccccccccccccccc

I shall never forget the time I was in Florence and first beheld the magnificent, massive *Primavera* (almost seven feet high and eleven feet long)—that allegory of cool colors, all swirling lines and quaint poses, suffused with a sweet-sad Gothic grace, a murmuring, melancholy elegance. Within a curious tableau of figures, Paris is posed at the left, reaching to pick an apple off a tree to give the most beautiful of the three ethereal maidens dancing; and at the right is Flora, a pensive maiden, wreath in hair, garland around her neck, who strews roses from the folds of a superbly adorned gown. Throughout this utterly bewitching, somehow archaic painting are patterned the most exquisite flowers imaginable, delicate tresses, diaphanous gowns, translucent gauzes. A pale, unearthly light touches all the restless rhythms, visual rhythms unlike anything I had ever seen. And in the darkening, green-blue forest glade I sought such images as one yearns to recover from dreams.

Can you believe that for 400 years, until the late nineteenth century, the paintings of Sandro Botticelli were ignored and forgotten? For four centuries, art historians and critics did not think Botticelli worth mentioning—or, when mentioned, deserving of more than perfunctory reference. Then the pre-Raphaelites rediscovered him, and today the

Primavera and *Birth of Venus* rank among the most popular pictures in the world.

It is a mark of Botticelli's singularity that he founded no school, led no movement, attracted no imitators. And in a Renaissance world that burst with drama and brilliance and flamboyance, his life was devoid of all three. He was a marginal, isolated figure, "whimsical and eccentric," said Vasari, who followed his own aberrant necessities. He finally repudiated the world's pleasures and rewards, refusing even to paint, and died poor, unnoticed, and unknowable.

Botticelli was born in Florence, in (we think) 1444, the son of a tanner, Mariano di Vanno Filipepi. The boy was baptized Alessandro but was nicknamed "Botticelli" after his older brother and mentor, who was called "Botticello," which means "little barrel."

At fourteen he was apprenticed to Fra Filippo Lippi, and when he began to accept commissions on his own, he won the patronage of the grand Medici. They must have regarded his talent as essentially decorative, very far from any promise of immortality, because they commissioned him to paint "fancy pictures for bed fronts and chests." But his *Adoration of the Magi,* for the Church of Santa Maria Novella, was "so beautiful," wrote a contemporary, "that every artist who examines it is astonished." It won so great a reputation that Pope Sixtus IV called Botticelli to Rome.

Botticelli was given a company of fresco painters and put in charge of covering the walls in the chapel, now called the Sistine, in the papal palace. His frescoes created no great stir. For Botticelli was entirely overshadowed by his contemporaries, an array of artists to stun the mind: Leonardo da Vinci, Michelangelo, Raphael, Titian. The Sistine walls support the astounding ceiling Michelangelo Buonarotti made the marvel of the world.

Botticelli, much chastened, returned to Florence. That incredible city was unmatched for the brilliance of its culture, the majesty of its architecture, the genius of its painters and sculptors and artisans. It was also the envy of Europe for the splendor of its life, the variety and juiciness of its pleasures. The Florentines especially loved pageants and panoply, tournaments and religious fêtes and resplendent carnivals. One of the most spectacular *divertissements* occurred in 1475, when Giuliano de' Medici, the younger brother of Lorenzo the Magnificent (and, later, the father of Pope Clement VII), sponsored a great contest of beauty in the Piazza Santa Croce. The coveted crown of "Queen of Beauty" was bestowed on Simonetta Cattaneo, young wife of Marco Vespucci, and known to all as Giuliano's beloved.

Simonetta died soon after, Giuliano was murdered in the cathedral by political rivals, and the bereaved Lorenzo de' Medici asked Sandro Botticelli to immortalize his brother Giuliano and the girl he had loved. Tradition has it that it is Simonetta's features that appear in Botticelli's *Birth of Venus*, in his *Mars and Venus*, in the incomparable *Primavera*. Some authorities think Simonetta was the model for the Goddess of Love; some believe she is the unforgettable Flora, that ethereal, alluring creature I find the most bewitching figure in all art. Was this really Simonetta—this pensive goddess who appears again and again in Botticelli's work?

Not that he was in love with her; his name was never linked in romance to any woman's. Like many a Renaissance painter, Botticelli was said to be homosexual. Indeed, when his cousin once urged him to marry, Botticelli answered with some anguish: "One night I dreamed that I was married, and the bare idea made me so miserable that for fear I should fall asleep and dream the same dream, I got up and rushed about the streets of Florence like a madman!"

Simonetta died before Botticelli painted the *Primavera* (around 1478). Whether she was Botticelli's model or not we may never know; nor does it matter. *Some* face so haunted the painter that he repeated it and idealized it into an image of an altogether unique beauty. That face always brings to my mind the words of Francis Bacon: "There is no excellent beauty that hath not some strangeness in the proportion." In Botticelli, everything is strange, evanescent, spellbinding.

After Botticelli returned from Rome, he occupied himself
with tasks unworthy of his talent: illustrations for *The In-
ferno,* sundry prints and engravings. Then his brother, Simone di Mariano, returned from Naples to live with Sandro.
Simone became a proselyte of a fanatical Dominican monk
—and Sandro, a man neurotic by any standard, was soon
caught up in the fantastic drama of this Fra Girolamo Savonarola, whose fire-and-brimstone visions, terrifying prophecies, apocalyptic sermons and jeremiads against luxury and
licentiousness threw Florence into such panic, such agonies
of guilt, such fears of God's wrath, that huge bonfires were
lighted in the public squares, and proud lords and ladies
threw the signs of their vanity—jewels, ornaments, costumes, priceless treasures from antiquity—into the flames.
The maddened mob sang psalms.

Botticelli was tormented by Savonarola's fierce demands
for self-denial and self-punishment. He is reported to have
tossed some of his own "worldly" paintings into the fires,
and his house became a meeting place for Savonarola's im-
passioned *Piagnone.*

Savonarola became prior of San Marco, and when the
mighty Medici were exiled it was the gaunt, cowled monk
who dominated Florence. His zealotry was as limitless as it
was warped; he turned his followers into a legion of spies,
who reported to him the vices they uncovered, suspected,
or imagined.

Savonarola attacked the Pope, the profligate Borgia, Alexander VI—who excommunicated him; whereupon Savonarola denied the legitimacy of the Pope's accession to St.
Peter's throne. This was too much for the Franciscan order
and the elders of Florence.

Savonarola was hanged for heresy, in 1498, after the
rabid monk, under torture, confessed that he was a false
prophet (at least the authorities announced that Savonarola
had so confessed). Simone Botticelli was one of the votaries
who was banished from Florence. . . .

It is surprising that Sandro Botticelli was able to retain
the patronage of the returned Medici. But his creativity

seems to have been burned out in religious ecstasy and terror. Except for some minor assignments, he never painted again.

"Not having any other means of living, he fell into very great difficulties," Vasari tells us. "[He] abandoned all labor insomuch that, finding himself at length become old and very poor, he would surely have died of hunger had he not been supported by Lorenzo ... and assisted by other friends and admirers of his talents."

So little imprint had Botticelli made on his own time that his death, in 1510, went unnoticed. And when, ninety years later, the Grand Duke Ferdinand published a list of the masters whose paintings he considered immortal, forbidding Florentine citizens to remove them from their homes or churches, Botticelli's name was not included.

I think he had the rarest of gifts: the capacity to create a realm entirely his own, a dominion of a strange and special beauty. His undulating lines and intertwined forms, his mastery of color, his magic of ornamentation, his flowing patterns and dolorous harmonies, transform his paintings into a kind of dream-like tapestry. He lures us into his own Arcadia, all the while himself self-absorbed, distant, never reaching out to us with that force that commands the eye in Velásquez or Breughel, Manet or Van Gogh.

Botticelli has always seemed to me an artist from some other race, poignant, unearthly, melancholy, spinning out his own private and ambiguous intimations of the spirit. Perhaps that is why we receive aesthetic vibrations from him that "few if any other artists can give us," as Bernard Berenson said. "He was the greatest artist of linear design Europe has ever had. ... He got music out of design."

Touch Me, Feel Me, Grunt, Growl, Purr

I have this caustic friend, Rodney, who has this sentimental cousin, Elmer, and they disagree over just about everything. The disagreements are, I should tell you, extremely friendly. That is because each man is mature, intelligent, and thinks the other an idiot.

Rodney once told me that ever since Elmer fell out of his highchair he had suffered from a lopsided cerebellum, and Elmer once confided that Rodney had contracted a virulent variety of mumps at fourteen, which left him parched in the *medulla oblongata*. "It's pretty tough to go through life with a parched *medulla oblongata*," said Elmer.

This might have made a deeper impression on me had not Rodney remarked, the preceding night, "Elmer is such a sweet fellow. Sensitive. Idealistic. Heart of gold. Wouldn't hurt a fly—only people, to whom Elmer gives the most mushheaded advice since doctors advised patients with worms to rub aloe and honey into their navels."

Politically, the cousins are as far apart as Poles. Elmer thinks Rodney is a reactionary, and Rodney calls Elmer the kind of ninny described by H. L. Mencken as a man who, upon discovering that a rose smells better than a cabbage, concludes it will also make better soup.

I was lunching with Elmer and Rodney at the latter's

favorite restaurant, the Ptomaine, when a long-overdue confrontation erupted. It began when Elmer announced that he had changed his entire life and *Weltanschauung* with an astonishing, uplifting, even revolutionary experience: a group "Liberating Weekend," in the Catskills, at Swami Ishmar Yonklowitz's "Nirvana Sensory-Expansion Sanctuary." Elmer's eyes moistened as he pronounced the name.

"Is that the sort of retreat I saw in the movie *Bob and Carol and Ted and Alice?*" asked Rodney.

"Yes," said Elmer, "although our guru stresses empathy more than punching pillows."

"It was a marvelous film," grinned Rodney. "So perceptive. All those hung-up kooks, chasing adolescent phantoms——"

"Kooks? Phantoms?" gasped Elmer in dismay. "No, no, you got it all *wrong*, Rod. The movie gives an honest insight into four emotionally crippled people, typical of our alienated generation, brainwashed by the false values of our materialistic society. The film shows how such people, lonely and isolated, can break through their inhibitions to free their deepest emotions and widen their sensual potentialities beyond anything they'd ever dreamed possible— through honest, frank self-exposure in discussions, no matter how intimate, telling bedrock truths——"

"You think people should go around telling each other the *truth?*" asked Rodney in horror.

"Absolutely," said Elmer.

"You have bad breath," said Rodney.

I dropped my fork.

"Oh," stammered Elmer, turning vermilion. "I didn't know. ... Thank you for telling me. I-I'll change to a stronger mouthwash!"

"Don't," said Rodney. "I was just testing your principles."

"That is a lousy trick!" cried Elmer. "Don't *you* believe in people telling each other the truth?"

"Good God, no," said Rodney. "It's too cruel, and it solves nothing. Why, if people went around telling each other the truth all the time, we'd have fisticuffs, bloodletting, homicides, divorces, ax murders ..."

"I, for one, have decided to defy social hypocrisy by being truthful at all times!" declared Elmer.

"O.K.," sighed Rodney. "What do you like best in bed?"

Elmer flushed. "This is not the right atmosphere for a question like that!"

"Here's one that is: What do you really think of Leo?"

Elmer hesitated. "Pass the ketchup."

"Good lad," said Rodney. "Leo always passes people ketchup."

I passed the ketchup.

"You're confusing the issues, using debaters' tricks," complained Elmer. "The Nirvana Sensory-Expansion Sanctuary teaches us not to be ashamed of our natural emotions——"

"You think that's *good?*" asked Rodney, agape.

"Certainly!"

"But our natural emotions have to be shamed, chained, threatened, and restrained," said Rodney, "or this horrid-enough world would become one big abattoir, rapery, and torture chamber."

"I meant man's good, noble feelings!" exclaimed Elmer. "You see how you twist my meaning? ! I meant feelings that hurt no one else! Touching, holding, embracing each other —those things are *beautiful,* not to feel guilty about."

"I don't feel guilty about embracing my wife, child, or secretary," said Rodney.

"Then why can't you show the same warmth to a stranger??"

"Male or female?" leered Rodney.

"Either!" said Elmer severely. "That's the point! A truly liberated person feels no guilt about showing physical affection to another human being, even one of the same sex. That other person is a human being, just like yourself!"

"Like hell he is," said Rodney. "I am unique. So are you. So is the waiter. Besides, *I* don't feel lonely or alienated."

"Then why do you balk at publicly sharing love?" asked Elmer.

"Because I see no need to go around proving my virtue,"

said Rodney, "or getting kinky sex kicks, or gratifying voyeurs, letting any freak intrude on my privacy—or moon over my privates."

"You have been crippled by this decadent society," mourned Elmer.

"Do you go to church?" asked Rodney.

"No," said Elmer stoutly. "I am a freethinker."

"Well, you're free to think about anything you want in church——"

"But it is an outmoded *institution*," blurted Elmer. "Man can worship God or Nature anywhere—in the hills, crossing a meadow, on a stretch of beach. We do not need the stultifying hokum of priests, ritual, prayers *en masse*——"

"Then why go in for mass snuggling, moaning, and weeping?" asked Rodney. "Pass the sugar."

"Again you distort my meaning!" complained Elmer. "Real or synthetic?"

"Either. The reason I suggest you go to church," said Rodney, "is that you should address your complaints about this undeniably baffling and iniquitous world to the responsible cause thereof: the Lord. He, after all, made two sexes, potent gonads, and arranged for babies to be very small, utterly helpless, and totally dependent. This cozied mankind into the family, and a social system, in both of which our 'noble, natural' feelings—incest, patricide, matricide—the Cain-and-Abel bit—must be harnessed——"

Elmer was sputtering objections all over his chicken à la king. "That's the Freudian fallacy! And we can overcome it! The time has come to stop our self-deception, and all our lying——"

"Suppose you have cancer," said Rodney. "Terminal. Do you want your doctor to con you with cheer or tell you the truth?"

"The truth!" said Elmer.

"You are a brave, fearless, admirable man," said Rodney, but not in a brave, fearless, admiring tone. "Now; suppose your child has leukemia. Would you——"

"Of course not!" retorted Elmer. "She's too young to be asked to cope with such hopeless tragedy."

"Right. And so am I."

"That's an extreme example," protested Elmer.

"Then let's take an unextreme one. You're going out to dinner. Your wife comes in, all dolled up, wearing a new low-cut gown and a hair-do she spent four hours and twenty bucks on. 'How do I look, dear?' she asks. What do you answer?"

"It—depends on how she looks!" said Elmer.

"You cad," said Rodney. "You heartless fiend. Can you really say, 'Sweetie, you look like an aging Algerian broad who has seen better days, not to say nights. Your Pucci dress looks like a pooch walked across it with his paws dipped in bubble gum. Your hair reminds me of nine snakes wrestling in aspic. And as for your décolletage, pussycat, let's face it: You're fifteen pounds overweight, in the bosom of the family, which is also where you're fifteen pounds overweight.' "

Elmer drew himself up into the huff that is known among the righteous as Elmer's Huff. "You mock my meaning! You caricature my ideas! You distort my reasoning——"

"Do I?" Rodney scratched his chin. "Didn't you tell your neighbors in Nutley, New Jersey, that Timothy Leary says LSD makes it possible to have a hundred orgasms a day?"

"Timothy was only giving that as a possibility——"

"Suppose you start having only ninety orgasms a day all over Nutley? Who will have enough strength left to bring in the milk, put on Junior's snowsuit, or turn on the six-o'clock news?"

Elmer wiped his palms. "You are very hostile! You're just not on my wavelength."

"Don't I turn you on?" asked Rodney.

"Certainly not!"

"I'm glad," said Rodney, "because 'wavelength' and 'turning on' refer to machines. It offends me when such barbarisms are used about people. After all, the basic difference between men and machines is that men have emotions; machines don't. . . . For dessert, will you have ice cream, cake, or tapioca?"

"Tapioca," said Elmer. "Or will you interpret that as a symbol of my soul?"

"Not your soul; your ideas!"

"Semantics! That's your undoing!" exclaimed Elmer. "Words! They distort ideas——"

Rodney said, "I always thought words were tools. Used with precision, they're irreplaceable; used by the zonked, they're gibberish."

"No, no, no," protested Elmer. "Take the poets, the mystics, the new generation of singers. Listen to them! Just *listen* to their basic, preverbal truths. They teach us to express ourselves by smashing old forms—to forget and transcend words, to release our gut emotions—to grunt, growl, purr, snarl."

"Then why don't we get down on all fours?" asked Rodney, unkindly. "We could cancel out a hundred thousand years of civilization—imperfect though it be, violent and vicious and disgraceful though the human race often is. . . . Will grunting, growling, purring, and snarling *really* redeem us? . . . Cousin, honest to God, don't you think that instead of going to Swami Yonklowitz you might try an old-fashioned shrink?"

"You are a pawn of the Establishment!" cried Elmer. "You are a goddam cynic! You throw cold water on every new, liberating idea!"

"First," sighed Rodney, "what you call new was old in Babylon—with unappetizing results. Second, what you call 'liberating' I think schizophrenic. Third, I prefer reason to daydreams, and experience to pipe dreams, as tests of truth or validity."

The atmosphere was growing so charged I knew there would be no quick reaching for credit cards, so I hastily said, "Elmer, is it true that your swami says that if everyone got a massage every day, there would be no war?"

"An interesting and original idea!" said Elmer.

"Oh, God," groaned Rodney. "Nero and Caligula went right from their *masseurs* to butcher Christians. In fact, the massages so relaxed their senses they needed *more* Christians than if they hadn't——"

"You son-of-a-bitch!" shouted Elmer.

"Elmer!" I protested. "Rod! You're both too intense——"

But I never finished my felicities. Elmer had popped two pills in his mouth. He was ashen, his lips parted, his forehead glistening. He was staring into space.

Rodney snapped his fingers. He did not seem at all worried, as I certainly was.

"Elmer . . . Stop that. . . . *Elmer!*"

Elmer made no answer. He was not dead, because he was sitting upright, not leaning right or left, and I could hear his breathing, which was exceptionally regular. Elmer had gone into a trance.

I hear that Swami Yonklowitz is now urging his acolytes to spread the faith without swallowing any pills at all.

Poor Hammerhead

THROUGH the open door clanked (I know no better word) a soldier who might have stepped right off a recruiting poster. His blouse, despite the heat, was absolutely crisp; a perfect knife edge ran along the forward edges of his sleeves; his tie was impeccably knotted; his belt buckle gleamed; his shoes glistened. This military paragon snapped to attention in a brace that would have done credit to a drill sergeant and, eyes fixed straight ahead, barked: "Private Albert Lawrence reporting for duty, sir!"

"At ease," said Captain Newman.

Private Lawrence broke his salute and handed a slip of paper across the desk stiffly. His cheeks were as scrubbed as prize apples. His blond crew-cut was as even as a brush. His bearing was so martial that he seemed to have been put together by an Army engineer: a bullet head, machine-gun eyes, teeth like cartridges.

"Sit down, Lawrence."

"Thank you, sir."

"Would you like a cigarette?"

"No, sir. I do not smoke while on duty."

"Well," said Captain Newman pleasantly, "let's say you're not on duty yet."

"In that case, sir, thank you, I will." Private Lawrence took a cigarette with a smart nod of the head and had a spotless Zippo burning under Captain Newman's nose before Newman had placed his cigarette between his lips.

"Thank you, Lawrence," smiled Captain Newman.

"Screw you, sir," said Private Lawrence.

I shall not try to describe the expression on Newman's face. Private Lawrence clapped his hands across his mouth, his cheeks flaming, stammering: "Oh, God! Excuse me, sir. Please. I did not mean it. That dirty, filthy word. I cannot *help* it, sir. It just comes out!"

It would be banal to say that Captain Newman looked as if he could not believe his ears; it would also be inaccurate, because he looked as though he did. And before Newman's stunned, incredulous expression, poor Lawrence became even more miserable and stuttered more abjectly. "I—could bite off my tongue, sir! It only happens when I am with an officer, sir. It just comes *out*, sir!"

"How long," asked Captain Newman at last, "has this been going on?"

"Since—I was fifteen, sir. It started with one of my teachers. It doesn't happen every time. Oh, no! Days go by, weeks, and it's no problem, no problem at all. Then all of a sudden, like you saw, sir, bang!"

"How old are you, Lawrence?"

"Twenty-two, sir."

"And you've had this problem since you were fifteen?"

"Yes, sir."

"Only with teachers or officers?"

"N-no, sir. With any superior, like a boss."

Newman studied the ceiling. "Well, Lawrence, you've got quite an original problem there for a soldier, haven't you? Tell me, does it get any better, any worse?"

"That's hard to say, sir. Sometimes—sometimes I'm sure I've got it licked. Like this past month: I went eight days and never once used a filthy word! Then—" Lawrence bit his lip. "Son-of-a-bitch! Goddam it to hell and Hong Kong, plus a flying pass at Santa Claus——"

"Is your problem always the same filthy word?" Newman cut in hastily.

Lawrence flushed. "No, sir."

"You mean sometimes it's *worse* than 'Screw you'?"

"Yes, sir. At first, when I was a kid, it was 'Go to hell.' That was bad—but it got worse. It began to be: 'Take a flying you-know-what for yourself, sir.' Then, lately, in the Army, where everyone uses bad words, it's—'Screw you, sir.' Sometimes worse. The word that begins with 'f' . . ." Lawrence stared at the floor miserably. "You could gig me, sir. You could send me to the guardhouse."

"Sure. But they don't need my business. You have to make a reservation to get into our guardhouse." Newman rubbed his chin moodily. "Lawrence, how the hell did they ever let you into the Army?"

"I was drafted, sir."

"But didn't your draft board know about your—compulsion?"

"No, sir. I was real good that day. I didn't have a single filthy impulse."

"Weren't you worried about what might happen once you were in the Army?"

"Oh, yes, sir! But I thought the discipline might help me get over the—habit."

"Did you ever see a doctor about this?" asked Newman.

"Yes, sir, about five years ago."

"What did he say?"

Lawrence knit his brow. "He told me I had to decide who was going to be master and who was going to be slave—— me or it! He said it was just a matter of will power."

"What did you think of that?"

"I thought he was a horse's ass."

Captain Newman glanced out of the window. I could see the heat rising off the parade ground like an evil vapor. "Who sent you here, Lawrence?"

"My lieutenant, at Santa Ana. He said you were just the man I ought to work for."

Newman reached for some water. "What was his name?"

"Kincaid, sir."

"Did you happen to remember his first name?"

"N-no, sir."

"Did he—uh—say *why* he thought I was just the man you ought to serve under?"

"He said—can I be frank, sir?"

"Please, Lawrence. Be very frank."

"Well, sir, he said you have a natural talent for dealing with nuts and screws."

Captain Newman winced. "Do you think you're a nut or a screw?"

Lawrence's lower lip trembled. "No, sir. He said you were desperate—to get men with hospital experience."

"Have you had much hospital experience?"

"Yes, sir! Back home, sir."

"Where was that?"

"Buffalo General," smiled Lawrence.

"Which wards?"

"Mostly mental wards, sir."

"Well," smiled Newman, "that's just fine! How long were you an orderly?"

"I never was an orderly, sir."

"I mean a wardsman."

"I never was a wardsman, either."

"Well, what jobs *did* you have?"

"No jobs, sir," said Lawrence earnestly. "I was a patient."

"*What?*" cried Newman.

"I was a patient, sir."

Captain Newman lunged forward. "You were a *patient?*"

"Five years, sir!"

"You were a patient in a psychiatric ward for five *years?*"

"Yes, sir. The doctors——"

"And you were *drafted?*"

"Yes, sir."

"They *knew* you were a psychiatric case and still inducted you into—the Army?! How the hell——"

"Sir," Lawrence proudly, "when I got out of the hospital I began looking around for a job. One day, the government wrote me about registering for Selective Service, so I did. I passed all the physicals easy, because I take tip-top care of myself, then I went in front of this special doctor who asked me how I slept and if I liked girls or had any emotional problems. I told him I liked girls a lot and my most emotional problem was to get a job and amount to something. I would have mentioned—*it*, sir, the swearing, but there was a real long line behind me, and the doctor looked sort of keyed-up, like people had their doubts about him. He waved me ahead to a sergeant, who was sitting at a table and filling forms out on a typewriter like a shot out of hell. The sergeant asked me, 'Occupation?' I answered, 'None.' He thought I was trying to be a wise guy, sir. He said, 'I suppose you are a retired millionaire?' real nasty. I said, 'No, my family are poor.' He said, 'You have to put *something* under Occupation, even if it's "Unemployed."' So I said that was true, I was unemployed. So he said, 'That's better. And what did you do *before* you were unemployed, buster?' I answered, 'I was in the hospital.' So he said, 'Now we're getting somewhere,' and typed on my form, after where it said 'Occupation,' 'Hospital.' Then he asked me how *long* I'd been in the hospital. I said 'Five years.' Then he asked if it was any special kind of hospital, and I said, 'Yes. Mental.' So he said, 'Good for you,' and typed in 'Mental.'" Lawrence paused. "In a way, it was all very logical."

"Logical?" Captain Newman echoed. "'Logical' doesn't begin to do it justice. It was wonderful! Standardized methods. Objective data. Foolproof. They took all those facts and coded them and transferred them to punch cards." He turned to me with a wicked grin. "Isn't that what you scientific psychologists do?"

"Yes," I said unhappily.

"Then they filed all the punch cards in the central files in Washington, right? Everything in place. And when *I* asked for assistants with hospital experience they knew exactly how to get the answer. They just fed all those beautiful punch cards into a wonderful machine, set it for 'Hospital experience,' flipped a switch, and the machine whirred and buzzed and sorted and a bell rang—and presto! Out came: 'Lawrence, Albert, private; Experience: Hospital;

How long? Five years; Specialty: Mental.'" He threw his head back and shook with laughter. "Oh, my aching back! Man, oh, man, in spades. Lawrence, I am indebted to you. Don't get worried. I'm not laughing at you. You have recharged my batteries. . . . Do you know what kind of ward I run here?"

"Yes, sir."

"Describe it."

"It's—like the one I was in."

"Very good. Now, do you want to work in a ward like that?"

"Yes, *sir!*"

"Why, boy?"

Lawrence hesitated. "I could help you, sir. I'll be a good orderly. I know a lot about hospital routine. I can make beds, scrub floors, empty bedpans, keep everything spick-and-span. I am very neat and tidy, sir. I *hate* anything dirty. There's no excuse for it! It takes no more time to be clean than to be dirty and filthy!"

" 'Dirty and filthy,' " Captain Newman repeated.

Lawrence blushed. "I know what you're driving at."

"I'm sure you do. . . . Lawrence, you know I can get you out of the Army, don't you?"

"I—don't want to, sir."

"Why not?"

"I think I'm better off in the Army, sir. Everything has to be clean. Everything happens on time!"

"But what about your swearing?" asked Newman.

"I—well, I try to avoid certain officers, sir, the ones who make the bad words slip out."

"Like me?"

"Oh, no, sir," Lawrence protested. "I don't feel angry with you!"

"But you swore at me. . . ."

"Because I was *nervous,* sir, not angry. I was sitting out there on the bench, twiddling my thumbs, waiting for you all the time you were interviewing that creep J. Laibowitz."

Captain Newman rubbed his chin. "I'll make a deal with

you. I'll try you out in the ward. Now don't get excited! We'll try it for two weeks. On probation. We'll see how it goes. O.K.?"

"Yes, *sir!*"

"That's fine."

Lawrence rose and saluted, holding the salute magnificently.

"Dismissed," said Newman.

"Screw you," said Lawrence.

I don't think I have ever felt as sorry for anyone as I felt for Lawrence at that moment. He turned white as a sheet, almost breaking into tears, and began to beat his fist against his thigh furiously. "Oh, Jesus! God! God *damn* it! Sir— please, sir. Excuse me. Give me another chance! Don't hold it against me!"

Captain Newman waved a hand carelessly. "Probation— that's the thing that threw you. No one likes to have a sword hanging over his head. The boner was mine, soldier. I'll have to think up something special for your kind of problem." He closed his eyes solemnly.

Poor Lawrence shot me an anxious glance, hoping, I suppose, for some sign of reassurance. I smiled idiotically. He swallowed, mumbling, "Thank you, sir."

I could not for the life of me figure out what Captain Newman would say or do now. When he opened his eyes he said, "Let's start all over. Private Lawrence, you will come to attention."

"Yes, sir." Lawrence sprang into a brace.

"Lawrence, I don't have to tell you that as a private in the United States Army you are under strict military discipline?"

"No, sir!"

"You understand, do you not, that when an officer gives you an order, that order *must be obeyed*?"

"Yes, sir."

"You understand that any order I, Captain Newman, give you must be obeyed to the letter, without qualification, evasion, ifs, ands, or buts?"

Lawrence was beginning to turn pale. "Yes, sir."

"Very well, Lawrence. I am going to give you an order. Ready!"

Lawrence snapped his heels together sharply.

"Private Albert Lawrence, I hereby order you to swear at me, Captain Newman, twice a day! You will swear at me once in the morning, when I check in, and once in the evening, when I check out. *That is an order!* Do you understand?"

"Yes, sir."

"Repeat the order!"

"Yes, sir! The Captain has ordered me to swear at him twice a day, sir; in the morning, when he checks in, and at night, when he checks out."

"Right! And you are *not to swear at me at any other time!*"

"Right, sir!"

"Repeat that."

"I am not to swear at you at any other time!" cried Lawrence.

"And you are hereby ordered not to swear at any *other* officer, here or on leave, at any time whatsoever." Captain Newman rose formally. "That will be all."

Lawrence brought his hand down smartly, thought of something, and brought his hand into a salute again. "Sir?"

"Yes?"

"May I ask the Captain a question?"

"You have my permission to ask a question."

"Thank you, sir. Should I stand at attention when I swear at you?"

Captain Newman's eyebrows arched in unfeigned admiration. "Excellent point, Lawrence. That is terribly smart of you. . . . Yes, I think it would be best if you swore at me from a formal military stance."

"Thank you, sir!" Private Lawrence's hand whipped down, he made a right-about face and marched out of the room. He was walking on air.

And why not? No one before had ever ordered him to swear. Men had chewed him out for swearing, or forbade him to swear, or punished him for swearing, or cajoled, threatened, chided or appeased him. But no one before had shouldered the burden of his need for him! No one had commanded him to do what he was driven to do, and dreaded. Reprimand, penalty, punishment—these were as useless as blood sacrifices after a hurricane. But an official *order*—! An order he could understand; an order he could execute; an order was someone else's will, with which Albert Lawrence could gratefully replace his own.

Within an hour after Lawrence entered Ward 7, he had a nickname. Sergeant Kopp studied that punctilious military dress and manner with disgust, turned to Pepi Gavoni, one of the other orderlies, and announced, "This character is in the wrong army. He's a hammerhead."

From that moment on, Lawrence was known as "Hammerhead." He did not mind. He was, indeed, grateful for the affection any nickname implies. He took to his duties as if they had been especially designed to fit his needs. He worked like a slave, ate like a horse, and slept like a log. He scrubbed, scoured, mopped, wiped, aired. He made Ward 7 gleam with that purity for which his inner self yearned.

Lawrence followed Captain Newman's orders to a T, swearing at him each morning, quite pleasantly, when Newman arrived, and swearing at him each evening, quite proudly, as Newman left. His compulsion seemed gratified by these fixed channels of disgrace. His profanity indeed began to take on a note of affection—or, at least, inoffensiveness—just as that which is familiar always does; for even the foulest words lose their meaning if repeated over and over until they become only sounds to which anxious men assign anxious meanings.

Each morning, when Captain Newman called, "Good morning, Lawrence," Hammerhead would snap to attention and rejoin, "Screw you, sir!" Every night, when Captain Newman left, Hammerhead would be waiting outside his office. "Good night, Lawrence," Newman would say, and Hammerhead would fling his hand to his forehead and descant, "Screw you, sir!"

There was no alteration of this ritual: Lawrence sought

neither variety nor originality in his symbolic defiance of authority. He was only at home with regularity.

Of course, the swearing caused a sensation in the ward, at first, albeit Hammerhead tried to swear at Captain Newman in a moderate and pleasant tone. The first time Laibowitz heard Hammerhead utter his fornicatory malediction, the startled corporal spread his arms wide and cried, "The Japs must be in Kansas City!"

But soon the swearing was accepted as part of that greater irrationality by which a military body is animated. Stranger, sadder, funnier things happened a dozen times a day in Ward 7. Laibowitz summed up the ward's consensus with that antiseptic disdain which was his metier: "*Nothing* in the Army makes sense."

Mr. Washington

WHEN I came to Washington, I was hired by Louis Brownlow, that bucolic, rumpled, immensely knowledgeable adviser to four presidents—and the John the Baptist of professional public administration in America. "Brownie" retained me, with White House funds, to make a study of the growth of the powers of the presidency, from the time of the Continental Congress down. I holed up in the Library of Congress and began to read. And soon, of course, I reached the point where George Washington dominated the stage of history.

I was, I should confess, no admirer of Washington. Like most of my young Turk friends, I regarded the Father of His Country as an icon of somewhat accidental immortality. His frigid, sniffish countenance had looked down upon me from the walls of grammar-school classrooms, and was hardly a face to inspire warmth. It relieved me to know I was not alone in my discomfort when I read Leigh Hunt's unforgettable line: "Washington's face was as cut and dry as a diagram."

True, I felt a certain awe for a lad who could say, "I cannot tell a lie, Father; I did it with my little hatchet," but the premature nobility of the confession soured my admiration until it curdled and became ambivalence. So I was doubly grateful when I ran across Mark Twain's judgment: "As a boy, Washington was ignorant of the commonest accomplishment of youth. He could not even lie." As for our Father's "All that I am I owe to my mother," I went moist-eyed when I first read it, feeling rather strongly obligated to my own mother, but in later, less shmaltzy days, whenever I encountered that paean to Mother I reached for an aspirin.

There was much of the prig in a man who could abjure "that unmeaning and abominable custom, swearing," or say, "Associate with men of good quality . . . for 'tis better to be alone than to be in bad company," or even, in uncharacteristic eloquence, "Labor to keep alive in your breast that little spark of celestial fire called Conscience."

All that my courses in American history (two) had taught me was that Washington was an excellent executive, and the embodiment of authority, rectitude, and pomp. The weak union of states was fortunate to find a leader so widely respected and, for a while, loved; so true a patriot, soldier, general; so patient a chairman of the convention that sweated to agree upon a Constitution; so calm a helmsman to guide the new nation through perilous domestic and international storms.

But intellectual depth or range or capacity to be original? Washington could not begin to deserve comparison with any one of the astonishing constellation around him: Franklin, Jefferson, Hamilton, Adams, Madison, Jay, Monroe. . . . Was there ever a more brilliant, a more able, a more politically sophisticated congregation of talent? Within that scintillating galaxy, Mr. Washington seemed a star of the third magnitude, a man indifferently educated, sparsely read, given to sanctimony. He was, to be candid, a stuffed shirt.

Those, gentleman of the press, were my solemn opinions. And I smiled the patronizing smile only graduate fellows can summon when I read Lord Brougham's panegyric:

> Surely Washington was the greatest man that ever lived in this world uninspired by divine wisdom and unsustained by supernatural virtue.

And so, with these predilections, I began to peruse Mr. Washington's letters, speeches, official papers. I was amused by the stilted phrases, the spelling, the abounding platitudes. But—but it began to dawn on me how much more complicated than I had ever dreamed were the violent pressures and refractory forces, the rival ambitions and suspicions, the harsh, willful oppositions, that swirled around Washington in that maelstrom of a revolutionary time. Nor could I help blinking when I realized with what poor resources Washington had led the Continental Army for no less than eight long, sometimes hopeless years.

Without knowing it, I began to slough off my disdain for the cardboard figure I had been asked to venerate by cardboard teachers, and the larger, vainglorious figurehead I had fabricated in my own Tussaud's Museum of the embroidered dead.

Here is what I came to think of him.

•

He was not the wintry patriarch of our folklore. He was a complex man: taciturn, proud, dignified, aloof—but surprisingly sensitive. After his last official speech, this courtly gentleman, the patrician quintessence of Virginia's lordly landed gentry, turned away from the plebeian crowd so that they would not see the tears wetting his cheeks.

He was reputed to be stiff, unemotional, overbearing. Perhaps that was because, as Artemus Ward dryly noted: "The prevailin' weakness of most public men is to slop over. G. Washington never slopt over." But he did harbor explosive emotions that, wrote Thomas Jefferson, made him "most tremendous in his wrath."

He was troubled by the adulation of the people: "The loud acclamations . . . which rent the skies as I walked along the streets, filled my mind with sensations as painful as they are pleasant." And he wrote a friend: "My movements to the chair of government will be accompanied by feelings not unlike those of a culprit who is going to the place of his execution."

When some of his loyal generals (many were not) and

friends and the soldiers themselves wanted to start a movement to make him king, Washington instantly composed a
blistering rejection: "It is an idea I view with abhorrence
and reprehend with severity."

And when he was elected President of the new United
States, he went into a depression, overwhelmed "with de-
spondence [about my] inferior endowments." It was a theme
that recurred again and again in his career, before and after
he became President. "Integrity and firmness are all I can
promise."

His detractors, who thought him haughty and condescending, poured calumnies upon him:

General Charles Lee called Washington "that dark designing sordid ambitious arrogant and vindicative knave."

A newspaper denounced him for "sounding like the omnipotent director to a seraglio [who has] thundered contempt
upon the people . . . as if he sat upon the throne of Indo-
stan."

John Adams called Washington "too illiterate, unlearned,
unread, for his station."

And Thomas Paine, who had praised him in *The Rights of
Man*, exploded maledictions in a sixty-page (!) letter of
which one paragraph reads:

> As to you, sir, treacherous to private friendship . . . and a
> hypocrite in public life, the world will be puzzled to decide
> whether you are an apostate or an impostor, whether you
> have abandoned good principles or whether you ever had
> any.

But I cannot forget the episode involving Washington as
he was being escorted down the street of a town in New
York by an official. An old Negro saw the General and
stopped and bared his head and bowed. Washington at once
doffed his hat, and returned the bow. The flabbergasted politician expressed surprise that the General had bared his
head to a slave. Washington replied, "But I cannot be less
civil than a poor Negro."

He was a majestic figure of a man, six feet two inches

tall, straight as an Indian, very strong, uncommonly grace-
ful, a superlative horseman. He thrived amidst the spacious
courtesies of the Virginia gentlemen from whom he came
and with whom he was at home. He dressed in elegant silks
and velvets; he loved to dance and hunt, play billiards, race
horses, play cards. He would have been entirely at home in
the England of his forebears, for he was the very model
of the country gentleman in taste, breeding and values.

Gilbert Stuart, whose portraits have given us the likeness
we all carry in our heads, said:

> There are features in his face totally different from what
> I ever observed in that of any other human being; the
> sockets of the eyes, for instance, are larger, and the upper
> part of the nose broader. All his features are indicative of
> the strongest passions; yet his judgment and self-command
> make him appear a man of a different cast in the eyes of
> the world.

Before Washington was sixteen he had taken long jour-
neys on horse, alone, to the frontier and wilderness of the
Appalachians. He loved the solitary exploration of mountain
and forest and Indian country. He became a public-land
surveyor, and fought in several battles with the British
forces, against the French and Indians.

Washington's experiences and wanderings made him one
of the best-informed men in the colonies and about the
colonies. And his reports from the frontier, his accounts of
the life of woodsmen and pioneer settlers, were widely read
in London.

He was not as in-bred or provincial as the gentlemen of
Virginia, because his life on the frontier and in the army
gave him first-hand knowledge of the different problems and
ideas and kinds of men—high- or low-born—bred in the
different parts of the thirteen colonies. He became, without
realizing it, national in outlook.

At twenty-seven, Washington made a most happy marriage with Martha Custis, a Tidewater planter's widow who
had two children, 15,000 acres of splendid land, and a
fortune. He made Mount Vernon one of the finest estates in

the colonies. He was an expert farmer who sent away for, and very carefully read, the latest books and journals on agriculture. He was one of the first men in the colonies to adopt the radical concept of rotating his crops. This wealthy Southern plantation owner (he had himself inherited 8,000 acres and many slaves) thought the institution of slavery unjust, immoral, and uneconomic. His will provided that his 119 slaves be freed.

His political career began as no more than a fulfillment of his duty as a landowner and taxpayer. For fifteen years he sat as a member of the Virginia House of Burgesses, during that period when England's colonial follies, imperial discriminations, and arbitrary economic repressions rubbed the colonists raw. British mercantilists, working through their powerful bloc in Parliament, strove to keep the colonies agricultural, a source of raw materials for England's factories; and they used tax and trade pressures to compel the American dependencies to sell to, and buy from, the homeland alone. The ultimate insult of placing high taxes on such essential commodities as stamps and tea, and the peremptory quartering of the King's troops in whatever private homes the King's officers selected, proved incendiary to colonial patriots who had thought themselves Englishmen, too.

The Crown's stupidities in governing and discriminating against the colonies in the New World offended Washington's pride and his innate sense of fairness. He moved from his Tory anchorage to become, of all things, "intensely republican."

During the first signs and sounds of friction, Washington envisaged no break with the King or Parliament or Mother England. He was no rebel by temperament, no crusader, and surely no rabble-rouser. But he was driven more and more to hate Britain's arbitrary actions and resent Parliament's odious taxes. He came to see that, as he put it, the Thirteen Colonies would soon be "drenched with blood, or inhabited by slaves. Can a virtuous man hesitate in his choice?"

In 1774, when open rebellion broke out in Boston, Colonel George Washington of the Virginia militia, that proper flower of the Southern elite, made this remarkable offer: "I will raise a thousand men, subsist them at my own expense, and march myself at their head for the relief of Boston."

The retaliation of Britsh and mercenary troops in Boston fueled the angers now sweeping the land. Washington was chosen, over considerable opposition from the nabobs of the north, to be commander in chief of the revolutionary forces. His salary: expenses.

He led a motley army of wayward soldiers and bickering generals, all ill-equipped for an extended war. He was chivvied almost beyond endurance by jealous, quarreling colonies oversensitive about the common, yet separate, independence they were trying to wrest from the English empire. Washington led such an army amidst the confusion of political indecisiveness, the fume of petty rancors and petulant parsimony, for eight uncertain and foreboding years. He clung to a faith in Providence and the virtue of his cause and the conviction he expressed in these words: "Liberty, when it begins to take root, is a plant of rapid growth." He also learned, from bitter experience with colleagues who sabotaged him or betrayed the revolution, that "few men have virtue to withstand the highest bidder."

Authorities on the craft of warfare agree that Washington was not a great military strategist. He committed many serious tactical blunders. He was in the habit of overestimating the power of attack; he often failed to plan for, or foresee, a professional adversary's responses. He often thinned his defenses rashly; he left his flanks so weak as to invite their turning; he consistently underestimated the ponderous role of supplies, food, and fodder.

But in one central requirement of command, Washington was a miracle: as a leader of men. In his poise, his confidence, his manner, his sense of honor and sheer character, he won the respect of his subordinates and the affection of his troops. His personal courage, his refusal to feel defeated, his calm acceptance of the disasters that beset him—these were priceless beacons to men who faced death for their captain.

Washington hammered out a fighting force from the most dubious material. He did not hesitate to order court-martials for deserters or public floggings for malingerers. But he used his power without favor, and with a profound understanding of the necessities of command. "Discipline," he wrote, "is the soul of an army. It makes small numbers formidable.... Defeat is only a reason for exertion." He despised "the sunshine patriot." And he was convinced to the very marrow of his bones that "our cause is noble; it is the cause of mankind."

His absolute resolution won his soldiers' confidence, his absolute fairness won their gratitude. The combination, in a fighting force compelled to retreat and retreat and live from hand to mouth, was infinite in worth.

Few commanders were ever so beleaguered. "Hideous civil strife" continued to erode the colonies' alliance. A suspicious, ununified Congress simply could not lead its squabbling constituents, each bristling over some possible breach of its autonomy. This Congress could not even tax the rambunctious colonies. Washington could not get enough men, guns, shoes, food. His recruits would serve for a few months— and disappear after rudimentary training and no combat. His army was paid in paper money so depreciated that a colonel's salary was not large enough to buy oats for his horse!

From top to bottom, this "revolutionary rabble," like the colonies themselves, was riddled by rumors, weakened by dissensions, ruptured by defections, shifts of purpose, or failures of nerve. But the Commander persevered.

Washington learned, through humiliating reverses, that his central strategy must lie in one direction: to avoid at all costs a direct, "set-piece" battle in which he risked losing his army. He avoided head-on confrontations, waging *his* war, instead, with sudden raids and prompt retreats. He led his hit-and-run regiments all the way from Boston to Philadelphia.

The policy was sure to provoke discontent. Furious critics —from governors of the colonies to their agents in the Congress—denounced Washington's repeated "procrastinations" and "dilatory" methods; such floundering, improvised tactics were doomed to fail; and even if Washington managed to outlast and outwait the British, the strategy was outrageously lengthening an already too-long, bankrupting war.

But Washington held fast: as long as he could keep an army in the field, England had not beaten him. It looked like an impossible cause. The army was badly battered, a desolate, shabby force of uncertain troops, whose commander's heart ached to see them, at Valley Forge, without boots, with filthy bandages on their bleeding feet, a horde of hungry, ragged, miserable survivors of bloody forays and despairing marches of retreat. They were so poorly provisioned that they had to sleep, Washington wrote, "under frost and snow without . . . blankets."

And now this lonely, altogether remarkable man, who wanted nothing more than to return to the ease and luxury of his beloved estate on the Potomac, trained and drilled these tatterdemalion soldiers, conducting himself as if there was no choice, as if final victory could come, as if he and his shivering band could expect to prevail. "Providence has at all times been my only dependence," he wrote, "for all other resources seem to have failed us." To his troops, he said, "Let us show the world that a Freeman, contending for liberty on his own ground, is superior to any slavish mercenary on earth."

That Washington could keep his army together over that brutal winter at Valley Forge, even though a full third of his men deserted (!), was unbelievable. Winston Churchill, no amateur where the facts and intangibles of war are concerned, called it Washington's greatest achievement.

The American commander scored his great military triumph by marching his men all the way down to Yorktown, to fight Cornwallis's beautifully attired redcoats. A force of 11,000 American and 9,000 French troops (let us not forget), plus the crucial naval blockade by thirty French ships under Admiral de Grasse that denied Cornwallis supplies and reinforcements, brought the colonists victory. The date was October 19, 1781.

And now ... ? Washington, the greatest of all heroes, praised and admired, could hardly wait to leave public life, and return to Mount Vernon. He rebuffed those who urged him to exploit his immense prestige. He scotched as despicable the revived suggestion that he wanted, or could have, the powers of a king.

But a leader so great could not be allowed to withdraw. The *ad hoc* government faced a welter of new crises and dilemmas. Who but Washington could preside over the deliberations of the Convention that had been called to draft a constitution that would formally unite, by their own free consent, the thirteen colonies?

And so, for five months, Mr. Washington, wearing no uniform, a gentleman in knee breeches and a powdered wig, presided over the debates, the committees, the pressures and tempers and compromises, the legalistic and philosophical battles, that characterized the Constitutional Convention in Philadelphia.

He presided, but rarely spoke. Yet his moral influence, his steadfastness, his impartial judgment, served immeasurably to cool the heated differences, to moderate the quarrels, to clarify the confusions about issues of the gravest importance: federal power and individual freedom; the independence of states—but under a central government; public debts and foreign affairs; the power to tax and the limits of taxing; the primacy of a constitution—but a method of making amendments to allow for change; the balance between authority and consent, between the elected and the governed; the accouterments of political legitimacy—without royal or divine sanctions; the riddle of how power should be transferred and transmitted, and how the democracy of the polls could be protected from usurpation, *coups-d-états,* conspiracy; the question of who should control which armies, and who should have the authority to declare a war; above all, the question of whose opinions and rulings should prevail, by what process, through what guarantees, in interpreting and adjudicating whatever document was agreed to. It is not hyperbole to say there might have been no Constitution, no union, no federal government without the immense and encompassing influence of Washington. The historian W. E. H. Lecky concluded: "In Washington, America found a leader who could be induced by no earthly motive to tell a falsehood, or to break an engagement, or to commit any dishonorable act."

And Fisher Ames reflected:

There has scarcely appeared a really great man whose character has been more admired in his lifetime, or less correctly understood by his admirers. . . . His talents were adapted to lead without dazzling mankind, and to draw forth and employ the talents of others without being misled by them.

The description of Samuel Eliot Morison is noteworthy:

[Washington] had the power of inspiring respect. . . . He was direct, not adroit; stubborn rather than flexible; slow to reach a decision. . . . The mask of dignity and reserve that concealed his inner life came from humility, and stern self-control. A warm heart was revealed by innumerable kindly acts to his . . . subordinates. Some men . . . found him stiff and dull; but the ladies never did. He talked with them charmingly, and danced with gusto.

And now, again, he hoped to leave public life for good, and go home. From every side came the clamor that he become the country's first president. When Gouverneur Morris urged Washington to accept the presidency, he saw, with uncommon percipience, what both the man and the moment were: "No Constitution," said Morris, "is the same on paper and in life. The exercise of authority depends on personal character. Your cool, steady temper is *indispensably necessary* to give firm and manly tone to the new government."

Washington could not refuse. He could never negate his sense of duty, or deny the paramount power of conscience, which he had called "that little spark of celestial fire." He was unanimously elected Chief Executive, and wrote one of his generals: "I face an ocean of difficulties, without that competence of political skills, abilities, and inclinations . . . necessary to manage the helm." His modesty was not feigned; he never overcame his anxieties about "my inferior endowments." He consoled himself by saying, "I consider the most enviable of all titles, the character of an 'Honest Man.' "

During the trip from Mount Vernon to New York to take office, the man from Virginia was accorded such adulation that, as Morison has written, "a lesser man might have thought himself a god."

He took office on April 30, 1787, a long, hard time since the Declaration of Independence, on the balcony of Federal Hall, which overlooked a street on New York harbor called Wall. It was a remarkable piece of judgment that led Washington to appear at his inauguration, watched afar by the kings and queens, the viceroys and rebels of Europe, not in the splendor of his uniform, with gold epaulets and silver sword and plumed hat, but in plain, brown homespun.

The symbolism was not lost on the world, or on the new breed called Americans. The man who said, "Let us raise a standard to which the wise and honest can repair," had written, in a less lofty mood: "Do not conceive that fine clothes make fine men, any more than feathers make fine birds. A plain, genteel dress is more admired, and obtains more credit in the eyes of the judicious and sensible."

We forget that unlike previous revolutionists, the American colonists did not take over an existing government. There were no federal agencies, no federal officials, no federal treasury, no central system of administering day-by-day affairs. And the national army Washington could now command consisted of exactly 672 officers and men!

"No successful leader of a revolution [was] so naked before the world." Credit was so scarce and so cautious that the new state found itself strapped for funds. Washington was a wealthy man, but the personal debts he had incurred as general, plus the expenses needed for him now to move to New York, made it necessary for him to borrow $3,000.

Washington endowed the presidency with a stateliness that won swift respect. He had to make his own rules for how the Chief Executive should conduct himself: where which protocol should be followed; when the national interest ought to be asserted, even at the displeasure of states; how national unity could be affirmed and national power abetted—by diplomacy or congressional action or the deployment of force.

His every act as president was triply scrutinized. His official entertaining was attacked by anti-Federalists as "aping the British." His driving in a coach and six horses was rumored "royal pretension." His sensitivity to the subtleties of status vis-à-vis foreign plenipotentiaries made him decide that the President would "receive" at the Executive Mansion, but not pay courtesy calls elsewhere—which was cited as a sign of unforgivable conceit.

Reticent in manner, plain in speech, he was a new kind of personification of what the Greeks called charisma. "Be courteous to all, but intimate to few; and let those few be well tried before you give them your confidence." Above all: "Undertake not what you cannot perform, but be careful to keep your promise."

It is a testimonial to his confidence that he could invite both Hamilton and Jefferson, bitter opponents, each much more brilliant than he, into his Cabinet. He had the rare capacity to ignore men's deficiencies when he needed their ability. Who but Washington would have suffered Alexander Hamilton's patronizing manner and outright insolence; or not have fretted under Jefferson's intellectual agility and devious inclinations? Washington did not know a great deal that his colleagues knew well: Latin, Greek, the classics, Aristotle, Plato, Montesquieu, Locke, Harrington. But his knowledge of the *fitness* of things, of governing as against commanding, of creating that aura that nourishes respect

and morale, of the practices of persuasion and agreement
—in these, he was a master.

Washington was no political theorist, but his political
judgment was superb:

> Government is not reason, it is not eloquent—it is a
> force. Like fire it is a dangerous servant and a fearful
> master; never for a moment should it be left to irresponsi-
> ble action.

He knew in his bones what more brilliant men could not
be taught: how to lead, when to act, when to resist, when
to compromise. He knew the power of honor, and the invisible leverage of dignity and grace.

In a remarkable passage, Jefferson wrote:

> His mind was great and powerful, without being of the
> very first order; his penetration strong, though not so acute
> as that of a Newton, Bacon, or Locke; and as far as he saw,
> no judgment was ever sounder. It was slow in operation,
> being little aided by invention or imagination, but sure in
> conclusion.

Washington fortified the Chief Executive's power against
incursions from other government branches. He staunchly
defended what the constitution provided: that the Senate
had the right to "advise and consent," but not decide, the
Supreme Court could adjudicate, but not legislate.

Washington persuaded the new Congress to assume the
states' debts; he reconciled the contending factions of state
and federal power; he threaded national policy between
ardent free-traders and rabid protectionists. He was visionary enough to proclaim "knowledge . . . the surest basis of
public happiness," and urged federal aid to colleges.

He was also driven to decisions he knew would make him
hated by those who had given him their trust and their
affection. He performed the galling task of putting down a
rebellion of American patriots in Pennsylvania's back country. Against tremendous pressure, he refused to send military help to France, hard pressed in her war with England—

and no man knew better how crucial French aid and arms had been to him and the Revolution. He refused, more surprisingly, despite a formal alliance with our best ally. Why? Because he saw "the national interest"; he knew the weakness of his resources, and the paramount need to husband them while his nation sank roots and began to grow.

This "betrayal" of France, and the ill-starred Jay Treaty, broke the dams of public opinion, drenching Washington with such virulent abuse that, he wrote bitterly, it was undeserved by "a Nero . . . or even a common pickpocket." But he would not answer the slanderers or the libelers. "To persevere in one's duty and be silent is the best answer to calumny."

This was more easily said than done. His temper was quick; he kept it under control, but periodically it boiled over in a way none who saw it could forget. Jefferson described one Cabinet meeting in which "the President was much inflamed, got into one of those passions when he cannot command himself [and said] that *by God* he had rather be in his grave than in his present situation!"

History pays tribute to the sustaining wisdom of his counsel:

> "To be prepared for war is one of the [best] means of preserving peace."

> It is a maxim founded on the universal experience of mankind that no nation is to be trusted farther than it is bound by its interest.

> It is folly in one nation to look for disinterested favors from another.

> The nation which indulges toward another an habitual hatred, or an habitual fondness, is in some degree a slave. It is a slave to its animosity or to its affection, either of which is sufficient to lead it astray from its duty and its interest.

His moving Farewell Address advised Americans to avoid "permanent alliances with . . . the foreign world," but it continued, as isolationists do not seem to know: "We may safely trust to temporary alliances for extraordinary emergencies."

He flatly refused to consider a third term.

How does one sum him up? Washington could not match Franklin in philosophic breadth; Jefferson in force of intellect or insight; Madison in the theory of statecraft; Hamilton in analytic power; the remarkable John Adams and the Boston Brahmins around him. But I think that no man in all that scintillating congregation could equal Washington in the sheer effectiveness of personal example.

He was one of that very rare breed of men whom power could neither seduce nor corrupt, nor even tempt into vainglorious adventures. We may thank our stars that Washington was no Caesar, no Cromwell, no Napoleon.

He died in 1799, aged sixty-seven.

No summation can equal the eulogy of Jefferson, who had differed with him and suffered his displeasure:

> ... his character was, in its mass, perfect, in nothing bad, in few points indifferent; and it may truly be said that never did nature and fortune combine more perfectly to make a man great. ... His integrity was most pure. No motives of interest ... friendship, or hatred [biased] his decision. He was ... in every sense of the words, a wise, a good, and a great man. [He merits] from Man an everlasting remembrance.

Arcturus,
We Greet Thee!

~~~~~~

YES, *there was (and maybe still is) a denomination or doctrine named the I AM. It will always occupy a special niche in my heart—even though Mr. and Mrs. G. W. Ballard, "our beloved messengers of light," ran into difficulty with the Department of Justice for hanky-panky diddles via the U.S. mails. The country may be better off because of this, but the cause of comedy (supernatural division) suffered a most grievous blow.*

Ever since I saw I AM, I have searched for a sect that could match it in richness of invention, or replace it, however pallidly, in my affections. I have found none. We shall have to wait until man reaches Arcturus (see text) to find the likes of it again.

The Temple of the I AM is a gleaming white mosque on Lake Street, just north of Beverly, in the City of the Angels. It is a big, clean, airy tabernacle, with nary a speck of red or black on the premises. That's because red and black are taboo to I AM-ers, who are also sternly opposed to liquor, tobacco, meat, onions, garlic, and sex. It's all part of the I AM creed, which is pretty complicated.

The I AM flock devotes itself to the teachings of the Ninety-Nine Ascended Masters of Saint Germain. These wonderful precepts have been transcribed for humanity by a Mr. and Mrs. G. W. Ballard, the celebrated leaders of the movement. They are referred to lovingly as "Our Messengers of Light," or simply as Papa and Mama Ballard. The head of this immortal household will go down in history as the man who started the I AM single-handed.

He was camping on Mount Shasta, in sunny California, when suddenly Saint Germain materialized before him and gave him all the dope on the Great I AM Presence, the All-Consuming Flame, the Coming of the Seventh Ray, the Blue Tube of Light, the illusion of "so-called death," and how to stop war, earthquakes, dandruff and traffic accidents, just by decreeing against them in a loud, firm voice. In all the years I spent in Los Angeles, no one ever died of dandruff while driving an automobile during an earthquake—which is a pretty potent testimonial, I think, to the power of prayer.

I went to an I AM meeting in the temple in Los Angeles on a Sunday night—a balmy Sunday night. An elderly gentleman—spare and tall and pale, and dressed in white from head to foot—led me down the aisle. There were some five hundred happy converts in the auditorium. Most of them wore the faint smile and peaked look of the uplifted. None wore red or black. The whole flock was on its feet singing a hymn. It was a nice, lilting hymn—entitled "Arcturus, We Greet Thee!" They sang it quite loudly. (Arcturus is 210,785,080,000,000 miles from the earth.) When the greeting to Arcturus was completed, everyone sat down and I found a seat.

On a lavishly beflowered stage (yellow, pink and violet flowers only) I saw two people and four panes of glass. The first pane of glass was about four feet high and on it was painted the manly visage of Saint Germain, illuminated from behind. The second pane of glass depicted Our Saviour. The third pane of glass had purple waves painted on it; when lit up, as it was, it looked like blue running water. The last pane of glass I had better describe slowly. Its central motif was a violet flame, within which were two nude male (but sexless) figures, one standing on the head of the other. I mean that the top figure was standing on the head of the bottom figure—only he wasn't really standing; because he had no feet. His legs kind of faded into a path of white light which blended into the head of the man underneath. In other words, the top man seemed to be melting upwards from the bottom man, like ectoplasm. In the background, behind the violet flame and the two androgynes, was a snow-capped mountain.

This work of art illustrates the subtle metaphysic of the Mighty I AM. It is called "The Chart." It was explained to us by one of the two mortals on the stage—an exalted young man, dressed all in white, who wore rimless glasses and spoke in a voice that suggested taffy dipped in fur.

"The I AM Presence is the perfect manifestation of the I AM principle," he began. "The original perfect bodies were of pure light substance, but of course not bodies that you can *see*. Now we have instructions from the Ninety-Nine Ascended Masters so we can rise above life on this octave of light." At this point our Saint Paul went over to the Chart and cleared up a few matters. It was fascinating. I gathered that the under-gentleman represents anyone—you or me or the man who calls for the laundry; by letting the light energy pour into him "until it fills every cell in the body, bursting with pure light radiance," the under-gentleman "rises" into the upper gentleman. Then he is in the Great I AM. Our teacher was a little vague about the mechanics of this elevation. He was, however, ultralucid about the mountain in the Chart. "That represents Mount Shasta," he said.

He told us many other things, terribly interesting, which I can only put down just as I heard them: "Mistakes are nothing but a disqualification of energy. . . . The Unfed Flame can burn anywhere, without oil or wood. Why, when you get pure enough you can call on the Flame and hold it right in the palm of your hand—and if you put a bar of steel or iron in the Flame it will be consumed at once but it

won't hurt *you. Every*thing manifests on inner octaves before manifesting here. Like a house on a blueprint."

At this, the other shepherd on the stage took the pulpit.
She was a serene, fat little lady—about five decades old—
with white hair and a distant look. She was dressed all in
pink—a shiny pink evening gown and a flowing pink cape
and a tiara of pink flowers in her hair and pink shoes and a
pink corsage and her face was all pink, too. Her eyes had an
ethereal look, even from where I sat. She spoke gently,
sweetly, with a beatific smile that didn't leave her face once
throughout that whole glorious evening. If anybody was
saved, she was. She called us "Dear ones."

I turned to a proselyte on my right—she was dressed
in pink, too—and whispered: "Who is that?"

The woman sighed ecstatically. "Ratana." A moment later
she added, "That is the name the Ascended Masters gave
her."

Ratana was saying that she was going to answer questions
that had been piling up all through the busy week.

"Is she an Ascended Master?" I whispered.

The woman on my right shook her head, ever so toler-
antly. "She is a Master Unascended. She *could* ascend, of
course, if she wanted to, she has been ready for such a long
time. But she has decided to stay on this octave of light to
do all this wonderful work with us. Like Mr. and Mrs. G. W.
Ballard."

"Who was the chap who explained the Chart?"

"Everybody calls him Stanley."

Ratana was waving a letter. "I have here a note from one
of the young people in our Ascension Class. You all know
about our Ascension Class every Sunday morning at eleven
o'clock, studying to make a public ascension? Well, this
dear one is a girl in that fine class and wrote me this letter."
She smiled and read: "'To whom it may concern: I have
just come down from Venus to usher in the Golden Age.'"
Ratana took thought with her I AM, then said: "I think that
is going a little too far."

The audience applauded.

"Of course we all know," Ratana continued, "that some spirits *did* come down from Venus to usher in the Golden Age. However"—Ratana gave us a particularly warm smile to soften the blow—"I do not think this particular girl is one of them."

The next letter was from "one of our most earnest and dynamic students"—a mail carrier. It seemed that this gentleman, putting his heart and soul into things, had donned the I AM veil by renouncing any and all forms of liquor, tobacco, meat, onions, and garlic. (The letter didn't say anything about sex.) What he was writing Ratana about was this: as he was making his rounds for Uncle Sam these days, his mail sack flung bravely over his shoulder, he was seeing steaks hanging before his eyes. This was accompanied by a strange hollow feeling in the stomach. Alarmed, he had consulted a doctor, and the doctor (a materialist) had told him to start eating meat at once. His letter ended simply: "What shall I do?"

A hush fell over the seekers of salvation. It was plain that a lot hung on Ratana's answer. I have nothing but admiration for the way she handled herself in the crisis. "Of *course* this dear one will feel a little weak for a while," Ratana smiled, taking the bull right by the horns. "But you can eat *poison* when you are in the Great I AM Presence, and take the quality out and change it back to its pristine purity. Why, even the scientists admit that meat-eating people get cancer and fish-eating people get leprosy. *What is the strongest animal in the animal kingdom?* The elephant! And he is a vegetarian."

The next letter was a pip. It was from an acolyte who wrote: "I demand that after so-called death my body be placed on a block of ice for seventy-two hours! No fluid, water, or blood whatsoever is to touch me! Then I am to be cremated at once!!"

This challenge didn't faze Ratana for a moment. "The Ascended Masters do not approve of this sort of thing," she proclaimed firmly. "When our earth-bodies reach so-called death, many relatives and so on want funeral services. Do not hurt them. So I do not approve of this dear one asking to have his earth-body laid on a block of ice for seventy-two hours." Ratana finished the whole problem off by remarking: "I want to warn you all that petitions about blocks of ice and cremation after so-called death are being circulated in Los Angeles by certain destructive forces. Watch out for them! Do not do anything fanatical. . . . Let us all stand up and give a decree! And make it loud and strong so the Ascended Ones will get plenty of energy to do their work!"

The audience of 500 rose as one and Stanley stepped forward and announced: "Let us give the decree for light! Let us give the three times three!" He waved his hands and the audience chanted the decree for light in mighty unison:

"Mighty I AM Presence! Ex–pand thy light in every cell of my body until its ra–di–ance *bla*–zes through my flesh— e–ter–nally sustained!"

Ratana cried, "Keep up the tempo! Do not let it drag!"

The lady at my right was decreeing like mad. Suddenly she shoved several mimeographed sheets at me with a cordial "The decrees!" There were three pronunciamentoes there, in violet ink, and they were wonderful to behold. The first was "The Decree for Annihilation of War in Europe."

There was also a jolly "Decree for Money," which began "Mighty I AM Presence! I must have money!!!"—and a special decree against "Spies, Agitators, Etc." "Spies, Agitators, Etc." was a number to make your hair stand on end. It began blandly enough, calling on Oromasis, the great Archangel Michael, and a Mr. David Lloyd; then it hit its stride and demanded that the Mighty Powers "project the Blue Lightning into every vortex of human discord in America and the world, and EXPLODE! EXPLODE! EXPLODE! everyone this instant!" There was also something about "dissolving all stolen airplanes."

Now Ratana beamed on her children and said, "I hope you will all decree to have the red traffic lights turned to violet."

Then Ratana exclaimed: "We just don't blaze enough light! How much light are you pouring forth?" A lot of people in the audience acted pretty sheepish when she put it that way. Whereupon Ratana lit into the evil forces. "I remember when I first got into this wonderful work. I was just an usher in the balcony. Well, a man staggered in and sat down—in the balcony. And dear ones, how that man smelled! Why, he smelled of liquor and tobacco and meat and all the destructive forces. The smell was so bad I decided to put the Tube of Light around me, but then I closed my eyes"—Ratana closed her eyes—"and suddenly I thought, 'Silly! Why don't you put the Tube of Light around *him?*'" There was a little explosion of laughter, and admiring nods over Ratana's ingenuity. "So I put the Tube of Light around him, and I put a tiny fragrance of roses around the edges!" We sat there breathless. "And after that beautiful service, dozens of dear ones came up to me and said, 'Ratana, Ratana, did you smell the roses in the Temple tonight?'" . . .

A letter challenged Ratana to reconcile the I AM's taboo on spirits (fluid spirits) with Jesus' miracle in turning water into wine. Ratana didn't bat an eye as she replied: "Jesus did turn water into wine—but times were different then! In that region they all ate fish. Well, he could not tell them not to eat *fish.* Why, Saint Germain once said, 'I will give you a ham sandwich but there won't be any pig in it.'" The congregation chuckled merrily at that. "Because it is pure substance. There is just a little *quality* of pig, to give it flavor . . ."

Stanley leered (I don't think he meant to leer; it was just the way he smiled) and relieved Ratana. "The Mighty I AM," he announced in his bold, blurry voice, "is opposed to secret orders and mysticism. There are *no mysteries whatsoever* in the teachings of the Ascended Ones! It is a simple thing which veritably any child can understand." Since no children were present, Stanley went on to explain things. "The ray intensifies and reintensifies and reduces disqualification, causing pure light to expand in our bodies."

Ratana floated to the fore at this point and interpolated: "I would like to say that our dear Papa Ballard has just gotten a message that during the past few weeks the

Ascended Ones have been walking around in Wall Street. They have also been walking around right here in downtown Los Angeles, in the business districts. They are working on the financial crisis!"

There was a roar of appreciation and applause. "Let us sing a hymn! That beautiful Number Twenty-three! And make it lively, for the Masters do not like slow rhythms."

I thumbed the numerous pages of the hymnbook and read the names of the following liturgies: "Beloved Leto," "O Presence of the Diamond Heart," "Great Sanat Kumara." Even more wondrous were two psalms, the names of which I shall never forget. One was entitled "To Nada, Rex, Bob and Pearl." The other was called "Visualize, Just Visualize."

And now Ratana stepped forward, smiled like an affectionate cherub, and said, "God bless you."

"God bless *you*," the audience echoed fondly.

"God bless you," Ratana called.

"God bless *you!*" chorused the followers of the Ninety-Nine Ascended Masters of Saint Germain.

"God bless you!" Ratana proclaimed for yet a third time.

"God bless *you!*" the voices of the saved rang out.

The service was over.

We all filed out. The ushers were standing in the foyer in their nice white suits and dresses, beaming at everyone, sending pure light all over the place. The air throbbed with I AM good nights. Little clusters of the unascended hovered around pedestals inscribed "Love Gift." The more fervent disciples of Mr. and Mrs. G. W. Ballard dropped dimes and quarters as their love gifts. (I didn't drop anything: I wasn't in love.)

Just as I got to the exit a clear-eyed woman with the look of an eagle trapped me. "God bless you," she sang out.

"God bless *you*," I murmured.

"Is this your first time here?"

"Yes."

"Oh, it is wonderful work. It is simply wonderful! You will see how wonderful the work is. Would you like to ask anything about anything?"

I heard some thirty voices chanting furiously from a room upstairs. "Whom are they decreeing against?" I asked.

"Grasshoppers!" she replied at once. "You know this terrible plague in Kern County that's destroying the crops and all? Well, we are working on it. We are working on it with all our powers. We have been decreeing all day just as hard as we can for the Ascended Masters to *drain* the energy out of the insects, to *drain* out their destructive forces. Generally, the Los Angeles chapter decrees against earthquakes and the San Francisco chapter decrees against strikes and revolution."

I started to ask her when Saint Germain had died, or lived, but I caught myself in time and asked instead: "When *was* Saint Germain?"

She blinked: "Oh, many times! You know, of course, that he was Sir Francis Drake. And he wrote all of Shakespeare." Before I could put the Blue Tube around me she had added: "He takes different forms, you see. For the last five years he has just been known as Freedom." She was so transported by her revelation that she was breathing heavily, and her eyes were bright as beads, and her cheeks . . . well, for one agnostic moment I could have sworn they turned r-d.

A Cheer for
Great Men

E VER since I sang the praises of such men as the genius who invented square spaghetti, or the man who wrote, "Beneath those ragged trousers beat a heart of gold," or the reporter who told mankind, "The ball game was held in Jackson's cow pasture, but ended abruptly when a runner slid into what he thought was second base," I have been deluged by letters from readers begging me to "go on . . . please . . . give us more."

Few requests are so easy to fulfill; and I hope that now Jasper P. Deluge, who wrote four of the five letters, will be happy. It is a pleasure for me to salute these benefactors of our inhuman race:

1. *J. Irwin Miller*, chairman of the board of Cummins Engine Company, whom I watched in a television "talk" show as he patiently tried to explain his views to three condescending panelists, indubitable highbrows, who insisted on demolishing points Mr. Miller had not made, and persisted in ridiculing policies Mr. Miller had never propounded.

When he saw that he could not persuade the deep thinkers to desist from their eloquent irrelevances, the deadpan businessman finally cleared his throat and sighed, with exemplary kindness: "In my house, we all try to follow a rule

I once suggested to my children. The rule goes like this: 'You can disagree with a man's position as much as you want— *after* you have been able to state it, to his satisfaction.'"

I consider this dictum, which belongs in all anthologies of great quotations, the best statement ever made about the basic rule men of reason ought to follow during an argument. I wish it would govern the dinner parties *I* get invited to, where the cross fires of political discourse remind me of nothing so much as the plight of the three cross-eyed prisoners who were brought before a cross-eyed judge.

JUDGE: *(to First Prisoner):* What's your name?

SECOND PRISONER: Henry Megilla.

JUDGE: *(to Second Prisoner):* I wasn't talking to you!

THIRD PRISONER: *I* didn't say anything!

P.S. I would like to follow J. Irwin Miller's lovely Law with Rosten's wistful Rule: "Those who raise their voice lower their effectiveness."

2. *Robert Benchley,* the prince of drollery, who once asked his doctor what he (the doctor) was going to prescribe for his (Benchley's) stuffed head, runny nose, clammy palms and romping fever. When the M.D. briskly said, "One of the new miracle drugs," Benchley, a devout and accomplished hypochondriac, complained: "But I don't *like* to try new drugs; they might have funny side effects . . ."

"Nonsense! This will make you fit as a fiddle," said the doctor, whose name, I think, was Stradivarius. "I'll drop in to see you tomorrow."

The next morning, Benchley arose to find his fever vanished, his head clear, his palms dry, his anxieties allayed. His spirit soared so high with well-being and gratitude that he decided to show his appreciation to the doctor by brightening the man's day, or expanding the man's horizons in some memorable way. Mr. Benchley considered several ways of doing this, then found a pot of glue, slit open the pillow, and, humming happily all the while, glued feathers on and to both thighs. This delicate maneuver completed, he drew the sheet up to his neck very carefully, high above his waist, cautiously lowered the sheet and, with a seraphic smile, waited for his healer.

The moment Dr. Stradivarius appeared in the doorway, Benchley exclaimed, "Doc, you're a whiz! That new drug you gave me certainly worked miracles!"

"You can say that again," said the doctor.

But instead of saying it again, Benchley blinked innocently and asked, "There's just one thing, Doc: What do you make of—" he lifted the sheet to reveal two thighs thick with feathers—". . . this!"

I have whiled away many a blissful hour imagining what the expression on that doctor's face must have been, and what horrified apparitions—of incredulity, panic, guilt— must have beset his thunderstruckness.

3. *Joseph Goldberger*, who, back in 1913, was assigned by the U.S. Marine Hospital to investigate pellagra, a baffling, debilitating, sometimes fatal disease that was afflicting 100,- 000 victims a year in the South. Pellagra broke out in epidemics, it seemed, and clearly looked contagious. Medical men were also convinced that pellagra caused insanity, because it was so frequently seen in the mental wards of hospitals and the state or county asylums for the demented. The local and state authorities appealed to Washington to send them someone who might possibly discover the cause of, and—if only that were possible!—the cure for this ugly, saddening pestilence. The U.S. guardians of health came up with Joseph Goldberger.

Dr. Goldberger had served as a health officer and germ detective in Cuba and Mexico, contending with disastrous epidemics of typhus and yellow fever—both of which, in the course of his work, he himself contracted. Now he set forth for the South, where he and his wife began to roam the hospitals and orphanages and asylums of Mississippi, Alabama, South Carolina, Georgia.

One thing soon struck him: nurses, interns, orderlies, and physicians who lived and worked with pellagra patients did not themselves ever come down with the disease. They seemed to enjoy "a peculiar exemption," he said.

Dr. Goldberger finally reasoned that pellagra could not be caused by a microbe, but must come from some—deficiency in diet! This theory was greeted with considerable skepti-cism by Goldberger's unpasteurized colleagues. To try to prove his point, Goldberger now injected into the bloodstream of sixteen volunteers (fourteen plus Goldberger and his wife) matter taken directly from pellagra victims. It was a bold, dramatic, dangerous thing to do. And not one of the six-teen "caught" pellagra.

To drive home his theory even more forcefully, Dr. Gold-berger then made up icky compounds from the skin scrap-ings, nasal mucus and even feces (!) of pellagra victims— and bade his squeamish volunteers swallow them! It is a tribute to man's courage in pursuit of truth, to say nothing of the dimensions of his intestinal fortitude, that the fourteen volunteers, and Goldberger *and* his very brave wife, did so.

The next days' waiting must have been a case study in the parameters of uneasiness. . . . But not one swallower contracted pellagra. It was hard for the hardest die-hard in the tribe of Asclepius to dismiss evidence like that.

Dr. Goldberger was an immigrant to our shores, by the way, who had volunteered for the medical branch of the U.S. Navy. That august service turned him down cold. The mahatmas from Annapolis seem not to have looked with favor, in those days, on oddities named Goldberger—or, later, Rickover. But millions of human beings around the world no longer suffer from pellagra's "awful crimson sig-nature" because of Joseph Goldberger's intelligence, inde-pendence, and courage.

4. *Lawrence Peter Berra*, the short, squat, lovable, beetle-browed, waddle-gaited, jug-eared, drum-chested, short-legged, long-armed, solemn-faced nonpareil of baseball, who is en-shrined in the temple of that sport as a giant, even though he played for the Yankees.

When Mr. Berra first took baseball's vows, as a catcher,

his somewhat freakish figure made him the instant target
of mockery, taunts, raspberries and other energetic sounds
of disesteem, not excluding all sorts of variations of the
Bronx cheer, aimed at him from the dugouts of his opponents. His adversaries accompanied their verbal fusillade by
Darwinian suggestions anent his ancestry, which slander
they illustrated most graphically by scratching their armpits,
grimacing like baboons, placing their tongues under their
upper lips to magnify their prognathism and simian deriva-
tions, all the while affecting to swing from branches whilst
uttering cryptic cries, croaks and grunts.

To these unfriendly salutations, which were based on
perfectly sound principles of primitive warfare, Lawrence
"Yogi" Berra responded with noble forbearance and increasing proficiency—whether crouched behind the plate or standing at it. He became the best damn catcher in baseball, a
fixture on the coveted All Star squads, and a slugger who
made fear endemic among pitchers in the American League.
Mr. Berra set no fewer than eighteen separate World Series
records. He set a high-water mark for consecutive games
caught without an error (148). He whacked 358 home runs.
He also got more hits (71) and drove in more runs (39)
than any player in a World Series before or since. One can
only stand reverent before such prodigality.

In addition to his other exceptional talents, Mr. Berra
was a rarity encountered, among professionals, once in a
generation: He was a phenomenal "bad-ball" hitter. This
means that he would not only "bite at" balls flung so remote
from the strike zone that most batters would sneer at them:
Mr. Berra welcomed, met, and clobbered them. He simply
luxuriated in very low, very high, very wide, or very close
pitches that no batter in his right mind would attempt to
hit. I do not mean to imply that Mr. Berra was of unsound
mentality; I mean that once the man was permitted to lift
his bat, his subsequent capacity to hit any ball within his
vicinity, however wild or "safe" the pitcher of that ball considered it to be, was of an order of excellence not seen since
the days of Shoeless Joe Jackson.

On one memorable occasion at Yankee Stadium, Mr.
Berra came to bat in the twilight of the ninth inning, with
two out for the Yankees and the Chicago White Sox two
fat runs ahead. With the count a near-fatal 2–2 against
him, Mr. Berra suddenly seemed to confuse baseball with
golf, for he dropped his bat like a driving iron and, brushing the ground, smote a veritable ankle-duster into the distant bleachers. This scored three runs and cruelly snatched
victory from the Chicago team in a game the Yankees clearly
deserved to lose. And when the understandably embittered
losing pitcher was asked for his expert opinion on the best
way of getting the incredible Yogi out, that White Sock
morosely replied: "With a pistol."

But I salute Mr. Berra in these pages not for his sparkling
achievements on the diamond, but for his astonishing originality as a linguist. Even Jacques Barzun would not deny
how greatly the redoubtable Berra has enriched our tongue
with his altogether new, breathtakingly fresh, and immensely creative use of ordinary words which he borrowed,
as it were, from English. I quote but five examples, each in
a separate branch of knowledge:

Education: "You can observe a lot by watching."

The Fourth Dimension (upon arriving five minutes late,
instead of his usual half-hour, for a radio interview): "I
guess this is the earliest I've ever been late."

Logic: "How can that pitcher stay in the majors, considering the stuff he keeps striking me out with?"

The Future of Fiction (to his roommate, a summer sec-
ond-baseman and winter medical student, who spent hour
after hour, when the Yankees were on the road, studying
his anatomy textbook, which he finally finished): "How'd
it come out?"

Etiquette (opening his acceptance speech on "Yogi Berra
Day" in St. Louis, his hometown): "I just want to thank
everyone who made this day necessary."

What can one say of such versatility? These days, when
I think back on the golden era Yogi Berra adorned, I think

of Byron—his immortal lines slightly adapted for the purposes of my paean:

> The isles of Greece, the isles of Greece!
> Where burning Berra swat and sung,
> Where grew the arts of war and peace,
> Where Mantle rose, and Musial sprung!
> Eternal summer gilds them yet,
> And none, except their sun, is set.

5. *J. B. Priestley*, that prolific novelist, essayist, play-
wright and civil libertarian: that sterling apostle of good
sense who gave vent (in London's *New Statesman*) to his
ire over student demonstrations in these words:

"I don't see ... why young men in universities, turning
themselves into mischievous and sometimes dangerous
mobs, should be treated as if they were different from
mobs of garage-hands. Indeed, there is a case for more
severity. Students ... should be the last and not the first
to create howling, destructive mobs.

"I do not care whose side they are supposed to be on. I
am revolted by these idiot processions [on TV], with their
banners and slogans and mindless grinning faces. . . . I
won't join a mob to smash *their* windows and overturn their
cars, but I'll be damned if I'll admire them. . . . I [would
welcome] some newsreels showing students ... studying."

P.S. Furious letters to Mr. Priestley should be written at room
temperature. Nasty letters to me should be typed on 13″ ×
16″ foolscap, then donned. Letters that are not on foolscap
should be carefully folded, placed in an envelope, and mislaid. Letters that are not mislaid may be cut into small
pieces with a scissors. Postcards—whether snide, riled, abu-
sive or apoplectic—should be swallowed, as a gag.

My Friend Montaigne

B LOOD poured down the map of France. For thirty-six long years, hideous civil war (no wars are less civil) had turned France into a charnelhouse. Politics, inflamed by passion, had joined religion, fouled by fanaticism, in the most monstrous of those crusades men conjure up out of their faith, their deliriums, their ambitions and their greed: war in the name of God—and some anointed king; war to spread God's faith—and an agent's sovereignty; war to give one House or another a monopoly on taxes, and one church or another a monopoly on worship.

Catholics burned Protestants, Protestants slaughtered Papists, and accident alone spared Anabaptists (the Albigensians had been totally exterminated for their heresy), backsliders, freethinkers, or Jews. Those whom the sword or the pyre missed fell victim to plague and pillage and famine.

In the year 1571, having witnessed such atrocities as "make me blench with horror," thirty-eight-year-old Michel Eyquem, *seigneur* of Montaigne, near Bordeaux, forsook his duties in this hideous world to retire to a study he built in the third story of the tower of the chateau he had inherited. On the walls of this refuge he inscribed: "To the learned virgins."

Montaigne loved this countryside. He had been put out to nurse in the village, where he lived as a babe, and he never lost his affection and respect for the peasants among whom he had dwelt. He loved to watch their work and study their crafts and talk to them about their life, their adversities, their convictions.

His first tutor was a German who taught young Montaigne Latin, an experiment which his sagacious father approved. Montaigne was a child prodigy, an intellectual sponge, a curious, inquiring, clear-eyed scholar. He was sent to the Collège de Guyenne at Bordeaux.

As a young man he fought bravely as a soldier, and his intelligence and poise soon recommended him to princes, who employed him as their envoy on diplomatic matters. He married Françoise de la Chassaigne in 1565, and three years later his father's death left him the lovely château and estate at Montaigne.

He served in the Bordeaux *parlement,* and in Bordeaux's court, for fifteen years—not because he was especially interested in politics or the law, but out of a sense of civic duty, and only after the King asked him to serve the state.

And now, in 1571, thirty-eight years old, what he wanted more than any riches or honors the lords of the land could offer him was—solitude. "In solitude alone," he was to write "can [we] know true freedom. A man must keep a little back shop where he can be himself without reserve . . . where he can be his sole company, where he can invite his kind, where he can lurk secure." He wanted to read, to study, to ruminate—and to write. Write what? He could not say, for there was no name for what he vaguely dreamed of doing. Not a treatise or book, not a journal or autobiography.

He edited some things written by his close friend, Etienne de la Boëtie; wrote notes and comments and interpretations of favorite authors; and then he began "to speak on paper as I do to the first person I meet," he put it. He began to write, in a most informal way, about himself: his appearance, his habits, his foibles and whims and ideas:

> I am of somewhat less than medium height. . . . I seldom dress in anything but plain black or white. . . . I scratch myself mostly on the inside of my ears. . . . I have madness or quicksilver in my feet, for they are always fidgeting. . . . You can't imagine how strangely all sorts of odors cling to me. . . . I like to sleep on a hard bed, alone, even without my wife, like royalty. . . . I seldom dream, and when I do it is of fantastic things commonly pleasant or absurd, rather than sad. . . . My father hated, and I love, every sort of gravy. . . . When I play with my cat, who knows whether I do not make her more sport than she does me?

Now, you must realize that there was no precedent in literature for such casual, trifling, formless reflections. This was not in the tradition of the West, of the Greek or Roman classics. This was no learned treatise on Ethics or Manners, Nature or God, Astronomy or Philosophy or Psychology. This was not a tract, a manual, a discourse, a commentary. There was, in fact, no name at all for such intimate, random revelations of the self. So Montaigne coined a name: *essais*—which means efforts, or attempts. . . .

It took him nine years to prepare his first collection of these "tries," these improvisations and these digressive *pensées*. All that guided him was the blissful sensation of a man whose motto was "Que sais-je?" ("What do I know?"), a man who had come through a bloody christening in men's madness to realize: "It is absolute perfection . . . divine to know how to get the very most out of one's individuality."

In 1580 his first collections of *Essais* were published; and Montaigne, suffering from "the stone," went off to travel, in France, Germany, Italy. He loved travel, which gave him fresh impressions and renewed introspective delights.

He returned to the "sweet solitude" of his tower, but was called to diplomatic missions and the mayorship of Bordeaux, which he tried to avoid until Henry III prevailed upon him. He was briefly jailed in the Bastille. . . .

His château was often threatened by marauders, and when plague broke out he wandered around the hungering countryside with his family for six ghastly months.

It was not until 1585 that he could return to the blessed refuge of his ivory tower, to pen more of his casual, crystal-line "tries," resigned to life and aging, unembittered by experience, strengthened in his bemusement and skepticism. He now sat down to his third set of verbal venturings. . . .

Was this to be all—this undesigned chronicling of *ad libitum* remarks? Was it to be no more than self-indulgent prattle? If it had so turned out, who would remember Montaigne's name? But the matter-of-fact, personal details are set down with such grace and ease, such lucidity, such a *directness* of rapport between writer and reader, that the reader is swiftly captivated.

This Renaissance dilettante is master of the rarest of writers' talents: the knack of immersing us inside his pri-vate, intensely personal world. His pages light up with trenchant observations, witty maxims, delicious fancies, ironic intuitions—on men, women, honor; on sex, passion, chastity; on books and pleasures and the laughter of the gods; on the follies of men and the function of kings.

To reveal one man, Montaigne said, is to explain all men. He wanted to gain the deepest, fullest understanding of him-self, because he dared to believe that "every man carries within himself the whole condition of humanity. . . . Within us, in our own breast, where nothing is forbidden and every-thing is hid, to be honest there—that's the rub! . . . Perched on the loftiest throne in the world, we still sit on our own arse."

His reflections on the human condition show us man as part tragic, part comic, part noble, part ludicrous. For he examined men's feelings and minds, their aspirations and confusions and urgings toward the divine, with a cool, in-cisive intelligence. He is always illuminating and often elec-trifying.

A woman is no sooner ours than we are no longer hers.

Few men have been admired by their servants.

The games of children are not sports, but should be re-garded as their most serious actions.

The man who [tries] to please the multitude is never done.

When I consider the absurd titillations of [love], the brainless motions it excites, the countenance inflamed with fury and cruelty during its sweetest effects; the grave, solemn, entranced air in an action downright silly, the supreme moment . . . bathed, like pain, in sighing and fainting—I then believe, with Plato, that the gods made men for their sport.

Montaigne was a devout man, not because he was sure his faith was true, but because, as he quoted a Greek skeptic, "everyman's true worship [is] the one he finds customary wherever he happens to be," and continued, "We are Christians by the same token we are Frenchmen or Germans." He loathed dogmatism, that "wretched disease which rivets a man so firmly to his own belief that he becomes incapable of conceiving other men may believe otherwise."

He ridiculed the self-anointed shamans of faith: "those who gull us with fables: our alchemists, astrologers, fortune-tellers [and those] who presume to interpret the designs of God himself." It is man who makes God in his own image, he remarked, not the other way around. "Religion is a thing of [our] own contrivance. What kind of truth is it that is true on one side of a mountain and false on the other?"

In a time when religious affiliations were forced by the thumbscrew and the faggot, this liberated spirit said, "I speak truth, not so much as I want, but as much as I dare." He urged "detachment and moderation in . . . opinions [and] hatred of that wrangling, self-satisfied arrogance that is the enemy of truth."

All this almost two centuries before Voltaire! And all this from the man who wrote: "A wise man sees as much as he ought, not as much as he can."

Reason, he said, is imperfect. Our convictions are but guesses. Our sacred faiths are accidents of geography. Then to what can man hold fast? "The height of wisdom is to take things as they are," he said, "to endure what we cannot evade. [We must learn] how to rule our behavior and understanding, how to live and die well. . . . Give every man a free rein to laugh, and we will all live in peace. . . . My trade and art is to live my life. . . . It is divine to know how to get the very most out of one's own individuality."

But how could this gospel of expedience, of the internal reservation of faith, of prolonged introspection, make any sense to the poor, the persecuted, those hounded by fate or by bigotry? Must not liberals despise Montaigne's apologia for an established yet evil order ("We owe loyalty and obedience to our kings, good or bad") simply because he preferred peace to bloodshed? Must not conservatives dislike his ironies about the hallowed certitudes? Do not reactionaries fear and hate his championing of freedom of opinion?

The answer is that for nearly four hundred years, men, whatever their political or religious bent, have turned to Montaigne for inspiration, for solace and for self-renewal. Michel Montaigne is the first *writer* we can call modern. (Call Roger Bacon the first modern philosopher-scientist.) Montaigne's subject was not Man, idealized and abstract, but man, that contradictory creature who eats, breathes, breeds, works, worships, doubts, laughs, hates, wonders.

Let me put together lines from various essays, to give you the thrust of his thought:

ON MEN AND WOMEN

There is no man so good, who, were he to submit all his thoughts and actions to the laws, would not deserve hanging ten times in his life.

An untempted woman cannot boast of her chastity.

A good marriage would join a blind wife and a deaf husband.

There is as much difference between us and ourselves as between us and others.

Virtue craves a steep and thorny path.

Only he can judge of matters great and high whose soul is likewise.

Life is a dream . . . we waking sleep and sleeping wake.

We, I know not how, *double in* in ourselves, so that what we believe we disbelieve, and we cannot rid ourselves of what we condemn.

As to fidelity, there is no animal in the world so treacherous as man.

ON RELIGION

Man is certainly stark mad. He cannot make a flea, and yet he will make gods by the dozen.

How many things that served us yesterday as articles of faith, today are fables.

Few men dare publish to the world the prayers they make to Almighty God.

ON PHILOSOPHY

Philosophy is doubt.

Men [are] more eager to discover a reason for ends than to find out whether the ends are so.

Nothing is so firmly built as that which we least know.

Of all the benefits which virtue confers on us, the contempt of death is one of the greatest.

ON POLITICS

Fame and tranquillity can never be bedfellows.

Eloquence flourished most . . . when public affairs were in the worst condition.

Those who give the first shock to a state are the first overwhelmed in its ruin.

Montaigne's third book of essays, from which many of these excerpts are taken, was his crowning work. He constantly edited, changed, refined a style that is a model of lucidity and charm. Elegant in texture, rich in wisdom, every line breathes with a modest radiance. Nothing seems forced, nothing strained, nothing florid or extravagant.

It is not surprising that from the beginning Montaigne's

writings were admired. But it is surprising that not until our
own century did the dating of his work appear, so that we
may judge the chronological flow of his thought. We now
can see how his meditations grew, from halting comments
to a larger, meaningful compass. It was by stages that he
circled in on a comprehensive self-portrait. Not until the
third volume did he reach for the larger attributes of the
human—not only personal—condition.

He started as a troubled Stoic; he matured into an un-
guilty Epicurean. ("My trade and art is to live my life.") He
never rids himself of his early admiration for the philosophy
of those unruffled by life's adversities. He owes much to
Plutarch, and more to Cicero, whose call to personal honor,
to the rectitude of one's own self, he admired.

He hated cruelty, in any form; he hated bigotry; he attacked the persecution of "witches"; he shrank from the bar-
barism of torture even when tortures were administered by
the authorized, pious clergy. He was so pantheistic in vision
that he could write: "There is . . . a certain respect and a general duty of humanity not only to beasts that have life and
sense, but even to trees and plants."

He was a just man, a humanist who sought an understanding of men's sorrows. His mind never ceased searching
for deeper truths. He held himself to standards that left him
discontented with himself.

For all the seeming candor of his confessions, Montaigne
is often elusive—or silent. "I [write]," he mourned, "by
halves." He does not once mention his mother, whose maiden name was Antoinette de Louppes (Lopes), who lived
with him. Is it because she was still alive and he was reticent to publish his impressions of her; or was it because her
family, expelled from Inquisition Spain, were Jews, and had
nominally been converted, and he did not want that widely
known—or, perhaps, feared for her safety in a feckless
world?

He found rationalizations for his incomplete revelation.
Perhaps he saw no reason to go beyond the bounds of
decorum or taste. "No man is exempt from saying silly

things," he said; "the mischief is to say them deliberately."
That he never did.

To the end he savored the immeasurable luxury of being
left alone. "The greatest thing in the world is to know how
to be self-sufficient." But to the end, too, he harbored
melancholy about his talents and his achievement—both
of which, given his reach and brains, he could not escape
underestimating. His evaluation of his own contribution is
sad: "It might well be said of me that I have merely made
up a bunch of other men's flowers, and provided nothing
of my own but the string to tie them together."

Emerson's judgment was far more valid; Emerson called
him the most honest of all writers: "Cut these words and
they would bleed."

Montaigne remains one of the most civilized intelligences,
one of the most widely read and loved authors, who ever
lived. His enduring miracle, to me, is this: Whoever picks
up his essays, in whatever time or circumstance, finds him
contemporary.

A Seminole with
a Hole in His Head

I always liked Larry. Some of my friends in Hollywood found him abrasive ("He comes on too strong") but I liked him. He was an exuberant gamin—all passion and indignations, short, sharp, intense, lean. He did not *stay* lean (success made him tubby) but his whole attitude to life—his abruptness, his irreverence, even his gestures—signaled a lean and hungry man.

Larry was a movie writer and, like most of that unique breed, a slam-bang raconteur. He told a story with unpoetic license and utter indifference to tenses, switching from one to the other when he felt like it, but always favoring the present. Now I know that professors of English look down (or turn up) their noses at the very idea of telling a tale in the historical present. I also concede that the present indicative is inelegant and infantile, fit for bartenders or train announcers. Yet there is a power, an immediacy, a sense of crisis in the present that the past simply embalms. The present tense endows a tale with a certain breathlessness, and creates the illusion that everything is happening before your very eyes and has not yet been resolved . . . Every yarn Larry told was a cliff-hanger, and every listener to it became a participant.

Larry also acted out his stories, shamelessly bolting from

his chair or falling to his knees, clutching his hair or bursting into sobs, groans, ominous va-ROOMs and blood-cur-
dling kee-OWs. Sometimes, as he jumped around the furniture, he reminded me of a jackrabbit in a judo match.

I am imparting all this because I want to tell you a story
in the succulent idiom Larry used when he told it to me. He
told it to me in New York, which he hated, on his way to
Rome, which he loved, from Beverly Hills, which made his
eyes itch. I omit the running quotation marks, which would
only get between you and him.

Here's one you won't believe, Buster Brown, but I got it
straight from a lady who wouldn't lie if her virginity de-
pended on it, which it doesn't, since she has two kids. She
happens to be Mrs. Alice _____ (Larry named a family and
a fortune as illustrious as, say, the duPonts; I'll call them
the Simoleons).

Well, it all begins, in a perfect Fade-in, when Alice mar-
ries Roger Simoleon III, in society nuptials it would cost
Zanuck two million bucks to duplicate. After the honeymoon
they come home and Alice has to meet the head of the clan,
Roger's grandfather, Brewster Croesus Simoleon, who is
around eighty-nine and a half years old and wasn't up to attending the wedding.

So Roger tells the chauffeur to crank up the Silver Cloud,
whose clock ticks louder than its motor, and off they breeze
to the family manse—the Simoleon Palace old Brewster built
in Pennsylvania over fifty years ago. Alice tells me her eyes
turned to popcorn as they drove down the lane of Lombardy
poplars, a good half-mile long, and she spotted the old man's
abode. It's one of those sugar-cane castles you see in fairy
tales, or on the Rhine. And that, pal, is exactly what it turns
out to be: A Rhenish castle, down to the last gargoyle. All
it lacks is a hunchback court jester named Toto.

Now, how come we find a dizzying Gothic château here?
That's the kicker. Flashback: It's early in this century. Young
Brewster Croesus Simoleon, a lively buck, with a yacht that
is slightly smaller than the Yale Bowl, is taking a trip down

der Rhein with his wife, kiddies, friends, governesses and secretary, whom I shall call Gus. Gus is Simoleon's man Monday-Tuesday-Wednesday-Thursday-*and*-Friday—a trouble-shooter who could rustle up matzos in Cairo. I think he was of Hungarian origin.

Well, as the Simoleon gondola glides down the historish river, full of Lorelei and Nibelungen, which sounds like vital organs you get in a German butcher shop, all marvel mightily over the castles that float by. Then they spot this absolute smasheroo of an acropolis, jutting up there in the sky. And Brewster cries, "Bless my soul! Shiver my timbers! Have you ever seen anything like that? By Jove, *that's* the place I want!"

The place he wants happens to be bigger than the Sixty-ninth Street Armory, but the longer he gazes at those aged turrets and medieval rainspouts the more his mouth waters.

Now Brewster C. Simoleon is not one to flinch before a problem. To him, everything is a mere matter of m–o–n–e–y. So he tells the captain to pull in at the next landing— where what does he do but give Gus, his jack-of-all-finaglers, these instructions: "Go back to that castle, find the owner, buy the joint, and ship it to me back home, stone by stone!" Oh, I know it sounds weird, but as Alice remarked: After all, if a William Randolph Hearst or Howard Hughes could indulge whims like that, why not Brewster C. Simoleon?

So, faithful Gus gets off the yacht, hires himself a carriage and driver, and gallops to the castle, which any Tom, Dick, and Heinrich in the neighborhood can lead you to blind-folded. They come to the Shangri-La, cross a real moat, and rear up before the portcullis or whatever-you-call a castle's front door.

Gus gets out, removes his snazzy goggles and duster, and pulls on a big iron ring. Presto! A smaller door in the port-cullis opens. Gus goes through it, and at the inner castle entrance there awaits him a butler in livery, with white bib and silver buckles on his Mary Janes.

Gus hands this stand-in for Arthur Treacher his card, which identifies him as Personal Representative for Brewster Simoleon. He also slips him a fin, confiding, "It is imperative that I see your master on a matter of international import."

Quick Dissolve as the totem pole returns, bowing: "His Most Gracious Highness, Prince Rudolph von Graffenstein zu Wienerschnitzel, will receive you." Now any jerk in the Hamburg fifth grade can recognize that name—one of *the* first families of Deutschland. Why, they have been hunting boars and beating peasants all the way back to Charlemagne, whose gunsels gave the Wienerschnitzels their first potroast and margravery.

The butler ushers Gus down a gallery of armor to a living room which is two feet longer than Roseland, and presents him to the prince, who is right out of *The Prisoner of Zenda* in glorious Technicolor: He is wearing velvet lederhosen, fingers his goatee, and is backed up by three beautiful daughters, draped on a sofa, two dachshunds at his feet and a Dalmatian at his knee.

Gus plays it like David Niven. "Your Most Gracious Highness," he murmurs, "it is kind of you to receive me in behalf of Herr Brewster Croesus Simoleon, the world-famous steel-smelting-and-strudel magnate, who extends his compliments, *en passant*. I have the honor to inform you that Mr. Brewster would like to—well, purchase this castle . . . the whole kit and caboodle. . . . The price, need I say, will present no obstacle. . . . In short, Prince, how much will you take for the premises?"

Well, Prince Graffenstein von and zu is stunned. He is also amazed, affronted, and homicidal. He draws himself up to his full archery-or-dueling height, and explodes: "My family has liffed in Puffenbrenner zince 1509, and I have no more indention of leaving, leazing, lending *or* zelling my anzestral abode than His Imperial Majesty Kaiser Wilhelm has of auctioning the Imperial Stables in Potsdam! Good day—*und get out!*"

The daughters sneer, the dachshunds snarl, the Dalmatian growls, and Gus takes a powder.

He hustles down the Rhine to catch up with the yacht

a day later, and there reports the bad news to Mr. Simoleon
—who splits a gut. He just can't understand *anyone*, not
even a blue-blooded Kraut with saber scars on his navel,
refusing to sell something before he even knows how much
he can make on it!

He rants and raves and swears and stamps his feet and
finally says, "Fee-fi-fo-fum! A pox on Fauntleroy *and* his
dachshunds. Let him keep that gingerbread garage, which
is probably Termites' Paradise anyhow. . . . We'll duplicate
it! You heard me. We'll copy it, copy it right down to the
last arch, buttress, and leak in the roof! . . . Gus, take yourself back there and set up shop. Hire photographers, archi-
tects, artists, whatever you need. I want drawings and pictures of that sauerkraut domicile from every angle! Forget
the inside. I would probably freeze to death in that barn.
It is the outside I crave for my own! Here is the name of my
banker in Cologne. Carry on!"

Fade-out.

Well, you have to admire a guy like that. The vision of a
Thalberg, the gall of a Goldwyn, backed by more soft green
bills than David Merrick, if possible.

So–o, we Fade-in on ever-loyal Gus, in Dusseldorf or Dor-
fendussel or some goddam village on the Rhine, assembling
his task force for architectural plagiarism. We move to a
Close Shot of a calendar, and it is June and we Dissolve
to a watery effect and the pages drop off, one by one, and it
says "October" and we Hold: Gus is coming down the gang-
plank in New York with eleven trunks full of pictures, drawings and blueprints of Schloss Puffenbrenner—which, on a
choice piece of real estate in Pennsylvania, Brewster C.
Simoleon reproduces!

And it is to *this* carbon-copy castle that Brewster's grand-
son, Roger, has brought our heroine, Alice, to end the Flashback. It is Now.

Well, old Simoleon takes a quick shine to Alice, which is
easy: A sweeter smile hasn't been seen since Lillian Gish,
who overcame that ludicrous last name—*Gish*, for God's
sake!—to light up the silver screen.

One day, the two of them are playing backgammon and old Simoleon cackles: "My dear, have you noticed the very wide brick—the back of the main fireplace chimney—in the corridor that leads to the guest wing you and my Roger are occupying?"

Alice says she has indeed admired the beautiful brickwork, which she has passed going to and from her suite.

"And do you know what is inside that brick wall, before you would reach the flue?" leers old Simoleon.

"No," says Alice.

"The body of a Seminole Indian," whispers Simoleon. "With a hole in his head."

Well, Alice gives a ladylike laugh—as who wouldn't?—but the old pirate nails her with a glare. "Do not laugh, child; I do not jest! While this mausoleum was being erected, I took a trip through the Seminole country with Howie Tailfeather, the Indian guide I used for years, since I love those Florida swamps and spent many a happy sojourn there. Following a lazy week, we come to a dock where a hundred Seminoles are waiting, wailing and jabbering, and as excited as the redskins who got General Custer. (*Imagine* getting into the history books for having yourself scalped!) Why are Howie Tailfeather's relatives awaiting us here? To tell him that Sitting Duck, his favorite cousin, has been murdered in a tribal fracas, shot between the eyes, and Howie must return to his village at once for the solemn burial rites. . . .

"Well, Alice," the old man chuckles, "suddenly I was struck by an idea—an idea so original, so piquant, so tantalizing, I knew it had to be executed! . . . I took Howie aside and told him it would mean a great deal to me, and a pretty penny to him *and* the family of the deceased, if instead of burying Sitting Duck they pickled him—then placed him in a crate, and shipped him up to me! . . . After all, an Indian has as much right as a Presbyterian to be buried wherever he wants. Just because Sitting Duck was a Seminole didn't mean he had to stay cooped up for eternity in that damp Okefenokee or whatever-it's-called bog where you can die of malaria! I again stressed to Howie that I would contribute a handsome sum to the widow, orphans, tribe—and Howie himself.

"Well, my dear, Mr. Tailfeather was torn between tribal honor and plain, wholesome greed. He also expressed an understandable squeamishness about the Florida police, who might not approve of pickling corpses and shipping them all over the country by Railway Express. I congratulated Howie on his foresight and assured him that I would attend to the palefaces—starting with the coroner, who no doubt yearned to retire, and going all the way to the county sheriff, whose kiddies no doubt needed Shetland ponies and music lessons. Howie, a soft-hearted Mongolian, felt an instant kinship for these underpaid public servants.

"Well, through methods I shall not disclose, since they involved *sub rosa* contributions to two unions, a disreputable mortician, and a carpenter devoted to the Demon Rum, the corpse of Howie's unjustly murdered cousin was properly enbalmed, placed within a stout crate marked FOSSILS:DO NOT USE HOOKS and shipped to a 'front' address I called 'The Traveling Museum of Indian Culture.'" Here Old Simoleon cracked his knuckles, cackling like a crow, though he looked more like a buzzard. "And it is that corpse, my dear, that is in an upright position, right now, inside the brick wall in the back of the fireplace you pass each day!" The old coot practically had a convulsion, Alice told me, the tears *gushing* down his withered, wicked cheeks.

Of course Alice wonders if the old man has lost his marbles, or is giving her the Munchausen bit in spades. But something tells her that any man who has so much money, and has always gotten what he wanted, is liable to be a wee bit eccentric, to put it charitably.

"But Grampa Simoleon," asks Alice, "what on earth made you *want* to put a corpse in a chimney?"

Cut to a huge Closeup, full-frame, of Simoleon as he reacts. "Why?" he echoes. "*Why?* Don't you see it? Can't you *visualize* it?" cries Simoleon. "A hundred years from now, when they tear this mausoleum down, out of that Gothic chimney will plop the *skeleton of a Seminole Indian!*" He slaps his thighs and doubles up like he just bust the bank at Monte Carlo. "Can you imagine the problem, the puzzle, the head-scratchings? The locals will go *crazy* trying to figure out how the skeleton of a Seminole Indian got walled up in the chimney of a German castle in an American suburb a thousand miles from the Florida moraine!...But that is not all!" guffaws the old man. "Oh, no! They will see that bullet hole in the Seminole's forehead—and realize *murder* was committed! Can you imagine what *that* will do? The police, the DA, the FBI, will have to move in—and they'll end up with a sieveful of nothing!...I can see it now—the funniest thing that ever happened! And I won't have to be alive to know it was worth every penny!"

Leo, that old buccaneer had laughed himself to sleep every night for fifty *years* gloating over the mishmash he had inflicted on the future.

Larry went on to Rome, and in time returned to Hollywood. A year or so later, I received a letter telling me he had gotten himself married to a Bel Air beauty named Frances and was coming to New York for a week. Would we invite them to dinner?

We spent a fine evening together. Frances was a lovely thing, rather quiet, who seemed to understand (and defer to) Larry's moods. They looked at each other, every so often, with the special affection of the connubial. We were leaving the table when a telephone call came in for Larry, from his agent. He took it in my study.

My wife and Frances and I went into the living room. I offered Frances a liqueur.

"Larry is very fond of you," she said.

"Well, I'm very fond of him. I enjoy his enthusiasm—his preposterous stories. Did he ever tell you the one about a Seminole Indian with a hole in his head?"

"Oh, yes," she laughed. "That *is* a wild one. Larry loves it."

"Who wouldn't? It takes genius to invent a story like that."

"But it happens to be true," she said.

"Oh, come on," said my wife. "You don't mean to say you believe——"

"Of course I do," said Frances.

"You are a trusting soul," I said, "and a true-blue wife."

"I'll admit that Larry tends to overdramatize," said Frances, "and sometimes gussies up the details for effect. . . . Did he tell you he got that story from Alice?"

"Yes."

"Well, that wasn't true. I mean, Alice wasn't her name. Larry was protecting her, because she was married."

"What was her name?" I asked.

"Frances," said Frances, smiling.

The Incredible
Professor

YOU must not expect me to write about him coolly. Nor will I try to mislead you by adopting that austerity of language behind which Harold Dwight Lasswell has always concealed his romanticism about "detachment." I begin this memoir with a confession: I respect, I admire, and I *like* him.

I met him two hundred years ago, in 1927, in a classroom at the University of Chicago. I was a grubby sophomore and he was the callow instructor of a course in political science —one of the earliest, I think, he ever gave.

I thought him a bit of a freak: pedantic, verbose, and quite ill at ease. He wore his hair in a short, stiff, Prussian cut, and his knowledge in a high, stiff, abrasive manner. He was only twenty-five, and he lectured us desperately, with a glazed stare into space, unaware of whether we understood him and unconcerned with what we might be thinking.

He talked so fast, so frantically, tumbling idea upon idea in a torrent of excitation, that his nonstop monologues became a polysyllabic blur from which only startling phrases emerged to penetrate my dumbfoundedness: "context . . . frame of reference . . . thanks to . . . anxiety . . . systematic

... rigorous ... quantify ... symbols ... expectations ... explicit ... insecurity ... participant-observer ... symbols ... thanks to ... world revolution of our times."

He baffled—nay, flabbergasted—me. He did not lecture so much as smother. He seemed unable to leave a moment of time unoccupied by language. I even wondered if he did not suffer from some strange speech impediment which he was trying to drown in a flood, or throttle in a glut, of words. I was not helped, of course, by the fact that he blithely scrambled together technical terms from a dozen unhomogenized disciplines: philosophy, sociology, political science, psychology, economics, anthropology, psychiatry, statistics, pediatrics, psychoanalysis, physiology, physics (oh, yes).

The play of his nostrils, as he monologized, intrigued me. Please do not scoff. His globular cheeks puffed out like those of a chipmunk with a nut in each pouch, and from those two round protuberances sailed forth a surprisingly thin nose—with most mobile and expressive nostrils. They flared and narrowed and quivered in tune with his meaning, signaling a disdain here, an esteem there, not expressed by his words—since he was in the grip, then as now, of a compulsion to be entirely objective. The goal was inhuman, to say nothing of inhumane.

I shall never forget my first têta-à-tête with him. I was considerably miffed because, apart from not understanding what this antiseptic pastor was talking about, I was groaning under the burdens of a bizarre assignment he had given me: to subscribe to two Arizona newspapers and to measure each story in them in column inches, classifying the figures in categories that ranged from city-hall shenanigans to astrological advice. After three weeks of this carpentry, which had not yet been elevated to the elegance of "content analysis," I mobilized my indignation (and my courage) and marched to Dr. Lasswell's office. It was the first time I had ever been alone with an instructor.

I gulped out my heartfelt complaints like a burgher at Calais. He listened steely-eyed and silent. Thrown off base by his clinical stare, which made me feel like a case study, I even quavered that I often did not understand what on earth he was talking about.

To these anguished protestations Lasswell at last sniffed icily: "Communication is, after all, but the fortuitous parallelism of biophysic variables." I staggered out . . . I could not repress reluctant admiration over the beauty and precision of that ad lib. Save for "fortuitous," I still know no better definition of communication, that hypnotic rubric under which at least five thousand earnest researchers are today buzzing away like mad.

It took me years to discover why H.D.L. resorts to such outlandish lingo: He is entirely at home with it. It is, indeed, his natural patois. When launched on a spree of euphoric cerebration, he does not choose words; he goes into an intellectual trance in which words choose—or, better, possess—him. Only after prolonged prayer did it dawn on me that whereas most men use language clumsily, in an effort to express their banal ideas and conceal their complex feelings, Lasswell uses words brilliantly to conceal simple feelings and express complex ideas. I think he has a passion to be comprehended, and defenses against being understood.

In those days, he always said "we"—never, never "I." He also shunned small talk, gossip, or the conventional exchange of nonideas. He would proceed directly from an obligatory "Greetings!" (he loathed all clichés, including "Hello") to his latest lucubrations on Ibn Khaldun. Emphatically egalitarian, he was likely to enlighten dazed coeds about both Pareto and penis envy. His totem was ideas; his taboo, boredom.

I once heard a harmless hostess ask him, "Isn't it wonderful weather we're having?" Only after Lasswell recovered sufficiently to analyze her motivations did he answer, "Yes." I was surprised that he did not diagnose the meteorological components of the weather we were having.

Lasswell mystifies the proletariat by his massive verbiage. What the Philistines do not see is that he thinks by listening to what he says, then mines it to separate gold from dross.

To him, talking is a form of testing, of dropping plumb lines into the gigantic reservoir of his knowledge. He talks the way other men daydream. His monologues are symposiums with invisible peers. Who has not heard him verbalize for hours without the faintest idea of what he was getting at, or even around, flitting from Peter the Great to projective mechanisms, from "equilibrium analysis" to "time-space manifolds," until—bingo!—he hit upon some attractive hunch or slant or self-illumination which he then seized with relief and embroidered feverishly?

Lasswell is a system builder, a cheerful cosmologist, an exuberant virtuoso of fancy-shmancy correlations, in which he revels. He finds connections between the Gothic arch and, say, feudal ambivalence about copulation, between German philanthropy and Oedipal guilt, between bureaucracy and breast-feeding. Sometimes he sounds like a cross between Machiavelli and Freud, as recorded by Veblen.

I remember limping out of one class stunned by a mischievous comment he had tossed off which ran something like this: "If one postulates that the conventional wisdom, encapsulated in the equilibrium (as opposed to configurational) analysis that underlies capitalistic mythology, is a makeshift evasion of those unconscious drives that account for persistent irrationality, and if one regards contemporary institutions as but functional arrangements designed to accommodate those contradictory symbols that emasculate ego-threatening impulses, then to support the League of Nations may be interpreted as a cynical concession to human perversity." I was never the same.

In lunches or dinners with him, which I came to prize, I was struck by the ballet of his hands. They are library hands, very pale, soft, unsullied by physical exertion. When Harold talks, over drinks or food, his hands make small gyrations, in the same ritual of gestures. The left hand is motionless, its thumb and forefinger forming an "O"; the right hand hovers over and dances around that "O." If, say, he is trying to illustrate Planck's constant or the dynamics of constipation, the right hand pulls an invisible thread through an invisible needle on a path horizontal to and away from the inert circle of the left hand "O." It is astounding how Harold hemstitches theoretical points into imaginary petit point.

I was also fascinated by his glasses—which were always spotless, as if perpetually cleaned by invisible wipers. Only twice in almost four decades have I seen him remove his glasses to clean them. His eyes look no different. They gleam.

Lasswell is essentially self-oriented, and exceptionally self-sufficient. He is the Compleat Intellectual—egocentric, not egotistic; he has not, I think, a shred of vanity. In language he might find more congenial, he is, *au fond,* narcissistic. I believe he is by all odds the most interesting man he has ever known.

The callithump* of his ideas never stops, never flags, never pauses for rest or recuperation or revival. I have dined with him hundreds of times, and, leaving for a moment to make a phone call, returned to find him scribbling notes as though he had just solved the last theorem of Fermat. I'm sure they were his words, not mine, that he was preserving in amber.

Our hero's erudition is, of course, Himalayan. It is coupled to the one lifelong passion that consumes him: the passion for omniscience. His mountainous knowledge may, in my opinion, inhibit a very high capacity for original thinking and sometimes sterilizes his most fecund insights. Some childhood overvaluation of Teutonic scholarship (which carries with it constraining anal values, I hear), or some residues of an early need to impress his elders in the academic dodge, has led H.D.L. to overload his works with references, footnotes, bibliography, and learned (if irrelevant) digressions. I yield to no man in my respect for reading, but I cannot help feeling that Harold uses his bibliography the way Ethel Merman delivers a "sock" number. He may not so intend it (I hesitate to probe beneath his surfaces) but his merciless use of citations serves not simply to fortify an argument but to clobber the reader. I wish that loyal friends

---

* It pleases me to think he may have to look this up.

would join with me in helping to emancipate him from the stultifying standards of academe, perhaps by giving him a plaque that proclaims him our ambulatory Library of Congress.

Harold luxuriates in company, but seems to need it less than anyone I have ever known. Not that he does not have friends. They came in legions, literally, and continental subdivisions. He has met, charmed, offended, or mesmerized a countless muster of people. Strangers, uncued by any comment from me, have brought up his name in places as far removed as Sebastopol and Council Bluffs. He is a zestful socializer but seems capable of spending unlimited days alone, happily reading, writing, ruminating. He is a triumph of autogeny.

Harold abhors anything that borders on sentiment or suggests dependence. No one is a warmer or more generous friend—but he is, essentially and quite oddly, *shy*. No one of my acquaintance has ever been so parsimonious in the revelation of personal data. Ask him a truly personal question and he will hem and haw and evade, and his face will swarm with as many hues of red as could be found in the American labor movement from 1932 to 1941. He is embarrassed not so much by affection as by the *display* thereof —on your part, surely, and more surely on his. He is like a Calvinist who has learned how to laugh.

He gives unstintingly of his time, encouragement, expertise, but he is embarrassed by intimacy—at least as others define it. I have never seen the knob on the door of any quarters he ever occupied.

He was raised in Decatur, Illinois, and spent summers in Indiana with an uncle who was an M.D. This uncle, baffled by his inability to relieve a patient of a paralysis of the arm that had no physical cause, heard of the work of a certain doctor in Vienna who was curing cases of "hysterical paralysis." The Indiana medic wrote to Europe and ordered some German books by one Sigmund Freud. Young Harold, then fourteen or fifteen, read them. They seemed rather sensible. "It was not until I was a junior at the University of Chicago," Harold once told me, "that I discovered that Freud was controversial."

At one point, in Chicago, Harold's reputation spread beyond the small, fervent circle of his apostles (Gabriel Almond, Philleo Nash, Edith Rosenfels, Dorothy Blumenstock, William T. R. Fox, and certain awed, though not baptized, followers, including an M.A. from Tennessee who mumbled to himself and spent all his time changing the Dictaphone cylinders Lasswell used while psychoanalyzing volunteer students and refugees from the Loop). At the beginning of one spring term I entered the classroom with our professor to discover almost thirty expectant students waiting. I had never known more than ten or twelve at a time to brave the hurricane of Lasswell's pedagogy. Harold looked as though he had stumbled into a Holy Roller festival, sniffed, and *sotto voce* said, "We shall reduce the number forthwith."

The forthwith Harold used, out of shame at finding so many peasants afflicted with *hubris*, was to expatiate on certain cases he had recently observed in a mental hospital. To make sure that the unworthies he faced would not turn up again in his classroom, Dr. Lasswell, fluttering those nostrils, quoted one psychotic inmate as having confided that he (the patient) was both a considerable genius and a titanic fornicator. A chair in the last row, tilted back against the wall by the student on it, promptly and explosively slammed down to the floor. Harold stared balefully at the flaming child who was picking up his notebooks and protective talismans, flared his nostrils outward, and icily continued his excursion into psychopathology. After the class, when the students were well out of earshot, Harold exploded with laughter—and how many men do you know who explode with such percussive resonance?

Lasswell is perennially youthful. His prevailing mood is ebullience. I have seen him distracted, but never, I think, depressed. And I have never known him to be frustrated. Even at sixty-five he seems precocious.

Harold is sometimes exhausting, but always inexhaustible.

This I attribute to his phenomenal and endearing capacity for enthusiasm. He has a ravenous, a ferocious, an insatiable appetite for every conceivable aspect of living. He is surely the most indefatigable talker, drinker, eater, traveler, conferee, collaborator, lecturer, bibliophile and notetaker in the world.

As my houseguest in California, he once delivered a three-hour monologue before cocktails and topped it off at dinner with verbalizing that went on until 2:30 A.M. It remains one of the most extraordinary exhibitions of brilliance and nonalcoholic inebriation I have ever heard. It started with China (Harold had just returned from a teaching stint in Peking), and from there made leaping gambadoes to British club mores in Shanghai, phallic artifacts in Cambodia, the paralysis of Marxist ideology, the latent homosexuality of geisha-loving Japanese, Jung on the persona, Freud on Jung, Lasswell on Jung and Freud and Adler (sniff), the journalism of Karl Radek, the delusions of French foreign policy in the Far East, the puerility of Thomas Wolfe, Los Angeles as an architectural projection of masturbatory fantasies, the partial insights of Melanie Klein, Georg Lukacz as a literary critic, the vectors of L. L. Thurstone, the illuminations of Sherrington and L. J. Henderson and Anton Carlson on brain and blood, the Bhagavad Gita, Lao-Tzu, the symbolism in Zuñi dances, Sapir's illuminations of linguistics, R. H. Tawney and Max Weber, Oriental "face" as an exercise in stylized hostility, Heisenberg and Schrödinger on indeterminacy, Rousseau's muddle-headedness and Catlin's pragmatism, leg fetishism in American high schools, Charles Merriam's beatification of credenda, miranda, and charisma, Malaparte's variations on the *coup d'état*—plus assorted comments, appraisals, footnotes and gibes at Sorel, Dicey, Sombart, Keynes, Bryce, Whitehead, Lenin, Eddington, C. I. Lewis, Boas, Roberto Michels and Spengler, to say nothing of the Dolly Sisters and the Comte de Guiche. This too-brief résumé must, I regret, omit those incandescent flourishes with which Harold customarily garnishes one of his hypomanic seizures. I have seen strangers, during one of these roaring improvisations, act as if they had fallen into an automatic washer with Immanuel Kant.

Of his many and original contributions to the sociosexual sciences, I want merely to say that I consider H.D.L. the most fertile catalyst and theorist of his generation. After the surface forays of Graham Wallas and Walter Lippmann, Lasswell—armed with a mastery of psychoanalytic theory, fieldwork among its practitioners in Vienna, Berlin, Boston, and Washington, and acquaintanceship with Einstein's revolution—carried the corpus of political behavior theory to the couch, there to be infused and invigorated by his insights and imagination. His analyses of psychoanalysis are, to me, unsurpassed among the keepers of the flame. His pioneering contributions to propaganda analysis, "the pyramid of power," content analysis, political symbols, and political psychology are indisputable and historic.

He is, of course, neither omniscient nor flawless. Because he operates best with high abstractions and adores the game of multivariable ping-pong, Lasswell will move heaven and earth to find the picayune meaningful. His unreserved interest in *everything* long ago drove him to seek some all-inclusive frame or scheme, which is understandable; but just as some men have no eye for color, Harold has an imperfect gauge for proportion. He may devote as many words to chiropody, should it happen to get on the roller coaster of his speculations, as to bank deposits. His work has remarkable range, pyrotechnic effects, profundity, brilliance, suggestibility, and insights galore—but haphazard proportion and uneven focus. This has always puzzled me, perhaps because I am a simple man who gets the bends when the rise and fall of Papuan hemlines pops up in the middle of a dissection of the class origins of post-office employees in Kenosha, Wisconsin.

Lasswell shelters not the faintest prejudice against serendipity, which is, in fact, the closest thing to religion he observes. He is easily seduced by an idea. He is often excited by what interests no one else. His infatuation with objectivity drives him to adopt the stance of a surgeon and the style of an engineer; most conversation strikes him as "the production of propitiating noises," and a speech by a ward heeler at a wake becomes "symbol manipulation." Much of this is meant to illuminate via irony, and is both elegant and witty, but sometimes it uses cannons to kill flies.

Yet Harold can be as simple and clear as Jello. (Children, for instance, get along fine with him.) Under duress, and given rigid word limits, he produces analytic gems: for example, his articles in the *Encyclopedia of the Social Sciences* (Bribery, Chauvinism, Feuds, Morale); his 1933 article on the rise of Hitler; his classic *Politics: Who Gets What, When, How;* part of *World Politics and Personal Insecurity;* truly original, trenchant pieces on public opinion, symbols, power, Marxist fallacies, international relations, the psychology of revolution, *et,* as they say, *cetera.*

Lasswell longed to be a "participant-observer" in every culture, society, revolution, and laboratory experiment of his time. This led him, years ago, into "world surveys" that were to be scooped up in regional dragnets labeled "focus of attention" studies. *Manibus pedibusque,* and hot as a pistol, he proceeded to correspond with brainwashed accomplices from Australia to Zagreb; all poured dubious nuggets of data into his inventory of critical factors in those political convulsions he was the first, I think, to dub the "world revolution of our time." ("Rising expectations" and "garrison state" are also his striking coinages.) Lasswell was often electrifying in his political predictions, but they bore little relation to the ragout of erratic guesses and peculiar *obiter dicta* he was receiving from excitable Serbs, Afrikaners, and Cretans whom he had conned into transcendental illusions. He is a most starry-eyed sophisticate.

I think it was God's manifest will that, in 1938, made a van bound for New York, which contained Harold's voluminous reports from the paranoid zones of the world between 1928 and 1938, burn to a crisp. The fire freed him from the prison of his files.

Shortly thereafter, prior to accepting a post in the Law

School at Yale, Harold proceeded to write a series of programs for radio, dramatizing traumatic moments in the life of Caesar, Muhammad, Napoleon, and others. The series remains one of the most sparkling applications of knowledge to public enlightenment that has yet appeared in the mass media. It also remains a striking example of Harold's capacity to be lucid.

My friend and mentor has a delicious sense of satire, but he is rarely malicious and never petty. He is, as a matter of fact, a very kind man, exceptionally generous in his professional judgments. Except where the evidence is overwhelming, he eschews derogation. (He once wrote the following book review: "Rhetoric." End of review.) He can be sardonic but not really cynical. And all this is so, I think, because he has always identified himself with the long, high line of theorists—past and future—and spurned the ad-hominem squabbles of his critics.

Harold has never displayed noticeable anxiety about his health or possible demise. His equanimity vis-à-vis the Grim Reaper has a certain bounce to it. I once heard him console an embarrassed companion, who had guzzled too much, with these gentle words: "One must, at times, defer to the banal demands of the soma." I have heard him mourn the death of a colleague kindly, sadly, yet somehow in the way a commuter might regret having missed the 6:10 to New Haven. Not that he is callous—far from it; he is just better at analyzing emotions than expressing them. He feels, I think, very deeply—when no one is watching. Neutrality is his shield.

I have never heard him tell a joke, but no one is a better audience for the risible. His laughter is Falstaffian. He adores anecdotes, but I have never heard him tell a story. He venerates the analytic rather than the discursive. His desired image of himself is cerebral—a 100 percent pure scientist who tries to maintain rigorous detachment in what he insists on calling "interpersonal relations." His humanness is ample enough, but hides behind transparent curtains. It is not surprising that people who do not know him consider him a mortician of ideas. They confuse their confusion with (allegedly) his.

Lasswell is a phenomenal generator of ideas but an ineffective editor—of either his writings or the work of others. This long puzzled me because he is a most acute critic. The trouble is, I suspect, his fear of confessing that something just may not be "relevant." Since *he* is always learning, arranging, recording, storing, what possible facts or speculations *might* not—someday, somewhere, somehow—be useful? Think of what Sigmund Freud discovered, after all. It was Freud who opened Lasswell's eyes to how important the "trivial" may be, and how common the bizarre.

One cannot give a true picture of this truly unique man without mentioning, however reluctantly, the vocal hopscotch to which he is prone. ("The—uh—possible extrapolations—mmh—of these neatly implicit categories may—er —be designed to—uh—expedite analytic clarity if only one conjectures that—well—the intellectuals of *Mittel-europa* were dominantly characterized—uh—by their preoccupation with literary, as distinct from systematic, formulations —er—mmh—thanks to the overvaluation of—mmh—solipsistic dexterity.") I think Harold falls into such faltering because he blames himself for not automatically producing instant, definitive formulas in answer to any question on any occasion. This is why one never hears him say, "I don't know," or "I haven't the faintest idea." I have heard him say, "*We* know little about this," but that meant that man's accumulated knowledge had not yet reached the point where an answer was possible; if it had, Harold would, clearly, have known it.

How do I rate him as a teacher? For 90 percent of the unshaven who dipped their toes in his raging waters, Harold was not a teacher but a torrent, to be resisted, resented, endured, and survived. They could no more understand him than they could understand the *Principia Mathematica* in Urdu. Easily bored in and by a classroom, the master often retreated into highfalutin' ambiguity—or reveries too arcane to convey meaning to anyone but an athletic symbolist.

For another 5 percent of his students, Lasswell was a galvanizing, unnerving, seditious comet who had roared in from some alien planet of the intellect (surely alien to the narcotic drone and tranquilizing platitudes of most college pedagogy). He required in students brain, discipline, fearful bibliography, and a determination to crack the stainless-steel cover in which the superego is enclosed.

And to the final 5 percent, Harold was an eye-opener, a mind-liberator, a horizon-widener unlike anyone they would ever run into again, in this world or the next. He was original, disruptive, challenging, derisive. He hurdled the barriers that block the efforts most of us make to communicate: differences in age, culture, temperament, style, metabolism, repression, orality. He proceeded on the sanguine assumption that he *could* be understood, and he was grateful to anyone who was interested in what he had to say. He was also fascinated by anyone who was fascinated by him. I was, unashamedly, in the latter group.

I learned, or was encouraged and jolted and inspired to learn, more from him than from anyone I ever met. One cannot easily measure, or hope to repay, such indebtedness.

Dime-a-Dance

I counted eight taxi-dance ballrooms between Forty-sixth and Fiftieth streets, on Broadway and Seventh Avenue, that time. They are pretty much alike. Each is on a second floor. Each plasters its entrance with come-hither pictures of its hostesses. Each has a grandly uniformed barker on the sidewalk who passes out cut-rate cards while he lures lonely men with extravagant intimations about the madonnas at one's beck and call just one flight upstairs. Each blares out canned, nerve-tingling music from the paradise above. All are invested with the same factitious promise of romance.

If you walk up Broadway or Seventh Avenue you can't miss them:

"50 BEAUTIFUL LONELY HEARTS TO DANCE WITH YOU!"
"75 GLAMOROUS HOSTESSES WAITING FOR YOU!"
"DANCE IN ECSTASY WITH 100 GORGEOUS BEAUTIES!"

These pulse-quickeners, designed to arouse the love-cells without alarming the conscience, are pitched at unattached young men and undated older salesmen who yearn for the voice and touch and smell of a female of the species. The image of lonely girls waiting, hoping, yearning just for you is shrewd bait for unsure males who dream of *liaison intime*.

287

PEOPLE I HAVE LOVED, KNOWN OR ADMIRED

And to out-of-towners, loners, sailors, ballroom-lizards, the taxi dances are a bright, beckoning oasis in the impersonal and intimidating clamor of New York.

I spent a dandy Saturday night in three of these temples to the dance, succumbing first to the siren call of Honeymoon Lane Danceland, on Seventh Avenue just after it leaves Times Square. The thing that settled me on Honeymoon Lane Danceland, aside from its honeysuckle name, was the sign in the entrance:

IF YOU AIM TO DANCE WITH A GLAMOROUS GIRL
SHOOT IN HERE!

That seemed pretty candid, so I took a free-dance card from the Grand Duke Sergei Alexandrovich Rachmaninov (what would *you* name a six-foot five-inch Cossack in a tunic, boots, and chinchilla fez?) and tripped upstairs.

At the entrance window I turned in my card to a stout girl's-basketball coach, paid the paltry admission, and received an admission ticket plus a ticket for "One FREE Dance" to replace my "Special Cut-Rate Tonight Only!" chit. Why the exchange, I cannot figure out. An agitated melody was being ground out of the loudspeakers, but I could see nothing because the glass in the doors leading to the soft heart of Honeymoon Lane were heavily painted in red and purple.

A very large, very broad-shouldered gent in a tux gave me a quick once-over as he took my ticket, then said "O.K.," satisfied I was neither drunk nor slavering: I swung back the doors.

Wham! Eighteen girls (I counted them later) in evening gowns, lined up behind a low railing directly opposite the entrance, began cleaving the air with mating calls.

"Honey, honey, *honey!*"

"Dance, handsome? Take me!"

"*Please* dance with me, sweetheart."

The corybants certainly seemed frantic in their loneliness. The mere sight of me had driven them wild: they waved their hands, smiled, winked, pouted, undulated, and bobbed up and down, all the while yodeling their unshy invitations. I sank onto a nearby bench.

The posse promptly sidled along the rail, still facing me, to train their guns with improved precision.

"Honey! Come *on!"*

"Don't be a meanie!"

"How's about it, how's *about* it?"

"Choose me!"

"Whaddaya say, lover? Let's do it!"

"Don't be bashful, dreamboat!"

The taxi-dancers were attractive girls, let me say. The youngest looked no more than eighteen, the oldest no more than twenty-eight. They wore iridescent gowns, their make-up was discreet, their bared backs and arms and unbared bosoms were lovely to behold. They were nowhere near as hard-looking as their photographs in the lobby. They did not cease crooning, cooing, pitching Indian Love Calls at me, and when, stalling for time and poise, I reached for my cigarettes, it set off a new barrage—with a shrewd shift in the strategy of seduction.

"Honey, c'n *I* have a puff?"

"How about *me,* baby?"

"Can I have one, doll?"

I approached the rail, bearing gifts.

Three girls took cigarettes, an act which I soon learned was no more than a maneuver to bring me closer.

"Come *on!"*

"I'm waitin' for you, you, you!"

"Dance, dance, dance, dance!"

One girl fixed me with Mona Lisa's slow, tantalizing smile, and winked, ever so significantly. The next thing I remember is leading her out to the dance floor.

Mona let her body, all marshmallow, flow against mine and squeezed my hand and murmured, "Mmmm—mmh!" It was a voluptuous "Mmmm—mmh!"

I think I said, "Good evening."

We danced for a moment, approaching ecstasy, when a

loud buzzer honked through the music. Mona stopped, disengaged her clutch, and said, "Honey, better get some tickets."

She had separated my complimentary ticket from my hand with a dainty gesture.

"I thought that ticket was for a dance," I ventured.

"It *was*, baby. A dance is every time the buzzer buzzes."

The buzzer buzzes every minute.

I hurried to a booth off the floor, bought ten tickets for a dollar, and returned to da Vinci's delight. She put her left arm around my shoulder, her cheek against my temperature, and, with her right hand, snagged all ten tickets. "It's simpler that way, baby," she whispered.

It was.

We danced along to "Avalon," which sings of lost and recovered love, and Mona was soft and warm and yielding in my arms—until the buzzer finished its tenth pecuniary decree. My soul-mate stopped. "That makes ten. You are ter*rif!* Why doncha buy five dollars' wortha tickets, doll, and save all that goin' back and forth?"

I bought ten more tickets and when I returned to positioning, I held the tickets in my right hand, behind Mona Lisa's back. She squeezed me, giggling, "You're pretty darn careful, aren't you, dear?" Then she came in very close, closed her eyes in imminent rapture, and hummed, "Mmmm."

"Why do you say 'Mmmm'?" I asked, boldly.

She trailed Delilah's hair across my cheek. "You're my doll, that's why."

The floor darkened now, and a revolving glass globe in the ceiling showered colored spangles all around us, and confetti of light fell upon us. A four-piece band, erasing the canned aphrodisia, slid into a glutinous waltz. My partner was all dappled, carmine and blue and diamond sparklings, no longer Mona Lisa but a Seurat, a Prendergast, a living Vuillard. This was Honeymoon Lane at its best. I heard her moan.

"What is it?" I asked, in a low, throbbing voice.

"Three so far," she murmured.

I gave her the ten tickets.

"My name's Jean," she smiled. "So what's yours?"

"Rudolph."

"What line you in?"

"Clothes."

Jean said, "That's *cute.*"

I waltzed her into a dashing whirl. "How late do you work here, Jean?" I asked, exploring the maximum yield on my investment ($2.35 by now, and the night was just beginning).

"Till four, baby. Nine to four, every night—I mean every morning. Why not just buy five bucks' wortha tickets more and take me to breakfast? At four?"

It took me a moment to collect my forces. "When do you sleep?"

Jean singed me with a sidelong flame. "Mmmm. . . . After breakfast."

Our conversation followed the immemorial protocol and I learned that Jean was a Brooklyn girl, an ex-model, and made between forty and seventy dollars a week as a taxi-dancer.* Not from salary, mind you. She receives nothing from the management, but keeps one-half of the price of all the tickets she collects. She is, in truth, a nickel-a-dance girl, and glad of it. "Forty to seventy a week isn't all," Jean smiled. "You have to add the *presents.*"

"Presents?"

Jean squeezed me. "*Silly.* Say a fella takes you out afters. Has breakfast with you. Or takes you out someplace, to eat and dance. Takes you home. Well, he gives you a—present."

"Oh," I said. "What kind of presents?"

She gave me a linchpin chuckle. "You're dumb, arncha? Oh, yes, I'll bet you are, ha, ha! . . . Well, like nice lingerie, a bracelet, a purse, a piece of jewelry, maybe an evening gown. Honey!" she cried. "Let's you and me go out tomorrow! Night. Dinner. Mm*mm!* . . . If you want to keep me out past nine, of course, you make up my time here."

* This was quite a while ago.

Milady's time, it turned out, was assessed at twenty dollars an evening.*

I suggested that that was a bit high, considering her weekly income.

She shrugged, "Gee, you have a mathematic-type mind. . . . O.K. Fifteen."

I said that I hated to put a beautiful friendship on a cold commercial basis. I think that impressed Jean. Not the words (she gave me a look you could sell to a rug peddler) but the fact that any male on earth would resort to such a cliché. "*Any*way," she mused, "you and me ought to step out. We'd have a real good time. I know. Mmmmh." She leaned her head way back so I could see her smiling. (The rest of her was not way back; I want to be accurate at all times.) "*Then* if you want to give me a little present, why that would be real nice. Just call me at——"

She gave me her telephone number. I had not asked for it, but Jean was a democratic maiden. The music faded.

I went to the bench for rest and rehabilitation. To my surprise, the girls at the mating rail ignored me. Apparently it was the Code: I was considered Jean's. Either that or they figured they had already wasted their blandishments on me. There were two men next to me on the recovery plank. One was sallow and bald and kept glowering at the girls, muttering "Some bims," or "Would you just look at them bims?" The other gentleman was sleek, plump, practiced, and blasé. He carried on a running line of banter with the damsels at the rail, whom he called "Toots," "Tootsie Roll" or "Tootsie Pie."

There were no fewer than twenty-seven glamorous hostesses on call now, by my count, and nine men, counting me. Only two couples were dancing. The girls who weren't dancing kept moving around, gliding, sliding, swaying, snapping their fingers. Occasionally, two girls would pair off and go out on the floor.

One of the men dancing was young, and wore an Ivy

* This was *quite* a while ago.

League suit, obviously a scholar being exposed to higher education elsewhere. The other was definitely not a college man: he kept flinging successive hostesses around in violent spasms. One of the girls at the hitching post snickered, "His idear of the Big Apple, the jerk."

In a back corner of the ballroom there was a chromium bar, where two males, snappy dressers, were drinking beer. Fenced off from the dance floor was an area filled with tables. Not a soul was seated at a single table. I found out why later.

I went to the window for ten tickets—and my previous conclusion was demolished: the minute the girls saw those tickets, my irresistibility returned. The front line resounded with pleas of alliance.

"Honey, honey, *honey!*"

"Me, dear!"

"Spin me around, hot shot."

"Me!"

"Look, look, look. You're for me!"

I had obviously been mistaken about the Code. Priority rights are dissolved the moment a male buys more tickets.

One girl in the lineup didn't make noises in the verbal barrage. She didn't even smile. Since I am incapable of controlling my empathy, I asked her to dance. She looked surprised.

As my hand slid around her waist she said, "It's funny your choosing me. I'm not so lively tonight." She grimaced. "Toothache. It's killing me."

I said, "Would you rather sit down—have a drink?"

She thought that over, then nodded.

We went to the tables. To do this we had to pass a slightly mustached matron at a desk; she wrote something down as we went by. I noticed that my sibyl was walking on the other side of a low, curtained railing; and when we sat down in the chairs, side by side, a fence separated us from the hips down.

"Police department rule," sighed my partner.

A waiter came up and I ordered two beers. Mine, at least, was unlike any malt concoction I had ever drunk. After a sip and a shudder from me, the girl leaned forward. "I ought to tell you. I guess you're new here . . . They charge for sitting."

"What do you mean?"

She winced, not for me but her bicuspids. "That woman at the desk. We come in, she checks you in. We get up, she checks you out. You pay for the time you spend sitting with one of us girls."

"How much?"

"Six dollars an hour. That's ten cents a minute. You see, there are sixty minutes an hour, so six dol——"

After she calmed me down, she explained that the benevolent management did allow you ten free minutes to drink the beer you paid for.

Her name was Blossom, she told me. Her last name was false: "All the girls use phony last names; you have to be crazy not to." She was from New Brunswick, New Jersey, and had been taxi-dancing for four months. She didn't mind it. She said she made "pretty good money." Yes, occasionally a client got fresh, but there were inconspicuous bouncers around to stop any hanky-panky on the premises.

"What about away from here?" I asked.

"Well, you don't date the pointed-head types—and the others, if you slap 'em in the puss once," said Blossom, "they behave."

Before taking the vows at Honeymoon Lane, Blossom had been a clerk in a five-and-ten-cent store, a waitress, unemployed, an usher in a movie theater. All she said about this last calling was, "Those damn uniforms. They got me down." Finding this taxi-dance job was a real break, she felt. Any girl could be a taxi-dancer. All you need is an evening gown. You don't even have to be much of a dancer, although most of the girls were pretty good at it.

Blossom wasn't at all like Jean. She didn't have the calculated murmur, the sedulous look, the perfidiously erotic emanations. Maybe it was her toothache. She kept saying,

"Gee, it's too bad you had to choose tonight to choose me. Usually, I'm lively." She gave me her telephone number.

So I forsook Honeymoon Lane for Parisian Danceland, a block further south, where the Fair Trade Practices Act permitted them to announce: "WORLD'S MOST RAVISHING GIRLS AS YOUR PARTNER!" The only difference I could see between Honeymoon Lane and Parisian Danceland was that the Parisian is laid out more like a rectangle.

The girls at the entrance rail erupted with the same predatory patois, begged for a cigarette, praised my appearance, fanned my emotions with the same bobbing mammary movements. Escorted from balustrade to dance area, they promptly launched their personal salesmanship. They suggested breakfast at four, soulfully expressed their love of dining and dancing, casually mentioned the matter of presents. They were not at all demure about offering me their telephone numbers.

I asked three of the girls where they lived, and their answers were fraught with such virtuosity that they are worth recording for historians interested in contemporary mores: The first dancer, Flo, said she lived with "two girl friends— and our cat. And say, if that cat could talk!"

The second balletomane, Hazel, lived "with my sister and Peewee. Peewee's our canary. And am I glad Peewee doesn't keep a *di*ary!"

The third nymph, Babe, resided with "a coupla girls from here and we got a Scotty and is he ever cute—but thank *God* he can't tell what goes *on!*"

The girls had strong views about animal magnetism.

My last port of call that evening was Majestic Danceland, which doesn't live up to its name. But I shall always remember it for two things: a girl named Honey and a girl named Cuba.

Cuba won my instant palpitations. She was truly ravishing—dark-eyed, ebony-haired, a skin like creamed-coffee, and the kind of mouth sonnets are written to. There's no point in trying to describe her physique. I waited around for a while, in the hope of holding Cuba in my arms, but during that entire vigil she danced with a sloe-eyed cavalier in a pearl-buttoned vest and pants that came up to his sternum. He held her very close, being a man of judgment, and danced cheek to cheek. He also displayed complete indifference to the beat of whatever music was being played: he tangoed all the while. He never talked; he just tangoed. And each time he reached the edge of the floor, he kicked his left foot backward, twirled around, pressed his other cheek against Cuba's other cheek, and proceeded to slide his suave, hateful path to the opposite edge of the hardwood.

After my faithful, fruitless wait for the dark lady of the sonnets, I took to the floor, with an importuning blonde who wore a cross on a chain around her neck and volunteered the wholesome news that her name was Honey.

I asked, "Who's that dark-haired girl with——"

She didn't even turn her head. "Her name is Cuba. All the boys ask. We girls do not like her."

Honey said taxi-dancing was a lot better than working behind a counter. "I ought to know. Fifteen, eighteen a week, and on your feet every minute! Honey, lis' . . ." (It took three or four "lis's" for me to realize that Honey was using her own diminutive of "listen".) "Lis', hon, why not just buy ten dollars' wortha tickets so we can relax and enjoy ourself without no other guy interuding?"

Honey said she especially likes to go out with college boys. "They drink beer and sing and they're just full of the devil." Some of Honey's best boy friends, she allowed, are Harvard and Princeton men. Yale, Columbia and Cornell products come up to the Majestic, too, "but somehow I go for the Harvard-Princeton type. What about you buy more tickets, dear, and——"

Honey doesn't mind going out with middle-aged gentlemen, of whom she has a loyal following. "They probably don't get satisfaction at home, so they come up here. Cheat on their wives. . . . Older men are easier to handle; I mean for we girls. Say, some of those Harvard-Princeton boys are practically engineers! I mean in getting a *hold*." Older men give nice presents, too. "Once," she said with a faraway look and underwriting dimple, "this real-estate dealer from St. Louis, he said, but how do you ever know, dated me and he leaned over in the cab he was taking me to some scrumptious Chinese food in, and without one single word he leaned over and kissed me—nothing rough or forcing, just a real sweet little kiss. Then he handed me ten dollars without a peep."

Each taxi-dancer has faith in her own special patter, Honey confided. "I can't yell, for instance, like some of the others. Maybe you noticed. I guess I'm just not the *type*. All I say when a customer comes in is, 'Honey, wouldn't you like to dance?' I hit the 'you,' to make it personal." She eyed me, languorous and powdery. "Why not let's you and me get away from all this? I mean right now! You see, for twelve dollars' wortha tickets, hon——"

Twelve dollars' worth of tickets, it turned out, would compensate Honey for the rest of the evening. (It was 2:00 A.M.) I declined, pleading an early case in court.

"Well, then how is tomorrow night?" she asked. "I love to go formal. . . . I guess you'd have to buy me an evening gown, because you won't believe it but I haven't a *thing* to wear. Nothing for going *formal*, I mean, like to a nightclub. I like soft pink or blue, with——" She described the garment in scrupulous detail. Size 10.

Honey wouldn't give me her telephone number for quite a while. She kept smiling mysteriously, eying me from the corners of her twinkletoe eyes. She said she never gave her number to a gentleman "for less than five dollars' wortha tickets."

I was ungallant, I'm afraid; I said nothing. And then the whole giddying weight of that unforgettable night in ECSTASY—dancing with Bevies of Glamorous Girls, holding Lonely-Hearted Beauties in my Embrace, whispering to America's Most Ravishing Hostesses, overwhelmed me. I yawned. Honey gave me her phone number.

"Gee, I guess I must like you," she sighed through all the magnolia and dimples. "I never have gave up my number so cheap before."

Leonardo

“**I** wish to work miracles," he wrote in his youth; and after a lifetime of creating miracles, in art and science and technology, in our knowledge of man and the secrets of nature, this altogether incomparable man lamented that the hours of his life had been "wasted."

History smiles. "The world knows of no other man of a genius so universal," wrote Taine, "so endowed with imagination, so thirsting for the eternal, so far pushed beyond his own century and the centuries to come."

I do not think the tribute excessive. I do not even think it adequate. But I know no way of improving upon it.

Most of us think of Leonardo da Vinci as a painter. He was: a painter never excelled, and never equaled for the innovations he introduced to painting. No painter showed more insight into how to invest a flat surface with the lyrical mystery we call art.

But Leonardo was far, far more than a painter. Before Copernicus, he wrote that it is the earth that moves, not the sun: *"Il sole non si move."* Before Galileo, he recorded the fact that a falling object must accelerate with the distance of its fall, said that "The earth is a star, like the moon," suggested that a pendulum be used to regulate a clock, and urged that a magnifying lens "be turned on the moon." Two centuries before Newton, Leonardo made striking observations on gravity and motion; he saw that inertia was the crucial key to movement: "a body whether moving or at rest changes unwillingly." He noted that light and sound move in waves, just as water does ("The air moves like a river and carries the clouds"), which explained to him why we hear church bells from varying distances. And 400 years before Darwin, if you please, Leonardo da Vinci speculated that our human species has evolved, and wrote this stupendous, heretical line: "Man does not vary from the animals except in what is accidental."

I never cease to marvel over Leonardo's assumption that he could understand everything. His mind was so curious, so confident, so swift and deft and original, that he approached the unknown with a sense of pleasure that never seemed to flag, and as if he expected to solve any of the puzzles of nature or mechanics he encountered. He called impatience the "mother of stupidity," knowledge "the "mother of love," and defined science as "the knowledge of things possible."

And in an age in which the most learned men knew Holy Scripture to be the definitive Word of God, and sought all answers in Aristotle or Ptolemy or Aquinas, Leonardo wrote this timeless epigram: "Those who argue by referring to authority are not using their minds but their memories."

Once, exploring the hills near Florence, he found fish fossils embedded in the rocks; he brushed aside the conventional explanation, in terms of Noah and the Flood, and deduced that the earth itself had changed down the eons: that hilltops had once lain under the oceans! The bold surmise led him to speculate further, from the evidence of the strata in rocks, as to how mountains themselves must have been born.

There seems to be no way of describing his achievements —his art, his theories, his observations, his inventions, the infinite range of his intellect—without resorting to superlatives. Let me catalogue his skills:

He was a painter, architect, sculptor; a poet, an accomplished musician, and a cartographer. More significant, in the stumbling chronicle of man, is the fact that Leonardo was among the first scientists who can be called a modern: a superlative investigator, an ingenious experimenter, an inexhaustible generator of hypotheses. He was a pioneer in physics, optics, acoustics, hydraulics. He was a superb naturalist, a gifted anatomist, a geologist, physiologist, zoologist. He was an audacious engineer and city planner, a designer of advanced irrigation techniques, a fabricator of canals, locks, weirs, and novel ways of draining marshes, raising rivers, channeling lakes, using waterfalls for power. He invented the tank, the submarine, a diving suit, a snorkel. He designed superior battlements, catapults, and new ways of scaling parapets. (He was for a time Cesare Borgia's Engineer General.)

He was the most gifted of trail-blazers in aeronautics: He invented a helicopter, a parachute, a glider. He defined the principles of steering and lateral balance. He described the function of wing slots and retractable landing gears.

His incisive intelligence extended to anatomy: "The span of man's outstretched arms," he wrote, "is equal to his height." He drew a marvelous male figure in a square set within a circle, the legs together, then set apart, the arms horizontal, then at a 45-degree angle, and explained: "The center of the circle formed by the extremities of the outstretched limbs will be the navel, and the space between the legs . . . will form an equilateral triangle."

Leonardo must have had phenomenal eyesight, a hyperacuity of vision that let him see minute things no one before had seen. He could "freeze" rapid motion, in his mind, breaking a single sequence into separate, swift actions that were not really made visible until the invention of the camera, and stroboscopic lights. Just as his passion for exactitude made him draw details of an insect's eyes, say, or the way light falls on leaves, so his exceptional sharpness of focus revealed the way a bird avoids turning over when the wind strikes it underneath, or how the spread of tail feathers and the flapping of wings cut landing speed. He saw how a whirlpool spins, how clouds shift and alter their shape, how the sea breaks on rocks, how water swirls in an eddy. He noticed so ordinary but revealing a thing as this: When the wind sweeps across a field, the grain moves in ripples "but the stalks of the grain do not move."

One can only marvel at the umversality of his mind, the prodigality of his talents, the unbounded bounty of his eye, hand, and imagination. He once wrote: "Iron rusts from disuse, stagnant water loses its purity . . . even so does inaction sap the vigors of the mind." His mind was incapable of inaction.

He beheld the kind of revelations that reward that rare few who never lose their engrossment in wondering. And he paid the price—moody impulse, incessant discontent, uncontrollable digressions, painful self-chastisement for the self's limitations—that the gods exact from those who dare aspire to Olympus.

•

Leonardo was a bastard. Born in 1452, he was taken away from his mother, a peasant girl named Caterina di Piero del Vacca, and legitimized by his father, Ser Piero da Vinci, a notary, who married another woman and left the upbringing of the boy largely to his grandfather, in a village near Florence. The fates showered Leonardo with gifts. He was a beguiling conversationalist, a fine fencer and horseman, a lute player, an improviser of lyrics which he sang in a beautiful voice, was strong enough to bend horseshoes with his hands. As if all this was not enough, "His personal beauty could not be exaggerated," wrote Vasari, "for his every movement was grace itself."

We shall never know what daemons drove him on and made him secretive, restless, reticent, inordinately sensitive. He feared crowds and never ate meat. He often failed to complete a commission; he was forever dropping one project to plunge into another. He so hated cruelty that it was his custom to purchase caged birds in the marketplace, and set them free. (I have no doubt he also wanted to see how they took off from his hands and spread and flapped their wings.)

He chose his apprentices more for their beauty than their talents: not one of his students amounted to much as a painter, unless, as a strong tradition has it, Il Sodoma was a pupil of his. He housed, fed and clothed the young men. He was almost certainly homosexual—in his affections, if not in practice.

Leonardo began his career as a painter, and transformed the entire realm of painting. He discovered how atmosphere changes with distance. He hit upon new ways of treating shadows, outlines, juxtapositions of color, light itself. He introduced individual comment, as it were, into portraiture. He rendered landscape with new modalities of feeling. The hypnotic *Mona Lisa,* the twilight intimations of the *Virgin of the Rocks,* the monumental *Last Supper*—each transfixes us with that evasive particularity that distinguishes genius from talent. Delacroix wrote:

> He freed himself with one blow from the traditional painting of the fifteenth century; without errors, without weakening, without exaggerations; and as if with a single bound, he arrives at judicious naturalism, equally separated from servile imitation and an empty, chimerical ideal. . . .

Leonardo drew the first landscapes *as* landscapes (not as backgrounds for figures) in Western art. He brought a breathtaking sensitivity to the drawing of a twig, a stone, a fern, a face. He painted his portraits with the most subtle adumbrations, setting his subjects against labyrinthine caves and obscure vistas to enrich the painting with supernatural penumbras.

His instructions on the techniques of art are as fresh today as when they were written:

> Be very careful to observe that among the shadows there are other shadows, almost imperceptible as to darkness and shape.

The painter should notice those quick motions which men are apt to make without thinking, when impelled by strong and powerful affections of the mind. He should make sketches of them ... then place a living model in the same position and observe . . . the muscles which are in action.

Black is the most beautiful in the shade; white in the strongest light; blue and green in the half-tint. . . .

Remember that young people have no sharp shadings: their flesh is transparent, something like what we observe when we put our hand between the sun and our eyes. . . . Place one of your fingers close to your picture, so that it will cast a shadow upon it. You can obtain the intensity of the shadow you desire by moving your finger nearer or farther from the picture.

Or consider his observations on character:

The artist who has no doubts about his own ability will attain little. When his work succeeds beyond his judgment, he acquires nothing; but when his judgment is superior to his work, he will never cease to improve, unless his love of gain interferes. . . .

His constant care should be to avoid conveying onto his own work the defects in his own person. For these defects, having become habitual to his observation, will mislead his judgment. . . . The mind, being fond of its own habitation, is apt to represent this prejudice to our imagination as something beautiful.

•

And the Mona Lisa smile, that bewitching expression, so enticing and elusive, "more divine than human," that seems to move before our eyes? For almost 500 years men have tried to solve the riddle of that alluring, dreamlike smile—from Raphael, who imitated it, to Sigmund Freud, who traced it back to Leonardo's memory of the mother he was separated from so young. Some have said the smile in the portrait is that of a woman carrying a child; others attribute it to the blissful reverie induced by the music Leonardo had a musician play for the model.

But that tantalizing smile is not limited to La Gioconda! You will see it on Leonardo's other women, and on John the Baptist, and on the faces of the Virgin and her mother and the angel in *The Madonna of the Rocks*, which he painted twenty years before *Mona Lisa*. The mystery of that smile, which Raphael and Andrea del Sarto and a platoon of Renaissance artists also painted, has been the subject of considerable conjecture (and nonsense) for almost five centuries. I like to think I have a solution—perhaps not *the* solution, but one that strongly recommends itself to my discontent with the alternatives.

First, all painters before Leonardo outlined their figures, so that they "stood away" from their backgrounds. Leonardo invented the technique the Italians call *sfumato* ("smoked"), painting in such a way as to omit sharp outlines, deliberately blurring and softening the corners of the eyes and mouth, blending light and shadow to tease our eye to find where one ends and the other begins.

Secondly, during the Renaissance, all well-born maidens were carefully schooled in the components of courtesy and decorum, flirtation and charm. In one primer on the feminine graces, *I Discorsi delle Bellezze delle Donne*, Agnolo Firenzuola advised the ladies: "From time to time, close the mouth at the right corner with a suave movement, and open it at the left, as if you were smiling secretely. . . ."

My theory is that a thousand Giocondas smiled that way, in the *palazzi* of Rome and Florence, Venice and Milan; and I maintain that dozens of painters painted that smile— but only Leonardo's technical mastery was able to imprison the transient, knowing intent to entice which is its secret.

•

What Théophile Gautier said of Leonardo's art explains Leonardo's originality in whatever he undertook:

> He worked after no set pattern or model; each of his creations was an exploration along a new line. He did not, like other painters, multiply his works, but once having attained his special ideal, abandoned that pursuit forever.

Leonardo filled hundreds of notebooks with an astonishing assortment of drawings, sketches, diagrams, outlines—*and* with written notes, descriptions, and specifications for further observation or invention. The notes, helter-skelter, were written backwards. (He taught himself this "secret writing," in which the words could be read only when reversed in a mirror, possibly to evade the Church's prohibitions against dissecting human bodies; he dissected over thirty!)

We do not know how many pages he filled, pouring out his ideas and wonderings, but at least 5,000 have so far been found: loose folios, bound notebooks in a multitude of sizes, unstitched sheets, pages large and small. The notes and sketches are a jumbled treasury of comments, questions, formulas, even fables such as no other man ever approximated. They are a priceless repository of findings: on anatomy, botany, physiology, human parts and expressions—from children's smiles to the grimaces of the insane. (For a time, Leonardo followed condemned men to the gallows, sketching the changes in their mien.)

For almost 400 *years* this incomparable richness of observation and experiment, original hypotheses and brilliant clues, was but partly known and never assembled. For when Leonardo died, in 1519, at the Château of Cloux, to which the admiring king of France, Francis I, had invited him, pages or volumes of those remarkable journals were given away, sold, stolen, bartered, auctioned. Separated parts ended up all over Europe, in all sorts of private collections: in Milan, Paris, Turin, Windsor Castle; in palaces, mansions, and museums from Madrid to Petrograd. The magnitude of the loss for so long of such a wealth of knowledge and invention and intuition is surely incalculable.

Consider a few details: Leonardo was the first man to build an actual model of the human heart. He also made a model of the eye. And the brain. He was the first man to draw an opened womb, with an embryo inside. He was the first to notice how leaves are arranged around a stem.

He was the first to understand friction and describe stream-lining. He was the first to recommend the use of air and steam as sources of power. He foresaw controlled explosions (an internal combustion engine) as a way of moving pistons. He described an air-conditioning device to diminish intolerable heat. He drew the first aerial map and it seems the first map of the world in which the name of America appears.

Leonardo would forsake painting for months on end to give his curiosity free rein: studying mathematics (he collaborated on a textbook), astronomy, geography; experimenting with motion and sound and leverage; marveling over a dragonfly's wing or conjecturing how the earth was born out of the universe. As for flight, which had dazzled men from the time of the cave, Leonardo wrote: "A bird is an instrument, working according to mathematical law, which it is within the power of man to reproduce."

Since the instruments of his time were very crude and unwieldy, Leonardo proceeded to invent better ones. He was a wizard with gears, pulleys, cogs, weights, springs. When he faced a problem, he analyzed the functions required to resolve it, and invented the artifacts needed to perform the functions. He mastered ways of controlling power through gear ratios. He dreamed up novel threadings in screws and bolts. He devised cams, pawls, flywheels, crankshafts.

Leonardo actually made, drew, or described a hygrometer, pedometer, odometer, inclinometer; portable bridges, band brakes, a jigsaw, double-decker streets. He invented a sprocket chain, an oil lamp with a water-lens to focus the light, machines to roll copper into even strips, an adjustable monkey wrench, an automatic "feed" for printing. He invented a clock that used a falling weight to mark the minutes, not only the hours. He dreamed up a wagon that moved without a horse, from the released energy of wound-up springs. He invented gadgets for measuring the mileage traversed by wheels, for improving the accuracy of weighing techniques, for recording changes in the weather.

He contrived a double-spiral staircase in which, because of the cunning use of the helix, passengers could go up or down without colliding with those moving in the opposite direction. He described prefabricated houses, a dredging machine, a giant earth-mover. He was the first man to analyze the carrying stress and the breaking points of certain materials. He figured out the optimum load a wire can carry. He discovered where an overloaded column will collapse. . . .

•

No one can explain him. In all the staggering, tumbling magic of his notebooks, this panurgic mind offers us only guarded, fleeting glimpses into his heart: "While I thought I was learning how to live, I have been learning how to die."

He was a miracle. He remains the most talented being this fumbling race of ours has ever known. I venerate him as the supreme example of that glory that is granted only to those who are prisoner to man's most sublime passion: to understand.

"How! Is It Already O'Clock?"

〰〰〰〰〰〰〰〰〰〰〰〰〰〰〰〰〰〰〰〰〰〰〰〰〰〰〰〰〰〰〰〰〰

THE most accomplished (and mystifying) Casanova I ever knew was my jeep driver in Paris. His name was Jud and he had the most fetching, melting, winning smile you ever saw. Its seductiveness was magnified by Jud's "Aw, shucks" manner, which was true, and his air of sublime innocence, which was false.

Jud's smile reached its most perfidious incandescence whenever, as he dreamily put it, "Ah git me a whiff of quail." When Jud said "a whiff of quail" he was not referring to the scent of the fowl whose mating call, any ornithologist will tell you, sounds like "Wet my lips"; when Jud said "quail" he was thinking of a featherless female of our own species.

Jud's vocabulary was as meager as that of most GIs, and just as fertile in synonyms for "girl." In the months Jud served as my driver, he used the following synonyms for the subject that dominated the thinking, day or night, of the brave Americans who were fighting to liberate Europe from Nazi tyranny:

broad	muff	yum-yum
job	stuff	skirt
dish	fluff	hubba-hubba
tomato	eyedrop	stack of hay
blinder	package	darb
piece of jam	twilly	chicken with fixin's

This list is far from complete, of course; it sternly omits synonyms of a more vivid, or anatomical, genre.

Jud usually looked sleepy. He could "knock me off forty-fifty li'l ole winks" at any hour, in any place, in any posture. I once asked him if he was so dopey during the day because he did not get enough shuteye at night. From the cryptic utterances he employed in place of speech I gathered that it was a point of honor with Jud not to enter a bed unless (or until) it contained a female cotenant. "B'en that way sence Ah was a colt, sir," he ruminated. "Ah'm from Tennessee."

Jud was crazy about Paris. This was not because of that noble city's architecture, history, museums or cultural *richesse.* Jud loved Paris because of *les girls,* and from the way he pronounced *"les"* it was hard to tell whether he was speaking French or English. The distinction is important, because if Jud was trying French, he was using the definite article, the most barren part of any tongue; but if he was speaking English, he was using an adjective, thus passing moot judgment on the girls' moral elasticity.

Jud especially admired the Champs Elysées, which, like most GIs, he called "The Champs." The reason for the Champs' popularity was not its fine trees or spacious splendor, but its endless droves of cyclists: since gasoline was drastically rationed, buses few and frantic, taxis rare and felonious, thousands upon thousands of sensible Parisians rode bicycles. And as *les girls* pedaled up the long incline to the *Arc de Triomphe,* or came free-wheeling down in a blaze of speed, their skirts would rise and billow and spinnaker in the breeze, thus providing Jud and his heroic comrades with renewed dedication to the cause they regarded as the Fifth Freedom.

Jud would take me to and from many crucial conferences by which the American Expeditionary Forces in Europe were not run, and he would wait in the jeep for me to emerge from a palace or hotel or the Shell Building, where my office was. When I came out of a building I often found Jud sitting behind the wheel of the jeep, staring/grinning fixedly at some damsel—who was at a café table, kiosk or traffic light anywhere from ten to twenty feet away. Most of the time, the nymph was staring/smiling back. It was uncanny. It sometimes reminded me of a snake and a rabbit hypnotizing each other, which contradicts the laws of the jungle. True, Jud grinned much more like a wolf than a snake, but I'll stand by the analogy, even though wolves don't frequent jungles.

The first time I observed this reciprocal mesmerization, I said, as I climbed into the jeep, "No hurry, Jud. Finish what you were doing."

"Wasn't doin' nuthin'," he sighed, clashing the gears.

We drove along, distrusting each other.

"I hope you got her name," I ventured.

"No, sir."

"Her address?"

"Nope."

"Too bad."

"Oh, Ah dunno," he shrugged. "She'll be back tomorrow."

She was.

I hope you are not expecting me to explain this. I can't. All I can tell you is that the same filly was stationed at the same mating ground (this was *long* before Robert Ardrey's lyrical description of courtship patterns among the African kob), Jud was giving her his Svengali half-Nelson, and she was responding with a trancelike goggle that signaled animal acquiescence.

One morning, a new driver from the motor pool picked me up at my hotel. He was an apple-cheeked lad from Oregon who, after wiping his forehead in what may have been intended to be a salute, introduced himself as Private Wentzel Sir and informed me that Private Jud Whatever-his-last-name-was was not up to reporting for duty.

"Is he sick?" I asked.

"I—don't know, sir."

"Then what's wrong?"

"He's just—run down," the earnest lad said.

"From what?" I asked. "He doesn't do enough driving to keep mold from forming on our tires."

"But, *sir*," blushed young Lochinvar, "Jud leads an awful active life!"

When Jud returned from his awful active life, three days later, he gave me that irresistible, corn-muffin smile.

"Welcome back to the ranks of the U.S. Army," I re-smiled, just as insincerely. "What was wrong?"

The valiant chauffeur scratched his neck. "Don't rightly know, sir. Ah jest had some miseries and went in for sick call, accordin' to regulations, an' when them docs got one peek at m' zoomin' tempacheer they said Ah jest had to ketch up on m' sleep!"

"Did they keep you in the hospital for three days?" I asked.

"Ah was there for sick call——"

"No, Jud. I mean 'catching up on your sleep.' Were you actually hospitalized for three days?"

"Well, not exactly, sir," said Jud, girding his brows, so to speak (I judged he was girding his brows from the canyon of wrinkles that appeared thereon, as they did whenever he was driven to the extremity of cerebration).

"What do you mean—'not exactly'?" I asked. "Either you were or you weren't."

"Well, them docs suggested Ah report for morning check-ups, which Ah did——"

"But you *slept*," I ventured, "elsewhere?"

"*Kee*rect, sir," Jud beamed. "An' that's what cured me!"

"It brought down your temperature."

"Sure did."

"And ended the miseries."

"Yup."

"Jud," I said, summoning all the funeral puissance of Rank (actually I had no *real* rank, being what was peculiarly called "Colonel, Assimilated Rank"), "tell me the honest-to-God truth: Did you shack up with that piece of cake?" I asked.

"Which one, sir?"

"The one I saw you putting the hex on, the day before you came down with the miseries and the ballooning temperature!"

"Yup," Jud clucked with radiant fondness. "Man, oh, man."

He spent the remainder of the week (the daylight hours, at least) in an emphatic languor.

The more I thought about Jud, the more I envied him, and the more I envied him the more I began to resent him. I crystallized my resentment, I suppose, around one simple point: How did he *communicate* with the dishes he hypnotized? I had never seem him actually talk to a girl.

When Jud had first been assigned to me, I had asked him whether he spoke French, and he had answered, quite manfully, "M' paw was over here in 19 and 18; an' he done jest fine, sir. An' *he* coont hinky-dink the *parlay voo* anymore'n Ah kin—so Ah ain't worryin'."

Now I wondered if Jud's extensive researches in Paris (he had, after all, spent three long months among the natives) had altered his monolinguistic bias. So one afternoon I asked, in a most casual way, "How's your French these days?"

"She's really sumpin'," he said.

"I meant the language."

"Oh . . . Well, cain't say Ah know more'n when Ah first hit Paree."

I cleared my throat. "Jud, do you *ever* speak French?"

"Nope," he said. "Ah jest point to it."

"What," I asked cautiously, "do you mean you just 'point' to it?"

He took a hand off the wheel, reached inside the left breast pocket of his combat jacket, pulled out a tiny red book, and flipped it open with his thumb. "Like this, sir."

I leaned over and read the random line to which he was pointing: "*You look so bloomy today I have not words to inform.*"

I lifted the tiny red book from his hand, thinking, I am

ashamed to tell you, of Keats on first reading Chapman's
Homer. On the left side of each page of the little red
book was a column of French sentences; and on the right
side, exactly opposite, were the English translations. The
page to which Jud had opened the tiny volume was headed
"Politeness Words." Some of the other "politeness words"
were:

"I suppose I don't mistake, it is you."

"Years pass over you without leaving a wrinkle."

*"You are so kind, how shall I ever discharge myself
towards you?"*

"How! Is it already o'clock?"

After the moment or two required to do justice to such
translations, I turned to the title page of that little booklet:
It read *La Conversation Usuelle* and employed this subtitle
(in French): "A Practical Guide for Travelers, through
the Aid of which You Will Avoid Embarrassment in the
Circumstances Which Present Themselves on a Journey."

The meaning struck me like a flash: what Jud had found,
somewhere, somehow, was a phrase book for *French*
travelers, written by a compatriot whose English left everything to be desired. The "Circumstances Which Present
Themselves on a Journey" were divided into categories that
still brighten my reveries:

> To Arise and Dress Oneself
> With a Washerwoman
> To Hire a Carriage
> At the Police Station
> With Health and Healing

A dawning suspicion reached high noon: I looked for
the publication date, and I found it: 1881.

That night, with Jud's permission, I studied *La Conversation Usuelle* at leisure, and I was wafted back into a
Victorian world of portmanteaus and poultices, walking
sticks and farthingales and archaic twilights in refulgent
gardens. I was so enchanted by this resurrected civilization, like Schliemann at Mycenae, that I copied out some

choice Anglicizations of Racine's (or even de Gaulle's) classic tongue:

> *"What a beautiful weather!"*
> *"Doctor, please auscultate me."*
> *"I like moonshine."*
> *"Coachman, stop! I no longer doubt you verge intoxication."*
> *"It sneezed the whole night long."*
> *(Il a neigé toute la nuit.)*
> *"Come dip your foot to wet in this rivulet."*
> *"What are these small, black pigs I behold everywhere?"*
> *"Has a thunderbolt struck on?"*
> *"My nose has bled these two hours."*
> *"By Jove! The bacon is quite rancid!"*
> *(Sapristi! Le jambon est fameusement rance.)*

But of *l'amour*, the line to which Jud presumably would "point" in his impudicious adventures, I found not a trace.

The next morning, when I returned the booklet, I asked Jud, affecting idle interest, "By the way, what part of this rare book did you say to 'point to'?"

"The part called 'In a Soiry,'" he said.

"I beg your pardon?"

"In a Soiry," he repeated, and riffled to a section entitled, *"En Soirée."* There, in a delicious "soiry," I read the well-thumbed lines:

> *"Madame, will you honor me with this mazurka?"*
> *"I never tire with gavotting."*
> *"Would you be amiable to dance vis-à-vis?"*
> *"How! Is it already o'clock to good-bye?"*

"Jud," I said, with dignity, "don't you realize that these phrases are very, very old-fashioned? Absurd? Even ridiculous?"

"Yup," he smiled.

"Well, then—" I fumbled for words. "I mean, when you point to a phrase, doesn't the girl bust out laughing?"

He nodded, grinning. "That's the real point, sir. She takes pity on me."

I flung my leg over the side of the jeep, not without a

certain bitterness, and Jud turned his head ever so slightly and said, "Once you git a muff smilin' *an* pityin' you, sir, you're roundin' third and headin' right for home." He turned the sun of his smile on my depression, saying, with bucolic charity, "Would you like for me to try an' latch ont' another li'l ole book like this one, sir? For you?"

The Indubitable
Laibowitz

~~~~~~

THE weeks came, the weeks passed. We broiled by day
and almost froze by night. The sun burned down and the
sands burned up and we gasped for air between. At twilight, the colors showered down on the Arizona desert,
clothing the ghostly yuccas in iridescence, and each night
the stars, so brilliant, so indifferent, burned cold on the
velvet sky.

I was working so hard that I lost track of time. I was
flooded by new patients, case histories, interviews, emergencies—above all, by the demands of Ward 7, the N.P.
(neuro-psychiatric) Ward at AAF Camp Colfax.

Captain Newman pleaded with Colonel Larrabee for two
more psychiatrists, four more nurses, six more orderlies.
We never did get the psychiatrists, but Area Command
dug up two live orderlies and hustled them to Colfax.
Within eight hours, the whole post was swapping yarns
about them.

I was in Captain Newman's office, giving him a run-down
on some admissions, when we heard a diffident knock on
the door and the first of Ward 7's priceless reinforcements
slouched into the room. He was a corporal, about five foot
ten, well built, tanned; but he carried himself as if death
was licking at his ear lobes.

"Good morning," said Captain Newman brightly.

The soldier touched a finger to his forehead, confirming its existence, and studied us through lugubrious eyes. He made no effort to conceal the fact that he did not approve of what he beheld.

"Sit down, Corporal."

The invitation proved belated: the lachrymose corporal had already deposited his weary coil in the chair across the desk.

"What's your name?" asked Captain Newman.

"Laibowitz," came a slow, sepulchral suspiration.

"First name?"

"Jackson." (sigh)

"How old are you?"

"Real age or felt age?" mourned the corporal.

"Stop that!"

"Twenty-five."

To my surprise, Captain Newman leaned forward and said frostily, "I *believe* it is customary for a soldier to address an officer as 'sir '!"

"Sir." Corporal Laibowitz shrugged. "What's 'customary' for a soldier can be tough for a civilian."

"But you aren't a civilian," said Newman acidly.

"I *feel* like a civilian," said Laibowitz.

"Congratulations." Captain Newman put on a propitiatory smile and held out his cigarettes. "Would you like to smoke?"

"Nicotine," announced Laibowitz, "is bad for the eyes."

"Oh. Do you have trouble with your eyes?"

"No, sir."

"Then why——"

"That's because I never touch nicotine," said Laibowitz.

Captain Newman looked startled. He leaned back in his chair to study the man before him with new interest. This did not present the slightest problem to Laibowitz, who suffered the scrutiny with the resignation of a man accustomed to the slow-witted. He was, all in all, rather good-looking—well-shaped features, a firm mouth, large liquid eyes. It was only his manner—an amalgam of acid stomach and apocalypse—which celebrated despair.

Captain Newman said, "I assume you've worked in a hospital before."

"Yes—sir."

Captain Newman waited. So did Laibowitz.

"Go on, Corporal."

"Go on where?" blinked the dour one.

"Tell me about your hospital experience."

"What's to tell? The camp I just came from, I don't want to knock the government, wasn't fit for a dog! Maybe a Nazi dog, not a U.S. citizen. They had me working in the wards day and night. I didn't like it."

"You mustn't hide your feelings," said Captain Newman dryly.

"I agree," said Laibowitz.

Newman winced. "What kinds of wards did you work in?"

"All kinds."

"Give me a hint," crooned Newman.

"It would spoil your lunch."

"I'll skip lunch."

"I advise you shouldn't; ask any doctor——"

"I *am* a doctor," leered Newman.

"Of nutrition?"

"*That* will do, Corporal. What–hospital–wards–did–you work–in?"

"O.K. General, general surgery, infectial diseases, where I caught everything, and O.B.—that was for the officers' wives. The rate they're getting pregnant, with free U.S. Army delivery, is enough so we won't need a draft in twenty years. I also did time in the V.D. department, which, to be frank about it, goes against my grains."

"Did you ever work in—an N.P. ward?" asked Captain Newman, rather too casually.

Laibowitz's eyes widened. "A *mental* ward?"

"I mean psychiatric cases——"

"Nuts?"

"They are not 'nuts,'" said Captain Newman firmly. "They're

men who————"

"My God, Doc," cried Laibowitz, "you gonna put me in a *loony* bin?"

"It is *not*————"

"I'll drop dead!" Laibowitz struggled to his feet, "I give you my word, Doc, inside one hour you can start digging my grave!"

"Sit down."

"Better ask me to *lay* down! I'm already a patient."

"Now listen!" said Captain Newman sharply. "I don't know where the hell you guys got all these cockeyed ideas! Most of the men in my ward are simply depressed————"

"So am I," proclaimed Laibowitz.

"—miserable————"

"*They're* miserable? Look at me!"

"Sit *down!*"

Corporal Laibowitz sank into the chair with noises suggestive of strangulation and verging on emphysema.

Crisply, firmly, sternly, Captain Newman launched into a lecture explaining the functions of his ward, the nature of our tasks, the duties of a wardman. He was simple, direct, and, I thought, remarkably reassuring. It made not the slightest dent on Laibowitz, who kept uttering woeful lamentations and embittered asides.

Captain Newman explained that we had a staff of excellent doctors ("For me alone you'll need one full-time," said Laibowitz), that the patients were not permitted razors, matches, blunt artifacts or sharp objects ("But *teeth* they've got?"), that an encouraging proportion of our cases responded favorably to therapy ("Don't spoil your record, Captain!") and were dismissed from Ward 7 to return to either army or civilian life ("I will gladly join them!"), that orderlies were pampered with frequent passes and off-post privileges ("You mean of their own free-will they come *back?*"), and that when he was off duty, Corporal Laibowitz, along with the other wardman, would sleep in complete comfort and safety in the finest barracks on the base, a good five hundred yards away ("Who will drag me back and forth?" asked Laibowitz).

"That's it," said Captain Newman efficiently. "Do you have any questions?"

Laibowitz raised his hand.

"You *don't* have to raise your hand," frowned Newman.

"I'm as surprised as you to see I still got the strength."

"Ask your question."

Laibowitz rose. "Doc, I appreciate your trying to raise my morale. But let us face facts. You are putting me in a booberino hatch. You are asking me to buddy up to cuckoos, crazies, dumdums, and scrambled-eggs-in-the-head. I got problems of my own, you know. I'm practically a nervous wretch. I'm high-strung, sensitive, and I promise you if you send me into your nuthouse, by Sunday—the *latest*—you'll have to fit me for a straitjacket!"

Captain Newman, who had listened to this oration somewhat open-mouthed, as if hearing a great Hamlet accusing his transfixed mother, cleared his throat, scratched his chin, braced his shoulders and narrowed his eyes sternly. "That will be all. You may go now. You will report to Sergeant Kopp."

"Who's he?" asked Laibowitz.

"My wardmaster."

"Where does he keep his whip?"

"Laibowitz," snapped Captain Newman, "what the *devil* is the matter with you? You look like an intelligent——"

"Don't be fooled by my looks!"

"You're making a mountain out of a molehill!"

"So I'm no good in geography."

"You'll get the best food on the post in my ward!"

"I already lost all my appetite."

"You have my deepest sympathy," said Captain Newman sarcastically.

"From plumbers I expect sympathy; from psychiatrists I expect understanding," cried Laibowitz, glancing toward the Judge in heaven.

Again, Captain Newman cleared his throat. "You may go now. . . . Ring the bell outside the door. Sergeant Kopp will show you the ropes."

"He should only give me a rope; I'll hang myself."

"Dismissed!"

Corporal Laibowitz gave his captain one last, imploring look. "Doc, can I just——"

"Send the other man in!" said Captain Newman in his most military manner.

Laibowitz reaffirmed the location on his forehead and sagged out of the room. He might have been en route to the firing squad.

Captain Newman turned to me. To my astonishment, his eyes were dancing. "What a break. That ambulatory Job will make a first-rate wardman."

"You really think so?" I exclaimed.

"Of course I do. Don't you?"

"I think he's closer to becoming a patient than a——"

Newman gave me a pitying look. "What the hell did they teach you jokers at Hahvud? Laibowitz is a natural. He may beef and buck and goof off for a while but the important points are: One, he's not afraid to voice his feelings; two, he understands suffering!"

I looked properly chastened, as I was supposed to whenever Newman said "Hahvud."

And Laibowitz did become, as Newman predicted, a superb wardman. Newman had said: "He understands suffering." Laibowitz did more than understand it; he welcomed it, he encouraged it, he embraced it. He had been raised in an ancient tradition that regarded misery as normal; and contentment as neurotic.

After his initial horror over being condemned to "a loony bin," after those first violent protestations and apocalyptic prophecies, Jackson Laibowitz found himself in the one place in the Army, perhaps the world, which he truly understood: a place where everyone else was unhappy, too.

If Captain Newman automatically took the side of the enlisted men against the brass, Laibowitz became the champion of the patients against the doctors.

With that blithe extension of his ego which was his most disconcerting characteristic, Jackson Laibowitz began to refer to the men in Ward 7 as "my patients." He was only one of five orderlies assigned to Master Sergeant Kopp, but within a week he had altered his status from menial to co-director. With a benevolence that spurned the niceties of Standing Operating Procedure, Laibowitz set out to improve the diet, the regimen, the recreation and the therapy for those souls whom, he took it as self-evident, fate had entrusted to his personal guardianship. What Omar Khayyám had preached, Jackson Laibowitz put into practice.

In this noble, humane enterprise, Laibowitz quickly enlisted the aid of another orderly, Pepi Gavoni. If Laibowitz was born to complain—and command, Pepi was born to endure—and obey. Everyone liked him. He was short, jolly, with thickish glasses, a musical voice, and an inextinguishable faith in men. Gavoni seemed to think that all human ailments could be cured with kindness and salami. He had an inexhaustible supply of both.

Every week a three- or four-pound Genoa salami, wrapped in brown butcher paper, arrived from Gavoni's patriotic sister in Passaic. He kept it under lock and key in his locker.

Gavoni dispensed salami as a reward, a bribe, a token, a sacrament. It was Laibowitz who supervised and sanctioned the dispensing. He also taught Gavoni the fine art and infinite finesses of standing military authority on its head.

Take, for instance, Laibowitz's methods of dealing with orders—orders from officers, his superiors, the Base Command itself. Written orders of which he approved, he executed with lightning dispatch; written orders of which he disapproved, he "mislaid," misread, misinterpreted, or misrouted.

His response to verbal instructions was even more exasperating: when he disagreed with a superior's instruction, he simply pretended he had not heard it; when it was repeated to him, he concluded it had not been communicated correctly the first time, which made the second exposition no more reliable than the first; when it was driven home to him in an indisputable manner that whatever his personal views, such-and-such a command *had* to be obeyed, he got "sick" and took to his quarters. Achilles had his tent; Laibowitz had his symptoms. Rarely has medical science been confronted with such symptoms—such coughs, aches, pains, wheezes, faintnesses and vertigos— as Jackson Laibowitz could summon to his cause, when that cause stood in need of reinforcement or camouflage, *blitzkrieg* or delaying maneuvers.

Laibowitz was not often forced to the extremity of malingering: *au naturel,* he displayed masterly skills in circumvention. He never directly *disobeyed* Captain Newman's will, for instance; he managed to modify it through reinterpretation. He never refused; he simply outflanked. He simulated deafness with an innocence that defied exposure, and stupidity with a poise that demanded admiration.

His intensely personal, protective concern for "his" cases grew by such leaps and bounds that he began to resent the way our psychiatrists tossed the word "sick" around. "Doc," he once asked Captain Mathieson, "why do you call that boy from Texas 'sick'? In my opinion, he is not sick; he is just miserable."

"He's miserable because he's in conflict."

"Who wouldn't be, going through what that poor guy went through?" Laibowitz cried. "Twenty-two days behind the Jap lines! In a stinking jungle, living like a rat, out of his head with fever. A Jap sentry is going to run a bayonet through his guts—Tex puts a switch-knife right in the Jap's heart. The blood squirts over Tex like it's coming out of a pump, and he throws up. From this you expect a man should come out singing 'I'm Looking at the World Through Rose-Colored Glasses'?"

"N-no," said Captain Mathieson, "but——"

"I'm glad you agree with my diagnosis," said Laibowitz, and promptly repaired to Captain Newman for "consultation" on the case of Tex Hovring. "Consider what he went through, Doc!"

Captain Newman nodded. "I have. But other men have gone through experiences as bad as Tex's and didn't end up in Ward 7. . . . He's getting therapy."

"That he needs like a shark needs teeth. Send him home to Dallas, to his wife and kids, and in a month, I give you five to one, he'll be as normal as me."

"Will he? It was on his way back to Dallas that Tex broke down. He can't *face* his wife and kids, Jackson. He says he's a coward."

"That's because he's so brave!" protested Laibowitz. "Brave enough to come right out and say what everyone feels but is afraid to admit."

"Everyone else doesn't try to jump out of a plane on his way home."

Laibowitz scowled. "So he flipped his lid *maybe* for a minute. From all the excitement! . . . 'Sick' I call the odd-balls who *don't* know when to take a dive. . . . Doc, there are times I do not understand you!"

"When you're around, Florence Nightingale, I'm not sure I understand myself."

The irony was wasted on Laibowitz, who nodded morosely, "That's what I figured."

No one ever won an argument from Laibowitz. He was like the prophets of old, absolutely convinced of his own righteousness. He rarely expressed an opinion without framing it as an axiom. He could not, indeed, conceive of having mere opinions; they were invincible propositions in a larger, majestic philosophical system.

Take a matter as mundane as shaving. Laibowitz hated to shave. But he would never say—simply, directly—that he hated to shave. He wrapped his prejudice in the raiment of cosmology: "If God meant men should have clean cheeks, *would He have invented hair?*" Or, "What distinguishes male from female? Except for sex, nothing but beards." Or, "I read where the Chinese are the most civilized people in the world, and *Chinese men do not shave.*"

"Indians don't shave either," I once kidded him.

"That puts you in my corner," said Laibowitz, "because the Hindus could give us aces and spades in culture!"

"I meant the American Indians."

"You just dug your own grave, Lieutenant! The *American* Indians were the bravest men ever lived!"

Laibowitz's resistance to barbering was made easier for him by the fact that patients in the ward were often permitted to go unshaved. One morning, when Laibowitz looked like the "before" version in an advertisement for razor blades, Captain Newman asked him testily, "Why didn't you shave this morning?"

"The major in Room C didn't shave this morning, either," said Laibowitz.

"You know perfectly well that the major is forbidden to use a razor."

"So please give me the same break; *forbid* I should use one."

"Major Slater is suicidal," said Newman.

"That's exactly what I'm becoming, with your fetish about hair."

"I asked you a question!" snapped Newman. "Why didn't you shave this morning?"

"Is this morning different from other mornings?"

"No. That's why you should shave."

"Excuse me. There is a hole in your logic. That's why I shouldn't."

"Laibowitz—"

"A man can be born with very delicate skin!" cried Laibowitz. "Touch it with metal, it bleeds. Scratch it with steel, it gushes. Douse it with witch hazel, my whole body breaks out in a rash."

"I'll report these original symptoms to the AMA," said Newman.

"Put in that I also itch from the brush."

"Shave!" said Captain Newman.

"Why do you treat me like I was *normal*?" complained Laibowitz. "If I was a patient, you'd call it a phobia and bring me breakfast in bed."

"But you're *not* a patient——"

"That, you can arrange in a second."

"—and you're not phobic!"

"So I'm *counter*phobic, like Goo-Goo Gannon."

Captain Newman assumed his most forbidding expression. "That will be enough, Jackson. Shave!"

Laibowitz rolled his eyes around in anguish and glanced up toward the Almighty. "I think I'll lay down. I feel dizzy."

"That–is–an–order."

"It's against human nature," muttered Laibowitz.

This apothegm, "It's against human nature," was the last unyielding bastion of Laibowitz's creed. Whatever he opposed, he transformed into an enemy of natural law. He believed that he knew more about "human nature" than any man on earth. He also seemed to think that *his* human nature was different from others' and required unquestioning acceptance. "Today I am depressed," he might announce, "so do not aggravate me with details. It is not advisable to get in God's way." Or: "Some men God gave big muscles; others He gave big brains. Don't ask me to move furniture."

I often heard him invoke the Deity—but in a peculiar way: He called upon God the way a coach sends in a pinch hitter.

Laibowitz's loyalty to Captain Newman was passionate. He would do anything for Newman—except change his behavior. This he defended with a certain pride and maintained with what I can only call a certain grandeur.

One day, I saw Captain Newman stalk out of the ward, his face a cloud, with Laibowitz in his wake. When they got to the office, Newman closed the door with a bang.

"Aha!" said Laibowitz. "A chewing-out is on the way."

Captain Newman sat down, very erect. "I suppose Sergeant Kopp is on leave."

"How did you guess?"

"I didn't have to guess, Corporal; I smelled. The bedding in the ward."

"What's that got to do with Arkie?"

"When Kopp is on duty, the ward is as clean as a whistle!"

"Today it's 110 in the shade," cried Laibowitz, "so naturally, the bedding smells!"

"If you *aired* it, Laibowitz, it wouldn't smell."

Laibowitz regarded his captain with solicitude. "I have been studying your behavior. When you're mad, you call me Laibowitz; when you're annoyed, you call me Jackson; when you're happy, you call me Jake."

"You're damn right I'm mad! That bedding is a disgrace!"

"*Today* you think it smells?" cried Laibowitz. "You should of smelled it yesterday! It's a miracle my patients didn't faint like flies! I could of bottled that smell and sold it to Secret Weapons!"

"All sheets, mattresses and pillow cases are to be aired each morning," said Captain Newman firmly. "Do you understand?"

"Deaf, I'm not."

"That is an order!"

To a direct command, which Laibowitz regarded as the unfair advantage the Chiefs of Staff had given officers as against GIs who might best them in man-to-man combat, Laibowitz unfailingly responded with a surprise maneuver on the flanks. "I'm only human."

"So are the men who have to sleep in those beds!" snapped Newman.

"I only have two hands."

"But you have four orderlies to help you!"

"They're human the same as me."

"That's enough!"

Corporal Laibowitz studied his captain with the utmost sympathy. "Doc, you look tired."

"Thank you. The condition of the bedding has tired me."

"If it tires you, imagine what it does to *me*."

"Stop playing ping-pong with my sentences! Get that bedding out of the ward and into the open air."

"That goddam sun could make the mattresses explode!" wailed Laibowitz.

"Then put them in the shade."

"By the time you get any shade around here it's time for my patients to go to sleep!"

"Don't talk like an idiot."

"That," Laibowitz grumbled darkly, "is what will lose us this war."

"Airing the mattresses?" exclaimed Captain Newman.

"Treating Americans like slaves."

"Welcome, Patrick Henry," scowled Newman.

"Sarcasm is for children; from psychiatrists I expect honestness."

" 'Honesty,' Jake, not 'honestness.' "

"So flunk me on English! A frank friend is better than a Park Avenue Charley!"

I thought it was Captain Newman's excessive indulgence that encouraged Laibowitz's unmilitary conduct, but I learned how wrong I was the day Laibowitz passed my office, on his way to Central Supplies, and asked if there was anything he could get me.

"Yes, thank you." I gave him a list. I needed PPS forms, red pencils, and thumbtacks.

In an hour, Corporal Laibowitz returned—with PPS forms, red pencils, and Scotch tape.

"Didn't they have thumbtacks?" I asked.

"You wanted *thumb*tacks?" he asked incredulously.

"Why, yes. That's why I wrote them down."

Laibowitz found fascination in the ceiling. "I can't read your writing."

"But I *printed* that list."

"Lieutenant, your printing is even worse than your writing!"

Suddenly I saw a rare opportunity to achieve a miracle— make Laibowitz admit that he had made a mistake. "Did you by any chance keep that list, Jake?"

"Am I the type to destroy official documents?" He reached into his pocket and produced the list with an expression that warned me that where trust is stunted friendship will soon die.

"Read it," I suggested.

"I already strained two eyes trying."

"Read it aloud."

"With pleasure. . . . Item number one," he read, "PPS forms."

"Check."

"Item two: Red pencils."

"I thought you said you can't read my printing," I smiled.

"*This* you call reading? I'm breaking a code."

"Try item three."

"Is that the one that says 'Thumbtacks'?"

"Ah!" . . . I sang out in triumph. "So you *did* understand."

"Scotch tape is better."

"Jackson, sometimes I wonder—"

"Put a thumbtack in deep, you need a crowbar to pry it out!" cried Laibowitz. "Stick your thumb, you get blood poisoning. Be honest, Lieutenant; did you ever hear a man should get hurt from Scotch tape?"

"That's not the point. I *wanted* thumbtacks!"

Laibowitz bestowed a considerate expression upon me. "You got too much on your mind, Lieutenant. I don't blame you for not knowing what's best for your own welfare."

I often wonder what duties Laibowitz is upsetting, ignoring, transforming or subverting now . . .

The Murder
of a Nit-picker

MY life as a writer was not always as pleasant as it is these days. I once served a six-month stretch in RKO, a penal colony to which I was sent after I had committed a movie. Before that, I tried to earn a living lecturing to ladies' luncheon clubs, but that career came to naught because the naughtiest title in my repertoire was "What the Well-Dressed Woman Should Know About the Smoot-Hawley Tariff." And before *that,* I was on the staff of an eximious (I had to look it up, too) trade journal in Chicago.

Writing for the *Foot-Locker Clarion,* which was not its name, was a living hell because of Roy Sludge, which is not *his* name but gives you a hint as to how I feel about him. He was tall, athletic, fastidious, and mean. He was also stupid. He was a squash player and a prig, a product of a southeastern Military Academy, which taught him to sit up straight and bark, and Lake Forest College, whom you shouldn't blame. I think Roy went to Lake Forest because his parents lived right in the lake, in a forest. How Roy ever got it into his head to go into journalism, as he called it, I never understood. His talents were more suited to attaching leg-manacles.

Everyone used to say, "Roy is very *efficient.* You have to grant him that." I granted nothing. Roy *acted* efficient,

which is a force of another color: He was always busy. But
he was always busy because it took him so long to unravel
the snafu of cat's cradles he had himself woven.

Sludge was one of those perpetual smilers who gives
people ulcers. He had two Achilles' heels (one on each
foot), he was literal-minded, and he was inflexible. (He
was also deaf to the rhythm of a sentence, but I don't think
you can call a tin ear an Achilles' heel.) He browbeat us
writers into squeezing all the juice and joy out of a story.
By the time a page emerged from the wringer of Roy's
infestivity, it was as exact as a ruler—and just about as
interesting. He was obsessed by the irrelevant.

I loathed Roy, who, being a moral cost-accountant,
loathed me, too. And I tried to escape the torture of his
blue pencil by sending our editor this playlet:

SCENE: *The office of* LEO ROSTEN.
Enter ROY SLUDGE, *brandishing a manuscript. His face resembles a knuckle. He is, at the moment, grinning, so he
looks like a grinning knuckle. This is not a nice way to look.*

SLUDGE *(cooing):*
Are you busy?

ROSTEN:
Yes.

SLUDGE *(snappishly):*
This story of yours for the Fourth of July issue: You should
identify "Washington," when you say, right here, "Washington crossed the Delaware." Some of our readers will wonder
which Washington you're referring to.

ROSTEN:
I meant Israel Washington, the head of Boy Scout Troop
27 in Muscle Shoals.

SLUDGE:
There you are! Some of our readers might think you mean
George Washington.

ROSTEN:
Who's he?

SLUDGE *(sternly):*
George Washington was a famous general in the American

Revolution, or "War of Independence," as it is sometimes called.

ROSTEN *(turning pale)*:

Roy, are you sure? Have you checked that out?

SLUDGE:

Certainly! It's on page 42 of *Girlcraft: The Journal for Pregnant Teen-Agers*. I think we should print "Israel" in 6-point Baloney Italics, right under "Washington" in the title, to sort of tip off our readers as to which Washington you mean.

ROSTEN *(crying)*:

Roy, you are a genius! But won't our Legal Department object if we come right out and say we mean Israel Washington—who, after all, stole $14,000 from the First Mortgage and Loan Church of Whitefish, Montana?

SLUDGE *(frowning)*:

N–no, we can run a box saying Israel Washington was illegitimate, according to the DAR, which stands for Daughters of the American Revolution.

ROSTEN:

I thought DAR meant Defenders of the Armenian Rabbinate.

SLUDGE:

Not according to Hugo Shimmelfarb's *Facts About Your Sump Pump!* I had Harriet check that.

ROSTEN:

Harriet who?

SLUDGE:

Our Harriet; she works down in Research.

ROSTEN:

Oh, I thought you meant Harriet Beecher Alcott, who wrote *David Copperfield*.

SLUDGE:

She only wrote the David part.

ROSTEN *(leaping up)*:

And if that's true, Roy, we are on to a real blockbuster! *Think*, man: Wasn't Harriet's sister, Jane Austen, Mrs. Washington's social secretary?

SLUDGE *(startled):*

That Mrs. Washington couldn't read or write.

ROSTEN:

But Mrs. *Israel* Washington was illiterate in only one eye, Roy. She comes right out and admits it in her autobiography, *How Cornea Can You Get?*

SLUDGE *(irritably):*

I don't mean Israel's wife, I mean George's wife, whose first name Harriet is running down. We think it begins with an "M."

ROSTEN *(crying out):*

With an "M"? Do you realize what that *means*? If Mrs. George Washington's first name begins with an "M," it's just possible she—was—*Martha* Washington!

SLUDGE:

Great Scott! Wasn't Martha——

ROSTEN:

Exactly! The manufacturer of all those goddam candies! She sat around all day stuffing cherries into marzipan. And that means that Washington—George, not Israel— was getting a kickback from the candy lobby in Philadelphia, which was our capital at the time.

SLUDGE:

Now do you see how important it is to check everything out?

ROSTEN *(kissing him):*

Oh, I do, I do! *(Opens drawer.)* Whenever you find an error in my copy—like not spelling out what I meant by "Hello," or "Old Glory"—be sure to barge right in on me, because I am a stickler for accuracy. *(Removes revolver.)* And since I just finished writing, "Roy Sludge, author of *You and Colonic Irrigation*, was murdered this morning," I cannot let our readers down. *(Shoots* SLUDGE.*)* Writhe in peace. *(Looks up.)* Why Harriet! Come *in*. Just step over the body.

Enter HARRIET KLUTCHKNOB, *a resolute researcher with an M.A. in Inducing Nervous Ailments.*

HARRIET:

We just had a conference down in Research trying to figure out, in your story on Christopher Columbus, what "1492" refers to.

> ROSTEN (*chuckling*):
> That was the year the Comanche Indians ran their first
> "The Family That Slays Together Stays Together" festival.
> . . . Say "Cheese," Harriet. Good girl. (*Shoots* HARRIET, *picks*
> *up phone.*) Ask Armand Pfeinkuchen, head of Legal, to
> come down. Tell him to bring his coat and hat.
> (*Curtain*)

That was the homiletic little play I sent, in post-adolescent frustration, to our editor. He must have read it, I'm sure, because the very next morning I was fired.

Romance in Vienna

SHELTON'S eyes are washy blue. Whenever I see him, which is not often, he gives me the impression that his thoughts are elsewhere—uneasy, uneasy.

Shelton lives in London. He edits catalogs: I mean, that's his profession. He edits a seed catalog, and one for office furniture, and one for a rug mill. It's a dreadful life for someone who wanted to be a writer. On the side, he writes poetry. I don't know if it ever gets published, but he told me once, in a rush of impulsive confidence, that his greatest pleasure was writing poems.

Now we were dining in his club, not at all what you think, but a rather chilly refuge for bachelors off the Bayswater Road. I had not particularly wanted to see Shelton, but he had phoned so often that I felt guilty; and when he'd rung up again that Sunday morning—a wretched, clammy Sunday to climax a weekend in London alone—I was glad to accept. His company was better than none.

We had barely lifted our cocktails before he said, "I hear you've just come from Vienna."

"Yes."

"Were you there long?"

"A week."

"And how did you like it?"

"Oh, I suppose I like almost any large city," I said; "at least I find something to interest me——"

"But you're not terribly fond of Vienna?" he cut in. "Was this your first trip there?"

"No."

He hesitated. "Would you mind telling me about your first time—I mean, your impressions?"

I said I had first seen Vienna in my college days, entranced by its history, thinking of imperial Rome, the Ottomans, the Magyars, the Habsburgs, churning with romanticism about Mozart and Beethoven, awed by the quite beautiful but moribund city, trying to be frivolous, but sad. Oh, it was *gemutlich* enough, all froth and bowings and I-kiss-your-hand-Madame, but I had never been able to shake off a sense of something cynical behind the courtesy, something contemptuous beneath the charm.

"How curious that you should think that," said Shelton. "How very strange."

"Why?"

He only shrugged.

"Do you know Vienna?" I asked.

Instead of answering, he said, "Tell me, if you were describing the place, I mean its appearance today, what would you say?"

I've forgotten what I answered, but not what passed through my mind, for I think of Vienna as a shell of splendor, a husk of glory gone to dust, a baroque museum, all flowing curves and arching domes, ornate cupolas and statues—so many statues, parading across the rooftop balustrades: kings, prophets, princes, angels, each caught midgesture, pointing, praying, turning, kneeling, rising in a sea of swirling robes and rearing horses, a surge of scornful figures in the sky, monarchs, prelates, schemers, saints —transfixed celebrants of Catholicism and Empire.

I noticed that Shelton was staring out of the window, then absently dabbed at his forehead. He was in another place, and he was sweating. How odd. It struck me that I knew almost nothing about him.

"Thanks . ." He frowned, then blurted, "You asked if I know Vienna. . . . Oh, yes. And I hate it. . . . Let's eat."

We talked about politics and Parliament, over dinner, then went into the deserted library, where—thank God!— a fire was going. We had brandy and cigars, and Shelton downed his brandy too quickly and called the waiter and tapped for a refill.

"Can I tell you something?" he asked impulsively.

"Certainly."

He relighted his cigar and tossed the match toward the ashtray, but missed it and flushed, apologizing, a man who never seemed to do things right.

After a moment, he began to talk, reticently at first, but soon, in the thrall of remembrance—and drink, he was pouring out the words.

You may think I dreamed all this (said Shelton) but it happened. Truly, old man. It happened just as I'll tell it to you.

You must remember I was in my twenties and, if I may say so, rather dashing: thirty pounds lighter, with all my hair, time on my hands, youth bursting at every seam, full of vinegar, all that sort of thing, you know, plus a pocketful of money I was burning to spend. You see, I was traveling around Europe, with Vienna set as my last stop, on the inheritance my mother had left me. She had also left me a letter, urging me to spend it all on travel, on the Continent, and especially to go to Vienna, where she'd been born. She used to tell me London was majestic, Paris elegant, but only Vienna was "grand." She called it "the sun of Europe, and all the stars."

So I went there and discovered the *Konditoreien*—those marvelous confectioners and coffeehouses, ambrosial cakes and pastries. . . .

I managed to locate an old aunt and a cousin—the rest of my mother's family was gone, dead, starved, killed by one side or the other in the war. . . . I had no trouble with the language, you understand, because Mother spoke Ger-

man to me when I was growing up. My father was ten gen-
erations of Wiltshire. . . . England and Austria—what a pair.
Me.

Well, in Vienna, at a party, I met her. Marianne. . . . I
didn't know she was a baroness. I soon enough gathered
she was rich, because she wore expensive clothes and drove
a Mercedes, a convertible, an oldish one, pale blue, molded
like a woman's body. Marianne loved to drive that car, and,
because she had nothing better to do—she was always
fighting off boredom—she began to chauffeur me around,
showing me the sights. We'd drive out to the *Wienerwald*,
or up toward Linz or out to Schönbrunn, and we'd picnic or
dine in some wine garden and talk and try the new spring
wine and dance until no one was left except us. Sometimes
we'd kill the night just driving along the muddy blue
Danube.

Late one afternoon, we were driving with the top down,
and Marianne at the wheel, as always. It was a sunset to
make you drunk—all warm and soft, shiny in the bur-
nished twilight you get only at summer's end. Vienna
glowed. . . . Marianne—the light lay on her face like copper. Her tawniness always made me think of a gypsy. I
wish she had been . . .

I should tell you that she was not really beautiful. She
was more—oh, arresting than beautiful: black hair, green-
ish eyes, a sharp nose, a swan's neck, too thin, a full-
lipped mouth, but too wide. Very provocative.

Provocative? In Rome, from which I'd just come, everyone fell madly in love, if only for a night; but in Vienna,
everyone flirted—and flirted and flirted. It seemed obligatory
to perform the practiced coquetries. Vienna's substitute for
small talk: Flirtation, and flattery. Austria's motto: "Flatter
the men; flirt with the women." It was as automatic to them
as it's unheard-of to the English. Perhaps I was too sensitive. I was too young to be blasé.

Well, we were driving.

"And where would Your *Excellenz* care to dine?" she
asked.

That night, I was "Your Excellency." Sometimes I was "Your Highness," sometimes, "Your Most Serene Highness." She loved to put me on. She said I was an *echt* Englishman. She meant stuffy, I suppose.

"Wherever you say," I said.

"Don't be stupid!" She loathed indecisiveness; even a moment's waiting annoyed her. "How about *Friedl's*—no, *The Three Hussars?*"

"You choose," I said. "Surprise me. After all, this is my last night in *Wien* . . . or have you forgotten? I'm going home tomorrow."

She laughed. "I should have known! You wish tears, toasts, swooning, sentiment. You wish a souvenir, *Liebchen,* of our eternal love?"

Our eternal love, my foot! *"Liebchen"*—that was her knife, and she liked to twist it. Oh, I had tried to kiss her, several times—dancing, or holding her wrap, or saying good night; and each time, with a mocking evasion, *"Such* passion!" or *"Putchy,* do be a *gentle*man!" she turned away, brushing her cheek against mine, or putting a finger to her lips and transferring a "kiss" to mine.

"So we celebrate! *Ja? Gut!* . . . How would Your *Excellenz* care to dine in a palace?"

"Why not?" I said, dryly. "Whose?"

"Mine."

"Good-*o!*" I snickered. "Take me to your palace."

She braked so abruptly my head snapped, and reversed her course and gunned ahead. She loved to do things that way. She was driven by impulse. I could never read her moods.

I remember we sped across the *Heldenplatz,* under Prinz Eugen's frantic stallion, and I leaned back, admiring that low, incredible skyline you talked about, that frozen procession of pomp wheeling overhead.

Marianne turned off somewhere and I heard gravel sputtering under the tires and she braked hard and jolted us to a stop. I sat up.

We were in a small courtyard, before a quite large and imposing mansion.

"Who lives here?" I asked.

"An illegitimate grand-niece of Franz Joseph and twenty-nine dwarfs."

"Very funny."

"Well, watch." She opened her door, crossed the courtyard, strode to a pair of high, carved wooden doors and, without knocking, turned a great brass knob. The door moved away from her and she was splashed with light from within. . . . You could have floored me with an eclair: she had used no key.

"Marianne!" I called.

She had gone inside.

I went after her, through the door, into a three- or four-story-high foyer, with stairways curving upward, left and right; and somewhere, softly, music played. A waltz. Not Strauss. Franz Lehar, I think, or Chopin, who can drug your senses.

I heard Marianne's heels clicking up the marble stairs, above me, and I hurried after her, and at the head of the landing I stopped. It was a scene I shall never forget: an exquisite oval ballroom, a fairy-tale chamber with crystal chandeliers. And there were candles, flickering in sconces. And a fresco, up high, of Greek gods and maidens and flowered chariots, up near the lovely dome. It was an absolute gem of a room. . . . I remember ballroom chairs, gilded, arrayed along the curving walls. And at the far, high, open windows, so opulently draped, silken curtains swayed, in a breeze from the garden.

Marianne came pirouetting to me from the end of that salon, holding her dress out with one hand, the other waving in time to the music, her hair floating as she danced, her gown green as desire. She danced into my arms. . . .

I asked, "Where *are* we?" and she gravely answered, "In my palace," and pressed against me and I waltzed her around deliriously, I suppose, in great Spencerian circles, both of us laughing. We whirled into another chamber, where, from the damasked walls, ancestral portraits watched us: women with alabaster skin and tiny waists, in cascades of tulle; side-whiskered cavaliers in silken breeches and purple sashes, their swords in gleaming scabbards; porcelain children in velvet pantaloons, with their pet dogs. . . . I waltzed her down that long gallery of the noble, arrogant dead, preserved to scrutinize the living with disdainful eyes.

Suddenly, I would no longer play her game, her not even telling me the rules, so I stopped dancing and took her by the arms and cried, "Where the hell *are* we? . . . Whose place is this? Why is it empty? Why was the front door open? How do you——"

She said, "You fool," and moved out of my hold into the room beyond. And now I thought I really was hallucinating, because this was a bamboo place, full of fronds and palms, where, in an elaborate cage, a *cockatoo* (yes, believe me), a cockatoo, that most improbable of creatures, cawed.

"Caw, caw, caw," went Marianne. "You silly bird . . . I am hungry, *Liebchen.*"

She led me through some high windows, onto an open terrace that jutted into and above the garden below, from which the trees sent a canopy of leafy branches up and above us. Many tables were set for dinner: candlelight, glasses, silver, linen—everything shining, snow white. And now Strauss murmured from hidden violins.

A *maître d'hôtel* materialized from the gloaming—bowing, fawning, snapping his fingers to servants in stiff dickeys and knee breeches, and he led us to a far table and held Marianne's chair. "Ah, *gnädige* Baroness . . ."

She ordered for both of us, the most expensive dishes, choosing the wine, as usual, treating my questions as if she had not heard them, chattering away about trifles, refusing to tell me where I was, enjoying my confusion and her evasions and mockery, until I could no longer contain my irritation and said something rather nasty. "Your teasing doesn't stop at your lips, ducky."

She paused—a flicker of anger—then smiled, but sarcastically, and laced her fingers across her eyes like a mask and peered through it flirtatiously. "All right, I tell you," she sighed. "You spoiled it. So British. You want a last-night souvenir of Vienna, no? What could I give you better? . . . Yes, this is a palace, Mr. Shelton. It was built by Fischer von Erlach—and for whom? Would you believe me? Count Rofrano, the real *Rosenkavalier.* . . . Ah, yes. The Auerspergs lived here, and just sold it—how *could* they?—to a coffee company. It is a restaurant now. Anyone can come. But few Viennese can afford it, and the tourists don't know. . . . I *hate* for people to come here. I never tell them. If you were not leaving in the morning, I would not have brought you."

"You said it was your palace."

She shrugged. "In my mind," she said, "it is."

I paid the bill and she held out her hand and led me back into the long gallery and past those paintings of the high-born on damasked walls. "My ancestors," sighed Marianne, play-acting. "Bid them *adieu.*"

We descended the marble stairway in silence, hand in hand; and in the courtyard she turned to me, the moonlight on her like a veil. . . . God, I *ached* for her!

"You're beautiful," I said.

That displeased her. "Liar. You are too long in *Wien.* . . . I am not unattractive; but 'beautiful'? Poof!"

She slid behind the wheel, raced the motor, and drove away and soon we passed the *Karlskirche.* . . . Clouds crossed the moon.

"I suppose you're in love with someone else," I blurted.

She wrinkled her nose. "Why must you think that? To save your vanity? . . . No. I love no one."

"How many—have many men fallen wildly in love with you?"

"Oh, yes. Many. Many many. . . . Men are fools."

When we reached my hotel, she did not cut the motor off. She just put her hand out. "So? This is good-bye? Or *auf wiedersehen?*"

I was angry. I waved the doorman aside and grabbed her arm and leaned over to kiss her—and this time, for the first time, for the only time, she let me.

"All right," she said.

I'll never forget that kiss: her lips were smooth and firm, and cold as glass.

She laughed, engaged the gear and tore away, her hair spinning out like a black scarf, waving to me, singing out, "*Auf wiedersehen . . . auf wiedersehen . . .*" then, from down the street called, "Come back soon, yes?" so loud it echoed under the portico.

I left Vienna next morning.

Shelton stopped. He was frowning. He shook his head, as if trying to clear it, or to shake it out of memory. "Never saw her again," he said thickly. "Wish—I wish I'd never met her."

"Really?" I said. "It's one of the things that happens when you're young, in love."

"Young? Love?" He snorted. "I hate her. I hate the thought of her.... And *was* I in love? Or was I just desperately lonely, romantically 'in love with love,' *wanting* to be in love, to be loved, trying . . ."

"All of us have done that," I said.

"But I was too young to know!" He stopped, blinking, fumbling for something in his fog.

"To know what?" I asked, after a moment.

He looked up, and a chill passed over me. Something unpleasant swarmed into those washy-blue eyes. "To know," he said, "that that bitch, that damned, cold, teasing bitch was using me, passing the time in titillation, amusing herself alone, too goddamn self-centered to know or care that *I*—would never—be young—again."

A Temple to Eros

$$\approx\approx\approx\approx\approx\approx\approx\approx\approx\approx\approx\approx\approx\approx\approx\approx\approx\approx\approx$$

THE Loop ends at Van Buren Street. State Street south of that is the sleazy sanctuary for burlesque shows, pawnshops, flophouses, chili parlors, and saloons where (when all this happened) you could buy a stein of beer for a nickel and a deadly glass of gin for a dime.

This was Chicago's Bowery: vulgar, lurid, putrid, and only two blocks from the sweep of the skyline on Michigan Boulevard and the cool, clean winds off the Lake.

The sidewalks were laden with cigarette butts on South State Street that day, and the air hung heavy with smells. The varmints who rambled up and down the impolite stretch were what is known as down-at-the-heelers: riffraff, misfits or, to be frank about it, bums.

I was exploring South State Street that muggy afternoon, and even though I was young and lusting for Life (raw or cooked), it was like walking through an especially gimcrack carnival. Values were all haywire there: a pair of socks sold for eight cents, a tie for nine, undershirts for eleven. You could buy razor blades for a penny apiece, and fifty cents got you tattooed for all time by "The Tattoo King." Rooms ran up to thirty cents a night with "Free Breakfast," and you could have all your tattoos removed ("No Needles Used") for a pittance. I noticed that the Tattoo Remover was only a few doors from the Tattoo King, which struck me as a pretty decisive revelation of the merits of a free society.

On the subcultural front, South State Street was right down there fighting. The artery was clotted with seedy temples of the silver screen: *Wages of Sin* ("Deceived and Deserted She Shot Her Lascivious Betrayer!") could be seen for ten cents in the coin of the realm; *Marihuana—Weed with Roots in Hell* ran into more money—fifteen. If neither of these parables promised to slake your thirst for art in the cinema, there was always good old *"White-Slave Racket Exposed!"* or *"Abyss of Shame,"* synopsized in opaline prose: "See Pure Maidens Devoured by the Shameless Passions of Men!"

The briefest of surveys was enough to convince me that more American males are interested in seeing pure maidens devoured by the shameless passions of men than in seeing the white-slave racket properly exposed.

It wasn't easy to steel myself against the seductive intimations from the *demi-monde*. Then, weakened by the strain of moral conflict, I fell under the spell of the evil eye of a place identified in railroad-poster type as

CONTINUOUS SHOW
Special Attractions Today
Admission: 5 cents

This bargain paradise displayed drawings, not photographs, of nude girls all over its open foyer. Tantalizing sell-lines under each drawing sent my metabolism way up:

"Daring!"

"Sensational!"

"Reveals ALL!"

"Straight from Paris Exposition!!"*

Above the nudes and the entrance doors I beheld a plaster entablature that gave name to the temple of Pan:

NICKEL—ODIUM

There is no telling *what* the mind that thought that up might

* It didn't say which year.

do next, so I went to the ticket booth, plunked down my nickel, and went inside, never to be heard from again.

The interior was bare and unclean. About ten men were crowded before a rough-planked platform. They were silent and seemed ill-at-ease, an odd cross-section of our native manhood: two bleary-eyed derelicts, a man in freshly pressed tweeds, several teen-agers who apparently held to the theory that hats cause baldness, a hollow-eyed young man in a brown raincoat, and a well-attired gentleman who was the spittin' image of the executive who proclaims "My Loved Ones Are Cared For!" in insurance ads. They avoided one another's furtive glances. So did I.

On the raised planking, before a burlap curtain, a decrepit piano rested. Its front had thoughtfully been removed so that doubting Thomases could see the way it worked. A man sat at this denuded instrument, and a sign informed us:

BLIND!
NO FINGERS ON EITHER HAND! HE PLAYS! !

The man at the piano began to assault the keys. The wooden hammers went like all fury, the piano wires whined in pain, and the strident strains of "Tiger Rag" howled in the fetid air. The piano player swung it (the one thing "Tiger Rag" does not need is swinging, if you ask me) until the instrument hovered on the edge of a nervous breakdown. You never heard such a rumpus. The man played very well, I think, for a blind man with no fingers on either hand.

He wrung "Tiger Rag" dry in sixty seconds flat, swept into "Hallelujah" (which he trampled underfoot), and tossed off "Collegiate" as if it were child's play. He had a deft left jab. The massacre ended with the shattering triad of "Collegiate" 's final "Rah-rah-rah! !" Then the quiet fell with a bang, not a whimper.

"Jeese!" breathed one of the oafish lads in front of me.

Suddenly a man appeared from behind the burlap curtain and raised his hand. He was a man you wouldn't want to meet on a sunny day. His lips formed a vulpine grin.

"No one can say this wunnaful playin' wasn't wort' five cents!"

No one was foolhardy enough to dissent.

"Now, men. Behind this here curtain is somethin' no live, red-blooded, he-man would ever wanna miss! T'ree *gor*-ge-ous dancin' beauties, in the flesh! Not one, not two, but—t'ree! No more'n twelve inches from your very eyes!" He dropped his voice confidentially. "You men all know why we ain't allowed to show our real girly show out here in fronta the curtain. I don't hafta go into details . . . an' I ain't sayin' nothin' about police regulations! . . . All right, all *right!* Behind that there curtain is the *real thing!* T'ree redhot cuties! A work of art, in the flesh. When you see this, man, you've seen everyt'ing! ! Only twenny-five cents, men, only two-bits . . ."

The two derelicts lunged forward as if propelled by an electric prod, paid their quarters (or so it appeared) and went behind that there curtain. (If those two weren't Judas sheep, my years of haunting phony auctions have been a waste of time.) Four or five art-lovers marched up and paid their quarters. The hatless minors consulted darkly, growled, and left the Nickel–odium in what a more innocent age called high dudgeon. I paid my quarter and went behind the burlap.

I found myself facing a tiny stage that was no more than four feet long, two feet deep, and about a foot off the floor. The backdrop seemed to be composed of sarongs sewn together by a hostile spastic.

"All *right*, men," the Man announced. "First attraction is our hot little Spanish dancer! O.K., Kenosha!"

A phonograph record began to wheeze and wail and out came the hot little Spanish dancer, Kenosha. She was neither hot, little, Spanish, nor a dancer. She was a mammal with the expression of a paper clip. She wore a feathery brassière, feathery tights, and a pair of well-worn street shoes. Her thighs, I regret to report, were bruised and resembled a relief map of Peru.

It took but a moment to persuade my congregation that Kenosha was not born to burn incense at the shrine of Pavlova. Her "dance" consisted of shuffling one foot cautiously before committing the other, all the while snapping two fingers with the vivacity of malnutrition. The feathers on the brassière were the only things that moved faster than her breathing. In a way, I was grateful.

Kenosha stopped, without an iota of warning, scratched her arm, and disappeared behind the limp sarongs.

"Next," the Man cried fervently, "we bring you that real, sizzlin' ball of fire—Ginger!"

Out came the sizzling ball of fire, Ginger. The fire had been extinguished long ago. Ginger was a blonde, older and more mature than Kenosha, who was no nymphet, and she was chewing gum. Ginger wore an opaque brassière, sensible tights and a pair of house slippers. I know you won't believe that, but that's what she was wearing: a pair of comfy slippers.

Ginger's dance can best be described as a drooping of the shoulders relieved by occasional twitches of the extremities. Once she raised a hand—then, depleted, fell back into the twitching. But she chewed her gum commendably throughout, summoned her resources to produce a halfhearted "bump," and drifted behind the Polynesian gauzes.

"And now, the girl the whole town's talking about!" cried the Man loudly, "the original, the one and only—Frenchy!"

Out came the one and only Frenchy. I could not question her singularity: a tallow-skinned biped whose hair color attested to a complex history and whose countenance had been frozen between discomfort and confusion. But Frenchy was a dancer, no doubt of that; she worked up a good sweat, throwing her arms and elbows around whilst aiming to fling her abdomen out of the front entrance. Her eyes were fixed on a distant star.

Frenchy went through all the hallowed epilepsies of burlesque: rolling, grinding, bumping, shimmying, and champing at the bit. When she stopped dead in her tracks it was not as a build-up to a smash finish: she stopped to stalk off.

The performance for real, red-blooded he-men was over.

"Now, men!" the Man instantly blared, with the air of a Hindu about to pull a cobra out of thin air. "That was only a weak *sample* of what we got waitin' for you. Back here—" he pointed to yet another curtain, at the side, a soft partition the color of Roquefort cheese—"back here's a certain booth, where the girls really go to town. *Dancin' on mirrors!* I guess you know what *that* means! No need to go into no details. . . . Any you men ever been to Gay Paree know exactly what I'm talkin' about!" The lurid larynx reached exultance. "When you see this, men, there's just *no more to see!* Only twenny-five cents, gents, two lousy little bits. . . ."

The two bums surged forward, waving their dishonest quarters. My confrères hesitated. Soon a client who must have come in late, a rabbity little gent with glasses, a sort of bookkeeper strayed out of Dickens, primly handed a coin to our cicerone and sidled behind the Roquefort curtain. The man in the business suit snickered, not hiding his skepticism—but he forked over the two-bits. As for "My Loved Ones Are Cared For," first he frowned, then he sighed, then he wet his lips, and then he followed the pioneers. I paid my quarter.

What I now beheld was a large, square, black booth, about eight feet high and four feet wide. On each of the four sides, at eye-level, were narrow observation slits. The other customers had taken up their posts expectantly; the shills betrayed their function by hanging back. I found a free slit, put my eyes against the opening, and saw the moist, beady stare of—all the other men's eyes. I hastily lowered my glance: inside the booth, a large round mirror adorned the center of the floor. Then, to my surprise, I saw a bench at one side of the bullpen, on which sat none other than our old friends Kenosha, Ginger and Frenchy. They were in the same unforgettable costumes. Ginger still chewed gum. Frenchy was scratching her back. Kenosha could not forgo the excitement of yawning.

The never-to-be revealed phonograph began to play some garbled aphrodisia and Kenosha got off the bench, stepped on the mirror, and began to dance the same dance she had proffered a moment ago, I think, but somehow this was more suggestive. I'm not sure what it was suggestive of, but it certainly was.

The burning eyes that were peering through all the slits dropped downward, to the mirror, with a unanimity rare in a democratic state. There was nothing special to see. Once you've seen a tight pair of panties, further panting will get you nowhere.

The Dionysian music changed. Ginger followed Kenosha, and Frenchy followed Ginger. Frenchy may have been playing charades, jerking and flailing like one of the Laocoons trapped by snakes.

The phonograph stopped. Frenchy stopped. Everything stopped. The excursion to the promised land was over.

The men now left the peep holes with distinctly negative mutterings. The businessman looked downright annoyed. The fellow with the sour look looked curdled. Br'er Rabbit blinked his eyes. "My Loved Ones Are Cared For" didn't blink his eyes; he just tightened his lips so hard that had you put a pitchfork in his right hand, Grant Wood could have done a new "American Gothic."

We started to leave, when suddenly someone called out to us from above, from a flight of stairs at the side wall I had not noticed: "Up here, men!" a new tempter called. "This is where the *real thing* goes on! It's free! Just follow me."

We trooped up the stairs as one. On the second floor, we entered a room with red walls and a red ceiling redly lit by dim red lights. My spirits lifted; here, at last, was Eros' inner temple. In the center of this concupiscent chamber was another booth, the same size as the one downstairs, but this enclosure was octagonal and it was covered with a top, and instead of open slits each side of the tantalizing bin was pierced by binocular peepholes. Next to each owlish aperture was a slot for a coin, and below each slot was tacked a pithy instruction: "Look Up," "Look Down," "Look Straight Ahead."

Our Pied Piper crooned, "Come closer, men, c'mon where

I can talk to you, private." He smiled us into a cozy corner.
"Come closer, men," he whispered. "C'mon ... Wait'll you
hear this. . . ."

My comrades wouldn't come too close, and I did not blame
them; our guide can be visualized, vaguely, as an enlarged
version of the sort of creature you see when you look under
a rock. He had a waxy sheath of skin, uncombed hair, pom-
aded sideburns, batrachian eyes. His grin revealed teeth
richly patinaed by time and cigars. I would not have been
surprised to hear a hyena howl nearby.

"Men," our mentor whispered, "this booth's been here—
for—eight—years. Which gives you a rough idea how popular this special booth is with the real *man* public in old
Chi! This special booth is run by the little girl in there, and
the management don't get one red cent from her special
show! ... I'm just here for your convenience, to make
change." He eyed each of us, man by man, gravely. Then,
with strategic hoarseness, he confided: "I ain't gonna give
you a speech, men. I don't hafta, that's for sure. But when
you see what you're gonna see now, over there, men, you'll
see *the end of the road!*" He paused. His eyes narrowed.
"You'll see *in the flesh,* the one and only—Fifi! Doin' her
famous Parisian dance! An' I advise you not to take your
eyes off that little girl a single minute! Pick your favorite
view, men—Bird's-eye, Worm's-eye, Head on, or Close-up.
The end of the road, men! I have plenty of nickels right
here. . . . Let's go!"

A miniature stampede sent the lords of creation scurrying
to their preferred view. By the time I changed a dollar, only
"Look Straight Ahead" was left.

Behind the binocular slot against which I pressed my face
was—tin. A tin plate prevented the indigent from enjoying
the scenery.

As a new phonograph crackled into action, the salesman
of sin yelled, "Drop your nickels, men! Fifi, let 'em have it!
Drop your nickels, men!"

I heard a waterfall of metal and the clack-clack-clack of
tiny plates flipping up. I dropped my nickel into my slot and

my tin plate swung up and I saw the face, neck, and philan-thropic bosom of Fifi. She looked more like a Thelma than a Fifi. Her eyes were mascaraed à la Aubrey Beardsley and she wore a shiny black brassière—with tassels.

The only part of the action I could see was Fifi's frenetic oscillation of her shoulders: the rest of her responded solely through the physics of sympathetic vibration. Before I knew it, in no more than fifteen fleeting seconds, the tin plate dropped. Eldorado was blacked out. I inserted another nickel. The tin plate flipped up. Fifi was still oscillating. The tin plate dropped down. I inserted another nickel. This piquant cycle continued for several minutes, until the men began to desert the peepholes.

Our friendly changemaker was watching us like a hawk. "Fifi!" he shouted. "Show them Fuzzy-Wuzzy!"

The kings of the animal kingdom rushed back to the peep-holes as though Gabriel had blown his trumpet. A veritable Yosemite of nickels poured down the chutes. This time I got "Look Down."

Fifi's short, lean legs were limply revealed to me. She was keeping her bloodstream active by going through the motions of a stately dance, on an indisputable mirror. She had on a pair of orchid tights and high-heeled slippers, and what her dance was supposed to be I never figured out. (In occasional recollections I think of it as "Diana at the Pump.")

The tin plates kept dropping to blind us voyeurs, the nickels poured into the slots, the tin plates kept flipping up again, and the frustration of the unfulfilled steamed in the air like a miasma.

The sour young man came over to me and grunted "Balls!" He lighted a cigarette. "If you see anything, let me know."

He stood right next to me, close, sullen, waiting for bul-letins, but all was quiet on the libidinal front. I saw nothing, and I let him know.

Again the men began to abandon their peep-posts. The rabbity bookkeeper chewed his mustache. The businessman sneered. "My Loved Ones Are Cared For" restuffed his dignity.

The Man from the netherworld yelled, "Fifi, give 'em old Sixty-six!"*Rekindled fires fueled a new race to the slots.

I got "Look Up."

Looking up revealed a heavenly mirror, in which I saw the inverted reflection of Fifi from head to waist, a bodily zone clearly *hors de combat*.

Yet once more the gulled turned away from the slots; and the son of Cain played his trump. "Just a minute, fellows! Hold it. I know how you feel.... I'm gonna ask Fifi if she won't put on a certain—" he whistled the call of the wolf "—well, a certain let's-call-it dance she did at Spider Kelly's down in Juarez, Mexico!"

He tapped on a side panel of the booth; it slid half-open.

"Fifi," croaked Beelzebub, earnestly, softly, but loud enough for the deafest mother's son among us to hear. "I was just wonderin' if you wouldn't put on that number you did down at Spider Kelly's. *You* know ... Aw, c'mon ... Just for this special group of men ..."

We heard a nasal soprano: "I do not put on that number for just *nickels*, Joe."

"Aw, come on, Fifi," our provider cooed. "Just this once."

"I do not think I *ought* to, Joe."

"Aw, go on. Be a sport. These men sure would appreciate it. I know they would."

They traded démarches with sovereign formality, then we heard sweet Fifi surrender to Joe's blandishments.

"O.K., men!" he cried. "She's gonna do it!"

The *homo sapiens* beat their heads against the booth for strategic views.

I got "Look Straight Ahead."

And now the phonograph sang nostalgically of "Sweet Sue," and the nickels dropped, the tin plates flipped, and we saw Fifi, the girl of no man's dreams, in the dance she had immortalized at Spider Kelly's. I had never been in Juarez, but I got a pretty good idea as to why Fifi was working in Chicago. The putative dance was the same erratic static she had been performing all along at a nickel a peek.

* I don't know what it meant either.

Two nickels per man was enough. The sound of coins dropping stopped. An icy silence followed.

The hollow-eyed fellow in the brown raincoat, his face brown with anger, went right up to Joe and said, "What a gyp!"

Joe smiled. I have seen more humane smiles in the cages of the Lincoln Park Zoo.

"Is that all we're gonna get?" seethed Hollow-eyes.

"Yeah," said Joe.

"Is that all you've got to *say?*"

"Yeah," snapped Joe, proceeding to tot up the coins in his hands. "Exit straight ahead. Let's go. Straight ahead and down them stairs."

I hoped Brownie would hit Joe in the jaw (he certainly looked as though he wanted to), but a hint of a shiv in Joe's nasty "Blow, bub" turned Brownie's bravado to butter.

We filed out of the Red Room, through another dingy corridor, down a long flight of stairs, and emerged from a door marked *Fire Exit*—to find ourselves in the soggy sunlight, at the side of the building, quite a way from the entrance. The men who ran the Nickel–Odium were no fools.

I had spent one dollar and seventy cents.

A new contingent of gudgeons was entering the Lorelei premises.

I walked up State Street, toward the Loop, taking very deep breaths.

Mr. Parkhill and
Mr. K·A·P·L·A·N

I T was a fine evening. The moon was washing the great behemoth of the city with silver. Mr. Parkhill looked at his watch. Forty minutes before he was due to meet his class. He decided to walk.

At this very moment, he reflected, from a dozen diverse outposts of this vast and clamorous city, his students, too, were wending their way to the school from which they expected so much. Miss Mitnick was probably subjecting her homework to yet another revision on the Fourteenth Street bus. (What a salutary student Miss Mitnick was.) Peter Studniczka was no doubt mumbling over his battered copy of *1,000 Words Commonly Misspelled* on the BMT express. (Sometimes Mr. Parkhill wondered whether Mr. Studniczka was as much influenced by the columns in which the words were spelled right as he seemed to be by the columns in which the words were spelled wrong.)

Miss Olga Tarnova was probably thinking up Open Questions on the Lexington Avenue subway as she brushed her excessively long eyelashes with mascara. (Mr. Parkhill often wished that Miss Tarnova, who worked for a milliner in Greenwich Village, would pay as much attention to her conjugations as she did to her cosmetics.)

What interesting, what *unusual* persons his students were.

They came from a score of lands and cultures. He had spent almost twelve years now introducing neophytes to the mysteries of English. Twelve years . . . Why, over three hundred students must have passed under his tutelage during all that time. Some he remembered quite vividly, others scarcely at all. Some had been swift to learn, others deplorably obtuse. Some were B.K. and some were A.K. . . . Mr. Parkhill frowned. His lips drew tight in a reflex of self-chastisement. Why on *earth* was he falling into that exasperating conceit again? It was absurd, perfectly absurd. Why, then, could he not shake it off, once and for all? *Qui Docet* should *discere*.

It had begun almost two weeks ago, when he had awakened with a frightful pounding of the heart, unaccountably short of breath and perspiring, from a dream—a dream that had recurred, to his dismay, again and again. There was nothing especially complicated about the dream; it contained no recondite symbols such as, Mr. Parkhill knew from rereading Freud, characterize the dreams of many men; and it surely contained nothing which could by the most fanciful stretch of the imagination be called "libidinal." No, it was just a plain, run-of-the-mill dream. This was its content:

A great crowd was gathered before the school, which was freshly painted, glistening with a strange radiance and bedecked with countless flags and gay banners. Some sort of ceremony was taking place. In one version of the dream, Mr. Leland Robinson, principal of the ANPSA, was addressing the throng; in others, the Chief Justice, in wig and black gown, was delivering the oration; and several times it had been none other than the Secretary-General of the United Nations himself who held the crowd spellbound. But it was not that part of the dream that always tore Mr. Parkhill's sleep asunder. The portion from which Mr. Parkhill awakened, his throat parched and his forehead damp, the only part of the dream, indeed, that repeated itself in identical form no matter *who* was delivering the main oration, came when the festivities suddenly stopped, a terrible hush fell upon the multitude, and Mr. Parkhill found himself the target of all eyes. They were glaring at him in peculiar accusation as (for reasons he could never make out) he began to mount a gigantic ladder, in excruciating slow motion, with a bronze plaque strapped to his back. The ladder seemed a hundred stories high, even though it rested just above the entrance to the school. What Mr. Parkhill seemed driven to do, from that awful ladder, was hang the bronze plaque above the doorway. Engraved on the plaque in great Gothic letters was this legend:

AMERICAN NIGHT PREPARATORY SCHOOL FOR ADULTS
Founded 1910
b. 25 years B.K.
d. "?" years A.K.

That "?" always blazed like a neon sign, the ? in bright red and the " " in blue. The "A.K.," however, was outlined in green.

A horn howling into his very eardrum caused Mr. Parkhill to jump back to the curb just as a truck whooshed by his nose. He heard a hoarse voice implore the deity to strike him dead. Mr. Parkhill apologized to the vacant air. The traffic light was indubitably red. He had not noticed it. Or had he mistaken the red of the light for the red of the "?"? He felt ashamed of himself. He waited for the light to change—to green, of course—and hastened across the street.

"B.K." . . . "A.K." Oh, he knew what those cryptic notations signified. They stood for "Before Kaplan" and "After Kaplan." In fact, that was the key to the whole dream. It simply raised, in symbolic form, a thought that must be churning and churning, unresolved, through Mr. Parkhill's unconsciousness: viz., that the American Night Preparatory School for Adults, which actually *had* been founded a good many years before Mr. Kaplan ever entered its doors, was doomed to survive only "?" years after Mr. Kaplan left. Left? That was just the point. Would Mr. Kaplan ever leave?

The question had haunted Mr. Parkhill long, long before he had ever had that distressing dream. For he did not see how he could, in conscience, promote Mr. Kaplan to Miss Higby's grade (only last week Mr. Kaplan had referred to

the codifier of the laws of gravity as "Isaac Newman"), and
he knew that he could not bring himself to advise Mr. Kaplan, as he was often tempted, to transfer to some other
night school where he might perhaps be happier. The un-
deniable fact was that there was no other night school in
which Hyman Kaplan could possibly be happier: Mr. Parkhill might be happier; Miss Higby might be happier; a dozen
members of the beginners' grade would surely be happier.
But Mr. Kaplan? That intrepid scholar displayed the strongest conceivable affection, an affection bordering on the
lyrical, for his alma mater.

That was another thing. Strictly speaking, of course, the
ANPSA could not possibly be the alma mater of someone
who had never been graduated from it; but Mr. Kaplan had
a way of acting as if it were.

That was yet another of the baffling characteristics that
made Mr. Kaplan so difficult to contend with: his cavalier
attitude to reality, which he seemed to think he could alter
to suit himself. How else could one describe a man who
identified the immortal Strauss waltz as "the Blue Daniel"?
Or who, in recounting the tale of the cloak spread in the
mud before Queen Elizabeth, insisted on crediting the gallantry to "Sir Walter Reilly"? Or who identified our first
First Lady as "Mother Washington"? True, George Washington was the father of our country, but that did not make
Martha the *mother*. It was all terribly frustrating.

Every way Mr. Parkhill turned, he seemed to sink deeper
and deeper into the Kaplan morass. If Mr. Kaplan could not
be promoted, much less graduated, what *could* be done
about him? Sometimes it looked to Mr. Parkhill as if Mr.
Kaplan was deliberately trying to stay in the beginners'
grade for the rest of his (i.e., Mr. Parkhill's) life. This
thought had begun to bother Mr. Parkhill so much that he
had brought it up at the last faculty meeting.

Right after Miss Schnepfe had reminded the staff to deposit their attendance reports in her office at the end of each
week, Mr. Robinson asked if there were any other problems
which ought to be brought to his attention. Mr. Parkhill had

cleared his throat. "What is the school's policy," he inquired, "toward a student who may *never* pass the final examination in—er—one of the lower grades?" He would not soon forget the cold, granitelike mask into which Mr. Robinson's features had composed themselves. (Few knew that under Mr. Robinson's stern exterior seethed emotions that led men to end up as what Mr. Kaplan had once called "a nervous rag.")

That left Mr. Parkhill exactly where he had been before. What could be done about Hyman Kaplan? The man simply refused to learn. No, Mr. Parkhill promptly corrected himself: It was not that Mr. Kaplan refused to learn; what Mr. Kaplan refused to do was *conform*. That was an entirely different matter. Mr. Parkhill could get Mr. Kaplan to understand a rule—about spelling or diction or punctuation; what he did not seem able to do was get Mr. Kaplan to *agree* with it. (Modern cities, Mr. Kaplan averred, consist of streets, boulevards, and revenues.)

Nor was that all. The laws of English, after all, have developed century after century, like the common law; and like the common law, they augment their authority precisely from the fact that men go on observing them, century after century. But Mr. Kaplan was not in the slightest impressed by precedent. He seemed to take the position that each rule of grammar, each canon of syntax, each convention of usage, no matter how ancient or how formidable, had to prove its case anew—to him. He seemed to make the whole English language start from scratch. (The plural of "sandwich," he had once declaimed, is "delicatessen.") Somewhere, somehow, Mr. Kaplan had gotten it into his head that to bend the knee to custom was but a hairbreadth from bending the neck to slavery.

And there was another perplexity. Whereas all the other students came to school in order to be instructed, Mr. Kaplan seemed to come in order to be consulted. It had taken a good deal of persuasion on Mr. Parkhill's part, for instance, to convince Mr. Kaplan that there simply is no feminine form of "ghost." If the feminine of "host" is "hostess," Mr.

Kaplan had observed, then surely the feminine of "ghost" should be "ghostess."

It was most trying. Not that Mr. Kaplan was an obstreperous student. On the contrary. Not one of Mr. Parkhill's three hundred abecedarians had ever been more eager, more enthusiastic, more athirst and aflame for knowledge. The trouble was that Mr. Kaplan was so eager, so enthusiastic, so athirst and aflame that he managed to convert the classroom into a courtroom—a courtroom, moreover, in which the entire English language found itself put on the stand as defendant.

How else could one describe the extraordinary process by which Mr. Kaplan had come to the conclusion that if a pronoun is a word used in place of a noun, a proverb is a pronoun used instead of a verb? It was outlandish, of course, and yet—when Mr. Parkhill had asked Mr. Kaplan, rather severely, if he could give one single example of a pronoun used instead of a verb, Mr. Kaplan, transported by that special joy that possessed him *in statu pupillari,* exclaimed, "I'll give t'ree: Soppoze in a rizort hotal is somebody hollerink, 'Who vants to svim?' T'ree pipple enswer: 'I!' 'Me!' 'You!' All pronons. No voibs."

Surely a student could not be permitted to go on that way, changing the tongue of Chaucer and Swift and Hazlitt as he went along. But if a student refused to accept authority, the testimony of experts, the awesome weight of precedent, to what higher court could one possibly appeal? There was the rub.

Mr. Kaplan did not deny that English had rules—good rules, sensible rules. What he would not accept, apparently, was that the rules applied to *him.* Mr. Kaplan had a way of getting Mr. Parkhill to submit each rule to the test of reason, and Mr. Parkhill was beginning to face the awful suspicion that he was no match for Mr. Kaplan, who had a way of operating with rules of reason entirely his own. Only a man with rules of reason entirely his own would dare to give the opposite of "height" as "lowth," or the plural of "blouse" as "blice."

In trying to grope his way through the fogs of his ghastly dilemma, Mr. Parkhill had even taken Miss Higby into his confidence. "Miss Higby," he had said during a recess, while they were alone for a moment in the room that served as faculty refuge, "it might just be that one of my students is a —well, a kind of genius."

"*Genius?*" echoed Miss Higby.

"I mean, he seems to take the position that since he raises no objection to our rules, why should *we* object to—er—his?"

Miss Higby had made a sort of gurgling noise, saying, "We get an extra day of vacation this term," and hurried out of the room.

That remark had made Mr. Parkhill quite cross. It was not at all a matter of an extra day of vacation. Vacation had nothing to do with it. The trouble with Miss Higby was that, like Mr. Robinson, she simply refused to face facts.

They refused to face facts just as Mr. Kaplan refused to abide by the laws and the customs to which other people were beholden. He was a kind of anarchist. But that did not absolve the ANPSA of responsibility; it only added to its burdens. What Mr. Parkhill had finally decided was that if Mr. Kaplan refused to enter their universe, they would have to enter his. They would have to try to teach him, as it were, *from the inside.*

For there was no longer any doubt in Mr. Parkhill's mind that Mr. Kaplan did inhabit a universe all his own. That would explain how Mr. Kaplan had come to define "diameter" as a machine that counts dimes, and once dubbed the waterway which connects the Atlantic and Pacific "the Panama Kennel."

Mr. Parkhill passed his hand across his brow. He wondered if it might not be best to think of Mr. Kaplan not as a pupil but as some sort of cosmic force, beyond human influence, a reckless, independent star that roared through the heavens in its own unconstrained and unpredictable orbit. Mr. Kaplan was *sui generis.* Perhaps that was why he so often responded with delight, rather than despair, when

Mr. Parkhill corrected him. It had taken Mr. Parkhill a long time to discover that Mr. Kaplan's smile signified not agreement but consolation.

One night Mr. Kaplan had delivered a rhapsodic speech on a topic which he had announced as "Amazink Stories Abot Names in U.S." New York, he had cheerfully confided to his comrades, was originally called "New Hamsterdam," Montana was so named because it was "full of montains," and Ohio, he averred, "sonds like an Indian yawnink." Sometimes Mr. Parkhill thought Mr. Kaplan would never find peace until he had invented a language all his own.

Ahead loomed the building in which the school occupied two floors. Tonight, bathed in gossamer moonbeams, it stood in ghostly grandeur. Mr. Parkhill removed his hat and went up the broad stone steps. Just as he was about to open the door, a voice behind him sang out, "Goot ivnink, Mr. Pockheel!"

He did not have to think or turn to know whose voice that was. No one else pronounced his name quite that way, or infused a routine salutation with the timbre of Archimedes crying "Eureka!"

"Vat's a madder? You not fillink Hau Kay?"

"I beg your pardon?"

"You vere lookink so fonny on de school."

Mr. Parkhill caught a glimpse of Mr. Kaplan's bland, bright mien, beclouded, for a moment, with solicitude. "It's nothing," said Mr. Parkhill hastily. "Nothing at all."

But he knew that he *had* been "lookink fonny on de school." He could have sworn that for a moment he had seen, glittering over the doorway:

b. 25 years B.K.
d. "?" years A.K.

They entered the temple together.

The Mocking Monk

RELIGION was debased by superstition and befouled
by bigotry. Piety was measured by subservience. Holy
men hounded the doubters, tortured "heretics," burned the
"witches." Miraculous cures and claims, supernatural visions
and impostures, were as common as fleas, and less honorable. Sacred relics—one saint's finger or another's tooth—
sanctified a thousand churches, in suspicious profusion. The
incantations that priests recited to confound Satan and his
ubiquitous demons were more worthy of voodoo than Christ.

From luxurious Rome down to the smallest village, the
Holy Catholic Church, mighty with spiritual power and political alliances, corrupted Christianity with its scandals.
Cardinals sold absolutions from sin; bishops hawked tickets
to Paradise; clerical salesmen toured Europe to sell the
sacraments and indulgences—through terror, threats and
shameless cozenings. Illiterate peasants were tithed for down
payments on salvation. The Church closed its eyes to sybari-
tic popes, indecent prelates, and brazen swindles in which
eternal bliss was sold on the installment plan. And in the
halls of learning, approved by the most illustrious theo-
logians, scholasticism throttled reason, to make thinking itself heretical.

It was the fifteenth century, into which Erasmus of Rot-

terdam was born. This remarkable Augustinian monk illuminated Europe with his humanism, regaled it with his
wit, and liberated it from cant and superstition through his
wisdom, his tolerance, and his unfailing good sense.

Erasmus was neither a philosopher nor a theologian. He
was a writer—that is, one of the first men in over a thousand years (since the fall of Rome) to earn his living by
his pen. He was the first scholar to gain a reputation
throughout Europe via the printing presses Gutenberg had
recently sired.

Erasmus was not a "creative" writer; he was an essayist,
a moralist, a critic, a crusader, a prolific correspondent. His
3,000 (!) letters remain the matchless record of the life,
the customs, the morals, the intellectual lemmas and dilemmas of his age. *The Praise of Folly*, which he wrote in
one week, and *Colloquies*, which set down his rules for the
instruction of the young, are sprinkled with the most acerbic
observations on the practices of the time—and were huge
bestsellers.

Erasmus galvanized scholarship by his independent com-
mentaries on Augustine, Chrysostom, Origen. He was a major
force in resurrecting the pagan classics of Greece and Rome,
after centuries of neglect, from flat disapproval in the universities, and sanctimonious prohibition by the papacy.
Single-handedly, he produced the first complete edition of
the works of Aristotle. He edited Seneca and Pliny. He published authoritative translations of Jerome (nine volumes),
Cyprian, Ambrose, Hilary.

He retranslated the original Greek text of the New Testament, placing beside it his own elegant Latin translation,
and exposed a succession of errors in St. Jerome's Vulgate
version, which had served as gospel for 1100 years. (Jerome
himself, we might remember, called the Bible translations of
his time "not versions, but perversions".) His marginal comments on the patristic texts were as impudent as they were
unconventional.

Erasmus was the first truly modern scholar of the New
Testament; and although he was often hasty and careless,

and more poetic than precise (he ignored Hebrew, and the Old Testament), he was animated by a freshness, a spaciousness of judgment, a fundamental humanity, that were irresistible. His fondest goal was neither exegesis nor erudition; it was the simplification and purification of faith. In one famous passage he wrote: "Would that the farmer might sing snatches of Scripture at his plow, that the weaver might hum phrases of Scripture to the tune of his shuttle, that the traveler might lighten with stories from Scripture the weariness of his journey."

Erasmus recast the very approach to Holy Scripture. His scholarship was so broad, his judgment so sane, that he made the pedants look either sterile or ludicrous. His *Paraphrases* of the Gospels were so admired in England that they were placed next to the Bible in England's churches.

He was at his best as a satirist, a sparkling stylist who rejected the linguistic affectations of his day. His Latin was so lucid, so muscular, so vivid and direct that it offered men a wholly new model of literary grace.

His book of *Adages* was read and cherished throughout Europe, for it salvaged countless maxims from the tomes accessible only to classical scholars:

Call a spade a spade.

Caught in his own snare.

As plain as the nose on your face.

One swallow does not make a spring.

In the country of the blind, the one-eyed man is king.

Of two evils, choose the lesser.

In front a precipice, behind wolves.

Talk of the devil and he'll appear.

'Tis a step toward health to know the disease.

Old wives' foolish tales.

Time takes away the grief of men.

The timid never set up a trophy.

An ape's an ape, though clad in scar et.

His own dancing wit added new epigrams in everything he wrote:

Almost everyone knows this, but it has not occurred to everyone.
Error is prolific.
Frugality is a handsome income.
Those who make haste in the beginning show least speed in the ending.
It is the worst madness to learn what has to be unlearnt.
This life of mortal man, what is it but a kind of stage play, where men come forth, disguised one in one array, and another in another, each playing his part?
The multitude . . . is a beast of many heads.
A good servant should be faithful, fierce, and ugly.
There is no satiety in study.
I am conquered by truth.

Humorous, fastidious, quizzical, urbane, this frail, sickly priest crisscrossed Europe on horseback, to study and teach and talk and advise. (Pope Leo X granted his petition to live outside the monasteries, and remove his monk's garb.) He often read while he rode, and dictated to one or another secretary astride a horse beside him. He did not suspend his reading or his dictating even while crossing the Alps.

He was an indefatigable traveler and correspondent (letters served as meetings and seminars in those days) and maintained a lively written dialogue with kings, popes, princes, scholars—in England, Italy, Holland, France, Switzerland, Germany. They revered him; they sought his advice; they chortled over his witticisms. At one point, Pope Paul III offered him a cardinal's hat. Martin Luther called him "our glory and our hope." Churchmen besought him to act as the major mediator in a council that might resolve the raging theological schisms, and unify Christendom once more.

And it was from this dazzling eminence that Erasmus's

reputation toppled—so far and so fast that even old friends cursed his name: Catholics, for betraying the Church; Protestants, for deserting the Reformation he played so measureless a role in inspiring. He was "John the Baptist and Judas Iscariot in one," the traitor incarnate to each side in the holocaust that would ravage the Western world. How did this happen?

Erasmus was born at Rotterdam (or Gouda) in either 1466 or 1469. We cannot be sure of the date because Erasmus kept pushing it back, to make it precede the date on which his father had taken holy orders. For Erasmus—like Leonardo da Vinci or Pope Clement VII—was illegitimate. In time he added the name "Desiderius" to Erasmus, to make the combination "desired beloved."

His mother died of the plague when he was fifteen, and his father soon after, which left Erasmus and an older brother, also born out of wedlock, at the mercy of three bleak guardians—who sent them off to a school of the Brethren of the Common Life at s'Hertogenbosch (where Hieronymus Bosch was born, thirty-four years earlier), near Antwerp. This gruesome academy prepared boys for the monastic life in a manner so severe, so heartless, that it gave Erasmus a lifelong hatred of the brutality that pedagogues used and defended. He all but starved or froze to death among the Brethren; his health was irreparably damaged.

At nineteen or twenty, Erasmus entered an Augustinian monastery, in Steyn, with little enthusiasm, almost in despair; but there, at least, he was allowed to immerse himself in reading not only the Church Fathers, but the ancient Greeks and Romans. He was ordained in 1492.

Erasmus was befriended by the Bishop of Cambria, and received permission to become the bishop's Latin secretary. When he discovered that his duties interfered with his studies, he moved to Paris, on a small pension from the bishop. There he entered "the house of the poor" section of the Collège Montaigu, a center trying to modernize or, at least, purify monastic orders whose scandals were becoming too frequent and too well-known. But the Collège Montaigu was entirely beholden to scholasticism, and entirely unresponsive to the Renaissance that was beginning to stir Europe.

Erasmus published a slender collection of poems, but soon his poverty and abstinence made him victim to a succession of illnesses, and he returned to Holland to recuperate. And when he returned to Paris now it was to live in the city, not the college, and earn his living as a tutor. He survived only because of pensions from one or another patron, none of whom he hesitated to flatter, sometimes in dedications so eulogistic that Tyndale waspishly remarked "Erasmus maketh of little gnats great elephants."

In 1499, on the initiative of Lord Mountjoy, one of his students and patrons, Erasmus first visited England. He was received with enormous respect and affection. Thomas More and John Colet, the most influential English scholars and clerics, and the Archbishop of Canterbury became life-long friends. Colet's disgust with the pedantries of the scholastics fortified Erasmus, who made a pilgrimage to Canterbury and wrote a withering description of "miraculous oils," the exhibition of "the Virgin's milk for money," and "the portions of the True Cross—enough, if collected, to freight a large ship." His irreverence was as fresh as his mind.

He visited Italy as the tutor to the sons of Henry VII's physician, and was sickened by the extravagances and profligacy of the princes of the Church. Nor could he summon enthusiasm for Rome's political machinations, her military alliances, her "holy" wars that exacted a tragic price from the pious poor.

Erasmus believed in the simple worship of God. He saw no conflict between Greek thought and Catholic creed, between Roman literature and Christian belief. "A heathen wrote this to a heathen," he once noted, "and yet his moral principles [contain] justice, sanctity, truth. . . . I can hardly refrain from saying, 'Saint Socrates, pray for me!' "

Erasmus brought reason to bear on the structure of faith. He had the rare capacity to excite men with his passion for knowledge, his sense of the infinite promise of freedom of thought, his scorn for blind reiterations of ritual. In one flashing sentence he cut through rigidified dogma: "By identifying the new learning with heresy, you make orthodoxy synonymous with ignorance."

Even cardinals applauded his caustic remarks about priests who "compute the time of each soul's residence in Purgatory and assign them longer or shorter [stays]—according as they purchase more or fewer ... pardons." Churchmen chuckled over his strictures on monks "allowed to fornicate, but not to marry," or his sardonic remark: "I do not see by what right we send a priest to the flames who prefers the wife to the concubine." He was admired by the brave, growing band of Reformers: Melancthon, Zwingli, Oecolampadius. And men great and small responded to his contempt for "religious imposters [who] play upon the credulity of the people" and promise "a seat at the right hand of the Saviour."

He drew the deadly rasp of his scorn across the casuists who determined "in what manner . . . our Saviour was conceived in the Virgin's womb." He mockingly asked whether "the first person of the Trinity [could] hate the second?" With artful solemnity he dared wonder "whether God, who took our nature upon Him in the form of a man, could as well have become a woman, a devil, an ass . . .?" He was a rare, bright mind in a Europe where, as Sydney Smith was to say centuries later, "The observances of the church concerning feasts and fasts are tolerably well kept, since the rich keep the feasts and the poor keep the fasts."

Among those who read Erasmus and rejoiced was Martin Luther. Erasmus defended Luther, saying to the hierarchy of the Church, "You may rid your bookshelves of him, but ... not men's minds." He saw in Luther a giant portent of that rebellion against unthinking enslavement to dogma that was anathema to him. (Erasmus, who disliked fish, once said, "My heart is Catholic, but my stomach is Lutheran.") In one form or another, Erasmus warned the holy fathers to moderate their obduracy and their absolutism.

Luther, an intransigent, roaring torrent of a man, hailed

Erasmus as Christendom's most shining son. And Erasmus said of Luther's crusade: "Luther was guilty of two great crimes; he struck the pope in his crown, and the monks in their belly." Erasmus wanted both pope and clergy to be cleansed by the new humanism.

But Erasmus was a sensitive, unbellicose spirit who became increasingly horrified by Luther's fury and coarseness and vituperations, Luther's rabid railing against "all of the offscourings of the Roman Sodom. . . . Why should we not wash our hands in their blood?" The German monk besought Heaven to send "plague, syphilis, epilepsy, boils" to Rome's theocrats. He called the pope "a Sodomite hermaphrodite." He labelled the Mass "blasphemy . . . idolatry . . . abomination."

Luther was a master polemicist, commander of a literary style that was in turn lyrical, slashing, sublime, and savage. He converted a vernacular, German, into a language. He wrote a whole new liturgy, a whole new catechism. He created hymns as majestic as "A Mighty Fortress Is Our God" and songs as endearing as "Away in the manger, no crib for His head." But he called reason "a whore . . . the greatest enemy that faith has." And that Erasmus could not stomach.

Contrast Luther's rage with Erasmus's rumination: "It has long been my cherished wish to cleanse the Lord's temple of barbarous ignorance, and to adorn it with treasures from afar, such as may kindle in generous hearts a warm love for the Scriptures." To the humanist Erasmus, Martin Luther was an angry, inflexible theologian: dogmatic, self-righteous, un-Christian in the violence of his views and the extremities to which he might resort.

Erasmus sought no break with Rome ("I will put up with this Church until I see a better"). He was a reformer; Luther was a revolutionary. Erasmus thought the papacy could and would redeem itself; Luther thundered that the pope was nothing less than the Antichrist. And Erasmus, a prophetic intelligence with a keen awareness of reality, realized that virulent nationalism and immense economic prizes (Church lands, huge incomes, personal properties, and riches such as no one could estimate) were caught up and concealed in the contest for religious power.

Politics, avarice and ambition would lead bishops, no less than barons, to oppose or support Luther's roaring challenge to the secular empire of Rome. The time was so explosive, the issues so intricate, the forces so complex, that nothing augured more tragedy and danger, to Erasmus, than a religious-economic-political-civil war. "The monarchy of the pope ... is a pestilence to Christendom," Erasmus wrote a friend, "but [it is not] expedient to touch that sore openly."

Beyond all else, Erasmus hated fanaticism. He opposed the neopagan cult of the humanist movement, whose fountainhead he was; he opposed the despotism of Rome; he found his sustenance in "the simple philosophy of Christ." But the central fact could not be denied: Erasmus had indeed, as one historian put it, "laid the egg that Luther hatched." Now he was caught in a maelstrom of zealotries.

Luther's cause spread with great speed. His supporters grew in numbers, in conviction, and in wrath. Open rebellions broke out against profligate Rome. Priests and nuns were attacked, abused, reviled or lynched. Churches were sacked, monasteries burned, convents pillaged.

And now the pope himself and King Henry VIII and Cardinal Wolsey appealed to Erasmus—to disown and disavow Luther, to join issue with them openly, to fight the peasant demagogue as only he could. And Luther, for his part, kept writing to Erasmus and begging for public support to advance their common cause.

Erasmus delayed and evaded and agonized within himself. He was torn by both conscience and fear. Finally, in 1524, he yielded to the mounting pressures and criticized Luther—but in a curious, moderate tract called *De Libero Arbitrio*, centering his censure on Luther's position that all human acts are determined by divine necessity.

To Luther, Erasmus wrote these blighting words: "I neither approve nor disapprove anything. ... I try to keep neutral, so as to help the revival of learning. ..."

Erasmus made the eminently revealing confession that he

simply could not "risk my life for the truth. All men have not strength for martyrdom. . . ." He wrote this candid and surprising defense of expedience: "I follow the just decrees of popes and emperors because it is right: I endure their evil laws because it is safe." I know of few figures in history so honest about their limitations or their pragmatism.

The storm that broke around Erasmus was shattering. Old friends, students, colleagues, admirers branded him a coward, a hypocrite, an opportunist, a Janus. He could only reply, "Christ . . . will look after me." He was soon forced to look after himself. Hurricanes of religious hatred consumed Europe. He had to flee from Basel when Protestant mobs went on terrible rampages of destruction.

Erasmus died in 1536—without the sacraments (to Luther's horror); and his will contained no provision for a Mass. Whether this was by accident, neglect, ambivalence or intent is difficult to determine. His last words on this earth were *"Lieve God,"* Dutch for "dear God."

All of his writings were condemned by Pope Paul IV, "even if they contain nothing against religion. . . ." The mighty Council of Trent put many of his works on the *Index Liborum Prohibitorum:* books Catholics were forbidden to read.

Desiderius Erasmus was no martyr. He was hardly a hero. He was, first, last, and foremost, an intellectual, a man in love with learning, a scholar who believed in the fructifying nobility of knowledge. In philosophy and temperament, he was a liberal, a mind that would have been much more at home in the eighteenth century than the sixteenth. He was the precursor of Voltaire and Rousseau, the deists and the *philosophes.* He was a man indeed beholden to truth, which, he sighed, had always "conquered" him.

"He, almost alone in his age," says Preserved Smith, "knew that truth had many facets. . . . Thomas More would die for his faith—and have you punished for yours; but Erasmus would be courteous . . . even to an infidel."

Erasmus devised no grand, systematic doctrine. He propounded no profundities. He cast no models for the Renaissance or the Reformation. But his contribution to our civilization was monumental. His sweeping sanity, his cleansing vision of worship, his comprehension of the human condition, helped men remove the blinders of self-abnegation and rebel against lifelong servitude to dogma. He showed how reason could nourish piety in a larger humanism. He encouraged scholars to be scholars, not parrots or servants or fuglemen to the past. He was free enough and bold enough to lampoon the flummery that had corrupted faith. He called on Christian doctrine to free itself from suffocating obscurantism, return to its purer sources, renounce its merchants and traducers. He blew a purifying wind of good sense across the fearful, darkened landscape of religion.

The simplest, most significant lesson Erasmus taught Europe was this: to celebrate Man does not derogate God. His pen pushed Europe beyond medievalism. "He contributed more to the liberation of the human mind," writes the author of his biography in the *Encyclopaedia Britannica*, "than all the uproar and rage of Luther's pamphlets."

In his last, unhappy years, many men reviled and despised Desiderius Erasmus. Today, Holland, England, Switzerland, Germany claim him as one of their national glories.

Peggy Dobell
Gets a Job

THIS is a sad story. *You* may think it's funny, but I think it's sad. In fact, it's so sad I can barely bring myself to write it.

It's about some friends of ours, an extremely nice couple in New York, Erwin and Dolly Dobell, and their teenage daughter. Erwin Dobell is a lawyer. Dolly is a psychologist who advises nervous mothers about their unnerving children. And their daughter Peggy is unlike any teenager my wife and I know. For instance, when her front door opens to admit us, she looks pleased, instead of glaring or wiping her nose on her sweatshirt. And she smiles when she meets you, instead of crying, "How can you be so *smug* when I'm searching for my identity?" She also brushes her hair! I even doubt that this kid has ever taken LSD or held up a gas station, the way normal American teenagers do.

Now, with a girl like Peggy, you'd think the Dobells would be in seventh heaven, not having to contend with the kind of problems that shrivel so many parental souls these days. That is not true. The Dobells have a terrible problem: the telephone.

I don't have to tell you what a phone means when you have an adolescent in the house. Frankly, something has happened to teen-age girls since I was one. The minute an American girl passes thirteen, a tormenting itch afflicts her left ear, an itch that can be soothed only by applying a telephone receiver to the irritated area for from one to two hours. That's why, the minute a teen-age girl comes home, she drops all of her risqué books and condemned tennis shoes on the floor and lunges for the phone. The longer she uses it, the less her ear itches.

When a teen-age girl runs out of friends, she proceeds to call classmates she "loathes," so that she can divulge her innermost secrets. The average American teen-age girl will talk to any creep, crud, nerd, or zook as long as there's something left to blame her parents for. When she can't think of another breathing body to phone, she goes into a depression.

The American teen-age girl's depression usually lasts until someone phones *her*. The National Mental Health Institute estimates that more time is spent each week on the telephone by teen-agers in New Rochelle than it took to build the great pyramid of Khufu, and they don't build pyramids like that anymore. As for the wear and tear of the occupied phone on the parents, who never get a chance to make or receive a call of their own, no one dares face up to this except Marshall McLuhan.

The traffic in the Dobell's hallway, which is where they keep the phone and support AT&T, grew so thick that the inhabitants of that household turned black and blue from bumping into each other. The number of times someone was on the phone when someone else wanted to use it greatly exceeded the number of times no one was on the phone when nobody wanted to use it.

One night, as the loving but high-strung family was having dinner, Peggy Dobell announced, "I think it's time I had my own telephone!"

After her father coughed up the fishbone (he was eating clear chicken broth at the time), he cried, "Your own phone?! Why I didn't have a phone of my own until I was——"

"Googie McGill and Muscles Shimmelfarb each—has—her

—own—phone!" Peggy said icily, prior to putting the Evil Eye on her mother.

"You can have your own phone, dear," said Mrs. Dobell, smiling psychologically.

Peggy's jaw dropped in joyous surprise. "I *can*? Honest to God and cross your heart? My own *phone*? In my own *room*?!"

"Certainly, dear," smiled Mrs. Dobell and, as her grateful daughter hugged her and kissed her, added, "All you have to do is pay for it. . . . Pass the salt, dear."

Peggy's jaw came apart. "*Pay* for it?"

"Uh-huh."

"*How*?"

"By working."

At this point, Mr. Dobell applauded.

"*Working*?" wailed Peggy. "I don't have a free half-*hour* all week!"

"What about Saturdays?" smiled Mrs. Dobel.

"Work *Saturdays*?" Peggy echoed, horrified. "Why, that would ruin my whole weekend!"

"How true," beamed Mr. Dobell. "People have been ruining their weekends for centuries to pay for such oddities as bread, clothes——"

"But—what kind of job could I get?" wailed Peggy.

"The supermarket," crooned Mrs. Dobell, "needs help, stuffing things into bags—"

"The stationer's!" chimed in Mr. Dobell. "Washing those windows, sweeping out his store——"

Without a word, Peggy, having rejected the idea of a nervous breakdown, flung her napkin to the floor, pushed her chair away from the table, and marched out of the room.

Mr. and Mrs. Dobell exchanged beatific smiles. He ate two portions of the *crème caramel* and she chipped up a *crème-de-menthe* mist.

Two nights later, Peggy announced, "Miss Grimshaw, who is in charge of student placement, got me a job—for Saturday."

"I am proud of you," said Mrs. Dobell.

"I can hardly wait," said Mr. Dobell.

At Saturday brunch, which is when, swimming against the Upper East Side tide, the Dobells have their bagels and lox, which Peggy hardly touched, the lass said, "I shall be working for Mrs. Hollingshead Forbes Eltington, who wants me to baby-sit for her daughter Lucy, who is nine. I get a dollar-fifty an hour. . . . I'd better get dressed now. The limousine is picking me up to lunch——"

"Limou*sine?*" choked Mr. Dobell. "Whose——"

"The *El*tingtons'. They're sending their chauffeur to——"

"To take you to *work?*" gasped Mrs. Dobell.

"*Mum*my! They live all the way over on Fifth Avenue."

"Where?" growled Mr. Dobell.

"At Seventy-third."

"That must be a whole ten-minute walk from here," glared Mr. Dobell.

"That's why they're sending their limou*sine,*" said Peggy.

So Mr. Dobell spent the afternoon watching the Yankees lose and hating the Eltingtons, whom he had never met; and Dolly Dobell shampooed her hair and paid her bills, hating only Mrs. Eltington, whom she was panting to advise.

At five o'clock, Mr. Dobell asked nervously if it wasn't about time for Peggy to be home.

At 5:30, Mrs. Dobell said maybe they should call the number Peggy had left and find out if their daughter had had a heart attack.

At 5:45, Mr. Dobell said he thought they should both have a martini.

At 6:15, as they were reaching the second plateau, the door was flung open. There stood their daughter, radiating pride, joy, and ergs. "Lookie, lookie!" She waved a check. "Nine real dollars!"

"God," said Mr. Dobell.

"Keep your religious beliefs out of this," said Mrs. Dobell. "Do you think it's easy taking care of a nine-year-old for six full hours?! You can go crazy trying to interest or amuse them. Isn't that so, dear?"

"No," said Peggy.

"Oh," said Mrs. Dobell. "What did you do?"

"Well, first, the chauffeur took me to the Eltington penthouse: *super*, Mum, it overlooks the park. Little Lucy and I lunched on the terrace. *Scrumpt*ious food, Dad, served by the butler, on the *groo*viest silver trays——"

"Lord," moaned Mr. Dobell.

"How did you eat?" asked Mrs. Dobell anxiously, thinking of her daughter's manners.

"Slowly," said Peggy, thinking only of numbers. "I get one-fifty an hour. After lunch—well, the Eltingtons had left us theater tickets to *Cabaret*——"

"Cab*aret*?!" shouted Mr. Dobell, jumping up and down. "I've been trying to get tickets for *Cabaret* for two months——"

"Oh, you'll en*joy* it, Daddy. It's *super*. Then after the show, I took Lucy to Schrafft's for chocolate sodas, and the chauffeur dropped me off here."

"For that you got *paid*?" bleated Mrs. Dobell.

"Sometimes I wonder if man will make it," said Mr. Dobell.

Peggy sighed. "They want me—next week—to take Lucy to Le Pavillon or the Colony, because they want her to develop poise in posh restaurants——"

"*I'd* like to develop poise at Pavillon!" shouted Mr. Dobell.

"—and we'll see either the Bolshoi Ballet or the Royal Shakespeare Company matinée——"

Mr. and Mrs. Dobell, I am sorry to tell you, were not even listening to their own flesh and blood. Dolly was mixing a fresh batch of martinis, muttering to herself, and Erwin was hunting through his law books for a state that goes light on fathers who chain their children to bedposts.

Peggy said, "I'd better pick out the exact place in my room for my phone. Tell them to install it on Monday."

As the Dobells returned to their martinis, they were silent, but then exchanged occasional bitter, cryptic monosyllables. An observer would have found them incomprehensible, but I think you will understand them: "Limousine . . ." "chauffeur . . ." "*Cabaret* . . ." "the Bolshoi Ballet . . ." "the Royal

Shakespeare . . ." "—and getting *paid* . . ." "—to eat at the Colony . . ." ". . . Pavillon" ". . . is there—no justice?"

Now you know why I said, at the beginning, that this was going to be a sad story. Think, if you can bear to, of how that innocent, lovely child has blighted the lives of Erwin and Dolly Dobell, forever.

Michio and the Fierce
American Conqueror

IT was in Kurashiki, an enchanting old town some 400
miles southwest of Tokyo, its diminutive river crossed by
pretty bridges and overhung by trees, that Michio Nagai told
me this story. It goes back to the time of the war, and I'll
try to tell it in his words, as I remember them, not mine.

When the Emperor himself told us, on the radio, that we
had been defeated and must now surrender, and that our
country would actually be occupied by soldiers of the American Army, we were all, naturally, full of apprehension. We
steeled ourselves for the arrival of the fierce conquerors, for
everyone knows how savagely battle-hardened soldiers do
behave. Some shopkeepers closed their shops and others
boarded shut their windows, fearing looters, and mothers
explained to their daughters where to hide the moment a
dread American appeared.

I was then in Kyoto, having just been graduated from
high school, and one fateful day I turned a corner and beheld—an American uniform! One soldier, in an American
uniform, and he was coming down the street. With my heart
fast-beating, and because I was also very curious and somewhat eager to test my stiff high-school English, I advanced

toward this first fierce conqueror and bowed and in a perhaps not-steady voice I inquired if I could be of assistance.

"Say, kid, you speak English!" the warrior exclaimed. "Sure, you can help me. Thanks a lot. . . . I'm looking for souvenirs."

These were the first words I heard from the American forces of occupation.

I accompanied him into a little shop that had many trinkets, of glass and such. The old shopkeeper and his wife were white-faced, trembly, bowing of course, and they showed this awesome military creature whatever thing caught his eye. Soon, the soldier selected several items, not costly, which were swiftly wrapped by the proprietor's wife and by him presented with hopeful bows and nervous smiles.

"How much is it?" asked the ferocious conqueror.

The shopkeeper and his wife could not understand English, and when I repeated the question, they appeared confused, as was I, and told me what to respond.

"Oh, sir," I said. "They wish you to have these small things as a gift."

"No, no, no," said the warrior. "That's not *right*. I can pay for these and I want to. Please ask them how much they are."

I translated this and the shopkeeper and his wife regarded each other in renewed astonishment.

So the American soldier paid the shopkeeper and said to me, "Thanks, kid. You were a great help." And when we were outside the shop, he handed me an American dollar.

I thanked him but observed that I had done nothing, except a small courtesy, and that it was not necessary to pay me.

"Nonsense," said the fierce American conqueror, "you earned this, kid. Take it."

So I took the dollar, the first American money I ever held in my hand, the first dollar I ever "earned."

Now this soldier and I walked along and he asked questions like a sightseer and I answered and pointed out things of interest. And on both sides of the street my dumbfounded compatriots were stopping as if in a dream to see this real, tall, fearsome invader from the West, and some were shrinking away in fear, which I tried for him not to notice by calling his attention to some historic or cultural feature.

He asked me personal questions too: what had I studied and what I hoped to become and so on, and when I said I had just been graduated, he grew quite earnest and told me it was very important to continue to study, to get as much education as one ever can. "Someday you ought to come to America, kid," he said, "to one of our schools, and perfect your English. That could be very important to you, you know, knowing English."

I said I would of course like to study in America if ever the opportunity arose, especially now that the war was over, and he said I would be surprised by what Americans were really like, and by how beautiful it is.

"If you do ever come over, kid," he said, "let me know, you hear? I would like to show you a part of America I know." And he wrote down his name and address and gave me the piece of paper. He lived in a place with the strange name of Buffalo, and it was not in the West but in New York.

We shook hands, I remember, because when I bowed my farewell he said, "Aw," and projected his hand and pumped my hand up and down and patted me on my back, thanking me again for helping him and for being his first Japanese to talk to. Then he waved and said, "So long, kid."

I bowed and watched him go away.

I was deeply puzzled by this whole experience, you can understand. I knew Americans were different from us, of course; all through the war and the fighting we heard how barbaric they were. I now was obliged to wonder. . . . Americans were assuredly a strange people.

Some years later, I was greatly pleased to receive a fellowship for graduate studies at Ohio State University, and I went to Columbus, Ohio. And I wrote this American soldier, who lived in Buffalo, New York, reminding him who I was and where we had met and telling him I hoped to be able soon to come and visit him.

Very quickly, I received a letter, a warm answer from him—plus a $10 bill inside. A student, he said, especially from abroad, could make use of a little extra spending money, so he was proposing to send me $10 each month. He asked me to try to come to Buffalo for a visit, and to be his guest and stay with him in his home.

I replied and thanked him for his generosity, but told him my fellowship was truly ample for my needs, and returned that $10 bill. I also said that during the Christmas holidays I would have an opportunity to go to the east, driving there with an American student, and I was greatly pleased and honored to accept his kind invitation.

Just before I left Ohio, I received a letter from my friend saying that unexpectedly some relatives would come to visit him, so his home would be too crowded, but he had made arrangements for me to stay with a nice lady, at a certain address, and he said to let me know when I expected to arrive and he would meet me there, at the lady's house.

A classmate drove me to Buffalo and to the address of the lady, and she received me very cordially and telephoned my American friend, the conquering soldier. Soon he arrived and we greeted each other with interest after all the years. Other people began to come in, too, many people, friends of his or hers whom he had invited to meet a friend of his from Japan. Of course, they were curious to see a live Japanese.

We all had dinner together and told many stories. I answered many questions about my country. It was a happy meal, but my friend, unfortunately, had to leave early because of the obligations to his relatives whom he had left at his own house.

Later, as my hostess was showing me to the room where I would sleep, I especially thanked her and explained that of course if my friend's relatives had not just arrived in Buffalo, I would be staying with him. I said how kind he was and how he had wanted to send me $10 a month.

The lady looked at me in a strange way. After some moments, she said, "You know, he was obliged to leave us early in order to go to his night job. He is a workingman. He does not have much money. There are no relatives visiting him. His aged mother lives with him—and there is no room for anyone more in that little flat."

That was Michio Nagai's story.

After I returned to America, I simply could not keep from wondering about that American soldier. Was he still alive? What was he doing?... I wrote Michio Nagai, now a professor at the Tokyo Institute of Technology, and asked whether he would mind if I wrote this story. And would he give me the name of his GI benefactor?

Nagai answered promptly. His friend's name was—let us call him "Harry Miller," and Nagai thought he still lived near Buffalo, on a certain street.

I found the telephone number easily and called from New York. I phoned several times, but there was no answer. So I sent Mr. Miller a telegram and asked him to telephone me at *Look* magazine, collect. He did, the next day. He seemed utterly mystified by why I or anyone at *Look* would be calling him. He even sounded nervous.

When I told him I had met Michio Nagai in Japan, he was delighted. He seemed surprised that Nagai had told me about him. I told him *Look* would like to bring him to New York, paying him a fee and all his expenses, to talk about the episode I have recounted. He seemed astounded. He could not understand why we would be interested in anything he had to say, and he was not sure he had anything to say I did not already know. He seemed worried that *Look* would be wasting its money. He finally agreed to come to New York, but it would have to be on his day off.

He appeared in my office several days later: a plain, quiet man in his forties, a bit short, intelligent, soft-spoken, simple in manner. What follows is his story, in his words, to the best of my ability. I have left only one thing out: the dialogue pertaining to whether there was a dependable kosher restaurant nearby; Mr. Miller is an orthodox Jew, and observes the dietary laws.

Well, I guess you know I was in the Sixth Army. I was in the records division, as a sort of accountant, which I had always wanted to be, but I never got enough education, which I've always regretted. But anyway, I did get to be a kind of accountant, keeping books, recording payments, checking bills, and so on.

The Sixth Army went in—to occupy Japan, I mean—and of course we didn't know what to expect, this being a very strange country and people, and us occupying it and all. But I certainly was glad to have a chance to see Japan, at least. I heard Kyoto was their most interesting beauty city, full of temples and shrines, you know, very old, something you could never see anywhere else in the world.

So I was lucky to get to Kyoto, and my first day there, after chow with my buddies, I decide to go out and see something of the town. You see, I do not drink or hang around bars or—those other places, the way a lot of the fellows did, so I always had more time, and I'd walk around, any place I was, really see a place and the people, talk to them. I used to take streetcars or buses, hanging on the straps like anyone else, and being that I was in uniform, they would be interested and sooner or later maybe someone would talk to me, in their English, and I had some very interesting conversations.

Well, in Tokyo, once, on a trolley or bus, they started a conversation with me, and I told them the terrible things the Japanese did—like Pearl Harbor, and what Japanese soldiers did to their prisoners, to our men, I mean, terrible, horrible things, like actual tortures and the terrible Bataan march and things like that—and you know, I have to say I think it made a dent, because the people on the bus didn't know anything about that side of the war, hearing only their own radio and propaganda in their newspapers. You can understand that, I guess, it's like people wherever you don't have a democracy and free press and all.

Well, to get back to the story, in Kyoto, like the second day I am in Japan, I come down a street, and a Japanese boy comes up and he asks, nice and polite, can he help me in any way. That was Michio.

I can see he is very intelligent. You don't have to hear much to know if someone is intelligent or educated, and this boy is. So I say, "Sure, kid, you can help. I don't speak Japanese and you can translate."

So we go into this store, where they have real nice lacquer boxes and pictures on rice paper and things like that, and I pick out a few items. Then, to show my appreciation, I give the kid a quarter ... Michio told you it was a dollar? Gee, I don't *think* so—I'm not sure—maybe he's right—but I still think it was just a quarter. . . . Anyway, we take a walk together and see some sights—that city, Kyoto! It's a really old and wonderful place. Very historic, with its architecture and all, beautiful Buddhist temples and Shinto shrines and unusual gardens—gardens with gravel and dwarf shrubs to kind of make you think it's a whole landscape.

Well, Michio is like my guide and because he has some education, I tell him he ought to go on, maybe improve his English, and if he ever gets to the States to let me know.

Well, he does come to America, you know, and he writes me a letter. I ask him to come to my town, near Buffalo. I want to show him Niagara Falls. I love the Falls. You ever see them? Oh, I know it's built up and commercial and all— but still, the *Falls!*

When Michio came to visit, I had to put him up at the home of a lady, a schoolteacher, a friend of mine. I called some of my friends, to make it like a party, and they come over, to meet Michio, and I thought it would be good for him, too, to meet some Americans.

We all had a great time, no fooling, had a good meal together and talked and told jokes, but I had to leave early because I had to work that night. *That* night I had to do the night shift.

What?

No, I couldn't let Michio stay at my flat because my

mother—well, she was old, and my brothers were gone, so
I was the only one to take care of her. She was living with
me, so I had no room for Michio. But I wasn't *poor!* Oh,
no! Michio must of got entirely the wrong impression somewhere! I always had a *job!* If you have a job, you're not
poor!

So I had to leave the party early. And the next day Michio
left. That's all. That's all that happened.

What is Michio doing now? . . . Really? A *professor.* . . .
Well, I'm not surprised. I knew he was a smart boy—and
good.

"Have you seen Michio since that time in Buffalo?" I
asked.

"Oh, no," said Mr. Miller. "I did get a little letter from him
a year—maybe two—ago. But, you know, he has his life, I
have mine, we're worlds apart, we just happen to meet because of the war, what else? . . One thing I will always regret—I mean, not being able to show Michio the Falls. I
have been in many places, in the Army, and seen many
wonderful scenes, but nothing in the world is more beautiful
—to me—than Niagara Falls. Have you ever been there?"

"Yes," I said.

"I really did want to take Michio there," he sighed. "I
really did want to show him that part of America."

You showed him a part of America that is more important,
I thought.

Front Men for God

~~~~~~

EVERY so often, after my name has appeared in print, or my face on television, I get a rash of hate mail. The strangest letters come from profoundly religious souls—who want to save mine. This always moves, and even chastens, me because the believers in God's mercy start their spiritual appeals with a friendly greeting, such as:

<div align="center">SINNER, FRY IN HELL! ! !</div>

If the pietist has been told to avoid deep-fat cooking, the opening fanfare may go:

<div align="center">JUGDMENT DAY IS HERE! ! !</div>

(For reasons I have never understood, the greater the faith, the less the likelihood that "judgment" will be spelled correctly.) Sometimes, to be perfectly fair about it, the soul-hustlers tell me that Judgment Day is only "near" instead of "here," and sometimes I am not scheduled to start burning until next Tuesday.

My devout correspondents love to brighten their dispatches with references to Scripture, like "EZRA 10:36 WILL OPEN YOUR EYES!!" or "COME TO GOD THRU DANIEL 3:5!" But these passages in the Good Book, which I always consult, turn out to be meant for someone else—an alcoholic Croat, for instance, or an Ashanti with the jim-jams: *Ezra 10:36* reads, in its entirety: "Vaniah, Meremoth, Eliashib," which causes me to *close* my eyes; and *Daniel 3:5*, far from leading me to God, leaves me floundering amidst a list of ancient instruments, including the psaltery and the sackbut.

I am even more baffled by the texts which the faithful shower on me after I have written something that has not the remotest connection with any religion, including Maoism. Why on earth should a satire on New York's waiters cause a lady in Pahokee (Fla.) to hurl *Exodus 28:25* at me? That passage begins: "And the other two ends of the . . . chains thou shalt fasten in the two ouches." And why should my lament over the turgid prose of a New York paper inspire a true believer from Desplaines (Ill.) to thunder: "THE ANSWER WAS GIVEN BY THE ALMIGHTY HIMSELF! READ DEUT. 27:23!!!" Well, I have read and reread *Deut.* 27:23 and still wander in unredeemed darkness, because *Deut. 27:23* starts, "Cursed be he that lieth with his mother-in-law . . ." and goes nowhere from there.

I really should no longer be surprised by the mental fandangoes to which the righteous are prone. I first met professional peddlers of salvation years ago, in that cult in Los Angeles called "The Great I AM."

My indoctrination in the lofty liturgy of The Great I AM so edified, not to say refreshed, me that I plunged into research on other self-appointed shills for the Lord. This was not difficult. History books simply glitter with unlicensed champions of one or another brand of theosophy; indeed, a good deal of history is little more than the record of the schisms precipitated by excitable interpreters of Scripture, the bloodbaths sanctioned by contending concepts of redemption, and the wars, massacres or inquisitions inspired by apocalyptic epileptics.

I hasten to add, lest I be thought irreverent, that religious evangelists range, of course, from true saints to true schizophrenics. (No one knows this better than the Church, which has long shown a sophistication greater than that of the laity in requiring much harder evidence for miracles than the credulous would dream of demanding.) The sad truth is that sincerity does not exclude self-delusion, honest holy men may be honestly demented, and spotless seers may be more paranoid than prophetic. My researches in this delicate field, aided at all times by friendly priests, ministers and rabbis, led me to the unhappy conclusion that the Lord must have a special love for lunatics: He created so many of them. Some messianic preachers were sublime; others were as ingenious as they were brazen, or as clever as they were cynical; and many, alas, would just have made excellent food for squirrels.

Whenever my faith in human creativity shows signs of faltering, I fortify it by recalling some salubrious members of the art of soothing souls with spiritual bubble-gum: wacky doxologists, derailed spellbinders, eccentric mystagogues, and more canny oilers of the pearly gates. Say what you will, the front men for God fatten on the one inexhaustible natural resource I know: man's gullibility.

Here are a few of my favorites. To what degree they were saints, and to what degree scoundrels, you may judge for yourself.

In A.D. 44, a stargazer named Theudas led his faithful dizzards to the River Jordan, which he had promised to part the waters of without any equipment other than his larynx. He parted not a single liquid yard of the Jordan, which is considerably narrower than the Red Sea, whereupon the Romans terminated Theudas, first by crucifying, then beheading him.

Or consider one Benjamin, a beatnik Egyptian who caused many to frown when he called himself "the Lord's anointed." In A.D. 59, Benjamin marched perhaps 20,000 loyal acolytes up the Mount of Olives, where, in the most frank and friendly manner, he asked the walls of Jerusalem to tumble down. When the walls did not so much as tremble, Benjamin took a powder, leaving many a minion dangling on the yo-yo of his faith.

In 431, on fabled Crete, once home to the Minotaur and

the Great Bull, an amateur ecclesiast named Moses tried to
lead his fervent followers to the Holy Land. Now there certainly is nothing wrong about a shepherd walking his flock
to Palestine, but Moses tried to walk his gudgeons there all
the way from *Crete*—i.e., across the water in between. Many
hymn-singing lambs drowned, in both their faith and the
Mediterranean, and unholy Moses fled to a drier jurisdiction.

In the ninth century, a religious rabble-rouser named
Eldad Ha-Dani proclaimed that the Ten Lost Tribes having
been located, he was authorized to inaugurate the Messianic
Age. Since the Lost Tribes remain unfound to this very day,
and signs of the Messianic Age were as missing in Eldad Ha-
Dani's time as they are today, I can only conclude that
Eldad Ha-Dani, who sounds like a magician at the old
Palace, was a dip.

We now leap four centuries to the thirteenth, when a pious
Spanish Jew named Abulafia heard a Voice from heaven.
The Voice commanded him to convert no one other than
Pope Nicholas III. Now it is unusual enough for a Voice to
tell you to set about converting a *pope;* what makes Abulafia's call all the more singular is that the Voice commanded
him to convert the Holy Pontiff to—Judaism. By sheer sincerity, persistence, courage and *chutzpa,* gentle Abulafia
succeeded in gaining an audience with the pope; but when
His Holiness sensed the general drift of what Abulafia was
up to, he (Nicholas) condemned him (Abulafia) to the
stake. Abulafia escaped ustulation because soon after ordering Abulafia to burn, the pope dropped dead.

This brings me to the unbelievable, but verified, story of
one David Reuveni or Reubeni, a dwarf. He came from the
Middle East, where so many quixotic souls flourished, and in
1524 made his way to Pope Clement VII, whom he told that
his (Reuveni's) brother, a desert king, commanded a secret
army of ferocious Jewish warriors beyond the Mountains of
Kush, and *behind the Turkish lines.* Given the homicidal
unfriendliness that existed between the Christian and Muslim folds, such an army, in such a strategically miraculous
position, clearly betokened Divine Providence, if not Direct

Intervention. The dwarf proposed a joint crusade that would crush the trapped infidels of Islam like eggs and free the Holy Land from the Turks.

The idea so excited Clement VII that he asked his astrologers for their opinion. These necromancers examined Reuveni's "credentials" (whatever they could have been), "certified" them (via criteria beyond my powers of comprehension), and gave the dwarf a glowing recommendation and his mission their occult blessing.

His Holiness promptly deputized Reuveni to sail off to Portugal to enlist the assistance of the most pious and Catholic king. Off to Portugal sailed Reuveni, in a fine ship, with sumptuous provender, financed by Rome, under a special, splendid flag he designed himself. Rarely has a boodler achieved such sacerdotal status.

In Portugal, the dwarf proved successful beyond his (and if not beyond his, then certainly beyond *my*) expectations. Not only did the hieropathic king approve of Reuveni's call for a crusade against Islam, but many simpler Portuguese hailed the gnome as nothing less than the Messiah. One local, *poco loco,* a Marrano known as Diego Pires, became so uplifted that he underwent circumcision of his own free will, changed his name to Molcho or Molko, and sailed to the Levant, where he steeped himself in mumbo-jumbo.

Sometime later, Molko/Pires appeared in Rome, where he made an excellent impression on one and all. Clement VII welcomed him into the Vatican and sheltered him from the unfriendly Inquisition. In due course, Molko/Pires announced that *he* was the Messiah. All sorts of confusion ensued, including an interview between Molko, the dwarf Reuveni, and the Holy Roman Emperor, Charles V, who was less gullible than Clement VII. In the end, Molko was burned at the stake, circumcision and all. The year was 1532. Reuveni was taken to Spain and his *auto da fé* soon after. (His diary is in the Bodleian Library, Oxford.)

The most spectacular of all soothsayers, for my money, was Sabbatai Zvi (or Shabbatai Zevi) of Salonika, then part of the Turkish empire, a mystic, much loved by children, given to reciting loftily and singing psalms, who, in 1648, after years of flirtation with the mysteries, announced that he was the Messiah—as his spellbound disciples had long claimed. Zvi must have been a persuasive preacher, for he struck the gyves of doubt from skeptics wherever he trod.

In 1662, he entered Jerusalem itself, there to inspire a new legion of believers. Although the elders and rabbis regarded him with distaste, to say nothing of distrust, judging him most charitably a lunatic and least charitably a charlatan, "Shabtsi" Zvi spread his gospel with undiminished zeal, fasting, preaching, and mortifying his flesh. He proceeded into Egypt, where he won the allegiance of one Nathan of Gaza, who began to precede him everywhere as a latter-day John the Baptist, announcing the glorious visitor as "The King" and unquestionable Messenger of the Lord. In this dangerous fashion, Zvi returned to Jerusalem, where the scandalized high priests anathematized him.

Perhaps to fulfill the Spanish proverb *Dios que da la llaga, da la medicina* ("God, who sends the wound, sends the cure"), there now appeared on the scene a most remarkable maiden, whose maidenhood many disputed, claiming she had for some time been supporting herself in quasi-theological ways. This charmer, known as Sarah, had found sactuary from a pogrom in a convent, back in her native Poland, pogroms being no less a lucrative industry of Poland in those days than they are in our own. After being raised and educated in the convent, Sarah visited cities in Europe, in one of which she announced that she was destined to marry the Messiah! Whatever her motives, or Sabbatai Zvi's needs, the two met, hit it off splendidly, and were married.

Sabbatai Zvi now announced that he was ready to set up the Kingdom of God. He chose Mount Zion for the proper locale. Ecstasy and hysteria ensued: A messianic fever raced from Palestine to Turkey to Venice to Hamburg to Amsterdam; it even possessed parts of staid London—where a sect of respectable Christians, having figured out (by numerical abracadabra with passages from the Bible) that the millennium was at hand, set the date of glory for 1666.

Far and wide, Sabbatai Zvi was acclaimed "The King of

the Jews," and many souls in Europe and the Middle East began to sell their homes, furniture, dry goods, livestock, and other worldly possessions that could not accompany them into the Elysian Fields. What they thought they were going to do with the money they received for the sale of their terrestrial chattels is something that both intrigues and perplexes me.

Sabbatai Zvi greatly enjoyed being "King of the Jews," but his reign was brief; for the Sultan, an adamant Mussulman, did not subscribe to the validity of the title. And when Zvi, the self-anointed Messiah, appeared in Constantinople with a contingent of consecrated yea-sayers for the purpose of deposing the Sultan, that swarthy son of the Prophet arrested Zvi, threw him into durance vile, and with surprising generosity, and potent motivational psychology, gave him this brisk choice: "Either embrace the faith of Islam or I'll chop off your head."

Zvi kept his head on his shoulders.

On the grounds of immediate survival, this decision is impossible to fault; on the grounds of potential posthumous benefits, it is impossible not to deplore. Whatever the faith to which he clung in his secret heart, Sabbatai Zvi played footsie with his larger duties, duties which, considering the thousands he had persuaded of his sweet divinity, required, at the very minimum, that he set a good example. He did not. His flight from martyrdom was bad enough; his embracing a non-Judaic and non-Christian creed was unforgivable. No other apostate broke so many trusting hearts. . . .

Sabbatai Zvi died quite obscurely, in 1676, but pockets of stout believers in his mission still grace Greece, Turkey, *Mittel-europa* and Brooklyn to this very day.

It is pointless to pinpoint the next three hundred years' supply of holy men, santons, celestial drummers, wowsers, heaven-stormers and taffyheads, there being too many to marvel over in these chilly pages. But my favorite will always be the ineffable Father Divine.

A Modest Man
Named Smith

CCCCCCCCCCCCCCCCCCCCCCCCCCCCC

I T is a clumsy, sprawling, elephantine book. The facts are suffocating, the digressions interminable, the pace as maddening as the title is uninviting: *An Inquiry into the Nature and the Causes of the Wealth of Nations*. But it is one of the towering achievements of the human mind: a masterwork of observation and analysis, of ingenious correlations, inspired theorizings, and the most persistent and powerful cerebration. Delightful ironies break through its stodgy surface:

> The late resolution of the Quakers [to free] their Negro slaves may satisfy us that their number cannot be very great. . . .

> The chief enjoyment of riches consists in the parade of riches.

> To found a great empire for the sole purpose of raising customers [is] unfit for a nation of shopkeepers, but extremely fit for a nation whose government is influenced by shopkeepers.

So comprehensive is its range, so perceptive its probings, that it can dance, within one conceptual scheme, from the diamond mines of Golconda to the price of Chinese silver in Peru; from the fisheries of Holland to the plight of Irish prostitutes in London. It links a thousand apparently unrelated oddities into unexpected chains of consequence. And the brilliance of its intelligence "lights up the mosaic of detail," says Schumpeter, "heating the facts until they glow." Sometimes.

Adam Smith published *The Wealth of Nations* in 1776—not as a textbook, but as a polemical cannon aimed at governments that were subsidizing and protecting their merchants, their farmers, their manufacturers, against "unfair" competition, at home or from imports. Smith set out to demolish the mercantilist theory from which those policies flowed. He challenged the powerful interests who were profiting from unfree markets, collusive prices, tariffs and subsidies and obsolete ways of producing things.

We must bear in mind the kind of world in which Smith lived:

Different kinds of money and measurements and weights were used in different localities of England. In some cities, laws hobbled the improvement of manufacturing, and punished any who attempted to introduce it. It was a crime to lend money for more than a fixed interest rate, which shrunk credit even though borrowers were eager to pay more than the law permitted. Business itself was viewed with suspicion by the lords of politics and privilege, as a selfish, déclassé activity in which personal gain is achieved at the expense of others. A free market in real estate or in labor, in the modern sense, did not exist, nor did corporations.

The artisans' guilds, no less than favored manufacturers, petitioned the king to outlaw labor-saving methods: a new stocking-frame was abolished by the Privy Council. To import printed calico was illegal. Farmers, driven off the land so that sheep could graze or aristocrats ride to hounds, were whipped—or branded for vagabondage.

Poverty was accepted as natural, indeed inevitable, part of the natural order and the divine will. Britain, it was assumed, needed an ample supply of the impecunious: especially those with strong backs, grateful hands and ignorant heads. "Nothing requires more to be explained than trade!" complained Dr. Johnson. By trade he meant that immense, unstudied structure of production, commerce and calculations that economics embraces.

It was this world, this semifeudal order that extended from the Caucasus to the Atlantic, that Adam Smith dissected, clarified, and revolutionized. Other theorists had meditated on isolated portions of economic life, but Smith attacked the nuclear concept of wealth itself: wealth is not gold and silver, as accepted doctrine took for granted, but the total sum of a nation's resources and skills and production.

He advocated a new cause, *laissez faire* (the phrase was Gournay's; oddly enough, Smith never used it), against the "self evident" advantages of having government guide and control the ways in which a nation produces and sells its food and goods. Smith proceeded to spell out in profuse detail why the supposed advantages were illusory: If all men are permitted to act freely, to work how and where they want, to charge whatever prices they can get; if men, that is, are given maximum freedom to try to maximize personal gain; if all men act out their rawest self-interest, pursuing whatever enterprises best satisfy their needs and their egotism and their cupidity; if the government keeps its hands off the economy—the result will be not anarchy or chaos or a jungle of selfish social destructiveness, but an ordered harmony in which the automatic forces of supply and demand, in a responsive and resilient free market, must bring about the most efficient utilization of all resources (labor, land, capital, skills, brains, ingenuity, inventiveness) to supply the largest and most lasting advantages to a nation.

Free, unregulated competition, Smith audaciously argued, converts "the private interests and passions of men" into consequences "most agreeable to the interests of the whole society"—as if by an Invisible Hand, and despite the intentions of rapacious landlords, greedy merchants, mendacious traders, ruthless profiteers.

It was a breath-taking revelation of the grand design that

is hidden within the mundane, workaday world of production and trade: The best guarantor of men's welfare, and the rock on which rests man's freedom, is—the profit system. Smith even offered the startling judgment that Britain's colonies and slave labor were more of an economic disadvantage than asset.

Smith illustrated this complex and paradoxical theme with matchless ingenuity, with a ceaseless cascade of facts and reasoning and analytic *tours de force*. And all that rolling, relentless argument came to focus on one conclusion: Government should get out of, and keep hands off, the economy.

Many men cried, as many still do, that Adam Smith offers an apologia for unconscionable aggrandizement by the heartless rich at the expense of the helpless poor. But only those who have not read him can think him inhumane, or cynical, or an apologist for a dog-eat-dog order. It was Adam Smith, not Karl Marx, who warned: "No society can flourish [where] the far greater part of its members are poor and miserable"; or castigated a social order in which "a mother who has borne twenty children" sees only two survive; or said that mass production would brutalize men's minds unless the government prevented it through energetic public education; or showed how road tolls help the rich "at the expense of the poor."

Smith knew perfectly well that businessmen are prone to possess a "mean rapacity [and] monopolizing spirit." "They seldom meet," he wrote, without concocting "a conspiracy against the public." In a typically dry, wry, memorable passage, he observed:

> It is not from the benevolence of the butcher, the brewer, or the baker that we expect our dinner, but from their regard to their own interest. We address ourselves not to their self-love, and never talk to them of our own necessities but of their advantages.

Not the least of Smith's charms are such shrewd and ironic arguments. Judges would try their cases faster, he said, if paid by the litigants instead of the state. Many religious sects are far better for a nation than one or two, because the need to compete, even in sacred persuasion, will ultimately foster a

> pure and rational religion, free from every mixture of absurdity, imposture, or fanaticism, such as wise men in all ages have wished to see established. The . . . zeal of religious leaders can be dangerous only where there is . . . but one sect [or two or three] tolerated in the society. That zeal must be altogether innocent where the society is divided into two or three hundred sects, of which no one would be considerable enough to disturb the public tranquility.

Who was this man who would change the intellectual structure of the world?

Adam Smith was born in Scotland, at Kirkcaldy, Fife, in 1723, and raised by his widowed mother. Briefly kidnaped as a child, by gypsy tinkers, and recovered by his uncle, he went on to live a life devoid of drama. At the University of Glasgow he concentrated on mathematics and moral philosophy, then went to Oxford for seven years.

We cannot be sure what he looked like: the best portrait of him was probably painted after his death. He is described as having been of middle height, "full but not corpulent," with large gray eyes that beamed with benignity. He was a shy man, embarrassed with strangers and inattentive to ordinary things. He was deeply devoted to his mother, and never married; after his mother died, a maiden cousin looked after him: *Someone* had to, for the professor was notoriously absentminded. He once brewed bread and butter, instead of tea. He walked fifteen miles down country lanes, still in his dressing robe, absorbed in some problem. On another occasion, he fell into a pit because he had not looked where he was going. He would stride along in his breeches and broad hat talking to himself, entirely blind to his surroundings, consumed by concentration on some problem.

In 1751 he was appointed to the chair of Logic, and later Moral Philosophy, at the University of Glasgow, where he was once reprimanded for the un-Scotsmanlike frivolity of smiling during a religious service.

He began by lecturing on theology, ethics, and jurisprudence, and he won such repute as a teacher that students came to him from as far away as Russia. This is all the more noteworthy because Smith had some sort of nervous disorder, often faltered in his speech, and became so lost in pursuing an idea that he was prone to forget where he was or what he had set out to demonstrate.

He never could organize his thoughts easily or quickly. He would walk up and down his study, dictating to a secretary, abruptly digressing or pursuing an impromptu hunch. His mind was an immense library and catalog system; he possessed a phenomenal memory.

He was a good if disrhythmic talker, but a better listener, who soaked up information and insights from the conversation of others. He loved poetry and could recite classics from English, Latin, Greek, French, Italian without a flaw. He was profoundly influenced by David Hume and Hume's writings and thinking; they were close friends; and Smith was at Hume's deathbed and wrote a moving account of the philosopher's last hours.

Smith could not resist buying books, and he assembled a vast personal library in history, science, astronomy, philosophy, physics. He loved the life of the clubs, in Edinburgh and especially London, where he reveled in the sparkling repartée and learned discourse of men whom history would place among the immortals: Edmund Burke, Samuel Johnson, Edward Gibbon. I drool over what that sparkling company spent their hours discussing.

At the age of thirty-six Smith published his college lectures in a volume called *The Theory of Moral Sentiments*. It was an investigation of how man's moral judgments can be explained, if men are primarily driven by self-interest. Smith postulated "social propensities" of Sympathy, Justice, and Benevolence. In a brilliant foray into psychology, he designated Sympathy as the human capacity to feel for others by imagining one's self in the place of another, as if by an impartial spectator. This construct anticipated Kant's categorical imperative, and what modern psychiatry calls identification and empathy.

The Theory of Moral Sentiments brought Smith international fame. One of its admirers was the Chancellor of the Exchequer, who invited Smith to tutor his son, to take the young duke, indeed, on the Grand Tour.

Smith went to the Continent with his pupil in 1763. He met the great Voltaire in Geneva and spent almost a year in Paris, where he discussed political economy with Turgot, Necker, and various luminaries of the thriving circle of *philosophes.* Quesnay, physician to Madame Pompadour (!), expounded to Smith the doctrine of the Physiocrats, who held that national wealth was not to be reckoned as the sum of the Treasury's supply of gold or silver, but as the total production a nation creates. But Quesnay thought only farmers produce real wealth; he missed the fructifying operations of the entrepreneur, the manager, the planner, the risk-taker.

When Smith returned to Kirkcaldy, he settled down to devote himself to his inquiry into the nature and causes of national wealth. He had pondered the problem now for over twenty-five years. He had often discussed it in Edinburgh, often with David Hume, often in London and France. He proceeded to dictate his masterpiece, slowly, haltingly, breaking off from time to time to travel down to London to consult others on special problems. (Benjamin Franklin gave him invaluable information about the economy and trade of the colonies.)

It took Adam Smith ten years to dictate and edit *The Wealth of Nations.*

He conceived it as a sequel to *The Theory of Moral Sentiments,* we should not forget, for he never ceased analyzing human behavior and moral obligations. Smith did not think of himself as simply an economist: He was a philosopher, a theoretical psychologist, a sociologist, an analyst of political and social institutions. He was, that is, an eighteenth-century intellectual. He examined the conduct of men in a constant search for the whys of ethics and the musts of morals. And because it is a sequel, *The Wealth of Nations* accepts, and does not try to stress, what Adam Smith had emphasized in his previous work: that man, for all his acquisitive and predatory appetites, is a social creature, put on this earth for God's purposes. His critics forget that central to all of Smith's thinking was his unshakable conviction about man's nobler social propensities: the instinct of Sympathy, the sense of Benevolence, the impulse to Justice.

Smith showed that a truly free market is a huge, sensitive polling booth. To buy an article or a service is to *vote*—for it and against others less desired or more costly or less useful. Prices therefore fairly reflect utility (or demand) and operate, in their fluctuations, to shift and channel and allocate resources with impartial efficiency, rewarding efficiency, quality, improved services. The decisive power is wielded in the most democratic of all methods: by the lowly, individual, sovereign customer.

The magic of the division of labor, Smith held, the specialization of skills, the encouragement of ingenuity and experiment and innovation, all energized by the potent magnetic lure of personal profits and the personal acquisition of riches, will serve to lead mankind to "universal opulence." And the freedom to venture, to risk gain or loss, in a class-free and depoliticized marketplace, must nourish, as no other economic system can, the priceless growth and strength of individual liberty.

Smith showed that the buyer profits no less than the seller (an unconventional idea in that time); that England's imports are valuable to those who buy them and in addition provide other nations with the money to buy England's exports. International trade must reduce international frictions, Smith held, and promote international peace.

Smith never tried to evade or rationalize what his eyes

and mind told him: "Landlords," he said, "love to reap where they never sowed." They are prone to "violence, rapine and disorder." Businessmen, in general, are prone to gratify "the meanest and most sordid of vanities."

He also knew that a system of enterprise deprived of special favors, and rules backed by governmental power, would be fought tooth and nail by "the insolent outrage of furious and disappointed monopolists." He knew that he would be ridiculed and misquoted by "that insidious and crafty animal . . . [the] politician."

But his analysis led to one unalterable goal: The government must enforce competition, punishing any who conspire to fix prices, or divide up markets, or restrict production.

Adam Smith knew that in human affairs the best must yield to the best obtainable, what is logical to what is possible. He favored certain public works and departures from free trade—for national defense, for instance. He denounced primogeniture, the hallowed custom under which only oldest sons inherit land, in a passage any socialist theoretician would be proud to have written:

> This custom . . . rests upon the most absurd of all suppositions, the supposition that every successive generation of men have not an equal right to the earth, and to all that it possesses; but that the property of the present generation should be restrained and regulated according to the fancy of those who died perhaps 500 years ago. . . .
>
> It seldom happens . . . that a great proprietor is a great improver. To improve land with profit . . . requires an exact attention to small savings and small gains; a man born to a great fortune is very seldom capable [of this].
>
> Every generation has an equal right to the earth and to all that it possesses.

I do not think many people realize that *The Wealth of Nations* is a *tour de force* of psychology and sociology, no less than economics. It offered men a theoretical scheme that, for the first time, encompassed the multitudinous intricacies of political economy.

The work is so rich, so germinal, that for a century it

gave Europe's kings, prime ministers, philosophers, politicians, their basic conception of human behavior, and guided their prescriptions for progress. The effect of Adam Smith on such men as Pitt, or Stein of Prussia, or Gentz of Austria, his influence on statesmen, social theorists, ministers of trade, would be hard to exaggerate.

Smith transformed the very way in which men *thought* about private economics or public policy. He lifted the national welfare above the special interests of the august and the privileged: the ruling lords, the landed gentry, the romantic, impatient builders of empire—and also above the special interests of the aggressive merchants, the clamoring protectionists, the clever traders, importers, exporters.

He heralded a new kind of freedom. He virtually founded a secular faith, Individualism, and *The Wealth of Nations* became its bible. "Next to Napoleon," one historian concluded, Adam Smith was "the mightiest monarch in Europe."

He never thought his system perfect; he did demonstrate how much better it was than any that existed, because his economic model operated independent of men's personal motives or monetary goals: it was governed and regulated by larger, impersonal *laws*. He had thought deeper, harder and better than anyone else about the dynamics of an economic order, and perceived the hidden equilibrium of interactions between contending forces.

I should interject that Adam Smith did not *invent* economics, or elevate it to a science single-handed. He owed much to Hutcheson, Hume, Quesnay, Turgot; and Professor William Lettwin has recently showed us how much Smith owes to John Locke, who discerned social laws "akin to the forces of nature," and to the astute Dudley North, who had related supply to demand, foresaw the functions of interest and rent, understood the balancing process in the movements of bullion, and extolled the spacious national benefits of free trade.

But Smith was surely economics' great architect, and remains its commanding theoretician. The gifted economists

who followed him—Ricardo, John Stuart Mill, Bastiat, Karl
Marx, Alfred Marshall, Irving Fisher, John Maynard Keynes,
Beveridge, von Hayek, Schumpeter—all began, as every
economist must, with Adam Smith's stupendous scheme.

The system was not (it could not be) without grave and
unresolved defects. Even perfect competition, notes Paul
Samuelson, "*could* lead to starving cripples; to malnourished
children . . . to the perpetuation of great inequality for gen-
erations or forever. If Smith were alive, he would agree." I
have no doubt he would.

Smith did not foresee the fantastic off-shoots of the Industrial Revolution: the role of gigantic corporations, the power
of unions, the problem of business cycles. Nor could he foresee how catastrophic depressions, frightful wars, and massive unemployment would create the most violent hatred for
an "inhuman, profit-mad, conscienceless capitalist system."

The visible hardships of life have animated powerful
movements for social reform. Governmental aid to the un-
propertied—farmer or worker, artisan or tenant—became
the battle cry for intellectuals, reformers, and labor unions.
Hunger, lost jobs, unfound work are intolerable evils to the
innocent victims of vicissitude.

To understand capitalism and its ramifications requires a
degree of sophistication that is much rarer than compassionate oversimplifications. In the competition for political
support, humanitarian appeals drown out reassurances
about necessary readjustments. And a nagging sense of guilt
about their self-enrichment weakens those who, one would
assume, would be the staunchest of capitalism's defenders.

The simple promises of a humane social order have
launched welfare states that respond to the demands of the
millions. For men want security, no less than liberty. Men
seek a proper share of justice and pelf no less than higher
wages for their work. Is it surprising that the gap between
the very rich and the very poor, between bourgeois luxuries
and widespread misery, between the discriminatory effects
of inflation or deflation, between war's profiteering and
war's horrors, would drive men to revolutionary protest?

Even had Marx or Engels never existed, the very objectivity of capitalism's operations would have imposed economics' penalties on men sooner or later angered by them.

It has become clear, I think, that voters want full employment more than national growth; they seem to prefer inflation to depression; they will vote for massive public debts to finance massive public services. Men may want freedom, but they want insurance against freedom's inherent risks.

How can *laissez faire* win advocacy among the weak, the unlucky, the dull, the unwilling, the inept? Those who fail— the incompetent or imprudent, the lazy or all those to whom the Lord gave mediocre talents and extravagant aspirations —such men do not comprehend or accept the market's unfeeling effects. Diligent men cannot reconcile themselves to the demoralizing verdicts of competition. How can those battered by illness or old age or sheer misfortune philosophically accept their hopeless prospect? Can they care about a system that does not seem to care about them?

It is folly to expect the dispossessed, the confused, the unskilled, the foolish, the scorned, the insecure, the jobless, the emotion-ridden, the impatient, the unanalytic, the failures of this world to accept an abstruse, unreachable scheme which they, in fact, blame for undeserved adversity and unjustified defeats.

The crucial point about democracy, I think, is that men who feel too poor to cast significant votes in the marketplace do cast very large votes in the polling booths.

And having said all this, believing in its verity and effects, what I find most amazing about Adam Smith is how much more often he is right than wrong.

He was to economics what Newton was to physics, or Darwin to the study of man: a giant in the kingdom of intelligence. The cheerful, absentminded master analyst of the great, invisible scheme that shapes a million variant acts and calculations into a harmonious and beneficent whole was far from being the desiccated priest of what Carlyle would call "the dismal science."

I think the best way to gauge Adam Smith's contribution

to mankind is this: List the six books you think have most profoundly shaped our world. Start with the Bible. Include Newton's *Principia* and Darwin's *Origin of Species*. Now, can you possibly name three more without including that astonishing "outpouring of an epoch," *The Wealth of Nations?*

Postscript

Now, finished, I must single out one whom I love, know and admire: my wife, who has survived long periods of Coventry from a husband locked within the blind, deaf, mute delirium of writing. Her forbearance is as much appreciated as her silences.

P.S. I like her mother, too.

About the Author

〰〰〰〰〰〰〰〰〰〰〰〰〰〰〰〰〰〰〰〰

Leo Rosten's *The Joys of Yiddish* brightened the bestseller lists for months on end, a season or two ago. A writer of remarkable versatility and range, Mr. Rosten is the creator of the immortal H*Y*M*A*N K*A*P*L*A*N and Captain Newman. His name has often appeared on the movie screen. His books on Hollywood and the Washington correspondents are standard works in social science. *A Most Private Intrigue, The Dark Corner, The Story Behind the Painting* have delighted legions of readers.

His feature page in *Look,* "The World of Leo Rosten," has been described as "the most interesting column being published in America today." His vignettes of men of genius—philosophers, writers, scientists, statesmen—were praised by the editors of *Great Books of the Western World* for "the brilliance of the analyses [and] the clarity of style . . . one of the most distinguished series ever to be published in a popular magazine."

A Ph.D. from the University of Chicago, Mr. Rosten studied at the London School of Economics, has taught at Yale, was Ford Visiting Professor of Political Science at the University of California, and is a Faculty Associate of Columbia University.

His writings have won many honors, including the Freedoms Foundation Medal and the George Polk Memorial Award.

He has served the government as Deputy Director of the Office of War Information and Consultant to the Commission on National Goals.

Mr. Rosten lives in New York, summers at East Quogue, and is a passionate traveler in between.